...nate Saturday, April 30ᵗʰ
...amendment.

B. F. Chapleau

Clerk of the Senate.

Bill in His Majesty's name

THE SEA IS
AT OUR GATES

THE SEA IS
AT OUR GATES

THE HISTORY OF THE
CANADIAN NAVY

COMMANDER TONY GERMAN

Canadian Cataloguing in Publication Data

German, Tony, 1924–
   The sea is at our gates

Includes bibliographical references.
ISBN   0-7710-3269-2

1. Canada.   Royal Canadian Navy – History.
2. Canada – History, Naval.   I. Title.

FC231.G4 1990   359′.00971   C90-093284-8
F1028.5.G4   1990

Endpaper illustrations: Alan Daniel

Front endpaper:

The Naval Service Act received royal assent from Governor General Earl Grey on 4 May, 1910. On 21 October, HMCS *Niobe* steamed into Halifax with a skeleton crew. Seventeen days later HMCS *Rainbow* arrived in Esquimalt and the young Dominion of Canada had a navy of its own.

Back endpaper:

In the mid 1960's the navy was at its peacetime peak of 20,000. HMCS *Bonaventure*, with her Trackers and helicopters, the Restigouche and Mackenzie classes and the St. Laurents, reconfigured to carry the Sea King helicopter, led the way with innovative equipment and special expertise in anti-submarine warfare.

McClelland & Stewart Inc.
The Canadian Publishers
481 University Avenue
Toronto, Ontario
M5G 2E9

Printed and bound in Canada

CONTENTS

DEDICATION

"The wholesome sea is at her gates – her gates both east and west." These words are carved in stone over the main door of our Parliament Buildings, sound reminder for a country with the longest coastline of any in the world, born and nurtured from the sea and depending for its way of life today on seaborne trade. But most Canadians live a thousand miles from salt water and know little of its works, and so our history shows those words have all too often been ignored. Yet those of us who had followed the lure of sea adventure have loved our ships, forged bonds with shipmates, and felt the sea shape our lives. To all who have sailed in Canada's navy, I dedicate this book.

FOREWORD

THE EIGHTY YEARS OF OUR NAVY'S LIFESPAN HAVE BEEN EXTRAORDI-
narily eventful ones in world history and decisive ones in the development of
our country. I was a schoolboy in Halifax when HMCS *Niobe* arrived to mark
the beginning of a Canadian navy. Of the Great War I remember troop trains
and transports and departing convoys and the Naval College in the dockyard,
and I vividly recall the Halifax explosion.

At the end of the Great War, Canada was enjoying the feeling of national
independence, but had formed no firm naval policy and continued to be dependent on the Royal Navy for advice, support, and defence. The arrival of HMCS
Aurora and two destroyers in 1920 signalled a second start, but it was short-lived.
I recall a period in the twenties when, with one small destroyer on each coast and
fewer than 400 officers and men, we couldn't afford to send the ships to sea. The
navy was a political football, ridiculed by the press, down but not out.

The thirties saw a relatively dramatic turn-around. Two fine destroyers
were built in the U.K. to Canadian specifications and a five-year plan resulted
in the purchase from the RN of four more, which enabled us to enter World
War Two with six modern, well-manned ships.

The war had a profound effect on all aspects of our lives. On the naval side
it called for ever-increasing numbers of escort vessels. Our Headquarters staff
and our dockyard and training facilities matched the size of our fleet, a long
way short of what was needed to plan, build, and support a whole new navy.
In the face of tremendous problems Canada achieved a remarkable shipbuilding effort, which called for an equally remarkable effort to provide and
train the crews. Much of the training had perforce to be obtained on the job, at
sea, in war. Officers and men alike learned by hard experience.

We entered the war with six small ships, built in Britain, manned by crews
trained in the RN and observing many of the customs and traditions of that

great service. We emerged with a fleet of ships built in Canada, manned by Canadians, trained in Canada, a sense of accomplishment, and a few customs of our own. There were problems of adjustment between old and new concepts of service and discipline, which were not overcome quickly or easily, but a more truly Canadian service evolved.

Our ambitions for the size and shape of a post-war fleet were soon to be determined by the formation of the Atlantic alliance. The Korean War gave us added confidence and brought home to Canadians the need for strong forces. Early NATO policy led us to concentrate our naval effort on anti-submarine forces. Our war experience in that special field enabled us to design and build ships that led the way. Our contribution to the combined ASW strength of the alliance earned us a share in the overall protection of the Allied fleets.

Before retiring in 1960, the year of our fiftieth anniversary, I visited Halifax and reviewed the fleet. At that time we had the ships to meet our NATO commitment, and we had in place a building program to replace the older vessels. Spirits were high! Unfortunately, government policies allowed wide gaps in replacement and before long the age of some ships exceeded the average age of the crews. In spite of the fact that Canada borders on three oceans, and much of our trade is seaborne, we lack a firm national maritime policy and continue to lean on our friends and allies.

The Sea Is At Our Gates is a valuable addition to Canada's maritime and military literature. Sailor, and son of a sailor, Tony German went to sea in war and commanded ships in a time of great technical advance. He is well qualified to tell this story, one I believe of special importance to those who have grown up without the experience of war. They should mark well that only in times of war or overwhelming threat have Canadians paid heed to their navy. At each such time the professional seamen they charged with the task of defending them had to build from nearly nothing, while our allies held the line.

The primary purpose of armed forces is preservation of peace. Armed strength and the fear of mutual annihilation have preserved a kind of peace for forty-five years. Now, as enlightened steps toward disarmament progress, peace will still be dependent on a balance of strength, hopefully armed with far less destructive weapons.

The security of our nation and our long-term interests are our responsibility. A nation has influence only to the extent it can assure its own interests, meet its international responsibilities, and back its commitments with force if need be.

May the lessons of our history, so well expressed in this book, not go unread.

Vice Admiral Harry DeWolf
CBE, DSO, DSC, CD, RCN *(retired)*

PROLOGUE

IN MARCH, 1964, I WAS COMMANDING HMCS *MACKENZIE* AND IN company with *Fraser* and *St. Laurent* and ships of the British, Australian, Indian, Pakistani, and New Zealand navies took part in a major exercise in the Bay of Bengal. This considerable assembly of Commonwealth might was without question a powerful deterrent to Indonesia's President Sukarno, just across the Malacca Strait, who was bearing hard on Malaysia. The effect was a lasting one, for naval force is highly mobile and this was Commonwealth solidarity with clout. Malaysia was emerging at that time as a vibrant independent federation and in Kuala Lumpur the Deputy Prime Minister, Tun Razak, told us Canadian captains in a private meeting just what our country's presence, in the shape of three modern ships of war, meant to his.

Curiously, the assembly anchorage for the exercise was inside the reef of an island I had last seen in 1944 with the RN's Eastern Fleet when we bombarded the Japanese airfield. More remarkably, the 1964 Commander-in-Chief of the Malaysian navy, the senior officer of the Australian frigates, and I had all served in the same destroyer in that operation. *Mackenzie* was new (fresh out of the builder's yard in the 1962 Cuban missile crisis when our navy stood firm with our American allies as Prime Minister Diefenbaker vacillated) and she and my superb ship's company performed admirably. But the most notable ship in that six-nation fleet was HMCS *St. Laurent*. Uniquely Canadian-designed and built in the fifties, she had just been converted on the west coast with hangar, flight deck, and beartrap to carry a big anti-submarine helicopter, plus variable depth sonar. She was in fact en route to Halifax the long way round and hadn't yet embarked her Sea King, but this radical and entirely Canadian development was hugely admired by that seagoing band of Commonwealth brothers.

Back in Singapore, I had a visit from another old shipmate – an RN lieutenant commander in the war, vice admiral at the time in question, and soon to become Britain's First Sea Lord. After his informal, detailed, eagle-eyed inspection of *Mackenzie* we raised a glass in my cabin. The genuine professional admiration he expressed for my ship and her company – he had spoken to many of them on the way around – and for the innovations in *St. Laurent* alongside was matched by my recognition that he had passed along to me so much that was of everlasting value. We stemmed, all of us, from the same centuries-old tradition of the sea and we followed the common aims, serving the vital interests of our respective countries around the world and preserving peace. At that very same time Canadian ships were keeping the Atlantic watch and working with NATO, *Bonaventure* was off-loading equipment in Cyprus for Canada's UN peacekeeping contingent, and her Captain was conferring personally with Archbishop Makarios.

In these encounters spanning the world lay many elements of the story that I have sought to unfold in this book: how Canada's navy was formed in the image of the Royal Navy in 1910; how Canada's failure to develop a naval policy of her own, compounded by excessive dependence on the RN, meant there was pathetically little on which a navy could be built when it was suddenly needed late in the Great War, and then so urgently called forth in World War Two; how Canada's greatest contribution to that terrible world struggle eventually succeeded, more than any other single factor, because of the quality of the people out at sea; how fifty years and three wars from its beginning our navy emerged in the sixties as its own vital, innovative, distinctive self, and a tangible expression of Canada's determination to take its destined international place in a threatening world; and how then, over twenty-five years, we lost the capability to defend our own shores – much less our growing trade. During that Far East operation in 1964 we got the first signals of that long demise. And now Canada, through years of looking inward, may still speak in the councils of the world, but her voice is scarcely heard.

My first notions of the navy came when I was very young because my father had been one of those first seven cadets to join in 1910. Though he was invalided out through loss of an arm he retained, along with his old shipmates who were often about the house and struggling to keep their little navy afloat, that twinkle of eye and tang of speech that always marked the sailor. Of course, I wanted to be one, too, and almost in a breath I found myself in 1942 on the bridge of the corvette *Weyburn* in the Strait of Belle Isle looking, quite literally downward, at the conning tower of a German U-boat racing off from the glare of the ship she had just torpedoed. I was seventeen, a mere cadet about to enter the Naval College and – courtesy of my father, who was back in for the war and Naval Officer in Charge in Gaspé – along for the ride. *Weyburn* went down a few months later with her Captain and many I had known. At the time I was far too unqualified to be afraid.

Wartime service "on loan" to the Royal Navy gave me a curious mixture of admiration for the way they did things, recognition that their ways were grown from centuries of hard-won tradition while rooted in a social structure far different from our own, and resentment at being patronized. It was not universal – certainly that outstanding officer who was my guest in Singapore never patronized anyone – and I am sure it was often unintentional. But it was there and it had, I feel certain, something to do with our post-war determination to be ourselves.

NATO gave us a clear sense of purpose. Our aim was to hold the line, making it too costly for the Soviets to step across it until the day came when the innate human force for freedom behind the Iron Curtain would inevitably break through. At the RN Staff College in 1956, we reasoned that it would take ten years and, with its historic resilience and deep cultural roots, Poland was the place where the first cracks in the East bloc monolith would appear. We were twenty years out.

Now in 1964, as we made our way back to Esquimalt via Hong Kong and Japan effectively advertising trade with high-tech Canada, we got rumblings from Ottawa of the integration of our armed forces. That move toward rational planning and economy was followed swiftly, and in my view disastrously, by unification. I left my happy and rewarding career on that account and watched sadly from the sidelines as the "sea element" over the years dwindled and shrivelled unrenewed.

Then in 1984, while working on a radio program to be broadcast during the navy's seventy-fifth anniversary, I was lifted by Sea King out to *Skeena*, thirty miles off Halifax. There she was on that dirty November day, at twenty-seven older than the average age of her own ship's company, butting into sixty knots of wind with waves to fifteen feet. The big helicopter, twenty years old herself, tucked down neatly on the heaving deck, to be clamped instantly in the maw of the beartrap. Spray lashed me crossing the tiny flight deck and I was back among friends: easy, courteous, professional officers and men doing their jobs with skill and élan in a demanding and highly technical game. It's quite outside the sailors' lexicon but, if they were to "work to rule," their obsolete old vessels would never get away from the wall, much less put up any kind of show against a modern enemy. If they had to fight for us today their blood would be on our heads, for we as a country have failed these best of men. And in so doing we have failed ourselves.

Extraordinarily, it is only now, forty-five years after the last depth charge, that the official operational history of the RCN in World War Two is being written by Defence Department historians. Recording events in war for subsequent analysis, as the Canadian army did, was given little attention by the navy. In the post-war retrenchment the partial draft assembled by Gilbert Tucker, the navy's very capable historian, was read with jaundiced eyes at senior levels and he went back to teaching with the task not done. Tucker finished his two excellent volumes, on the navy to 1939, then its shore activities during the war; but the only official account of operations was Joseph Schull's *The Far Distant Ships*. It is a very well-written, stirring, popular account of the exploits of Canadian ships and sailors, but it is neither properly analytical nor historically complete.

Into the eighties some first-rate scholars and a few sea-dog memoirists added immeasurably to Canadian naval historiography in war and peace and provided the likes of me with a real trove. The picture of World War Two that emerges has all the colours of gallantry, skill, sacrifice, extraordinary fortitude. It is underlaid, though, with the dark hues of inadequacy and ill-judgement at high levels. Above all – and the inadequacy stems directly from this – it shows a country, pretending independence, but so bereft of policy in peace that its navy had next to nothing on which to build in war. It only met the crucial challenge on the Atlantic through the dogged leadership of a few, good fortune, and plain sailors' guts.

As a result of the failure to write the real history after World War Two, British and American accounts give only passing, and sometimes scornful, mention of Canada's key part in the all-crucial Battle of the Atlantic. Worse, Canadians have had a rose-coloured picture of success at sea – perpetuating the myth that volunteers can always leap in and save the day – without grasping the fact that failed long-term policy courts disaster. If Canada were to heed her history, she could hardly keep her back turned to the sea, as she most often has in this century.

But for better or for worse, the navy is adventure and ships are wondrous things; the sea opens a world to be grasped beyond our gates and those who follow it have a certain lightness in their hearts, steadiness of spirit, and sparkle in their eye. Yes, there are rogues among sailors, too. But at sea not one would ever let a shipmate down. They simply are the best people going and in my certain knowledge Canadian sailors are the best of the lot. They have earned their country's trust.

Tony German
Commander, RCN (retired)
February, 1990

CHAPTER ONE

THE TIDES
OF HISTORY

WITH THE DAWN OF THE FIFTEENTH CENTURY, TEEMING EUROPE BURST outward from its shores. In less than forty years, between 1487 and 1523, resolute mariners in their stout little caravels – new ships that could effectively beat to windward – rounded the great capes, sailed into the Indian Ocean and the China Sea, crossed the Atlantic and Pacific, and circumnavigated the world. Trade followed exploration and the flags of monarchs followed trade.

English claims in North America were established by John Cabot in 1497. His discoveries told Europe what Columbus's had not: a whole continent stood in the way of Asia – a continent for the taking. Cabot's reports of the fabulous Newfoundland fishery drew Portuguese, Basque, French, and Spanish vessels, as well as English, by the hundreds; there were bloody clashes on the fishing grounds. Portugal and Spain, with lush new worlds in southern seas, had no territorial interests in the fog-bound north. But France did; Jacques Cartier staked her claim at Gaspé in 1536 and opened the St. Lawrence in pursuit of furs.

There were, as yet, no "royal" navies. Merchant ships were armed for their own defence and the crown hired them when in need. All monarchs issued "letters of marque" authorizing ships to attack their enemies. This was privateering, not piracy: a legitimate, if risky, business. Prizes brought profit for the captain and the owner, something for the crew, and a good slice for the crown. The first real naval engagement between fleets of sailing ships was the great running battle of the Spanish Armada in 1588. Here grew the notion of ships as fighting units, not just soldiers' transports, and of fleets concentrating force and firepower. Organized fighting tactics and signalling systems soon followed.

COLONIES AND CONFLICT
In 1603 Henry IV of France appointed a viceroy to Acadia and French

colonization began. A decade later this French toehold worried Virginians enough that they sent a fleet to level every settlement in the Bay of Fundy. James I claimed Nova Scotia, as he called Acadia, in 1621. There was little in the way of colonization but the lines of conflict were clearly drawn.

Seven years later Champlain, backed by Cardinal Richelieu, led a strong expedition to Quebec with stores, arms, and a solid group of colonists. But in the next two years David Kirke, sailing under letters of marque from Charles I, sacked Port Royal, ravaged settlements along the St. Lawrence, captured Champlain's supply ships, and besieged Quebec. Champlain, starved and desperate, had no choice but surrender. English seapower could have decided possession of all North America there and then, but Charles in his struggle with Parliament desperately needed money. He got it from France; France got back Canada, Acadia, and all her fishing stations.

In the seventeenth century, seapower emerged as a new element in the international balance. The riches of empire would be reaped by the nation with superior fleets of both merchantmen and fighting ships. The Dutch built a formidable navy. It overtook Spain's and won commerce and colonies, including New Amsterdam and the Hudson River route to the fur trade. A growing English navy ousted the Dutch from New Amsterdam in 1665 but the French, using Dutch technology, built an outstanding fleet and by the 1670s could challenge the English and the Dutch together. New France was safe behind its shield.

In 1691 Frontenac easily repelled a seaborne attack by English colonists from Massachusetts. The year before, Pierre le Moyne d'Iberville had taken New Severn in Hudson Bay from the English and snatched prizes, including two frigates, as far south as New York. Then, in a ruthless campaign he captured St. John's, razed thirty-six outposts, and almost ran the English out of Newfoundland. There was no French colonial navy and French seapower never held sway long enough to build trade with the West Indies. D'Iberville, born of an energetic seigneurial family in Ville Marie, had joined the French navy in its heyday. He was a brilliant, resourceful sea-officer and the ideal man to command North American sea operations. From 1699 he led the expedition that established France in Louisiana, and he was its first governor general. He took Nevis and twenty-four ships from the English in 1706, but died in Cuba that year at the age of forty-five. He was a hero in France as well as his native Canada.

Through Queen Anne's War, slaughter and the torch, raid and counter-raid through Acadia and Newfoundland cost ships and lives and solved nothing. Louis XIV had lost faith in his navy. French corsairs roved the seas but Britain's trade moved safely in convoy. With no effective fleet to oppose it an expedition sailed from England for Quebec in 1711. Once more, success would have settled Canada's fate. But the fleet was ill-led and foundered on the lower St. Lawrence shoals. The Treaty of Utrecht in 1713 gave Britain Hudson Bay and Acadia while France kept Ile Ste. Jean (Prince Edward Island), Cape Breton Island, and limited fishing rights.

The French then set about fortifying Louisbourg on the Cape Breton shore as a shield for Quebec and a base to win back Acadia and their fishery. It became a nest for corsairs and in 1745 the enraged New Englanders mounted their own assault, supported by three Royal Navy ships. The naval blockade sealed the port and captured supply ships as the colonists blazed away. The governor, like Champlain at Quebec, had no choice and the great fortress fell.

French attempts to retake Louisbourg in 1746 and British plans to capture Quebec came to nothing. Then, to the fury of New Englanders, Louisbourg was handed back to France at the peace of Aix la Chapelle in 1748. In fact, the fortress on its own was next to worthless; only a superior fleet could guarantee Quebec. But its mere presence forced Britain to settle mainland Nova Scotia. On magnificent Chebucto harbour they founded Halifax, the counterpoise to Louisbourg. Within easy reach of the great circle routes to Europe, Halifax had strategic significance beyond its founders' dreams. In the twentieth century it became a crucial lynchpin of the North Atlantic.

THE SEVEN YEARS' WAR

William Pitt saw clearly that without great armies, only Britain's trade would bring her full weight to the European balance, so he stiffened the languishing fleet. Pitt's strategy was to strike at the heart of French strength in North America. Though they could have sailed straight for Quebec, British forces took the safer option of taking Louisbourg first, then attacking from three directions: from seaward up the St. Lawrence; north up the Hudson Valley; and eastward from Lake Ontario. In June of 1758 Admiral Boscawen concentrated 180 ships off Louisbourg. The fortress surrendered in late summer, to be levelled two years after, stone by stone.

In spring, 1759, the greatest amphibious assault ever mounted – over 200 transports escorted by a quarter of the Royal Navy – sailed up the St. Lawrence through channels precisely surveyed and marked by Warrant Officer James Cook. It was always a difficult passage but fine seamanship and masterful ordering by Vice Admiral Charles Saunders brought the great fleet to Quebec without a single loss. There were, in fact, three times as many seamen as soldiers. In a smoothly co-ordinated operation Saunders gave young Major General James Wolfe all the mobility and gun support he needed for landing along the thirty miles from Montmorency to Pointe-aux-Trembles. Finally the landing at Anse au Foulon and the battle on the Plains of Abraham won for the British the occupation of Quebec.

But it was very late in the season. The fleet was chased downriver by the ice and in spring a strong French force that had wintered comfortably in Montreal ranged against Brigadier General James Murray's half-starved, scurvy-ridden soldiers in Quebec. They barely hung on for the first ships up the river – the squadron from Halifax with the inbound French supply ships they had captured on the way. Quebec was relieved, Montreal taken, and Canada was no longer a French possession. The matter had been clinched, in fact, not on the Plains of Abraham, but six months prior right across the Atlantic. Boscawen had smashed the French Toulon fleet off Portugal, then Admiral Hawke shattered the Brest fleet among the shoals of Quiberon Bay. France was without a navy, her colonial empire in shreds. With British dominion of the seas all her trade, North American included, could flourish unopposed.

THE AMERICAN REVOLUTION

At the first shots of the American Revolution, Britain assumed her navy could control the thirteen colonies by blockading their trade. In fact, the colonies, unlike Canada, were largely self-sufficient. Too, the American merchant fleet represented about a third of British shipping and 18,000 sailors; and the New England forests were one of Britain's prime sources of timber, masts, and spars. Confident she could always move her armies about at will, Britain made her final mistake by underestimating the power of France and Spain to challenge her pre-eminence at sea.

In the Great Lakes the British hold was clinched with a few more ships. On Lake Champlain, though, a fast-moving American force snatched all the British craft and opened the way to take Montreal and besiege Quebec. When the British squadron brought General Burgoyne up the St. Lawrence in the spring of 1776, the Yankees pulled back to Lake Champlain. By the time British tars could build a green-timbered fleet to control the lake and protect Burgoyne's flank on his drive south, he had lost the season. Then he lost next year's battle at Saratoga.

Britain's fleet had run down badly after the Seven Years' War, but France in the meantime had rebuilt much of her naval strength. She declared war on Britain in 1778 and next year, with the Spanish fleet, actually controlled the English Channel. The French squadron that sailed to American waters might well have taken Halifax and Newfoundland, too, but French ambitions lay in the West Indies. Thus, in 1780, the British were able to land at Charleston and support Cornwallis marching to Yorktown on the shore of Chesapeake Bay.

Admiral de Grasse now sailed up from Martinique with reinforcements for Lafayette and the Americans fighting Cornwallis. Just outside the Bay he mauled a British fleet, then blockaded Yorktown. Finally Cornwallis surrendered and the war on land was over. It was the only time in modern history that Britain lost control of the sea to lose a major war.

By the Treaty of Paris the United States got access to the Great Lakes, the Hudson's Bay Company got back the forts the French had taken, and France kept St. Pierre and Miquelon. The war had not been over fishing rights, but to the fury of Nova Scotians the Yankees could now fish their waters and cure the catches along their shores.

A GENERATION AT WAR

Through the wars that convulsed Europe from 1793 until Napoleon's end in 1814 at Waterloo, Britain's navy by and large controlled the sea. The Revolution gutted the French navy of its officers: they were deemed aristocrats. Weakened, they resorted to *guerre de course* again: raids on commerce by corsairs and isolated flying squadrons. But British trade moved, safe in a vast transatlantic web of convoys, and the colonies prospered. The timber trade boomed in Canada, supplying the navy and the Mother Country. Maritimers traded salt fish, flour, and timber in the Sugar Isles and nourished the slave economy that financed Britain's wars. Shipowner-merchants reaped their profits, did some privateering, and built more ships; the Cunards of thriving Halifax laid the foundation for one of the greatest of all Atlantic shipping lines.

THE WAR OF 1812

But now American western war-hawks wanted to grab Florida and the British colonies to the north while England was busy with Napoleon. "Free trade and sailors' rights" was a rallying cry without foundation. "Mr. Madison's War" of 1812 was roundly condemned by northeastern shipowners and manufacturers, who were thriving nicely on the European war. Now they were bottled up by the Royal Navy's 500 ships against the Americans' sixteen and Napoleon could send no help. New England secession came very close. Seven Yankee frigates, well designed and built, powerful, and very well manned, scored some fine single-ship victories that stoked patriotic fervour but achieved little else. Nova Scotian and New England skippers – often blood relations – took out letters of marque and snatched prizes from each other by the hundreds. Some made fortunes. Coastal traffic was in a turmoil, but the strategic effect was next to nil.

In the summer of 1812 the Provincial Marine controlled the Great Lakes well enough to ship supplies and reinforcements freely from Kingston to Niagara and Detroit. By fall the Americans had surrendered Detroit and Major General Isaac Brock had won death and victory at Queenston Heights. Now it was a shipbuilding race for naval control. The Americans had the advantage of shorter supply lines, and by April, 1813, had built enough ships on Lake Ontario for a major raid on York. They burned a nearly finished brig there and carried off mountains of naval stores and armament. A lot of it was intended for Lake Erie, and that crippled the drive there to keep pace with the Americans.

Lieutenant Robert Barclay, RN, clung to control of Lake Erie until Lieutenant Oliver Perry, the American Commodore, got two new ships to "sea." Barclay had a third of Perry's manpower and only fifty of his 450 men were naval seamen; the rest were Canadians: voyageurs, militia soldiers, lake sailors, farm boys, and some of Tecumseh's Indians. Sixty per cent of Perry's sailors were navy men from the coast and with heavier guns and a couple more small ships his broadside was double the weight of Barclay's. But General Proctor at Amherstburg was doomed without supplies and Barclay attacked Perry's squadron at Put-In Bay. The ferocious battle, muzzle to muzzle, went on for hours. When Barclay stopped the hopeless carnage and surrendered his squadron, half his men and a third of Perry's lay dead or wounded – a far more murderous bloodletting than Trafalgar. The leadership and bravery of two fine sea officers inspired deeds beyond duty in their men. But Perry held Lake Erie and Proctor, short of supplies and savaged by the Yankees, retreated to Lake Ontario.

There, Commodore Mortimer Yeo, RN, and Commodore Isaac Chauncey, USN, gingerly plied the waters, each a little more boldly when he had an edge with a new and bigger ship. The final colossus was HMS *St. Lawrence*, a 101-gun line-of-battle ship, bigger than Nelson's *Victory*, that swept Lake Ontario clear without firing a shot at the end of 1814. Meanwhile there was a standoff on Lake Champlain.

The forced abdication of Napoleon in 1814 freed Britain to turn her military might on the United States. Naval superiority got Wellington's veterans across the Atlantic unopposed and armies landed in Chesapeake Bay, burned Washington, and attacked Baltimore. General Prevost, with 14,000 seasoned troops set to drive down Lake Champlain, waited until enough green-timbered warships were thrown together by Captain Peter Downie, as Burgoyne had waited in 1775. In a blazing naval battle in Plattsburgh harbour, casualties were frightful. Downie was killed early in the point-blank carnage; command broke down and the Americans prevailed.

Prevost declined to press on, even against such slight opposition, without a navy to protect his rear. The freshwater navies' Battle of Plattsburgh decided the campaign and so in fact determined the shape of Canada. No one now wanted to prolong the costly war. Peace fixed the boundaries where they were before it started. The Rush-Bagot agreement in 1817 limited British North America and the U.S. to one warship each on Lake Champlain and Lake Ontario, and two each on the upper Great Lakes combined.

The Royal Navy was reduced after 1815 but still sailed supreme. The U.S. built a huge merchant fleet but had no naval strength until the Civil War. Britain fortified Halifax, Quebec, Kingston, and supporting points, but her main spending on Canadian defence was the Yankee-proof route from Montreal to Kingston via the Ottawa River and Rideau Canal. Disputes between the U.S. and Britain sent regular shivers down Canadian backs, and border issues raised temperatures to flash-point.

In 1837 William Lyon Mackenzie declared a provisional government on Navy Island in the Niagara River. He was supplied by a steamer called *Caroline* from the American side. A party of naval militia rowed across on a winter night, drove the crew ashore, set the ship afire, and cut her adrift. Over the falls she went, hard ablaze. Both countries were enraged. Rush-Bagot faded in the mounting tension. But conciliation triumphed and peace prevailed.

The Maine border dispute in 1845 and armed confrontation on San Juan Island in 1859 brought things to the boil. From the start of the American Civil War Britain was pro-South; she needed their cotton and their market, and the northeast states were industrial competitors. When a Union warship snatched Confederate emissaries from the British ship *Trent*, Britain was enraged. War loomed and 11,000 British troops rushed to Canada, many in Cunard's steamships. Confederate commerce raiders roved the seas for prizes but had no real effect on the war. A strong new Union navy blockaded southern ports, crippled their economy, and had a major bearing on the outcome. Meantime, Halifax boomed as a port for blockade running, and this identified Canada the more with Britain's pro-South stance. Canadians had leaned toward the North and abolition until a belligerent American press got to work. Fear of invasion rose and stayed very much alive well past the Civil War. It was a major stimulus to Confederation and governed British defence policy in the Western Hemisphere.

The only actual aggression, however, came from the Fenian Brotherhood. One feeble foray galvanized naval volunteers, and armed steamships appeared in the Great Lakes and St. Lawrence, Rush-Bagot notwithstanding. The feeling was growing that Canada might look after her own naval needs.

THE SEAGOING CENTURY

Shipbuilding boomed in the 1800s. Size, speed, price, and innovative design sold Canadian sailing ships to British owners. The 1,600-ton *Marco Polo* launched at Saint John in 1851 was known as the fastest ship in the world. The Shipping Register of Liverpool in 1858 showed 85 per cent of ships above 500 tons as Canadian-built. Shipping was the great business of the Atlantic provinces. For almost a century their ships traded round the world. Ships by the hundreds, laden with timber, sailed from Quebec and brought immigrants back – huddled, miserable, and dying in droves, but with the heart and mind and muscle to build a nation. But the wooden sailing ship's years were numbered and by the 1870s the government of the new Dominion and the financiers had turned inland to a burgeoning industrial heart.

The northwest coast of North America was one of the last areas of the globe to open up. Spain had claimed the whole of the Pacific in 1494, but it was almost 300 years before Hernandez, then Quadra, sailed the coastline north to Sitka. Britain contested Spain's claims as mere sightings and Captain James Cook, of St. Lawrence fame, landed at Nootka Sound in 1778, refitted his ship, traded with the Nootka, and claimed the land for King George III. Fur trade conflict brought Britain and Spain close to war, but in 1792 George Vancouver established Nootka Sound as a free port. He also surveyed the coast from California to Alaska and was at Bella Coola scant days before Alexander Mackenzie arrived there overland from Canada in 1793 – thirteen years before Lewis and Clarke from the United States descended the Columbia to the Pacific.

By that time Canadian fur traders had moved firmly in and built a rich trade with China. There were confrontations between Russians, Spaniards, Americans, and British, but Northwest coast trade grew without the great conflicts that plagued the East. By mid-century Russia had Alaska and the panhandle, Spain was out, the Canada-U.S. border was settled at the 49th parallel, and the Hudson's Bay Company ruled, rich and serene, in Victoria. Britain's need for naval bases grew with Empire and the demands of machine-driven ships for fuel and technical support. When the drydock opened in 1887, two years ahead of the one in Halifax, Esquimalt was firmly fixed on Britain's strategic map. The Canadian Pacific Railway, just completed, forged a great new link in the imperial chain.

Provincial Marines had grown by necessity for local defence and all the chores the RN wouldn't do. For years after the War of 1812 colonial governments chartered private vessels for essentials, from controlling smuggling to servicing lighthouses. Protecting the fisheries was a special problem. After endless disputes, unsatisfactory agreements, and fights on the fishing grounds, the Treaty of Washington was struck in 1871. Britain had authorized her colonies to raise their own local naval defence in 1865; at Confederation, fisheries became a federal matter. When bellicose Americans repudiated the treaty's fishing clauses in 1885, Maritimers watched angrily as Royal Navy warships swung at anchor. Britain effectively had dropped out. The little Canadian Fisheries Protection Service coped alone, quite capably. It became a permanent force and the base, eventually, for a Canadian navy.

The 1870s and 1880s saw new national powers emerging and a reordering of naval pre-eminence. Britain dropped to the "Two Power Standard," i.e., a navy equal to the combined strength of numbers two and three. In 1877 she came close to war with Russia. Canada, she said, would have to protect her own ports, fishermen, and coastal trade from commerce raiders. She had 90,000 seamen, after all, and in 1880 Admiralty donated an ancient steam corvette, HMS *Charybdis*, to train naval reserves. She was a broken-down pig in a poke and costs to make her useful proved sky-high. She slunk back to England under tow, a bad dream for any who might have naval notions. It would take another crisis to push Canada toward a navy of her own. Response to crisis, rather than strategic vision, became the hallmark of Canadian naval policy for over a hundred years.

At the first Colonial Conference in 1887 Britain said she would take care of Imperial Defence but she couldn't carry all the traditional burden; the colonies and dominions should contribute cash. Sir John A. Macdonald dug in. No act of Canada's would start a war calling for a navy and the CPR was a big enough contribution to imperial defence. But he really understood the importance of seapower to Canada and the need for naval forces of her own. His chief nautical adviser, Andrew Gordon, Lieutenant RN (retired), proposed buying Rattlesnake-class fast torpedo gunboats from Britain.

Rattlesnakes would be first class for the prime role in the fisheries. With their guns and torpedoes a flotilla could handle marauding cruisers, and they could dart up the canals to the Great Lakes if required. Macdonald liked the idea. It would meet peace, contingency, and war needs at reasonable cost and with Canadian control. But Admiralty knew better and their counterproposal of ships unsuited to Canadian conditions was haughty and unhelpful. An election was at hand. Two months after the Conservative victory of 1891, Sir John A. died, and with him went hope for the beginnings of a navy. For close to twenty more years Canada had no naval policy at all.

Canada's seagoing nineteenth century left a strangely prophetic mark. Horatio Nelson's victory and death at Trafalgar in 1805 stirred a great tide of emotion and a subscription was started in Montreal to raise a monument. It took twenty-one years to scrape the money together and at that the column fell eight feet short. Then, when they placed on it the figure of this most brilliant naval hero, his back was to the sea. And so was Canada's in the 1870s and 1890s; again in 1911; between the two terrible wars; after World War Two; then in the 1960s and 1970s when the Cold War was wishfully thought to ease; and the most recent dismal failure of naval policy came in 1989. Born in a country shaped by seapower and nourished by seaborne trade, with three oceans and the longest coastline in the world, Canadians have proved as fine sailors as can be found around the globe. Most often, though, except in times of driving need, their countrymen's backs have been turned, unthinking, to their navy and the sea.

CHAPTER TWO
THE BARE BEGINNINGS

COLONY OR NATION?

A VAST RANGE OF NEW FACTORS FACED THE NAVIES OF THE WORLD AT THE dawn of the twentieth century: steam, steel, electricity, wireless telegraphy, torpedoes, submarines, accurate long range guns, and soaring costs and rapid obsolescence. Britain's Royal Navy was no longer solely supreme. Japan was a new and formidable naval power. The U.S. Navy, since the Civil War, had moved to world status. Germany, united since 1870, industrially strong, and with aggressive Prussian leadership, built up a navy that was rapidly and ominously tilting the international scales.

At the Colonial Conference in 1897, Britain pressed for financial support for her navy. History supported the British view that "the sea was one," that the navy protected every corner of the Empire by neutralizing the enemy fleet wherever on the globe it might be. This was sound principle, but tell a Dominion voter he should pay for a navy he might never see and that could be moved at will by someone else's admiral. Strategy was one thing, politics another.

Wilfrid Laurier, newly elected Liberal Prime Minister of Canada, was in London to hear Joseph Chamberlain of the Colonial Office rub Canada's nose in the hard North American fact:

> . . . if Canada had not behind her to-day and does not continue to have behind her this great military and naval power of Great Britain, she would have to make concessions to her neighbours, and to accept views which might be extremely distasteful to her in order to remain permanently on good terms with them.

Laurier understood this very well but he would make no commitment on naval collaboration. Just as business and government looked inland, so most Canadians thought – if they thought of defence at all – in terms of an army. The myth persisted that the militia had won the War of 1812 and could be turned out to defend the borders once again if need be.

Navy-minded pressure groups then went to work. The Toronto branch of the Navy League of Canada proposed formation of a naval reserve in 1898 and consistently supported Canadian naval development. The pro-English Victoria branch favoured direct payments to the Royal Navy. The basic question – whether to support the Royal Navy financially or build Canada's own navy – was to be one of the most contentious issues since Confederation. Laurier had to move with care.

No longer able to take on the world, Britain leaned on alliances: a defensive one with Japan in the Pacific in 1902, an entente with France in 1904, and a similar agreement with Russia three years later. Her relations with the U.S. steadily improved. Arrayed on the other side were Germany, Austria-Hungary, and Italy. Keeping the Royal Navy just ahead of Germany alone was costing a huge amount, and Britain wanted help from the Empire that flourished under its protection.

Raymond Prefontaine, Laurier's Minister of Marine and Fisheries, went to London with him for the Colonial Conference on Defence in 1902. This time Chamberlain actively discouraged colonial or Dominion navies in favour of straight financial support of the RN. Again there was no Canadian commitment, but the British approach cut right across Laurier and Prefontaine's strong sense of Canadian nationalism. Things at Marine and Fisheries, the largest government department, began to move.

Marine and Fisheries handled everything to do with the sea and inland waters: hydrographic services, lighthouses and navigation aids, port facilities, fisheries, regulation of shipping, and so on, and it was responsible for Arctic sovereignty. It had substantial resources, including the Fisheries Protection Service, begun in 1886. In 1904 its fleet was eight armed fishery protection cruisers, six icebreakers, and eighteen other vessels. It ran thirteen Marconi marine wireless telegraphy stations on the east coast and five were added to the west coast in 1906. Much could be done within the department's existing structure and budget toward establishing a Canadian naval service.

Prefontaine's Commander of Marine Services, O.G.V. Spain, prepared "An Act Constituting the Naval Militia of Canada" for first reading in the House (it didn't get there) and a proposal for a naval academy. In 1904 the department bought Canadian Government Ship (CGS) *Canada* from Vickers Barrow in England. She had the lines and performance of a torpedo gunboat. CGS *Vigilant*, "the first modern warship to be built in Canada," was bought from the Polson Iron Works in Toronto. CGS *Falcon* arrived the same year. *Canada* and the others were in fact small warships with ram bows and quick-firing guns, and they were run like crisply disciplined navy ships. This was just what Andrew Gordon and Sir John A. Macdonald had in mind in 1887.

At Prefontaine's prompting, *Canada*, "armed and manned in all respects as a man of war," took a training class of young fishermen on a cruise to the West Indies in 1905. It was a fine carrot for winterbound fishermen and they did well. Mr. Spain proudly wrote: "The material we have in the Canadian Naval Militia is probably the best in the world." The Caribbean winter training cruise is a popular part of the annual training cycle to this day.

Prefontaine's successor in 1905 was Louis Phillipe Brodeur, a close friend of Laurier's and every bit as keen on having a navy. Progress in Canada was slowed by other political matters, but in Europe the arms race went inexorably on. It focused on a new word in the naval lexicon – "Dreadnought."

Over the years Admiralty in London had been very conservative about major innovations for fear they might wreak instant obsolescence on a huge fleet. But great improvements in the range and accuracy of naval gunnery demanded a completely new approach to the design of the line-of-battle ship. In 1905 Britain laid down a revolutionary new type and called her HMS *Dreadnought*. She was the first all-big gun ship.

The age-old criterion of power was now calculated in Dreadnoughts. If Germany built three, Britain must build five. The Hague Peace Conference of 1907 tried to cool the race. But Germany, in the catch-up position, would not stop building without political concessions, and those Britain would not give. The finish line was war.

Without a world-wide empire, Germany could keep her growing fleet at home. To counter it, Britain needed more and bigger ships in home waters. The Pacific Squadron was pulled out of Esquimalt in 1905, except for the old sloop HMS *Shearwater* and a survey ship. The Halifax dockyard became Canadian-owned for practical purposes in 1907, and Esquimalt in 1910. They would be kept up by Canada and the RN could use them as required. The garrisons of British regulars had left along with the Royal Navy. Canada, it appeared, must do something serious about defence.

The dockyards were strategically vital. Add fishery protection, hydrographic services, and marine wireless stations and Canada was making a measurable contribution to the overall scheme of imperial naval defence. So said Marine and Fisheries Minister L.P. Brodeur at the Imperial Defence Conference in 1907. Lord Tweedmouth, the First Lord (i.e., the political head) of the Admiralty, underlined the British stance of "one sea, one Empire, one Navy," and again pressed for help but with Admiralty running operations as it saw fit. But he acknowledged the value of local squadrons. Torpedo boats and submarines, for example, would be effective against commerce raiders and thus a contribution overall.

With European storm clouds gathering Canadians were getting far more interested in the naval question. In January, 1909, Hon. George Foster, one-time Minister of Marine and Fisheries under Macdonald and now a leading member of Robert Borden's Conservative opposition, gave notice of a motion that Canada should provide for naval defence of its own shores. He lobbied hard. It took him two months to deal with objections from F.D. Monk, leader of the Quebec Conservatives, and others of his own party, but by the time he rose in the House of Commons in late March his motion rode the crest of dramatic events.

A few days earlier the British Prime Minister in the House in Westminster had rung the alarm. By 1912 Germany would have twenty-one Dreadnoughts to Britain's eighteen, and that was a mortal threat. New Zealand instantly offered a Dreadnought, and Australia proposed immediate support. Foster's motion had stuck to coastal defence, but Sir Wilfrid Laurier exploited the opening with consummate skill. A series of amendments transformed the motion from the Opposition into the basis for a Canadian navy. The guts of it said:

> The House will cordially approve of any necessary expenditure designed to promote the speedy organization of a Canadian naval service in co-operation with and in close relation to the imperial navy, along the lines suggested by the Admiralty at the last Imperial Conference, and in full sympathy with the view that the naval supremacy of Britain is essential to the security of commerce, the safety of the empire and the peace of the world.

This first statement of naval policy in Canada's history passed the House unanimously. Brodeur took it as a ringing endorsement to a hastily convened Imperial Defence Conference in London in July. The atmosphere there had changed, for Britain agreed to the principle of Dominion navies and Admiralty was prepared to talk.

With Brodeur was Rear Admiral Charles Kingsmill, a Canadian who retired from the Royal Navy in 1908 to take the post of Director of Marine Service. They asked for outline plans for various squadrons with cost options. Admiralty recommended cruisers and destroyers, deferring submarines because of the special skills required. They would lend two old Apollo-class cruisers as interim training ships and provide RN volunteers to man them until replaced by trained Canadians. Officers and instructors would be loaned and Canadian cadets could be trained at the Royal Navy's preparatory school, Osborne, and the Royal Naval College at Dartmouth, in southern Devonshire. Australia stood with Canada on the matter of an independent navy and

Admiralty made similar arrangements with her. So the navies of the two senior dominions were born out of the same imperial events.

THE COUNTRY DIVIDED

Canadians were generally behind the Foster resolution except in Quebec. Opposition there was led by Monk, for the Conservatives, and Henri Bourassa, leader of the Nationalistes who had been a Liberal colleague of Laurier's but broke with him in 1905. Bourassa was a brilliant and fiery orator and an influential writer through his paper, *Le Devoir*. Now he uncompromisingly opposed introducing any naval policy without consulting the people.

The Naval Service Act came before the House in January, 1910. With it Laurier announced a program of eleven ships – a Boadicea-class armoured cruiser, four Bristol-class light cruisers, and six destroyers. Insofar as possible, they would be built in Canada. He acknowledged the cost would be about a third greater than buying from Britain, but it was the only way to develop the industrial base that a navy needed.

Robert Borden hedged. A Canadian navy would take years to build. The crisis was now and Canada should vote money now: Dreadnoughts for the RN it should be. Monk proposed a national plebiscite. In Montreal, Bourassa said the choice of ships proved they were not only for local defence, that in fact this was just a ruse for replacing the RN's overseas squadrons and thus for making the dominions pay the cost of Empire.

But the Naval Service Act became law on 4 May 1910, and L.P. Brodeur became the Minister of Naval Service. Rear Admiral Kingsmill was named as director, a position he held until 1921. As well as a Regular Force, the Act provided for a Naval College, a Reserve, and a Naval Volunteer force. Seven Royal Navy officers were loaned. Openings were advertised for the Royal Naval College of Canada, located in Halifax, and the first entrance exams were set for November, 1910. The British Naval Discipline Act of 1866 applied to all members of Canada's Naval Service, as did the venerable King's Regulations and Admiralty Instructions (KR&AI). Forty years and two wars would pass before Canada's navy replaced these revered documents with home-grown basic "bibles" of its own.

THE NAVY BEGUN

The first ships in the new Naval Service were the RN–built cruisers HMCS *Niobe* and *Rainbow*. *Niobe*'s full complement was 700 but she left England with only a skeleton crew of RN volunteers, each with the option of transferring to the fledgling navy. Her Captain was a British Columbian, Commander W.B. MacDonald, RN. *Niobe* arrived in Halifax on Trafalgar Day, 21 October 1910, fired a twenty-one-gun salute, and "dressed ship" – the old custom for special occasions of hoisting signal flags between mastheads, bow and stern. The Liberal *Halifax Chronicle* was effusive; the Conservative *Herald* sniffed over the nouveau HMCS for His Majesty's *Canadian* Ship instead of the time-honoured HMS; the Tory press in Toronto scoffed at her as "on her way to the scrap heap." Bourassa and Monk joined forces in a huge rally in Montreal and railed against Laurier's naval policy. *Le Devoir* called *Niobe* "canadienne en temps de paix, imperiale en temps de guerre." The new navy did not slide smoothly down the ways.

Niobe was an aging but in fact substantial ship – a "protected cruiser," launched in 1899, with sixteen 6-inch guns, a dozen 12-pounders, and two 18-inch torpedo tubes. *Rainbow* was a third *Niobe*'s size, an Apollo-class light cruiser with a main armament of two 6-inch guns. She left England headed for Canada's Pacific coast nearly two months before *Niobe*, but since the Panama Canal didn't open until 1914 she had to steam 15,000 miles via the Strait of Magellan to reach Esquimalt on 7 November. B.C. was pro-Navy and Victoria gave her a rousing welcome. Right away she set about a local cruise program combined with fishery protection – basically chasing Americans out of the three-mile limit – and on-the-spot recruiting. Twenty-three young men joined up on her first trip to Vancouver. The west coast sun shone on the new navy, happily distanced from eastern political storms.

Rainbow's Captain from mid-1911 was Commander Walter Hose, a widely experienced RN career officer with several seagoing commands under his belt. His wife was from St. John's, Newfoundland. That and prospects of quicker promotion in an infant service no doubt spurred him – adventurous and energetic as he was – to write to Admiral Kingsmill for a post. He was loaned at first to command *Rainbow*, and then in 1912 he resigned from the RN for a career in the RCN. The future at that time was shaky at best and the navy and Canada were lucky to have him.

Undismayed at *Niobe*'s mixed reception and proudly waiting in Halifax to step aboard their first big warship were six newly appointed midshipmen. They had actually joined as cadets several months before the Naval Service Act was passed and already had close to a year's hands-on instruction in seamanship and navigation in CGS *Canada*. Now they were ready for the next phase of their training as Canada's first home-grown naval officers before the Royal Naval College of Canada had opened its doors.

The Minister had taken a personal hand in this flying start to an officer corps. Naval Cadet Victor G. Brodeur was his son; Barry German was the son of the Liberal MP for Welland-St. Catharines; Percy Nelles's father was a retired senior army officer; Charles Beard's father was a senior government official; John Barron's was a judge; Trenwick Bate was the son of a Liberal millionaire. All were insiders. They had written no entrance exams – the method of selection was informal to say the least.

And brisk. Admiral Kingsmill's interview with seventeen-year-old Barry German in his office in Ottawa went thus:

W.M. German, MP, with pocket watch in hand: "This is the young man, Admiral. I have an appointment in ten minutes to introduce him to the Prime Minister."

The Admiral: "Can you swim?"

The candidate: "Yessir, I can swim the Welland Canal in ninety seconds."

The Admiral: "Catch the next train to Halifax."

It would certainly not do today, but the fact is this first class of naval cadets produced leaders who served the navy through years of struggle and despair, tremendous growth, and great achievement.

Their new shipmates in *Niobe* included Engine Room Artificer George Stephens, who turned over from the RN to the new navy. He rose through the ranks to become the Royal Canadian Navy's first Engineer Rear Admiral, Chief of Naval Engineering and Constructions, and member of the Naval Board. He directed the extraordinary naval shipbuilding program and technical expansion of World War Two and laid the base for building the highly sophisticated ships of the fifties and sixties.

Recruiting young Canadians for the lower deck started right away. Stoker J.O. Cossette signed up from Quebec early on and served in *Niobe*. He transferred from the boiler room to the ship's office as a Writer, a naval clerk, and worked his way up to head the Supply Branch and become the first Rear Admiral (Supply) in the RCN.

In those days matters of importance between governments went through the Governor General. Lord Grey, a strong supporter of Canadian initiative, backed a proposal that RCN ships fly the traditional White Ensign with a distinctive green maple leaf in the middle. The answer from Britain was the White Ensign unadorned. Next Grey proposed a West Indies training cruise with himself as a passenger, which was not approved "until the status of Dominion navies was settled." Further, Canadian ships would not cruise outside the three-mile limit without Admiralty approval. Brodeur was justifiably furious.

He was frustrated, too, over the matter of language at the Naval College. He asked Deputy Minister Georges Desbarats, who was also French, to see that the entrance exams were available in both languages and that the staff had a command of French so French-Canadian cadets would have a chance to adapt. Admiral Kingsmill's two senior staff officers, both from the RN, dug in their heels, and Kingsmill backed them – English in toto it must be. Hindsight is easy, but those two matters, a distinctive flag and a bicultural officer corps, could have given the RCN a Canadian distinctiveness that it never really found in the nation's eyes.

Canada lacked the marine engineering and shipyard capacity to build warships. Admiralty offered technical support and proposed a cautious start. Build the first few ships in Britain, they said, with some key Canadians learning on the job. But Laurier plunged in: British know-how, yes, but in Canada and from the start. The added cost and time were a reasonable price for the solid base a modern navy needed. The money would be spent largely in Canada, and the nation would be the richer for a major new industrial enterprise.

Tenders were called to set up plant and build four cruisers and six destroyers and a subsidy was offered to build drydocks. The deadline for bids was 1 May 1911. Canadian and British firms jumped at the chance, with bids around $12 million, but before a contract could be signed the election plug was pulled.

Parliament dissolved in July, 1911, and *Niobe* showed the flag – electioneering for Laurier, by any other name – in Quebec City, Charlottetown, and Yarmouth, but in thick weather she ran aground off Cape Sable, suffered underwater damage, and had to be towed back to Halifax. It was certainly bad news for the Liberal campaign, and for the navy. In the inevitable Court Martial the Navigating Officer was dismissed his ship and the Officer of the Watch reprimanded. It was a salutary lesson for the young Canadian officers. Being laid up alongside was no way to train midshipmen, though, so they were packed off to the RN to finish their training in the mighty HMS *Dreadnought* herself.

The election was fought on reciprocity with the U.S. Only in Quebec was the navy a major issue, and there the Conservatives and Bourassa's Nationalistes branded it the instrument of Empire and conscripter of young men. Laurier lost support in Quebec and lost the election, and the navy lost its champion. Quebec retained resentment of the navy for years. Robert Borden and the Conservatives formed a majority government. In Borden's first Speech from the Throne the navy wasn't even mentioned, and soon thereafter the shipbuilders' deposits were returned – there would be no ship construction program, no industrial base, and, for practical purposes, no navy. Repairs to *Niobe*, meanwhile, took over a year, and by then there was no money to send her to sea.

Winston Churchill, as First Lord of the Admiralty, proposed a scheme worthy of his agile mind at the following summer's meeting of the Committee of Imperial Defence. With a new threat in the Mediterranean from Austria and Italy, he said, Britain would be short three Dreadnoughts. If they were laid down for Canada as her contribution to Empire defence, then Germany would have no reason to lay down more ships herself. This, Churchill suggested, would be an interim solution to an urgent problem and not a permanent naval policy for Canada.

The proposal suited Borden. He in fact agreed with a scaled-down Laurier-style naval service but had to thread his own party's internal minefields. In December, 1912, he introduced the Naval Aid Bill, asking Parliament for $35 million for three Dreadnoughts as a one-time emergency contribution to imperial defence. The ships would be part of the Royal Navy but could be called back at some future date to form part of a Canadian unit of the RN. Laurier's Canadian-built navy would have cost one-third as much.

The Liberals fought the new bill tooth and nail. In the committee stage they used every obstructive trick in the book. Finally, on May 9, Borden introduced closure for the first time in Canadian parliamentary history, saying at the same time that he favoured a modest navy for coastal defence. A week later the bill passed third reading and went to the Senate for approval. But the Liberals had been in power since 1896. The Senate, packed with Laurier appointees, easily defeated the bill, and despite the predictable uproar and the fact that the Naval Service Act stayed on the books, Canada had no naval policy.

One brave pioneering light still burned in Victoria, B.C. A group of young men there started something akin to Britain's Royal Naval Volunteer Reserve with an unofficial blessing from the Minister. They got no support from Admiral Kingsmill, but Commander Hose, the man on the spot, pitched right in. They trained in the dockyard and on board *Rainbow* with her officers and petty officers as instructors. They had no uniforms, official status, or pay, only their own enthusiasm. Ten years later Walter Hose would harness that kind of spirit to virtually save the navy's neck.

But now its neck was wrung. The RN volunteers went home. Naval prospects in Canada were nil. In 1912 and 1913, 126 new enlistments were more than offset by 149 desertions. High hopes had vanished with the political wind. By 1914 the Royal Canadian Navy had dwindled to 330 officers and men and two old ships wasting in harbour without the funds to put to sea. It was not much of a basis on which to fight an approaching war. And no one in the country seemed to care.

THE ROYAL NAVAL COLLEGE OF CANADA

Quite remarkably, the infant Royal Naval College of Canada escaped Borden's axe, continued through the Great War, and survived until 1922. The Royal Navy had opened the doors of its colleges and gunrooms from the first suggestion that any Dominion was interested in its own seagoing service. Where better to become a naval officer than in the greatest navy in the world, which had produced the likes of Drake and Anson, Cook, Nelson, and Jackie Fisher, the current First Sea Lord? Where better, from the British point of view, to cast young colonials in the British mould?

Historically, the RN officer went to sea very young, usually as a servant first, then as a midshipman sponsored by some senior officer. From the age of twelve he was under the eye of the Captain and learned his profession from professionals at sea. The non-commissioned midshipman had authority over sailors, at least in theory. But he could learn from them, too, without losing face. He messed and slung his hammock in the gunroom, a partitioned corner of the gun deck that he shared with others of his ilk, men with warrants of promotion from the lower deck (like James Cook), and a couple of 32-pounders. A piping voice was no protection from being torn apart in battle.

For those who survived gunfire and disease, the commission as lieutenant was earned by time, diligent study, and rigorous examination. The ethos – the all-important basic outlook, moral standard, sense of duty, behaviour, self-discipline, and professional attitude – rubbed off from one's seniors. By and large they were capable men, and for centuries the system worked.

With new technology more formal preparation was needed ashore. The Royal Navy trained cadets in moored hulks from 1857, then founded the Britannia Royal Naval College ashore in Dartmouth in 1903. Still, RN cadets went off to sea as midshipmen in their middle teens. The United States Naval School, later the Academy, started at Annapolis in 1845. In the USN, midshipmen graduated from the Academy and went to sea as ensigns four years older with far more formal education and less horny-handed experience than their RN opposite numbers.

The first move toward a Canadian navy in 1904 included the concept of its own academy. The Naval Service Act of 1910 authorized the Naval College of Canada "for the purpose of imparting a complete education in all branches of naval science, tactics and strategy."

The easy, cheap, and obvious solution was to use the RN training system. But, as with building warships, Brodeur and Laurier saw the long-term importance of educating officers at home. Also, it was the only way to attract French candidates. They didn't choose the well-established Royal Military College at Kingston either – a navy was a navy to be led by naval officers, and they would be Canadian trained.

Space was found for forty-five cadets in the old Halifax Dockyard Naval Hospital. Twenty-one fourteen- to sixteen-year-olds passed the first exams. After 1912 the original two-year course was lengthened to three and the curriculum broadened. Admiral Lord Jackie Fisher, who towered as the ruler of the Royal Navy through these years, believed upper deck and engineering officers should be interchangeable, so there was a strong practical engineering element in the course. The little College was run with naval gusto and produced spirited young men, giving them a sound start for an adventurous life.

Applications had slowed to a trickle in 1913-14 when career prospects were nil. Curiously, though, the government kept the College going. The first class had just graduated in August, 1914, when the cruiser HMS *Good Hope*, flying the flag of Rear Admiral Sir Christopher Craddock, coaled in Halifax. Short-handed in the gunroom, she took fresh-minted Canadian midshipmen Malcolm Cann, William Palmer, Arthur Silver, and John Hathaway. It was a prize! Off to sea with the first guns of the Great War. They were the envy of their classmates.

Good Hope went down fighting on the 1st of November, sunk by Admiral Graf von Spee's Pacific Squadron off Coronel, South America. The four young midshipmen went down with her. They were Canada's first casualties of the war.

In the Halifax explosion in 1917 several cadets were hurt and the College was wrecked. It moved for a while to the Royal Military College, Kingston, then on to Esquimalt in September, 1918. There the old *Rainbow* served until space was found ashore. Finally, in June, 1922, with no money in the naval budget the College closed.

Today, the Royal Naval College of Canada seems to have been run on a shoestring, but it did a fine job. Commander A.E. Nixon – initially the First Lieutenant, then in command himself from 1915 – was its heart and soul, planting in young Canadians the seeds of that all-important, timeless naval ethos. He was the essential example of what a naval officer should be.

The College passed out a mere 150 graduates in its eleven years. But this vision of Laurier and Brodeur was an invaluable investment in people. It produced a generation of Canadian naval officers that the country sorely needed when the time came. And they served their country well.

CHAPTER THREE

THE
GREAT WAR

BRITAIN DECLARED WAR ON GERMANY ON 4 AUGUST 1914. SO, WITHOUT A by-your-leave, did the British Empire, Canada included. Thanks to utter lack of naval policy there was nothing more than a rundown cruiser on each coast, 350 officers and men, and some 250 slightly trained members of the Royal Naval Canadian Volunteer Reserve (RNCVR).

Germany, Austria–Hungary, and Italy mobilizing their armies against France and Russia had seemed a pretty remote broil. Canadians didn't even know about Britain's military understanding with France. When she honoured it and war came, the expectation – in Canada, as elsewhere – was that the bands would play, the flags would wave, the boys would march off, and it would all be over in a matter of months.

Young Canadians answered the ringing call to arms. If they didn't get in quickly they'd miss the great adventure. By the 8th of September 32,000 volunteers had poured into a half-constructed army camp at Valcartier. By the end of the month, barely kitted out and knowing little more about soldiering than the refrain of "Tipperary," they boarded transports at Quebec City. Downriver they sailed to assemble in the great anchorage at Gaspé. On 3 October the biggest body of men ever to cross the Atlantic sailed in convoy. Thirty-two passenger liners, mostly regulars on the Canadian run, carried them across. Only three were Canadian-owned. The escort was four RN light cruisers.

Prime Minister Borden, putting first things first, cabled London: "Probability elections makes it desirable to ascertain . . . what course would Admiralty advise if we decided offer naval aid." The reply: "Admiralty inform don't think anything effectual can now be done as ships take too long to build and advise Canadian assistance be concentrated on army."

In November, Borden pressed for destroyers and submarines to be built in Canada and for RN units on loan in the interval. Churchill repeated: no ships to spare; building in Canada not practical; send soldiers. Canada had neither a navy nor a shipbuilding industry, or, by now, an ocean-going merchant fleet with which to fight a war. Had Laurier's plans been realized Canada could have been far more a naval resource and arsenal for the Allies. As it was, Canada's answer was soldiers, a generation to die in the awful shambles that was France.

THE SUBMARINE

The naval war was seen as protecting Britain's trade, with the great fleets reaching the final resolution in cataclysmic battle, which the Royal Navy would by custom win. But what of the submarine, the great, new, admittedly unblooded naval weapon of the century? All the major powers had embraced it for their special needs. None, though, had yet divined its truly crucial role.

At the turn of the century the Holland submarine, devised by an Irish-American of that name, was developing quickly and being bought from the U.S. or built under licence by major navies. It was in essence the "conventional" submersible of today, driven underwater by electric motors and recharging its batteries as it ran on the surface on diesel engines. The threat of cheap, invisible little submarines torpedoing their behemoths gave the Dreadnought builders nightmares.

The Royal Navy wisdom of the day was that submarines would defend the fleet at sea and counter raiders in coastal waters. Oddly, they hadn't figured in Laurier's naval plan of 1910. A handful of submarines would have been a bargain for Canadian coastal defence against marauders. But Rear Admiral Kingsmill, Laurier's adviser, had plainly missed the point.

As to attacks on shipping, the Hague Conventions of 1899 and 1907 had, of course, fixed that. The Rules of War said a warship had to search an unescorted vessel for contraband prior to sinking her. Then it had to ensure the crew safe passage to shore. Lifeboats weren't counted as "safe passage" and submarines could carry few prisoners. So submarines wouldn't be used against shipping! Even a realist like Winston Churchill didn't believe a submarine campaign on merchant shipping "would ever be done by a civilized power."

Germany's Admiral von Tirpitz refused to spend money on submarines as long as they could cruise only in home waters. But in 1906 U-1, the first in the iron line of deadly Unterseebooten, completed a 600-mile cruise. Tirpitz moved fast. Inside three years Germany was building boats with four torpedo tubes, a gun, and a twelve-knot surface speed. By 1913 they had a 3,000-mile range at eight knots and carried efficient periscopes and powerful wireless transmitters. They would certainly be used against Britain's huge Grand Fleet.

New weapons breed counters. Ships could zigzag and use high speed. Screening destroyers, there to protect the fleet from torpedo boats in any case, could snag them with towed explosive paravanes. Periscopes could be sighted and smashed with gunfire. Hydrophones could detect their underwater sound. Surfaced, they could be rammed. They might indeed be spotted by that other new device, the airplane.

Aircraft, of course, brought the third dimension to naval warfare just as the submarine had added the second. Its potential was equally obscure. The Wright brothers' first piloted flight with a gasoline engine was in 1903. Louis Bleriot flew the English Channel in 1909. The first successful flight by a French seaplane came in 1910. A U.S. Navy plane took off and landed on a special platform on the battleship *Pennsylvania* in 1911. The RN ran trials on spotting submarines from aircraft in the same year.

By 1913 the new Royal Naval Air Service had some non-rigid airships and fifty-two Short seaplanes, which could stay airborne for three hours and had an operating radius of seventy-five miles. They were for reconnaissance and gunfire spotting. The potential was clear enough against submarines, but no one had an air-dropped or even a shipborne anti-submarine weapon. And no one had any notion of what the U-boat really held in store.

By 1914 the Royal Navy had seventy-five submarines, the French sixty-seven, Russia thirty-six, Germany thirty. Of the German boats, twenty were operational and battle-ready. Then, on the very day war broke out, Canada had a chance at two. The matter had come up over whisky and cigars at the Union Club in Victoria on the 29th of July. J.V. Paterson, president of the Seattle Construction and Drydock Company, was in town on business and told Captain W.H. Logan, surveyor for the London Salvage Association, about two submarines he had just finished for the Chilean government. He was having a wrangle with the Chileans over the specifications and they still owed some money. With the current threat of war, perhaps Canada would like them?

Captain Logan strode down Government Street to the Premier, Sir Richard McBride. The Dominion Minister of Agriculture, Hon. Martin Burrell, was on the coast and telegrams flashed to Ottawa on political and naval nets. Cables were exchanged with Admiralty. Paterson's price was $1,150,000 for the pair. His $332,000 mark-up on the Chilean deal raised eyebrows, but he was onto a good thing.

Logan dashed to Seattle on the 4th of August with a young Victoria Naval Reserve officer in civilian clothes. The cloaks were out, if not the daggers. If the American authorities or the Chileans or the German consul got a sniff of the wind the game would be up. That day the war news exploded in the streets. The boats would have to leave that very night or not at all. Logan haggled but the price was final and the sale was COD.

By phone, the Premier agreed to have a B.C. treasury cheque at the border at dawn the next day. It was a foggy night. The two subs silently crept out of the shipyard on electric motors with Logan and Paterson on board. Clear of the harbour, they blasted off on their diesels at full speed through the fog.

At first light SS *Salvor* waited, five miles south of Trial Island, just outside Canadian territorial waters. On board with the B.C. government's cheque in his pocket was Lieutenant Bertram Jones, RN (retired). Several years' experience in submarines made him a rare bird indeed, and during the summer's war rumblings he had presented himself at the Esquimalt dockyard.

Jones and the Chief Engineer Officer from Esquimalt set about a systematic inspection of the two submarines. No one was going to sell them a pig in a poke. In Seattle, of course, the fat was on the fire; in Washington, President Wilson was in the very act of signing the neutrality proclamation to slam the door on such transactions. The wires hummed. The Germans raged, as did the Chileans.

Four hours dragged by. Paterson fidgeted at the inspecting officers' heels. Logan scanned the horizon for the U.S. Navy. Satisfied at last, Jones handed over the huge cheque, hoisted the White Ensign on the two submarines, and set course triumphantly for Esquimalt. Next morning USS *Milwaukee* sternly combed American waters for the rascally Canadians, a good show of official indignation but nothing more.

The new prides of the west coast navy were named *Paterson* and *McBride* on the spot. Ottawa reimbursed British Columbia and damped local pride by ordering the anonymous names *CC1* and *CC2*, "C" for Canadian and "C" for their rough equivalent, the RN's C-class subs. The hard-nosed Paterson got something more to his liking in a handsome $40,000 personal commission from the Electric Boat Company, and Premier McBride got B.C.'s money back from the Dominion government. The submarines were commissioned into the RCN and, like *Niobe* and *Rainbow*, their operational control was turned over to Admiralty.

No torpedoes came with them. They had 18-inch tubes and *Rainbow*'s were the older 14-inch type, so *Niobe*'s stocks in Halifax were raided. Crews were the next problem. By a stroke of luck a very experienced submarine commander, Lieutenant Adrian Keyes, RN (retired), was working in Toronto. Admiral Kingsmill signed him on and in days he was taking charge of his two boats, bare minimum support facilities, and 100 brave and largely uninformed volunteers. Lieutenant Jones had lined up Lieutenants Wilfrid Walker, RN (retired), and Barney Johnson, RNR. Johnson was an experienced Master Mariner and B.C. coastal pilot. Fresh from the College in Halifax came Midshipman William Maitland-Dougall.

Admiral von Spee's cruisers were at large in the Pacific and there was no way of knowing where they might strike. Fears fanned by the press conjured bloody scenes – bombardments of Vancouver and Victoria, attacks on the coal mines at Nanaimo, slaughtering of fishermen. One Victoria family out-fitted their vault in the cemetery as a bombardment shelter. But no prudent cruiser captain half a world away from friendly repair facilities would risk damage from a submarine-launched torpedo. Consequently, the mere presence of *CC1* and *CC2* was vastly more effective than the dubious protection offered by the venerable *Rainbow*.

RAINBOW'S WAR

Admiralty had pulled most of the Royal Navy back to home waters and the far corners of the world were thinly held. The northwest Pacific boasted two other ancients, the steam-and-sail sloops HMS *Shearwater* and *Algerine*. In August they were off the Mexican coast with an international squadron protecting foreign interests in the Mexican civil war. The modern German cruiser *Leipzig* was in the squadron and in July had exchanged courtesies with *Algerine* in Mazatlan. Another German cruiser, *Nurnberg*, was about. As war began the two nigh-defenceless RN sloops were a long way from home and in real danger.

Rainbow, under Commander Hose of the RCN, was at sea on 3 August. He had done his best to whip his ship into shape, yet still she had less than half her proper complement and over a third of those were local volunteer reservists, keen but with no seagoing experience. Her wireless had a nighttime range of only 200 miles. Her ammunition outfit, quite incredibly, included only ancient gunpowder-filled shells. Modern high-explosive (HE) shells were stored at an inland magazine but the railway company was not organized to handle big shipments of explosives. Hose had just received a signal saying his HE shells had arrived in Vancouver when he got another from NSHQ:

> *Nurnberg* and *Leipzig* reported August 4th off Magdalena Bay [Mexico] steering north. Do your utmost to protect *Algerine* and *Shearwater* steering north from San Diego. Remember Nelson and the British Navy. All Canada is watching.

A stirring exhortation cum epitaph! Should Hose head for Vancouver and his shells? Being Hose, he turned south immediately at his best fifteen knots, pondering the tactics for his two old 6-inch guns and four 12-pounders versus two fast twenty-three-knot cruisers. Each of them had full complements, modern gunnery control, ten 4.1-inch guns with longer range than his – and they had high-explosive shells. The scene could be a quick and ugly one for all of Canada to watch.

Hose went into San Francisco seeking news, but there had been no reports of *Shearwater* or *Algerine* and they had no radios. The enemy cruisers, though, had been seen off San Diego heading north. One day's steaming at twelve knots! Hose steamed out, patrolled near the Farallones Islands west of the Golden Gate, right across the enemy's path, plotting time, speed, and distance on his chart, waiting for the two sloops – or the German squadron.

Preparing for battle, the ship's company ripped out and ditched all the inflammable peacetime woodwork. On 10 August, with his coal running low and when he reckoned the sloops must be safely to the north, Hose headed up the coast. Next day, unknown to Hose, *Leipzig* was sighted off the Farallones. Hose worked *Rainbow* slowly north, not running from the Germans but keeping himself between them and where he estimated his unseen charges were. At eight a.m. on 12 August a big, three-funnelled ship was sighted ahead, approaching fast. Hose rang full ahead, put the wheel over, sounded action stations. All hands stood to with pounding hearts and dry mouths, ready for a desperate battle. Then the "enemy" was identified. She was SS *Prince George*.

Back in Esquimalt it had been quite clear that *Rainbow* was on borrowed time. Those who saw her leave seriously doubted she would return. But there were no reinforcements to send. There weren't even torpedoes for the submarines. At least, though, wounded could be cared for. *Prince George* was hastily complemented with medical staff, marked as a hospital ship, and sent south. With her three funnels and tidy lines she'd been taken by *Rainbow* for the enemy.

By now *Shearwater* was almost at Esquimalt, but there was no sign of *Algerine*. Hose dashed into harbour for a quick coaling and – wonderful sight – his outfit of high-explosive shell, but no fuzes came with them and none were to be found. Regardless, he set off and next afternoon met *Algerine* getting some badly needed coal from a passing collier. *Algerine* signalled: "I am damned glad to see you." As *Rainbow* turned north to escort her safely home, Walter Hose and his whole ship's company no doubt echoed the words.

Now the Germans were reported off San Francisco taking British prizes and on the 17th *Leipzig* steamed in for fuel. Her captain held a press conference, saying the German navy would sweep the seas, presented the city zoo with two Japanese bear cubs, and sailed again by midnight.

Commander Hose got the news of *Leipzig* the next day, and *Rainbow* took on her fuzes at Esquimalt. Hose signalled for permission to go south and fight and sailed immediately. He was well on his way when Admiralty's signal arrived with permission to "engage or drive off *Leipzig* from trade route . . . off San Francisco." The following day, though, both German cruisers were reported there and Admiralty recalled the pugnacious *Rainbow* to await HMS *Newcastle*, now on her way from Yokohama.

Within a day, a three-funnelled cruiser was reported off Prince Rupert and *Rainbow* raced north. Imaginations get inflamed and reports can grow quickly in transmission during war. *Nurnberg* was never within 2,500 miles of B.C. Rumour notwithstanding, she took not a single prize. None of that, of course, in any way diminishes the problems, pressures, and hard decisions faced by Commander Walter Hose.

By the end of the month *Newcastle*, a fast Bristol-class cruiser, had arrived. Japan was now an ally and her powerful armoured cruiser *Idzumo* joined the force. *Rainbow* was useful mainly as a radio link. But no more was seen of the Germans. Admiral von Spee's task of destroying Britain's trade in the Pacific was wrecked by Japan's entry in the war. Now he was simply trying to get his ships back home.

Leipzig and *Nurnberg* joined von Spee. Then, at Coronel on 1 November, he met Craddock's RN squadron and dealt the British an overwhelming defeat. The Allied squadron in Esquimalt braced for von Spee to come north. Walter Hose signalled Admiral Kingsmill to ask Admiralty that *Rainbow* ". . . be in company with squadron when engaged with enemy." Such was the unquenchable spirit of the man. Kingsmill turned him down. If the ship were lost "there would be much criticism on account of her age in being sent to engage modern vessels." Fear of criticism – such was the Ottawa mind.

Von Spee's success was short-lived. Off the Falkland Islands on 8 December he met Rear Admiral Sturdee's squadron, including two powerful battle cruisers. All but one of the German ships were sunk. Only *Dresden* remained in the South Atlantic, a thorn in the RN's flesh until she was destroyed in March, 1915.

The danger to the west coast had passed. Japan controlled the Pacific. *Rainbow* made some forays south, took two prizes, and tied up German ships in neutral ports. When the U.S. entered the war in April, 1917, the last vestige of a threat was gone and *Rainbow* was at last paid off. If old ships dream in their retirement as old sailors do, she had some memories to warm her rusted heart.

NIOBE'S WAR

As in the American Civil War, the commerce raiders drew great public attention, brewed myth and rumour, incited near panic along the seaboards, and in fact achieved little in the total scheme of war. Admiral Tirpitz had no illusions. In late September he wrote: "The cruisers out at sea must one after the other perish for lack of coal, provisions, and refitting stations." They lived on borrowed time. Their chief value, as always, was in tying up large hunting forces.

In the northwest Atlantic the 4th Cruiser Squadron had to deal with the raiders, and also round up German merchant ships or bottle them up in neutral harbours. To handle the job, until his ill-fated cruise west, Rear Admiral Craddock had five cruisers. The fast cruisers *Dresden* and *Karlsruhe* were somewhere along the Atlantic coast. In the first few days of war Craddock actually spotted *Karlsruhe*. His ships were too slow to catch her but he cut her off from shipping in the rich hunting ground off Newfoundland. Big ocean liners and a stream of freighters passed as usual off Newfoundland and Nova Scotia. It was the focal point for raiders. Convoys weren't organized, though, except for troopers, and these were well protected: the first million men from overseas reached England without loss of a single life.

On the outbreak of war *Niobe*, like the west coast ships, was turned over to the RN for operational control with Captain R.G. Corbett, RN, in command. Stirred from her state of near decay in Halifax, she was ready for sea in three weeks. The two old sloops on the west coast were of no use as warships. *Algerine* became a depot ship and *Shearwater* the submarine tender. Most of their companies were rushed across to man *Niobe*. Volunteers across Canada with some kind of experience found their way on board. Still short-handed, she steamed to St. John's. The Royal Naval Reserve branch there had been going since 1900 and provided 107 trained seamen. *Niobe* for the first time in her Canadian career had a full complement of 700.

She took a trooper with the Royal Canadian Regiment to Bermuda in September, but defects stopped her from escorting the great October troop convoy out of Gaspé. She searched among the icebergs off Belle Isle for a raider reported – falsely – inside the Gulf of St. Lawrence, then joined the RN cruisers blockading off New York. Sheltering in neutral ports from Cartegena to Boston were some ninety enemy merchant ships; thirty-two were in New York. Blockading was tedious work: sixteen days off New York, boarding and searching every vessel for contraband and for German reservists trying to get home, back to Halifax for the filthy job of coaling ship, fresh provisions, then on station once again. The winter chill was warmed by the friendliness of the U.S. Navy, whose ships would raise a cheer in passing, and by British liners who stopped to send over lush goodies from their galleys.

By midsummer 1915, *Niobe* was worn out. Her funnels were collapsing, her boilers and main bulkheads were in bad shape. She needed a major overhaul, but at her age and stage it wasn't worth it. Admiralty offered a replacement cruiser three years younger, but by now the RCN couldn't find the men. Its hands were full trying to maintain a modest fleet of small ships for coastal patrol and trade protection.

THE U-BOATS

On the other side of the Atlantic the U-boat had surfaced dramatically as a tremendously potent weapon of war. Within the first few weeks four RN cruisers had been sunk, three of them by a single U-boat in a span of two hours. U-boats began sinking merchant ships in October, scrupulous at first about the rules. Most sinkings were by gunfire or by scuttling or placing explosives on board after the ships' crews took to the boats. Torpedoes were saved for large, fast merchant ships, troopers, and warships. The RN had only the imprecise hydrophone and the naked eye to detect U-boats, and nothing but guns or ramming to fight them. The simple depth charge only started development in 1915 and got its first kill two years later.

In February, 1915, with his hopes dashed for a quick victory in France, Kaiser Wilhelm declared the approaches to Britain a war zone. Allied ships could be sunk without warning or any guarantee for safety of the crew. Neutrals would be respected but they took their chances. The gloves were off. Sinkings increased dramatically – by summer of 1915 they had climbed to nearly 100 a month. Still, ships sailed independently. Admiralty made no move toward convoy for protecting trade. Escorts were for troopships only.

In May, the twenty-six-knot Cunard luxury liner *Lusitania* sailed from New York, her departure advertised as usual in the *New York Times*. Right below the ad was the German embassy's announcement that British flag vessels were "liable to destruction . . . and that travellers sailing in the war zone on ships of Great Britain or her allies do so at their own risk." She sailed with a full passenger list, streamers flying, the band playing, champagne corks popping. In sight of the south coast of Ireland in broad daylight she was hit by a single torpedo from a submerged U-boat and went down with loss of 1,000 lives. Among the drowned were 128 Americans.

The U.S. was outraged. President Wilson didn't go to war – that would take another two years – but the seeds were firmly planted. Germany reined in the U-boats for a time. They had a hey-day in the Mediterranean and off Africa and were careful with neutrals. Still, by the end of 1916 they had sunk 1,360 ships.

During this period the U-boat fleet continued to grow and the sinkings continued to climb. The RN tried everything: blockading the submarine ports; anti-submarine minefields; search and patrol by sea and air in submarine transit areas and in shipping focal points. They hatched desperate tricks like the "Q" ships, little coasters or fishing vessels with concealed guns that lured U-boats close, then dropped their disguise and blazed away.

An Okanagan fruit farmer, Clarence King, was a "Q" ship Navigator, First Lieutenant, then Captain. He'd come to B.C. from England before the war and had a merchant service Master's ticket and in 1915 got a commission in the Royal Naval Reserve. King duelled one U-boat to death, got two possibles, and won a Distinguished Service Cross. His confirmed kill was one of fourteen by the "Qs" through the war.

Naval intelligence had broken the German codes early in the war and the RN held that enormous advantage right to the end. There was also a fast developing direction-finding net to fix U-boat positions by their wireless transmissions. *U-20*, which sank *Lusitania*, had been accurately plotted by Admiralty from intercepted signals on the day of the attack. But it all did little good.

MADE IN CANADA

In spite of Admiralty blocking destroyer building in Canada there was some complex warship construction. The technical know-how came from the United States. In 1914 Admiralty had ordered twenty H-class submarines from Bethlehem Steel and the Electric Boat Company of Groton, Connecticut. Electric Boat held the Holland patents, which were the basis for most of the submarines built before the war, *CC1* and *CC2* included. U.S. neutrality caused problems so ten of the H-boats were built at Canadian Vickers in Montreal under American supervision.* Six completed in July, 1915, were the first submarines to cross the Atlantic under their own power.

Shipyards build on building. Seamen learn by doing. After the first crash training with *CC1* and *CC2* out west, Adrian Keyes rejoined the RN. Young Maitland-Dougall joined *H-10* completing at Canadian Vickers. He then qualified formally in RN submarines and spent a lot of time at sea in them on anti-submarine patrols. In January, 1918, he took over command of submarine *D-3* from Barney Johnson, who had been with him in *CC1* and *CC2*. That March *D-3* was taken for a U-boat by a French airship, bombed, and sunk. There were no survivors.

Barney Johnson had taken to submarines quickly, too. In 1915 he got command of the RN's *H-8*, building at Vickers, a first for a reserve officer – and a Canadian at that. Johnson took *H-8* to the U.K., stayed in command, and won the Distinguished Service Order for courage and seamanship on hazardous operations. He commanded RN submarines with hardly a break, including *D-3*. In May, 1918, he went to the States to bring back the new *H-14* and *H-15*, which were transferred to the RCN to replace the worn-out *CC1* and *CC2*.

Johnson retired as a Commander, RNR, at war's end, went back to the marine business in Vancouver, and joined the RCNR at the first gun in 1939. On his sixty-fifth birthday in 1943 – also the fiftieth anniversary of his seagoing career – he was back at sea commanding the depot ship *Preserver*. In the meantime, his son had been through the Royal Naval College of Canada and gone to sea in merchant ships in the lean years between wars. Cast in the Johnson mould, Barney Junior commanded the corvette *Agassiz* and two

---

* Canadian Vickers was a productive shipbuilder in World War Two as well. It was the lead yard in building the high-tech St. Laurent classes in the fifties and sixties, and fifty years after the H-boats Vickers was building nuclear submarine hull sections under contract for its old mentor, Electric Boat.

frigates, fighting submarines during World War Two. Seagoing runs in the blood.

JUTLAND

An intercepted German signal in late May, 1916, warned Admiral Jellicoe up in Scapa Flow that at long last the German High Seas Fleet was coming out. Admiral Scheer was heading up the North Sea, racing for the open ocean. The Grand Fleet put to sea. With Beatty's battle cruisers from Rosyth, it was an enormous fleet of 150 ships: thirty battleships, eleven battle cruisers, thirty-four cruisers, seventy-four destroyers, and one seaplane tender.

Near Jutland Bank off the entrance to the Baltic, Jellicoe joined battle with Admiral Scheer and his somewhat smaller force. He lost six ships to the German's five. British communications didn't measure up, and Scheer's ships proved better at night fighting. He got his fleet back to harbour pretty well intact. Jellicoe had failed, and he found himself behind a desk as First Sea Lord. The High Seas Fleet never seriously put to sea again. But intact and snug in harbour, it pinned the RN's Grand Fleet down.

As for centuries whenever Britain fought, the crux of any long and grimly grinding war was trade – the food and fuel, the sustenance for people, the material of war, the men in millions who must move across the sea. The privateers and corsairs and flying squadrons of the past had never won a war. But *guerre de course* by U-boats with their speed, their killing power, their sheer numbers, and their near invulnerability could very well succeed. In a single week in 1916 three of them sank thirty ships on the south coast of England, then eluded a huge search-and-patrol force. Widening the U-boat war, however, risked bringing in the United States. To the little ships patrolling around Nova Scotia and the Gulf of St. Lawrence this was all very far from Canadian shores, but in the summer of 1916 there had been a grim note of warning.

The British naval blockade was squeezing Germany very hard and in August their *Deutschland*, a big, unarmed cargo-carrying submarine, ran to the U.S. for a cargo of nickel, tin, and crude rubber. To the American public it seemed a rather glamorous venture. Then *U-53* entered Newport, Rhode Island. Without even topping up with fuel and within a few hours of sailing, she sank five British ships just outside territorial waters. USN destroyers stood back and watched, then rescued survivors. So U-boats could carry their attack clear across the Atlantic when they chose.

UNRESTRICTED WAR

In January, 1917, Kaiser Wilhelm weighed the odds. Germany's economy was in deep trouble and her armies were mired down on two fronts, quite unable to force a decision. She had 100 operational U-boats, and the U.S. would come into the war sooner or later with her big, capable navy and huge resources. An all-out effort now could drown Britain and resolve the issue, so on 1 February unrestricted submarine warfare became the order of the day – no holds barred, no ships spared. In three dark and bitter winter months 800 ships and 8,000 seamen went to the bottom of the sea. Fully a quarter of the merchant ships that sailed from British ports were being sunk. By spring, losses were so great that Admiralty's analysts baldly projected the effective destruction of the merchant fleet by November. That meant defeat for Britain, whatever miracle might be wrought in France.

The ghastly statistics of loss were almost entirely of unescorted shipping. Yet general convoy, the ancient device proven over centuries of sail in time of war, was still resisted at the highest level. Admiral Jellicoe and Rear Admiral Duff, his choice as head of the new Anti-Submarine Division, wouldn't have it. The arguments were various: congestion of ports; slowing down traffic; inability of merchant ships to keep accurate station; ships gathered together like sheep for slaughter; too few escorts to go around; the chronic resistance of shipowners. Not one of these objections was new – all had been overcome down the centuries. Technology had changed, and that was what the admirals saw. Basic principles had not.

Convoy was as old as war at sea. Henry III had ordered English ships into convoy in 1226. Acts of the British Parliament from 1650 had made convoy mandatory in time of war. Shipowners, to be sure, didn't like it, and merchant captains chafed at being held back to the speed of the slowest, tied into formation with the risk of collision, and pushed around by the navy. And delays, delays, delays. But convoy worked. In the War of the Austrian Succession, 300 unescorted British ships were taken by the enemy while ninety-six convoys sailed without a single loss. At Lloyd's Coffee House in London underwriters' rates reinforced the law. Between 1793 and 1815, for example, premiums for convoyed ships were a half to a third of those for independents.

And here was a very important point: convoys brought the enemy to battle. He couldn't snatch prizes at random using single cruisers in *guerre de course*, so he must come to the convoy, fight the escort, and risk battle with the supporting squadron. For almost 150 years nearly every major naval battle that had been fought was over a convoy, merchant or military. Admiral Lord Nelson said himself, "I consider the protection of trade the most essential service that can be performed. . . . No ship, even the fastest, shall sail out of convoy."

In February of 1917 the French government insisted the decimated cross-Channel coal trade be put in convoy. The colliers crossed almost untouched. The Scandinavian trade was losing a quarter of all its sailings, and Admiral Beatty finally got authority to try convoys there in April. Losses dropped immediately to one-quarter of one per cent. The case for convoy was clear.

At the end of April, faced with overwhelming evidence, the urging of some junior admirals, and pressure from Prime Minister Lloyd George himself,

Admiral Jellicoe made the decision that was long overdue. Convoys were quickly organized for inbound ships. The first reached Britain in May unscathed. Halifax and Sydney became assembly ports and the first trade convoy left Sydney on 10 July. Eastbound convoys were marshalled and escorted seaward by little ships of the RCN. Royal Navy and U.S. Navy cruisers and auxiliary cruisers served as ocean escort; destroyers and aircraft met them in the U.K. approaches and successfully held off the U-boats.

By August, outbound vessels from the U.K. were in convoy. Sinkings dropped below half of those in April. By October, losses in convoy were less than one in a hundred, one-tenth the rate of independents. Convoy was restored to its historic place in spite of the First Sea Lord's dilatory hand and in the barest nick of time.

That April, too, the United States declared war. The U-boat certainly was a strong factor – by far the largest in the public view. USN destroyers arrived at Cork in southern Ireland to heavily reinforce the British escorts, and their aircraft gave the Royal Naval Air Service a major boost.

It was not detection or weapons but the very nature of the convoy that won, as it had for centuries. Unlike a scattered stream of independents, a convoy could be routed around danger areas. Ships swept together into convoys meant the U-boats had to search a vast empty ocean for a fraction of the number of targets. To attack a convoy meant closing with the enemy, risking a fight with the escort, and convoys could be reinforced with surface and air escorts when they got to dangerous areas.

U-boats might slip in for torpedo attack, but the old days of finishing ship after lone ship at will with cheap and easy gunfire or by boarding and scuttling were no more. As unescorted ships grew rare in British waters the U-boats had to reach further and further for their targets. With the U.S. in the war from April, 1917, new hunting grounds for the Germans opened off North America.

THE EAST COAST PATROLS

Against this darkening background the Canadian navy organized the East Coast Patrols. Canada had requisitioned auxiliaries from the beginning of the war and armed them with 3- and 6-pounder guns, and a 12-pounder when one could be found. In 1916 seven vessels scratched together from government service and yacht basins were the core of the east coast navy. With eight more small auxiliaries they ran coastal patrols in the Gulf of St. Lawrence and along the shores of Nova Scotia and Newfoundland.

Admiralty pointed out gratuitously that RN cruisers couldn't protect transports against submarines and advised the RCN that year to triple its force to thirty-six ships with 12-pounder guns, at least. The RN would provide nothing but an officer to advise or take command.

Canada fired back. Britain had said from the start the Canadian effort should be on land, and Their Lordships had blocked all Canadian proposals to build warships in Canada. The RCN had rounded up every gun and every volunteer it could find and sent them to the RN as they'd asked. The Overseas Division of the RNCVR had sent 1,200 men and forty-seven of the best-trained permanent force officers to the RN. The RN had demanded and got much; it had given little.

Kingsmill ordered a dozen trawler/minesweepers from Canadian Vickers (an experienced yard now, no thanks to the RN) and the Polson Iron Works in Toronto. Admiralty ordered twenty-four more. They also released some trained men, including a number of Canadians, and sent a commander for the East Coast Patrols.

He was an ill-considered choice. Sir Charles Coke had been Vice Admiral in charge at Cork when *Lusitania* was sunk. He fared badly in the furore and he was being shunted off. For him it was a dead end. The last thing Kingsmill needed was a high-blown flag officer with a chip on his shoulder. Coke wouldn't adapt. He put his fingers in everything except his own business, got people's backs up in Ottawa and on the coast. Then he was dumped. An RN relief was on the way, but Kingsmill, unusually quick and decisive, chose his own Captain of Patrols, the redoubtable Walter Hose.

Captain Hose had his problems. The operational chain of command was a jungle: a Royal Navy rear admiral in Sydney ran the ocean convoys and reported to Admiralty, while coastal shipping and convoys were controlled by the RCN reporting to Ottawa. Captain Hose, in charge of patrols, provided escorts for all of them, including the first leg to seaward of the ocean convoys. He had a deputy, Commander Newcombe, in Halifax who ran the patrol ships stationed there.

But Rear Admiral W.O. Storey, RN (retired), the superintendent of the Halifax dockyard, had charge of all local defence forces, including mine-sweeping and patrols in his area. He, like Hose, answered to Ottawa. On top of this, the RN's Commander-in-Chief America and West Indies co-ordinated all the British and Canadian authorities in Canada and the U.S. involved in protection of trade. He dealt with Washington, went often to Ottawa and Halifax, and frequently eclipsed Kingsmill as naval adviser to the government.

To the RN the RCN was an appendage, and an awkward one at that. Kingsmill wasn't the man to sort things out. His experience was at sea. He had had no staff training and was not a notable administrator or an assertive or colourful man. With a tiny staff he had to deal almost alone with these tangled threads of command and try to build his untidy little navy into something far bigger. That needed support from his political masters. But with the country sucked completely into the terrible carnage of France, with the shattering issue of conscription and an election looming in late 1917, politicians were little help to the navy they had never understood.

Watching developments in the U-boat war, aircraft were clearly essential. Admiralty recommended Canada get its own, but Kingsmill couldn't get the money from Prime Minister Borden. It was a blessing the U-boats didn't come west that summer. In the fall Admiralty warned Kingsmill that the success of the convoy system would likely push U-boats across the Atlantic to find easy targets. Attacks by big, powerful, heavy-gunned U-cruisers should be expected any time after March, 1918. They could lay mines, too. Admiralty ordered another thirty-six trawlers plus 100 drifters from Canadian yards. Some would be available in spring to strengthen the patrols, but Canada would have to man them.

Transatlantic convoys sailed from Hampton Roads, New York, and Sydney from July, 1917. The fast convoys of British and U.S. troopships and big cargo vessels ran from Halifax starting in September. Feeders came down from Quebec. In December, when the river froze, the slow convoy terminal shifted from Sydney to Halifax. This meant even greater strain on port facilities: loading berths, fuelling, supplies and provisions, stevedoring, maintenance and repair. And for the navy this called for more minesweeping, more patrolling, more escort work. Demands grew as winter came.

HALIFAX CATASTROPHE

On the morning of 6 December, SS *Mont Blanc* of French registry steamed into Halifax harbour to anchor and await her convoy. She passed the dockyard, then, going through to Bedford Basin, she collided with another ship. On deck was a cargo of benzol. Some drums ruptured, bursting into flames, and the *Mont Blanc* crew scurried off and abandoned her. She drifted, blazing and out of control, down the harbour.

On board the old *Niobe* in the dockyard the alarm was raised. Through the flames the red flag at *Mont Blanc*'s masthead said she carried explosives. In fact, in her hold were 2,700 tons of guncotton, picric acid, and TNT. In double time *Niobe*'s bosun, Warrant Officer Albert Mattison, was away in the ship's pinnace with six men. They swarmed up *Mont Blanc*'s side aiming to scuttle her and at that moment she exploded.

Mattison and his crew were gone in a flash. It was the biggest man-made explosion ever, until Hiroshima. The force of it levelled a full square mile of the city. Sixteen hundred died that day; 9,000 were injured, including 200 blinded by flying glass; 6,000 people in the city of 50,000 were homeless with winter setting in. *Niobe* was badly damaged and naval installations suffered heavily. The College had to be abandoned. When the ensuing fire threatened the naval magazine, the city was evacuated until that danger was over. The explosion was a terrible catastrophe for Halifax and its people; as well, it crippled naval, shipping, and transport operations at a most crucial time, especially since Russia was out of the war and the battle in France was in a very bad way.

THE BATTLE OF 1918

A monumental task fell on the undersized Royal Canadian Navy. In March, 1918, American troops, Canadian reinforcements, and masses of material moved in convoy across the ocean. By April, Captain Hose had fifty ships operating. New construction followed the ice down the St. Lawrence and he had 100 by July, working out of Sydney, Halifax, and St. John's. There was a cruising base with fuel and essentials at Gaspé for the Gulf force and another at Louisbourg. The little ships, half-equipped and thinly manned, had all the endless wearying services on their backs – approach and harbour patrols, daily minesweeping of harbour approaches, assembly of convoys, local escort, escort of ocean convoys for a day or two outbound.

Hose needed 2,300 men for his ships and he had 1,500. Admiralty returned 200 RNCVRs and a few RN specialists. Three hundred more came from the Newfoundland Reserve. He urgently needed fast sloops, destroyers, or fast trawlers. Without them, he reported, his force had "not one gun which would be able to get within range of a U-cruiser before the patrol vessel would, in all probability, be sunk." Admiralty could provide no ships, other than lending some of their Canadian-built trawlers. As for the USN, the RN Commander-in-Chief was squeezing everything he could get for Britain's approaches.

But the U.S. Navy did provide valuable help where the Royal Navy didn't. In spring they took over patrols eastward to the longitude of Lockeport, Nova Scotia, and sent six sub-chasers and two torpedo boats to Halifax under Canadian control. They also agreed in April, 1918, to help the RCN start its own Naval Air Service and sent planes to Halifax and Sydney in the meantime. Now Borden had to foot the bill.

With the submarine season at hand and new trawlers coming down the river, Hose had more problems: hasty construction in inexperienced yards meant hull and machinery defects; dockyard facilities were wretched; the new crews were high on new-entry seamen dead low on experience, and he had no trained people to work them up into effective ships' companies. In addition, equipment was terribly short, with everything having to come from the U.K. There were not nearly enough hydrophones to go around, and some ships went to sea without guns. Half a dozen depth charges was the ration.

The first U-boat crossed the Atlantic in May and found what she wanted – coastal traffic wasn't convoyed. Off Maryland in one month *U-151* sank twenty-two ships in the old familiar way. Not one was under escort. The same boat also laid mines off Delaware that sank a tanker. Next came *U-156*. She announced her arrival by sinking two big sailing ships southeast of Sable

Island in early July. Then she ran to the U.S. coast and laid mines. The cruiser USS *San Diego* struck one off Fire Island Light and sank. The submarine then sank ships off Boston and Newport, in plain sight of vacationers on Cape Cod. Tracked by Admiralty's communications intelligence, she moved to the Gulf of Maine for more sinkings, then to Canadian waters.

On 2 August U-156 stopped a big four-masted schooner called *Dornfontein* off the Fundy shore and set her afire. The crew rowed ashore in their dories and the news flashed to Halifax. In the next two days seven schooners were sunk further around the Nova Scotia shore. In Halifax the effect was electric. A vital convoy, HC 12, was about to sail with seventeen ships and 12,500 Canadian and American troops. Escort forces were thin and ill-equipped. The enemy could be right at the harbour mouth. And the 130 miles of continental shelf was a fertile field for planting mines: U-cruisers carried forty each.

But the convoy was ready and it sailed on the afternoon of 4 August. The trawler minesweepers led, then came the three U.S. sub-chasers on an anti-submarine sweep. A close escort of ten trawlers and drifters led the troopers out, but they were too slow and gradually dropped behind. Luck was in, though. As HC 12 cleared to seaward U-156 was dawdling over far smaller fry – a fishing schooner near Shelburne and two more the next day off La Have.

That morning, the 5th of August, a British tanker cleared Halifax for Mexico at first light. The Master of *Luz Blanca* had ignored Naval Shipping Control's warning to wait till dusk and he didn't bother to zigzag. Just before noon, thirty-five miles south of Sambro Light, he took a torpedo from the Halifax-bound U-156. *Luz Blanca*, damaged but unbowed, turned back and bravely fought off the surfaced U-boat with her 12-pounder. After a lopsided exchange of gunfire the tanker lay stopped and afire with her gallant company pulling for shore. They were seventeen miles from Sambro Light.

The alarm spread from a steamer that saw the attack and the trawlers and drifters returning from convoy HC 12 got the message from Halifax radio. But they got the wrong position, for they found nothing in the haze. Other ships arrived very late. First on the scene were the submarine-chasers. They picked up survivors from the boats five hours after the torpedo struck. Sweeps for the submarine by every ship available turned up nothing. Wireless procedures were poor and no one showed up very well. U-156, in fact, had raced south to American waters where she sank three more steamships before having another go off Nova Scotia en route home.

Those four frantic days had immediate repercussions. C-in-C immediately suspended Halifax as a convoy terminal. The next HC convoy gathered at Sydney while ships due from American ports gathered at New York. The two sections joined well out to sea for the ocean leg. Shipping control was tightened. Canadian coastal shipping and traffic for convoy assembly were grouped into local convoys and escorted to the limit of meagre resources.

Quebec became the terminal for Canadian convoys so more escorts were needed for the vulnerable 600 miles of the river and the Gulf.

No lone Canadian ship was, as Hose had said, any match for a U-cruiser on the surface, but they were all Canada had. Admiral Kingsmill had time to sign a tactical instruction on 7 August. It was drafted by his newly arrived and sorely needed RN Staff Officer Operations. Apparently the first issued to the fledgling flotilla, it warned that they'd be out-gunned by a U-cruiser. But, the Admiral said, press in, fire at the pressure hull, zigzag to avoid being hit, and try to cause some damage. U-boats were a long way from home, their aim was sinking merchant ships, and they'd be rash to risk damage. They'd most likely submerge and could be attacked with depth charges. More succinct instructions followed, and these were crystal clear. And timely.

The first U.S. Navy air detachment, as promised, arrived at Dartmouth, Nova Scotia, on 19 August and an American escort squadron swept Nova Scotia waters just about the time *U-156* came back. The U-cruiser struck first near Cape Breton. Her captain, a real innovator, captured a Canadian steam trawler called *Triumph* off Canso, put a gun aboard, and sent her off as a mini-raider. *Triumph* was a familiar vessel on the fishing grounds. The German crew gleefully deceived and sank six Canadian schooners. When the coal ran out they scuttled her. The word came ashore when *Triumph*'s crew rowed into Canso. *U-156* sank another small steamer west of St. Pierre on the 25th of August and later that day caught a group of four schooners and set about sinking them with explosives.

Right at that point over the horizon hove a Canadian search line. They were *Cartier*, the senior officer, *Hochelaga*, and two trawlers all in line abreast and four miles apart. *Hochelaga* spotted two schooners and turned toward, followed by *Trawler 32*, to warn them about the latest U-boat scare. At about four miles *Hochelaga* saw one of the schooners suddenly disappear, then sighted the enemy – the low ominous shape of the big U-cruiser.

Hochelaga's Captain put his wheel hard over and rang on full speed – not zigzagging right for the enemy with his 12-pounder blazing, but back toward *Cartier*. As soon as *Cartier* read *Hochelaga*'s "enemy in sight" he ordered all ships to go for the U-boat full speed. But it had submerged and the four warships combed fruitlessly through the wreckage of the schooners. The golden moment for Walter Hose's East Coast Patrols was gone. There were six more sinkings from Sable Island to the Grand Banks in August, one of them to *U-156*. But she didn't make it home. Off Scotland she hit a mine and became one of the thirty-five U-boats sunk by mines during the war.

Hochelaga's failure in the face of the enemy wasn't for inexperience or lack of training. Her Captain, Lieutenant Robert Legate, had been on active service since the start of the war, was commissioned in 1915 in the RNCVR, and had held command at sea for nearly two years. Kingsmill's instruction must have been fresh in his mind, but in the moment of decision his nerve had failed. Now he faced Court Martial. The judgement: he failed to "use his utmost exertion to bring his ship into action." He was dismissed from the service. Captain Hose, who always took a warm interest in all his people, must have been a deeply disappointed man.

The last marauder, *Deutschland*, again laid mines near Sambro Light and another field off Peggy's Cove, then sank a trawler. The Quebec convoys now were routed north through the Strait of Belle Isle. Thanks to the patrols they, and the Sydney convoys, all got through unscathed.

The U-boat and its truly destructive powers had been hysterically portrayed by the press. Its sinister spectre had mesmerized Canadians in their armchairs for over three years. Now these U-boats were right at Canada's door, wreaking havoc as they pleased. Where was the navy? The press blasted it as ineffectual, helpless, while fishermen drowned. Twenty-eight vessels had been sunk in Canadian waters in a little over a month. Nineteen were victims of *U-156*. But twenty-three were fishing vessels. Only *Luz Blanca* and one other independent ship were significant in the scheme of war. Convoy was the important thing, not trying to be everywhere at once, and convoy had proved its point. The U-boats themselves all reported a shortage of major targets in Canadian waters while there were plenty off the States. The ragged, half-trained East Coast Patrols made convoy possible at a crucial time in a crucial place. The RCN did the job.

Captain Walter Hose had the art of getting the best out of whatever he was given – ships or people. But he had to report that fall: "The officers and men of the vessels are untrained, not only in the technical knowledge required to handle the weapons and offensive appliances on board the ships, but also in service discipline, being drafted to ships as hardly more than raw recruits." And the war wasn't over. The U-boats had had such a time along the U.S. Atlantic coast they'd surely be back in strength. Again the Minister, C.C. Ballantyne, asked Britain's First Lord for equipment and expertise for building destroyers in Canada. Again the request was turned down. With all the rebuffs from Britain and all the generous aid from the U.S., still no one ventured to stretch the apron strings of Empire and ask the next-door neighbour for a hand with building ships.

Ballantyne had little confidence in Kingsmill now, but the government had given him practically nothing to work with. Time and again he had appealed for ships and staff and equipment. But neither his political masters nor Admiralty had paid effective heed.

THE ROYAL CANADIAN NAVAL AIR SERVICE

The one bright light in the darkness of approaching winter was the presence of U.S. naval aircraft. By September they were covering convoys eighty miles to seaward of Halifax and Sydney and responding quickly to sighting reports.

A USN-RCN-RN meeting in Washington in April, 1918, had put things together and Borden had belatedly agreed. Canada built air stations at North Sydney and Eastern Passage, south of Dartmouth. The U.S. Naval Reserve Flying Corps brought six Curtiss flying boats to each station, all under command of Lieutenant Richard E. Byrd, USN. Dirigibles were ordered. Kite balloons went aloft from ships with submarine lookouts. Naval air was in business under a very capable man – Byrd became famous as the Antarctic explorer – and a vast relief it was to Walter Hose.

At the same time, Canada's first air force, the Royal Canadian Naval Air Service, was begun. The Royal Air Force lent an officer to command. Flight training of eighty cadets and 1,000 airmen began with the USN in Boston. A few cadets and some sailors went to England to train as airship coxswains. Within a month, though, the war was over and none of them saw action. The USN gave Canada the aircraft, equipment, and spares.

Canadians had flocked to the Royal Naval Air Service from the beginning of the war, the brilliant Raymond Collishaw among them. John Barron of the old *Canada* cadets was the first Canadian to qualify as an RNAS pilot. He flew airships, was mentioned in dispatches for an attack on a U-boat, and was decorated by Italy for commanding the naval air group at Taranto. Only seven U-boats were actually sunk by British air/sea co-operation in the war. Five of them were by Canadian pilots. The only U-boat killed solely by a British aircraft was hit by Canadian Sub-Lieutenants N.A. Magor and C.E.S. Lusk in September, 1917, flying an American Curtiss flying boat. Here was a fine pool of experienced naval aviators for the Canadian Service, but they could not be spared in 1918. With peacetime, however, the people and the planes were all disbanded. At the same time, the Canadians serving in the RAF, who had formed a Canadian air force overseas, were also discharged.

THE MERCHANT SHIPS

Canada's great merchant fleet had practically disappeared by 1914 and there was virtually no capacity to build. A new policy for a government-owned merchant service began to stir in 1917. Losses were soaring. Borden was angry at Britain's offhanded requisitioning of Canadian-owned ships. Canada built shipyards and a steel rolling mill, and building boomed. By the end of the war twenty-six steamships had been built for Britain and sixty-three for the Canadian government. The sixty-three new ships were completed just after the war and formed the first national flag fleet, the Canadian Government Merchant Marine. It was operated by the newly formed Canadian National Railway. Hold-over technology from the days of sail produced forty-five wooden-hulled steamers for Britain. To cover losses some sixty Great Lakers went to sea as well. Altogether, the U-boats sank forty-five Canadian steamships.

THE RECORD

The first U-boat war was foreseen by no one and it was a turning point in the history of sea warfare. Command of the sea by a superior fleet like Britain's now was not enough. Striking directly at trade, the awesome and economical new weapon, the U-boat, could actually win.

The record was there to read. The German U-boat fleet was not vast. At its peak in mid-1918 there were fifty-five operational boats on patrol. The Germans built 345 during the war and lost 178 in action. Of 13,000 who went to sea in them, fully 40 per cent died. But in four years they destroyed over 5,000 ships – 11 million tons – and killed 15,000. Of those ships, only 5 per cent were sunk in convoy – a mute indictment of the admirals' stubborn stand against it. Only one-tenth of one per cent were sunk in convoy escorted by ships and planes together.

The only answer to the U-boat was convoy. That meant escorts in great numbers, small enough for economy but long in endurance, fast enough, and specially equipped to detect and fight an elusive, dangerous enemy. And it meant aircraft co-ordinated closely with the ships.

The U-boat men came within a hair of winning the Kaiser's war. And they had found out plenty for themselves, which they wouldn't forget if others did. Late in the war, frustrated at trying to slip through convoy screens submerged, they tried something new: get well ahead, then run in on the surface at night, like a torpedo boat, but submerging if attacked. It worked. It worked for young Leutnant Karl Dönitz on a convoy in the Mediterranean. From this he built his *Rudeltactik*, the wolf-pack attack that would nearly win for Dönitz and for Germany another battle, another war, only twenty-five years later.

THE NAVY'S PLACE

Twelve of the minesweeping anti-submarine trawlers commissioned in the RCN in late 1918 were named for the wrenching land battles of France and Flanders – *Ypres, Vimy, Armentieres* – where thousands of young Canadians had died. That the navy should wear the army's battle honours said what was foremost in Canadian minds. That so many died in the mud can, in some part at least, be put at the door of the failed naval and maritime policy of the young Dominion. From Britain and its Admiralty, beset with war on a great scale, had come no encouragement, little help for Canada, and an insatiable appetite for her manpower. Mother England's priorities were hers. If her children wanted a set of their own they were on their own.

By November, 1918, the Royal Canadian Navy had scratched together some 9,600 all ranks, over 100 ships, and an embryo Naval Air Service. A national flag merchant fleet was emerging, too, and modern shipbuilding had begun. But the public mainly scorned the navy, tiny compared with army numbers and without a victory to its name. Neither public nor politicians understood its very real achievement. The witnesses to it were the U-boats themselves that found no worthwhile targets when they came to Canadian waters. The young and struggling RCN filled a certain vital gap in the whole great net of trade protection. Without that net the war in Europe could never have been won. For trade, as always, was the key.

Another old lesson was new to Canada, steeped as it was in the myth that militias won the wars. A navy must have a solid professional peacetime base; a navy can never be built overnight. Neither could the industrial base, and a navy and a country must have that if it would survive. For those who faced the tumult of expansion in the RCN in World War Two and who, with untrained men, ill-fitted ships, and weak air cover, did desperate battle with Admiral Dönitz's U-boats, this whole story had a terribly familiar ring. Every act, except the long delay in starting convoy, had been played through tragically before.

History's lessons are there to see. But one must always look.

CHAPTER FOUR

INTERMISSION

POST-WAR POLITICS

ON 11 NOVEMBER 1918 THE GREAT WAR WAS OVER. SIXTY THOUSAND OF Canada's young men and women were dead, as many more broken in mind or body. The survivors picked up their lives. The navy that had just begun to find itself dispersed. Canada wanted nothing more of war.

During the Imperial Conference of 1917, Admiralty had proposed again their single-navy notion with contributions from the dominions and colonies. Sir Robert Borden had learned a good deal in the war about British thinking, British generals and "colonial" troops, and their dedicated self-interest. Flatly, he said no. Canadians would control their own forces, their own men, where and when they fought. They would control, too, what they paid for – though when peace came that meant next to nothing.

In late 1919 Admiral Lord Jellicoe swung around the globe. The man whose Grand Fleet in the eyes of the world hadn't met the mark, and who had been so slow to make the one decision that beat the U-boats, now advised Commonwealth governments on their navies – a used warship salesman by any other name. In Ottawa he found Kingsmill a Vice Admiral and knighted, too. Sir Charles's staff was smaller than a squadron's and his navy even smaller. It was down to 500 officers and men, two useless old cruiser hulks, and a couple of submarines. The Naval Air Service was gone, the dockyards in decay. Naval policy did not exist.

The U.S. Navy equalled Britain's now, but war with the United States was unthinkable. The enemy of the future was Japan and her navy was growing. If Japan and the States fought, Canada would need a decent-sized force on the west coast to preserve neutrality, and there were two coasts. Jellicoe knew Canadians had never agreed on naval policy and he whipped out a whole menu of options complete with prices. At $4 million Canada could have a minimum local defence: eight submarines, four destroyers, eight anti-submarine patrol boats, and four minesweepers. A tidy two-ocean navy able to contribute to Empire defence could be had for $20 million tops: two battle cruisers, two aircraft carriers, seven cruisers, sixteen submarines, thirteen destroyers, and local defence vessels and auxiliaries.

Before the war Borden had been pushing $35 million for three Dread-noughts for the RN, so this was certainly a bargain. But no policy decision came from cabinet. If ships were going free, though . . . Canada took the two U.S.-built submarines, *H-14* and *H-15*, that Barney Johnson had left in Ber-muda at the end of the war, and the light cruiser *Aurora* and destroyers *Patriot* and *Patrician*. *Aurora* was commanded by a Royal Navy captain and the destroyers by RCN Lieutenants Charles Beard and G.C. Jones. Both were cadet-trained in Canada and since midshipman days had been at sea with the RN.

Arthur Meighen, briefly Conservative Prime Minister, argued at the Imperial Conference of 1921 that Britain shouldn't renew her treaty with Japan. It wouldn't go with the League of Nations idea. Besides, it could stir mistrust in the U.S. – for Canada, a live consideration. Then President Warren Harding invited the world powers to Washington to confer on disarmament. They agreed to a ratio of capital ships – Britain 5, U.S. 5, Japan 3, France and Italy 1.75 – and a limit on total tonnage. That meant scrapping many ships. Canada grandly agreed to a 40 per cent cut of next to nothing.

Later that year the Liberals and Mackenzie King were in power. King had deep-rooted anti-military views. So did his diverse caucus, which was about all they had in common. King said at the next Imperial Conference that any future decision for Canada to go to war was "a matter which her own Parliament will wish to decide." But he cut defence spending to the point where such talk was meaningless.

The League of Nations, not the old system of alliances, seemed to promise peace. The temper of the world was certainly to reduce armaments. But Canada's defence spending in the roaring twenties was a whisper at the bottom of the heap. In 1922 cabinet slashed the navy estimates from $2.5 to $1.5 million. In 1923-24, for example, Canadians spent $1.46 per capita on defence. Britons spent $23.04; France somewhat more than that; Australians $3.30. The isolationist Americans spent around $7.

MERE SURVIVAL

Canada had won the real feel of independence in the war. But she hadn't faced the hard reality of looking after herself. Captain Walter Hose, having taken the helm from Kingsmill, faced the crucial question. How, on less than a shoestring, would he keep the navy alive? Since Laurier in 1910, no sort of consensus on a navy had emerged. It had stumbled into a real *raison d'être* late in the war but produced no gripping Canadian feats at sea. On the contrary, Canadians still had no idea what a navy was about.

Britons were weaned on theirs. Americans understood their navy well in terms of their own place in the world. Vital as a navy was for a sovereign trading nation, Canadian politicians wouldn't generate the leadership. Captain Hose remembered his experience helping the self-generated Victoria RNCVR of 1913, with Reserve sailors in *Rainbow*, in the submarines, and in the patrols. Canada, Hose argued, never would have a navy until it found a place in the hearts and minds of Canadians. His answer then was to take the navy to the people, to start Reserve units right across the country. Where militia regiments had for years been such a part of the local fabric, Naval Reserve units must go, too; and, of course, they would provide a pool of naval-trained civilians and the machinery for inland recruiting in event of war.

Hose made the hard decisions. He returned *Aurora* and the submarines to the RN and shut the Youth Training Establishment for young sailors in Halifax. The Naval College – the only continuous thread since the navy's birth – closed its doors. From then until 1942 junior officers for the RCN were trained with the Royal Navy's cadets in England. He pressed Admiralty to find billets at sea and on advanced courses for his handful of RCN officers. The RN was offering junior officers a year at Cambridge University, but Canadians interested in broadening their education were told their navy couldn't afford the cost of £1 per day.

Walter Hose deliberately scrapped the navy as a force and spent every penny he could find on the Royal Canadian Naval Volunteer Reserve. One destroyer and two trawler minesweepers remained on each coast and they were devoted to training Reserves. He made it quite clear to the tiny permanent force that "its main role was to foster, encourage and train the RCNVR." History would prove his decision sound.

THE WAVY NAVY

Hose's two staff officers plugged away tirelessly, spoke to service clubs, cajoled, encouraged, found a few dollars here, a few there. Local effort had to do it. In each town it was a handful of keen people, usually with wartime experience at sea, who got on with it in the resourceful sailor's way. They found corners in drill sheds, quarters over laundries and in old factory buildings. They dipped in their own pockets. They scrounged equipment, devised training aids, organized seamanship training camps at summer cottages. A naval wireless net linked them and trained telegraphists, too.

The RCNVR (not the old RNCVR, which was a recruiting device for the Royal Navy) grew steadily. By 1925 there were "half companies" at fifty men each in fifteen major cities. Montreal had one English, one French. They all grew, and there were nineteen Naval Reserve divisions by late 1939. The main ports had registries of trained merchant service officers and men who agreed to serve in emergency. That was called the Royal Canadian Naval Reserve or RCNR.

RCNVR ratings got twenty-five cents per drill and such uniforms as could be found. Most were kitted out with old wartime flat caps and collars with wavy tapes stitched around the edge, which had distinguished Reserves from the permanent force. Officers were paid nothing and had to dig in their own pockets for their uniforms. It was quite an outlay – regular blue uniform, greatcoat and burberry raincoat, plus the ceremonial frock coat, sword, and mess jacket and several sets of high-necked summer whites. They must at least look the part.

The war-surplus sailors' caps and collars disappeared, but RCNVR officers kept the same "wavy" shaped gold rings on the sleeve that the Royal Navy had devised for their RNVR. In the same RN mould, the professional merchant service officers of the RCNR wore rings of narrow interwoven gold lace on their naval uniforms. Only permanent force officers could wear the solid straight rings with the round "executive curl."

This kind of distinction, between those who were and those who weren't quite, was the sort of English aberration that Canada's navy could well have done without. It served no useful purpose. An officer must stand or fall on capability, not cosmetics. It was divisive. When war came, the navy was so largely "wavy" that the few straight-ring RCN officers seemed to be a some-what snobbish elite. A standing British jest was transplanted to Canada: "The RCNVR are gentlemen trying to be officers; the RCNR are officers trying to be gentlemen; the RCN are neither trying to be both." That difference in the rank rings persisted until after World War Two.

Summer training at the coasts, and learning from the few professionals at sea, was the highlight of the Reservist's year. And for that period he was actually paid! In the lean depression years the naval divisions provided a lot of support for those on tough times. The Wavy Navy built up a special esprit of its own.

And as it was, in 1939 the RCNVR had some 2,000 officers and men and that about equalled the number in the permanent navy. As well, in every city in Canada the navy was there. A man could join it by taking the streetcar downtown. In fact, the great majority of Canada's wartime sailors had never seen the sea before.

INTEGRATION, 1922

Government economies that forced the 1922 cuts put the three services into one Department of National Defence and "integrated" them under one Chief of Staff. Major General J.H. MacBrien now controlled the three services and became chief adviser to the government on all military, air, and naval matters.

Walter Hose dug in his heels. He would simply not accept a situation where he, as head of the navy, had no direct access to the Minister. Small as it was, the navy's voice must be heard at cabinet level. There were some very difficult and acrimonious times, but Hose had an astute ally in Georges Desbarats, the deputy minister, who had been with the navy from the start. Doggedly he pressed the navy's point. MacBrien resigned in frustration and the post of Chief of Staff disappeared. Finally, in 1928 Commodore Walter Hose became the first Chief of Naval Staff. The RCAF, formally in being since 1924, stayed under the Chief of the General Staff until 1938.

THE MERCHANT FLEET

The war-built merchant ships managed by Canadian National Railways were slow and coal-fired, and few could carry passengers. Thus, they were uneconomical and one by one were sold or scrapped. No government merchant service policy emerged so they weren't replaced.

The sole addition was a prestige service begun in the mid-twenties to the Caribbean by the five "Lady Boats" – *Lady Rodney*, *Lady Nelson*, etc. But great shipping names like Canadian Pacific and Cunard had only the memory of Canadian roots. The Canadian Government Merchant Marine dwindled away. Foreign flag ships enjoying their own governments' subsidies prospered on Canada's huge overseas trade and passenger traffic. In the United States the Jones Act made it illegal for non-American ships to ply the coastal trade. It kept their shipping alive and applies to this day. But in Canada, as before 1914, there was no policy at all. By 1939 there were only thirty-eight Canadian ocean-going ships, averaging little over 6,000 tons.

NEW SHIPS, NEW LIFE

In 1928 two used RN destroyers renamed *Champlain* and *Vancouver* replaced the worn-out *Patriot* and *Patrician*. Commodore Hose got approval for two brand new ships to be built in Britain, the first-ever ordered to RCN specifications. They made some concessions to the North Atlantic, which the Royal Navy had never deigned to admit – hull strengthening for ice-infested waters, extra stability to counter icing, and steam heat.

Their sailors – as in all RN-built ships from the days of sail – still lived in messdecks where they slung their hammocks, stowed their gear, ate their food, and spent their off-watch hours. Showers (quite new in RN ships!), improved ventilation, and extra refrigeration made life a little more amenable for all. HMCS *Saguenay* and *Skeena*, by RN standards, were luxurious. When they were commissioned in 1931 they were dubbed the "Rolls-Royce destroyers."

Commander Percy Nelles was appointed Captain of *Saguenay* and Commander Victor Brodeur of *Skeena*. Since leaving the crippled old *Niobe* as midshipmen in 1911, they had spent most of their time with the RN. Nelles had edged Brodeur by a hair on promotion to Commander. That one place on the Navy List defined their careers. Brodeur in 1939 was Commodore in command on the west coast. Nelles had taken over as Chief of Naval Staff in 1934.

The year the Rolls-Royce destroyers were commissioned Japan invaded Manchuria, and the League of Nations failed to act. From then on that international body carried only the hopes of the naive. At the same time the world sunk into the Great Depression and there was another drive toward disarmament. Canadian defence estimates were slashed and slashed again. Classmates of Nelles and Brodeur and the Naval College graduates were mostly gone. Ken Adams skippered tugboats on the west coast; John Grant was a schoolmaster; Pip Musgrave was a physical training instructor. Barney Johnson's son, following his father, had gone through the Naval College and to sea with the merchant service. Sam Worth struck a bonanza – he ran an efficient communications network for the rumrunners on the east coast but slipped out with a whole skin when the underworld took over.

In 1933 came a major round of government spending cuts. The Chief of the General Staff, Major General A.G.L. McNaughton, offered the opinion that air and ground forces alone could deal with any invader. There wasn't enough money to properly run three services. So why not drop the navy? With Canada's geography – unless McNaughton was still thinking 1812 – that was absurd, but no doubt the proposal appealed to the Treasury Board. Because Walter Hose had stuck to his guns in 1922 there was till a navy head to speak for the navy. Now he ran the guns out again.

Hose closed the range on the ministers and the mandarins at Treasury Board and fired away. Canada needed a navy to prevent being drawn into a war between the U.S. and Japan, which was by no means unlikely. Next there was Canada's very big trade to protect if she did go to war. No navy could be run with any kind of effectiveness or economy below a certain size, nor could it be improvised from nothing if and when war came. If government insisted on reductions that would effectively destroy it with its 900 men, he, Walter Hose, would have to resign.

He won the day. Had he not, Canada's navy would have disappeared in 1933, the very year that Adolf Hitler became chancellor of Germany and set the world on the road to death and devastation once again.

Canada is lucky that young Walter Hose married his lady from Newfoundland. He brought full measure to the infant navy's struggles. He was a fine, experienced seaman, a brave fighting officer, and an inspiring leader. All of that he showed in the *Rainbow* days. Organizing ability, energy, and the talent to make the most of meagre resources had pulled the East Coast Patrols into an effective force; it was the first that Canada's navy really had. Professional capacity, wise judgement, and the courage of his convictions nursed the navy through those famished years. His soundly built Naval Reserve took some notion of a navy across the land and gave a base for expansion when the time did come to fight. Walter Hose was, in truth, the father of Canada's navy.

PEOPLE

Percy Nelles, who took over from Hose, had been Kingsmill's Flag Lieutenant. After commanding *Saguenay* he had had brief command of an RN light cruiser. He was short on experience to be chief of any naval staff, and he wasn't cut from the same cloth as Walter Hose.

Nelles was a small man, bouncy and affable, with unsailor-like horn-rimmed glasses. He carried little weight in his presence, more the comfortably situated senior public servant than the professional seadog. He was a sound administrator, thoughtful and considerate, but not a resounding leader, and he lacked the toughness to act in spite of personal feelings. Therein lay a problem. Friends were friends. The tight and tiny club of naval officers went through lean and bitter times together. They looked out for each other and their families, too. They knew each other well. Too well. Navy pay was so low that to have some comfort in life, much less meet the social obligations of senior rank, a private income was considered *de rigeur*. Nelles had married a lady of substantial means and forceful character. Woe the young naval officer whose bride failed to pass the social tests.

Victor Brodeur, senior officer of destroyers on the west coast, was a prickly character and a stern disciplinarian who kept some distance even from his own officers. In his young days with the RN he took more than a fair share of the condescension and ribbing that "colonials" got from many of their British messmates. A Canadian accent was one thing, but with his French–Canadian accent Brodeur really stood out. The RN sailors who couldn't fathom it dubbed him "Scottie." While others shrugged off the joshing and simply made up their minds to beat the Brits in due course at their own game, Brodeur retained suspicion, if not actual antipathy. He admired the RN as a service, but he was certainly no Anglophile.

When officers spent so many of their early years with the RN some of the British manner, custom, and accent was almost bound to rub off, on some more than others. The young men who joined the lower deck from the farms and small towns and cities across the land brought initiative and independence but not much education. Bill Manfield was a rare bird because he had some schooling when he joined as a Boy Seaman in Esquimalt in 1927. Few of his messmates in the bleak new entry block where they slung their hammocks could read or write. Manfield was quickly singled out. He was helped by the resident "Schooly" and by Lieutenant Harry DeWolf studying navigation.

He passed the educational tests and worked up rank by rank to retire as Commander Manfield with some forty years of outstanding service.

The British social structure that from time immemorial set officers and men on such different levels in the RN didn't fit well with Canadians. Manfield and his shipmates ran into the caste system in the British West Indies and Bermuda, where sailors weren't allowed on "white" beaches and signs proclaiming "Sailors and dogs not allowed" weren't unknown. And in the ships there wasn't much rapport between officers and men. Something rather like guerrilla warfare simmered between messdecks and wardroom, buffered by the chiefs and petty officers. But the younger RCN officers, Manfield found, were good men, without the biases of class.

These were depression days. An ordinary seaman made fifty cents a day, a lieutenant $5, and there was no marriage allowance. Still, the navy was a job and there was a line-up to get in. So they quickly learned to choke down the spartan life, the rigidity of new entry training, and some absurd restrictions. In the early thirties the destroyers *Saguenay* and *Champlain* were on the east coast and *Skeena* and *Vancouver* out west. By carefully husbanding fuel all four got south in winter. They met in the West Indies when there was enough money to transit the Panama Canal. It was a tight-knit little service. Everyone knew each other and even with so little to work on, at sea it ran very well. Indeed, one-on-one the smartly handled, sparkling clean fighting ships of the RCN were every bit as good as those of the big-name navies.

PLANS AND POLICIES

Military plans in the pigeonholes of National Defence, thick with the dust of 1812, still dealt with invasion from the south, and indeed there were U.S. plans on file for the invasion of Canada. Every armed force has to have at least a paper enemy. But attack on either country could really come only from outside North America and the U.S. must then be Canada's ally. The other new factor, and a great unknown, was airpower. It was the looming spectre of the thirties. By 1936 the U.S. had a bomber that could strike Europe with one refuelling stop. So what was to stop a European enemy from landing at some remote Canadian coastal point, clearing airstrips, and destroying North American cities with their bombs?

Contrary to MacNaughton's muddled view it would take a navy and an air force. From 1934 to 1939, defence estimates increased fourfold to a tentative $8.8 million. Mackenzie King, with home defence in mind and dreading being drawn again into European war, put the militia at the bottom of the pile. The air force got top priority. The navy, modest though its allocation was, came next.

Fraser and *St. Laurent*, used RN C-class destroyers, replaced the worn-out *Champlain* and *Vancouver* in 1937. The same year a fine Nova Scotian-built three-masted schooner, HMCS *Venture*, commissioned as a new entry seamen's training ship. She cruised mainly in the Caribbean and turned the modest intake of sixty recruits a year into first-rate young seamen. Two more C-class destroyers, renamed *Restigouche* and *Ottawa*, made six all told in 1938. Four Canadian-built minesweepers – coal burners to satisfy Cape Breton and Nanaimo miners – topped off the tiny fleet. Then, in May, 1939, the government announced plans for quite a respectable navy.

Canadian-American military talks had gone on from 1937 without much result. King noted in his usual circuitous way in the House of Commons that year that if Canada did not want to become a belligerent it at least had to defend itself against a belligerent operating from Canada against "some other country with which it may be at war." In plainer words, Canada should be prepared to stop Japan from gaining a lodgement in British Columbia to attack the States.

President Franklin D. Roosevelt said clearly in Kingston the following year that the U.S. "would not stand idly by" if "domination of Canadian soil was threatened by any other empire." This was a momentous statement of policy. King responded in the House that Canada had obligations to a friendly neighbour to make itself "as immune from attack or possible invasion as we can reasonably be expected to make it, and that . . . enemy forces should not be able to pursue their way, either by land, sea or air, to the United States." There was no move though for any kind of joint naval exercise.

The Ogdensburg Agreement between Roosevelt and King put the two countries' joint concerns on paper and set up the Permanent Joint Board on Defence in August, 1940. By then France was overrun and Britain at bay. Ogdensburg was the basis for the ongoing Canadian-American hemispheric defence alliance of today. It was natural and inevitable. Just as inevitably, it led later to the comfortable Canadians' conviction that whatever they did or didn't in their own defence, they were safe behind the shield of Uncle Sam.

In 1935 Italy had invaded Abyssinia. The League of Nations proved as impotent as it had with Manchuria and it was finished as a force for peace. The following year Hitler repudiated the Treaty of Versailles and signed the Axis pact with Mussolini. The Spanish Civil War, a proving ground for German and Italian arms, began; Addis Ababa fell to the Italians; and Hitler marched into France's Rhineland unopposed. Germany at that point was militarily weak but no one had the guts to call Hitler's bluff. In 1937 he annexed Austria without a shot and moved on the borders of Czechoslovakia. That same year Japan invaded China. Japan's navy, like Germany's, was growing fast.

In September of 1938 Britain and France traded Czechoslovakia for Hitler's meaningless guarantee to go no further. Britain's deluded Prime Minister Neville Chamberlain called it "peace in our time" – and only a small group of British politicians led by Winston Churchill inveighed against him.

Mackenzie King, another appeaser, heaped Chamberlain with praise and wrote to Hitler lauding him for stabilizing Europe and preserving peace. But seeking to appease by tossing bones was futile. Hitler understood the sword alone and he was forging navy, army, and air forces for a Third German Reich that would last "a thousand years."

Canadian opinion on defence ran the gamut: pacifism; let Britain and the U.S. do it; territorial self-defence and no truck with European affairs; no involvement in foreign war; back the Mother Country through hell and high water. It wasn't Quebec versus the rest by any means, though certainly Québécois were against foreign involvement and dead against conscription. As far as a navy was concerned, few Canadians had any interest. In Mother Country-minded B.C. the *Vancouver Province* said in May of 1939: "What our money should be spent for is to make the most weighty contribution possible to the combined military strength of the British Empire. We cannot do that by frittering it away in piffling little adventures in coastal defence."

One newspaper editorial in the four years before the war dealt seriously with naval policy. The *Montreal Gazette* on 4 May 1939 editorialized: " . . . the proposition is that Canada must go on sponging on the Mother Country and, what is even worse, upon the goodwill of a foreign nation, the United States, for the protection which Canada itself should provide, having regard to the position it occupies as a trading country. The Dominion should be either in a position to protect its own trade routes or to cooperate adequately with Great Britain in providing the protection that is necessary. It is absurd to suggest that anything like this is possible with six destroyers, four of which are antique, and a few minesweepers."

By March, 1939, King's cunning had brought consensus in the House of Commons: neutrality was out; if it came to war Canada would fight along-side Britain; there would be no conscription for overseas service. Canada's loyalty to the Mother Country was clinched that summer by the stunningly successful Royal Tour of King George VI and his warm and gracious Queen Elizabeth.

The Throne Speech after Munich had firmly talked defence, and in May, 1939, the Minister of Defence, Ian Mackenzie, announced the goal for a navy of eighteen destroyers, sixteen minesweepers, and eight anti-submarine vessels – all divided evenly between the coasts – and eight motor torpedo boats for the east coast. Apart from lack of submarines it was a respectable force for guarding Canada's approaches.

Lieutenant Commander Harry DeWolf, a Naval College graduate of 1921 and one of the rare trained staff officers in Naval Service Headquarters, had developed the expansion plans for Percy Nelles. Now with six destroyers in hand and the grand plan announced, DeWolf could let out a hearty cheer. He'd been appointed to command *St. Laurent* and with war in the wind that's

HMS *Shannon* leads her prize, USS *Chesapeake*, into Halifax. Powerful American frigates had won several ship-to-ship victories. In May, 1813, to redress the score, *Shannon* sent a written challenge in to Boston and *Chesapeake* came out. With many pressed Nova Scotians in her crew *Shannon* won a fierce boarding action. Commerce raiding and privateering drew a lot of attention but the Royal Navy controlled the sea and Canada stayed British. (*Maritime Museum of the Atlantic*)

HMS *Cormorant* formally opens the Esquimalt drydock in 1887. Steam-driven vessels needed fuel and technical support and the Esquimalt dockyard and drydock brought the North Pacific into the orbit of Britain's seapower. With the new Canadian Pacific Railway a great new link in the imperial chain was forged. (*National Archives of Canada*)

The first class of naval cadets, under training in CGS *Canada* in 1910. From left to right (back row): Charles T. Beard, P. Barry German, Victor G. Brodeur, Wright; middle, Fisheries' officers Fortier, Stewart, Woods; front, Henry T. Bate, Percy W. Nelles, John A. Barron. (*Maritime Command Museum*)

HMCS *Niobe* anchored in Digby Basin in 1911. She had arrived in Halifax on Trafalgar Day, 21 October 1910. *Niobe* was a powerful coal-burning ship, 11,000 tons, 15 knots, with sixteen 6-inch guns. (*National Archives of Canada*)

Commander Walter Hose joined the Royal Canadian Navy from the RN in 1912. He commanded *Rainbow*, then became Captain of Patrols on the east coast in 1917, Director of the Naval Service in 1921, and Chief of the Naval Staff in 1928 before retiring in 1934. A remarkable leader in very thin times. (*National Archives of Canada*)

A heavy-gunned U-cruiser holds up a merchant ship. The U-boats found plenty of unescorted targets along the American seaboard after the U.S. entered the war in 1917. Their campaign of 1918 brought the war right to Canada's shores, sinking mostly small vessels and stirring panic in the press. (*Imperial War Museum*)

HMCS *Fraser* in the Panama Canal in 1937 en route to Esquimalt. She had just commissioned in England, the third modern destroyer to join the little fleet in the thirties. Off the coast of France, on 25 June 1940, she was cut in half by RN cruiser *Calcutta* and lost forty-seven of her company. This was Canada's first loss of World War Two. (*National Archives of Canada*)

His Majesty King George VI presents the first King's Colour to the Royal Canadian Navy in Victoria, in the summer of 1939. The triumphant royal tour on the eve of war firmed Canadians' resolve to back Britain. The colour officer is Lieutenant J.C. Hibbard, who commanded *Skeena* and *Iroquois*, then after the war the cruiser *Ontario*. (*National Archives of Canada*)

Bedford Basin, with over fifty ships assembled to form a convoy. Through the Narrows lies Dartmouth on the left, and on the right the dockyard with the port of Halifax beyond. McNab's Island shelters the harbour from the open sea. Miles of steel-wire nets across both channels protect it from the U-boats. Trade and troop convoys have gathered and sailed from this magnificent harbour since the mid-1700s. (*National Archives of Canada*)

A Convoy Conference in Admiralty House, Halifax, March, 1941. Commander Richard Oland (the tall officer in the middle) was the first Naval Control Service Officer in Halifax. The elderly officer with the broad stripe at the head of the right-hand table is the convoy Commodore. Seated left of Oland is the Captain of the RN heavy ship escort. Few merchant service masters wore uniform. (*National Archives of Canada*)

Left to right: Lieutenant Commanders Harry DeWolf, Horatio Nelson Lay, and James C. Hibbard. They commanded *St. Laurent*, *Restigouche*, and *Skeena*, respectively, in 1940 during the evacuation of France, the threat of invasion, and then battling the U-boats in the Western Approaches. They all commanded other ships later in heavy fighting and went on to Flag rank, DeWolf to become Chief of Naval Staff. (*National Archives of Canada*)

HMCS *St. Croix*, one of the seven American four-stackers that the RCN manned in late 1940, nears the gate-vessel at Halifax. The four-stackers were miserable at sea but they had 28 knots, which was badly needed to catch surfaced U-boats. *St. Croix* sank two U-boats and was sunk herself by an acoustic torpedo in 1943. There was one survivor. (*National Archives of Canada*)

Winston Churchill comes aboard *Assiniboine* in Hvalfjord for passage to Reykjavik on 16 August 1941. He was visiting Iceland after drawing up the historic Atlantic Charter with President Roosevelt in Placentia Bay, Newfoundland. *Assiniboine's* Captain, Lieutenant John Stubbs, is ignored as the Prime Minister looks for someone more senior in command. On the left is Lieutenant Ralph Hennessy. Able Seaman Moody and the Chief Bosun's Mate, CPO Orr, man the side. A year later *Assiniboine* sank *U-210*. Stubbs went down with *Athabaskan*, his last command, in the Channel in April, 1944. (*National Archives of Canada*)

The corvette *Battleford* on convoy escort in November, 1941. Her open well-deck can be seen between bridge and forecastle. The forecastle was extended to enclose the well and provide more space and more comfort, but not until mid-1944. She has SW1C radar atop the foremast. The minesweeping gear (the davits project forward from the stern) was retained for some time "in case," which precluded carrying a full load of depth charges. (*National Archives of Canada*)

The destroyer repair ship HMS *Hecla* at a mooring buoy in Hvalfjord, Iceland, with corvettes nested either side. Essential support was provided afloat by the RN in this bleak gale-swept anchorage from April, 1941. It was the turn-around point for the Newfoundland Escort Force until they switched to the Newfy-Derry run in February, 1942. (*Imperial War Museum*)

Relaxing time in the stokers' mess, HMCS *Assiniboine*, November, 1940. Living was tight, even in destroyers. Each man had a "ditty box" for personal items (on the table), a tin hat-box (on the shelf), and a small built-in locker for his clothes (they're sitting on them). Food was carried from the galley and served at the table using dishes kept by each mess. They washed them there in a dishpan. They slung their hammocks overhead. (*National Archives of Canada*)

where he wanted to be. But the government's show of support was political eyewash. The money actually voted in 1939 did no more than buy the drawings.

The "anti-submarine vessels" in the plan weren't described. Admiral Jellicoe, who had learned something, said in 1927 that fast anti-submarine convoy escorts would be needed in another war. Further, they could not be improvised in a hurry. But nothing happened until the urgent expansion of the Royal Navy in 1938, when a "coastal escort" was quickly designed for Admiralty by a Yorkshire shipyard. The lines came from a successful whale-catcher, *Southern Pride*. Production began in 1939. The dumpy little work-horse and the rust-streaked vision of slogging along escorting merchant convoys held no appeal for fighting navy men. Winston Churchill, who knew his sailors, ruled out the drab name "patrol vessel, whaler type," dipped back in history, and crowned the little ship "Corvette." She was designed as a coastal escort but by default became the mainstay of the ocean convoy lanes. In the great battle to come she would fight her way to naval immortality.

But Canada's navy wasn't thinking convoy escort. The plan tabled in the Commons showed that. An enemy seeking lodgements, carrier- or land-based air attack, surface raiders, mines, bombardment of ports by surface ships or U-boats, torpedo boats launched from mother ships – these, it was deemed, were the threats on either coast. The new destroyers would be the most powerful ever built – the RN's Tribal class with eight 4.7-inch guns and four torpedoes. A flotilla of eight Tribals could give any raider a hard time. They were short-range ships, but this kind of defensive operation was close to home. The undefined anti-submarine vessels plus mines would keep off marauding U-boats. Naval officers, of course, could see those big destroyers fighting in surface actions alongside the Royal Navy. Convoy escort didn't get a word. Dockyards and repair facilities, the vital shoreside back-up that had fallen so short in the Great War, hardly got a cent.

THE THREAT

In the RN mind, and the RCN followed, the submarine threat had waned. With Japan the prime enemy it would have been a blazing big-ship war of the glamorous kind, not another grubby battle of attrition on the trade routes. Hitler on the scene changed things. But surely he'd never risk bringing in the United States with unrestricted U-boat warfare as the Kaiser had in 1917. He had a few U-boats, yes, but also very powerful surface units. *Scharnhorst*, *Gneisenau*, and three new pocket battleships were formidable ocean raiders. *Bismarck* and *Tirpitz*, two super battleships, had just slid down the ways. Those were the big threat to the shipping lanes, and the Germans would send out merchant raiders, too. The big ships of the Royal Navy would contain them all. The worldwide organization for wartime naval control of shipping was in place to marshal the convoys as and when necessary and Canada had its important place in that.

There was less resistance to convoy than in 1917, but naval thinking favoured hunting groups rather than using ships as convoy escorts. Modern wisdom added that convoys would be sitting ducks for air attack. In practice, though, gathering ships together and concentrating defence around them applied to aircraft as it did to surface ships and U-boats. Convoy could be introduced if really needed for the surface threat, or if the U-boat really did prove to be a problem. Convoys with surface and air escorts had, after all, beaten U-boats in the last war when there were no effective detection devices. And really clinching things was asdic.

Now called sonar, asdic was a highly secret device developed by the end of the Great War but not early enough to get in service. Basically, a sound transmitter housed in a dome sticking out from the ship's bottom projected a narrow beam of high-frequency sound. The operator turned a hand wheel to point it in the direction he chose and he listened on headphones to the reverberations from the sound transmission. They tailed off in the familiar P-I-I-I-i-i-i-n-n-n-g-g . . . which was the random return from all the minute sea life, bubbles, fish, and foreign bodies. With a solid object in the way, like a submarine, back came a metallic echo. *Beeep*!! Sound travelled at a known speed through water so range as well as bearing could be quite accurately read. "Doppler," the changed pitch of the returning echo, told if the submarine was steering toward you or away. The maximum range for asdic was about 2,000 yards.

To those reared on hydrophones, this was an amazing leap ahead. Spoken of in hushed tones only, it attained an unearned and mystic reputation as the final answer. Because of its "secret weapon" status very few in the RN knew much about it. Even the name was barely known. It was probably coined in 1918 as a cover for the key word "supersonic" and derived from "Anti-Submarine Division–ic." Not even the word became public until Winston Churchill used it in the House of Commons in 1939. The erudite Oxford University Press, seeking its etymological root, was handed the hastily fabricated story that it came from the "Allied Submarine Detection Investigation Committee" of the last war, a body that never in fact existed.

Partly because so little was known about asdic and so much expected, the U-boat was seen by the RN, and so by the RCN, as no serious threat. The First Sea Lord in 1936 said the RN's anti-submarine measures were 89 per cent effective. The next year an RN destroyer was completely baffled in an encounter with an Axis submarine in the Spanish Civil War. Anti-submarine exercises were rare, but when they were conducted they normally were set-pieces favouring the defence of the fleet with a tidy screen of destroyers "pinging" ahead of a battle group. The submarines nearly always slipped through but that was conveniently ignored. Convoy escort and exercises against submarines simply never took place. Neither did ship-air anti-submarine co-ordination. If there was little interest from the ship side, there was none at all from the air. At the end of the Great War Britain's Royal Flying Corps and the Royal Naval Air Service had been amalgamated into the Royal Air Force under the new Air Ministry. Whatever the rationale, for the navy it was disaster. Not until 1936 did the RN finally wrest back aviation afloat and form the Fleet Air Arm. In those eighteen years aircraft and techniques stagnated. The shore element, Coastal Command, stayed RAF, and remained the poor relation.

Coastal's role was spotting surface raiders breaking out. Or, in the case of the Royal Canadian Air Force, breaking in. They paid no heed to anti-submarine warfare. In fairness, the RN hadn't pushed and neither had the RCN. The RCAF had some 4,000 men and eight permanent squadrons in 1939. Only one, nominally a torpedo bomber squadron, had any notional attachment to the maritime scene, but they never worked with the navy on anything resembling defence of shipping against the U-boat.

The U.S. Navy had even less interest in ship anti-submarine capabilities than the RN. They and the Japanese, though, were streets ahead in carriers, naval aircraft, and naval aviation techniques, and controlled their own shore-based maritime air.

NAVAL DIRECTIONS

RCN thinking followed the RN's like a shadow. In 1937 Commodore Nelles wrote:

> If international law is complied with, submarine attack should not prove serious. If unrestricted warfare is again resorted to, the means of combatting submarines are considered so advanced that by employing a system of convoy and utilizing Air Forces, losses of submarines would be very heavy and might compel the enemy to give up this form of attack.

Percy Nelles was a wishful thinker, not an original one, and he sorely lacked technical understanding. His staff was minute. There were too few with the time, professional knowledge, staff training, and experience to do much systematic and detached Canadian naval thinking. The RCN was far too small to have effective training or staff schools of its own, where such thinking usually generates. Officers trained with the RN from cadet right through to the advanced staff courses. Higher specialist and technical courses for ratings in gunnery, signals, torpedo, the mystic submarine detection, and engineering all took place in Britain.

Administration and discipline came from the Royal Navy, and uniforms were identical except for "HMCS" on sailors' cap tallies and a tiny "Canada" on officers' and chief and petty officers' buttons. Ships flew the White Ensign unalloyed. For practical purposes the RCN was a tiny carbon copy of the RN. It seemed, externally at least, to lack an identity of its own. And that was the root of a long and underlying problem.

Through the thirties the east coast destroyers, sometimes joined by those from the west, exercised with the RN's America and West Indies Squadron and some big ships from the Home Fleet who followed the sun. "Fleet work" was exciting stuff: dashing around with battleships and cruisers, high-speed screening and torpedo attacks, smokescreens and night encounters. But the West Indies Squadron was no training ground for anti-submarine warfare. The RCN wasn't dead on the subject. Captain Leonard Murray wrote an appreciation of the submarine threat to the St. Lawrence, and the RN was asked to loan a submarine for exercises but declined.

The acronym ASW hadn't been coined. In the RN, the subject wasn't top drawer. The few anti-submarine specialists were counted as rejects from the glamorous fields of gunnery and torpedo and signals. Only two RCN officers had done anti-submarine courses, in 1927, and they hadn't worked at it since.

Reared as they had been, it is hardly surprising that sea-going RCN officers gave no more weight to anti-submarine warfare than did their own Chief of Naval Staff. The RCN had exactly eight trained submarine detector ratings in September, 1939, and one officer who had done a course in England ten years before. No Canadian destroyers had ever trained with a live submarine. When the war started two of the six did not even have asdic.

U-BOATS RESURFACED

The Germans didn't forget the U-boat war they nearly won. When Hitler repudiated the Treaty of Versailles in 1935 they were set to move. The Krupp steel empire had run a German-staffed design and engineering office in Holland since 1922, advancing the U-boat art by building them for other countries. They had also secretly stockpiled key long-lead components like diesel engines.

Commodore Karl Dönitz was in charge of the U-boat force. Drawing on his own Great War experience, he expounded *Rudeltactik*, which concentrated many U-boats on a single convoy, positioning ahead in daylight and racing in on the surface to attack at night. Staying on the surface would foil underwater detection; speed and low profile would get them past the escorts. Dönitz drilled his elite young U-boat force incessantly and instilled his own extraordinary esprit. He ran a major convoy-killing exercise in 1938. Also, he wrote it all down in an article, publicly available in the magazine *Nauticus* in 1939: U-boats would destroy Britain's trade, he said; they would slaughter the independents first, then decimate the convoys with the deadly wolf pack. It should have been required reading at every British naval school.

Dönitz estimated 300 U-boats would beat Britain. Hitler, though, put priority on the surface fleet with its visible prestige and power. Dönitz had to start the second U-boat war with only fifty-seven operational boats. But that was three times the German force of 1914.

PREPARING FOR WAR

Neither naval force nor thinking was in gear to fight the U-boat, but a very important element was in place when war broke out. Commander Eric Brand, RN, became Director of Naval Intelligence at NSHQ in Ottawa in June, 1939. He collected intelligence and collated and reported shipping movements in all North and South America to feed into Admiralty's global net.

Brand was an experienced first-rate officer who had lost out in the RN promotion stakes. He was quite unlike the up-stage RN officer who had blustered out to show Canadians how to run the patrols in 1917. He was friendly, cultivated, highly competent, an outstanding organizer and leader with the art of getting on with people and getting the best from them. Like Walter Hose, he threw himself into the RCN and later joined it. He later became Director of Trade and his dedication and brilliance fashioned a major Canadian contribution to the war.

The whole complex shoreside business of ship movements, naval control of shipping, convoy organization, plus gathering, digesting, and disseminating operational intelligence was Brand's work. His office in Ottawa was a vital part of the vast Allied network that kept trade moving and alive and so finally resolved the war. Raiders or U-boats, battle squadrons or anti-submarine escorts, in 1939 the organization and control of trade was firmly in place. The convoy system could be implemented whenever a decision was made, and it came very early in the game.

Navy life during those pre-war years had been as lean as the navy itself. Twice, without the heroic Walter Hose, it would have disappeared. Knowing that your own country resented you as a burden or ridiculed you as "tin-pot" or a "piffling little adventure in coastal defence" was hard to take. Being in the navy was a job in the depression years, yes. But going to sea, as it had been forever, was a challenge, a life of its own fit for the young man with adventure in his blood. In the little RCN there was a tight-knit camaraderie, a special esprit, a pride in doing things right – and better even than the RN could – that kept hearts high.

That last peacetime summer the four west coast destroyers held their largest exercise. They dashed in full speed, as destroyers should, on a target vessel representing an enemy battleship. Each ship had its eight torpedoes finely tuned and tipped with practice heads. Signal flags snapped at the yardarms. Beautifully co-ordinated, with precise skill, over went the helms; four destroyers heeled, carving foaming wakes, fired, and raced away making thick black smoke. Thirty-two torpedoes fanned the Straits of Juan de Fuca. The "battleship" was "sunk."

In truth, though, this two-thirds of the RCN was on the wrong coast dealing with the wrong target and firing a weapon only very few would ever use again. These Canadian sailors would have to learn a new kind of war, and when it came they would show others what they quietly understood themselves – they could fight at sea with the very best.

CHAPTER FIVE
BUILDING A NAVY IN WAR

THE STORY OF CANADA'S NAVY IN WORLD WAR TWO, AND INDEED ITS history thereafter, was overwhelmingly shaped by the Battle of the Atlantic. It thrust on the tiny service a vast expansion. From a token force, the RCN became the third largest of the Allied navies. By 1943 fully half of the convoy escort on that most crucial artery, the North Atlantic route from America to Britain, was provided by the RCN. By mid-1944 Canada carried it all.

The Royal Canadian Navy went to war with a permanent force of about 1,800 and 1,700 reserves. It had six destroyers, five minesweepers, and two small training vessels. In five years it multiplied by a factor of fifty to reach 100,000 men and women and over 400 fighting ships, with more than 900 vessels all told. By comparison, the RN multiplied by eight and the U.S. Navy by twenty. Numbers alone, however, don't spell effectiveness. The dramatic rise itself brought huge problems and revealed serious shortcomings. As a small offshoot of the RN, the RCN lacked the essential base for a self-sufficient navy.

Right to the very brink of war, successive governments failed to develop a naval policy. So, quite apart from ships and sailors, critical ingredients – experienced staff, specialist and technical expertise, scientific liaison, training facilities and organization, shipbuilding and repair capacity, dockyard facilities and logistic support – scarcely existed. As the Battle of the Atlantic built to its crescendo, these elements all too often fell far short. A sound naval policy for Canada, as Laurier well knew in 1910, would have produced the essential industrial and technological base. In 1939 it didn't exist.

Pre-war plans for a respectable Canadian fleet were too little, too late. Canadian shipyards had scant capacity and none at all for building modern warships. The only naval vessels built in Canada since the drifters and trawler-minesweepers of the Great War were four coal-fired minesweepers completed in 1938. A whole new industrial base had to be created. It took time to muster the resources of a nation with such tenuous naval roots. Many elements were lacking still in 1942 and early 1943 when the Battle of the Atlantic reached its crucial peak. But in times of dire necessity remarkable things are done, and for the first time in Canada's history the strands finally pulled together into a fighting navy. It built a proud tradition of its own.

Any seagoing ship demands special skills and experience, which scarcely exist in the civilian world. The small Canadian professional merchant service provided about a thousand first-rate people – deck officers, engineers, seamen, and technicians who were used to living in ships and getting them and their cargoes safely about the ocean. But even they were a considerable step away from taking a full and effective place in a fighting ship.

The neophyte – and the great majority of officers and men alike had never even seen the sea – had to fit into a disciplined organization, grasp mysterious nautical customs and language, and learn a whole new range of skills. He had to live, day after seemingly endless day, in extraordinary discomfort in a small ship battered incessantly by a hostile sea. He had to conquer seasickness, bitter cold, chronic fatigue, and the suppressed fear of an unseen enemy. He had somehow to carry out wearying, often complex duties in situations where failed alertness could mean disaster to his ship, death to his shipmates. The transformation – from farm boy, factory hand, bank clerk, or stockbroker to fighting seaman – had to happen, not in years, but in a matter of weeks.

Canadian sailors fought in every element of the war at sea – in battleships, cruisers, fleet destroyers, motor torpedo boats, landing craft, carriers and naval aircraft, minesweepers, submarines – and in every theatre of war, many "on loan" to the RN. The great majority, though, were in Canadian ships, and three-quarters of them served in the battered, unglamorous little escorts that had such a vital role in winning the most crucial, long-drawn-out struggle of the war.

Fighting the U-boat was not supposed to be the greatest task. The threat had all but been dismissed. But wars don't run as expected. Soon the need for more convoy escorts, and Britain's inability to build and man them, raised demands for ships and men that Canada valiantly answered but found nigh impossible to bear. What made it work at all was the eternal, intangible, greatest single factor in the sea-fighting equation – the quality of people.

In Ottawa the Naval Service Headquarters staff – all of ten officers under Rear Admiral Percy W. Nelles – was hard at work before the first gun. On 29 August 1939 Admiralty flashed the codeword "Funnel" by wireless around the world. With that signal, all British registered merchant ships, Canadian included, came under naval control. The compulsion was very simple. Acceptance of naval control meant Admiralty provided the war risk insurance, far beyond any Lloyd's Coffee House capacity to write. So the first and fundamental act was to take control of trade. Commander Eric Brand's skeleton Naval Control Service (NCS) instantly became a vital element of the worldwide organization that controlled the movements of every Allied merchant ship for the next six years.

In spite of events in Europe four of six destroyers were still on the west coast. On 31 August *Fraser* and *St. Laurent* were showing the flag at a civic celebration in Vancouver. Headquarters ordered them to Halifax. In under three hours they were off across the Georgia Strait at twenty-five knots. Esquimalt was their home port but the only good-bye to families and friends their people could manage was a wave as they raced by. To their astonishment they were going to war. Many never returned. Heading south for Panama they heard Britain had declared war on 3 September, and within a day the Cunard liner *Athenia* had been sunk by a U-boat. On 10 September, the day Canada declared war on Germany, the destroyers were transiting the Panama Canal. Five days later they were in Halifax.

Admiralty immediately asked Canada to turn over control of the destroyers to the RN. Nelles leaped at it; being part of the imperial fleet was something he took for granted. Mackenzie King, though, had a deep-seated aversion to British control, stemming from the debacle of the Great War. Only Canada would decide where Canadians would fight; cabinet authorized full co-operation, but not control. The implications of this crucial decision only struck home when the RCN launched its huge expansion. Admiralty provided total logistic support for the Allied navies-in-exile it controlled – Norwegian, Free French, Polish, Dutch, and Belgian – but not for an independent Canadian navy. Help was not denied, but fundamentally the RCN must now provide all those critical ingredients to run a navy for itself.

The Cunard liner *Athenia* was first blood of the war and her sinking was directly against Hitler's orders to observe the Hague Convention Prize Rules. He expected to make peace with Britain quickly before he turned on Russia, and he didn't want to rouse the neutrals, especially the United States. But Fritz Lemp, Captain of *U-30*, thought the ship he had dead in his periscope was an armed merchant cruiser. *Athenia* was carrying 1,000 civilian passengers; 118 of them went down with her, including twenty-two Americans. It was all too reminiscent of *Lusitania*.

Winston Churchill, back in his Great War post as First Sea Lord, saw this as a declaration of all-out U-boat warfare and ordered convoy on the spot. In Halifax the Naval Control Service Officer (NCSO), Commander Richard Oland, dragooned eighteen reluctant merchant skippers into the unpalatable business of convoy. On 16 September HX 1, the first transatlantic convoy, steamed out of Halifax for the United Kingdom. The "H" in the British convoy numbering stood for "Home"; "O" convoys were "Outbound" from Britain. Adding an "S" meant "Slow." For some 350 miles HX 1 was escorted by *Saguenay* and the newly arrived *St. Laurent*. To seaward, RN cruisers *Berwick* and *York* took over as ocean escort. The U-boats were most certainly at sea, but they were in the rich and ready hunting ground of U.K. waters. The convoys picked up their anti-submarine escorts in the Western Approaches to the British Isles.

But there were too few escorts. The RN, perhaps mesmerized by asdic's magic, deployed a big effort on search and patrol of focal areas and U-boat transit routes. It proved as fruitless as it had in the previous war and robbed the convoys of needed escorts. Fleet aircraft carriers confidently patrolled the Western Approaches as part of this offensive. They were prime U-boat targets. *U-39* narrowly missed torpedoing *Ark Royal* before being sunk by screening destroyers. Then *Courageous* was torpedoed and sunk. Asdic was certainly not infallible. Neither were the scouting Swordfish or even the defences of the great fleet anchorage at Scapa Flow. In October Gunther Prien in *U-47* crept through a narrow channel with brilliant seamanship and sank the battleship *Royal Oak*. The blockship that would have barred his entry arrived one day too late.

Dönitz, however, had too few U-boats for an all-out campaign. During the winter between two and ten were operating in British waters, sowing mines and attacking ships in harbour approaches. But they had easy pickings – forty-six ships in October alone. They didn't have outstandingly greater performance on paper than the U-boats of the Great War, but they were far more efficient. In the first six months shipping losses reached 700,000 tons – over twenty ships per month. (An "average" ship was 5,000 tons.) Independents suffered heavily, but the convoys, with only one or two anti-submarine escorts, had heavy losses, too.

The U-boats had no need to reach far for easy targets, so beyond 15° west, halfway between Ireland and Iceland, convoys had surface escort only. The threat on the broad Atlantic was surface raiders, such as the pocket battleships *Deutschland* and *Graf Spee*, both loose at the outbreak of war. In the same period these raiders between them sank less than one-tenth of the U-boats' score. As in any *guerre de course*, though, they tied up forces out of all proportion. *Graf Spee*, for example, sank only eight ships with her 11-inch guns but she drew every cruiser in the Atlantic and the attention of the world until she ended her career, scuttled on a mud bank in the Rio de la Plata estuary off Montevideo.

Ottawa and *Restigouche* came round from the west coast, leaving nothing there to mind the shop other than the little vessels of the Fisherman's Reserve. It had been formed in 1938 by enlisting fishing vessels, owners, and crews willing to serve in time of war. Close to fifty lightly armed craft, some fitted with minesweeping gear, were on patrol soon after hostilities began. They were the sole defence of the west coast until the first corvettes came out of

B.C. yards in 1941. *Assiniboine*, a secondhand flotilla leader similar to the other RCN destroyers, came straight to Halifax from her commissioning in England. Remembering that the Halifax harbour approaches had been mined in 1918, the minesweepers plodded away at their monotonously essential work. To counter surface raiders the venerable heavy ships of the RN's 3rd Battle Squadron were based at Halifax. Their Royal Marine bands played lively airs as the great grey shapes slipped through the fog, reminding the historic waterfront of more gracious and less fatal days.

Merchant ships assembled in Bedford Basin. The convoys sailed on an expanding schedule. On 10 December the first troop convoy sailed with the First Canadian Division, 7,400 strong, in five ocean liners. The destroyers saw them on their way and a heavy surface escort then took them across the sea.

By the end of the year the Royal Canadian Navy had gathered a curious collection of some sixty vessels. Armed merchant cruisers were a useful counter to the surface raider so the navy bought *Prince Robert*, *Prince David*, and *Prince Henry* – 6,000-ton, twenty-two-knot luxury liners – from Canadian National Steamships. They were converted and each armed with four old 6-inch guns from Admiralty stocks. But the shaky technical organization took a whole year to convert them.

Auxiliaries came from various government departments. Luxury yachts were extracted from the U.S. by devious means. Some fishing vessels were requisitioned. Mostly, their crews donned uniform. The dockyard fitted a gun if it was available, they hoisted the White Ensign, and they were in the navy. Theirs were the endless chores around the defended ports – minesweeping, local anti-submarine patrol, examination service to check the papers and cargoes of incoming vessels, harbour duties. Some of the yachts, though quite unsuitable, were used as A/S escorts. The venerable *Acadia*, which had served as an anti-submarine escort in the Great War with her kite balloon, came on strength again. The least mobile became gate vessels for harbour anti-submarine net defences. All the dreary but essential harbour defence paraphernalia – booms, anti-submarine nets, detector loops, shore signal stations, and communications systems – had to be installed and experts found to run them. It was a good thing the U-boats had plenty to keep them busy elsewhere.

Canada's first concern was defence of her own coast. It might have been the "phony war" in Europe, but at sea the war had been all too real from day one. The Tribal-class destroyers called for in peacetime plans couldn't be built in Canadian yards, and Britain's first corvettes were just getting to sea. The RN needed many more and agreed to build two Tribals in England in return for ten corvettes built in Canada. The corvette seemed to meet Canada's need, too, for a coastal escort with minesweeping capability. The RN also had a suitable minesweeper called the Bangor. Both designs could be handled in ordinary commercial yards and the ships were small enough to navigate the canals from the Great Lakes.

And now politics was on the navy's side. Downgraded to a mere token in peacetime, it found new favour in cabinet – though not for the sound strategic reasons that certainly prevailed. Mackenzie King feared that another huge 1914 army in Europe would bring dreadful casualties and the political nightmare of conscription. Thus, it was deemed politically wise to put the country's effort toward the navy and air force. They were far less manpower-intensive and demanded much greater industrial effort. The country could profit from that. If war must be, then reap the industrial harvest, save your citizens, and sell your wares! The RCAF had the British Commonwealth Air Training Plan; the RCN got the go-ahead for ships and men.

This was easier said than done. Armies could be expanded and trained quite quickly in war, building on the organized militia Canada had always kept in place. But building ships, training sailors, and combining them into effective fighting units was a far more sophisticated process. A tiny handful of officers had to figure this out and somehow make it work.

Sixty-four corvettes and eighteen Bangor minesweepers were to be built in Canada. Simple vessels though they were, it was a mighty plunge. Not only ships, but an entire industry had to be built, requiring yard capacity, tooling, and a trained work force with a multitude of special skills. Capacity for steel plate was lacking and boilers, main engines, condensers, pumps, propellers, fans, anchors, compasses, radios, direction finders, echo sounders – the items that go into any ordinary ship – were not made in Canada. Nor were the special items of naval equipment – asdic sets, guns, depth charge throwers, and later on, radar sets. But the job simply had to be done. By February, 1940, fifteen shipyards – East, West, up the river, and in the Great Lakes – were busy building corvettes and Bangors. Fourteen corvettes were commissioned by year's end, including the ten slated for the RN; fifty came in 1941, forty-nine more later. Over fifty Bangors were commissioned in 1941 and 1942.

Captain Angus Curry, the lone engineer officer on the staff in Headquarters, began the monumental task. At the end of 1940 he was relieved by Engineer Commander George Stephens, who had been a non-commissioned Engine Room Artificer 5th class in the old *Niobe* in 1910 when Curry was a sub-lieutenant. Stephens was promoted to Captain and Engineer in Chief and later became Canada's first Engineer Rear Admiral and Chief of Naval Engineering and Construction. He masterminded the massive naval shipbuilding program through to the end of the war, then well beyond. Remarkable times bring forth remarkable people.

By late winter the destroyers were finally let off the leash, rotating to the Caribbean to help the RN. In March Commander Rollo Mainguy's *Assiniboine* joined the cruiser HMS *Dunedin*, which had intercepted a German merchant ship, *Hanover*, west of Puerto Rico. Her crew had set the cargo afire and crippled her engines and steering gear. But boarding parties kept a belligerent crew in line, fought the fires, and towed their prize to Jamaica. Repaired, she ran the U-boat gauntlet in convoy under the Red Ensign. Then, with a flight deck added, she became HMS *Audacity*, the first auxiliary aircraft carrier. In a renowned and bitter convoy battle in December, 1941, she took a decisive part but fell prey herself to a torpedo from the frustrated pack.

Otherwise, held home by Ottawa, it was local escort and patrol for Canada's destroyers. They could only read of the mounting toll on trade and fret at being so far from the action until the disaster of Dunkirk in the spring of 1940 pulled them across the Atlantic to the vortex of the war.

THE FRONT LINE

In April, 1940, the sinkings dropped, but it was only because Dönitz redisposed his U-boats for Hitler's lightning blow on Norway. The Luftwaffe leapfrogged planes to forward airfields there, and in the fierce inshore fighting up the narrow fiords, the RN lost precious destroyers. The U-boats were back at the convoys quickly, in renewed strength. Germany had what it wanted from Norway: airfields, valuable new bases for U-boats and the surface fleet with open access to the northern seas, and – an ace in the hole when the time came to attack Russia – the flank of the sea route to Murmansk.

Then, with hardly a breath, the blitzkrieg slashed through Holland, Belgium, and France and hurled Britain's army to the sea at Dunkirk. The RN, desperate for destroyers, called on the RCN. Winston Churchill and the Canadian staff convinced Mackenzie King that the English Channel was Canada's first line of defence. The fate of North America, as history told, would be decided there. *Restigouche*, *Skeena*, *St. Laurent*, and *Fraser* raced across the Atlantic; *Ottawa*, *Assiniboine*, and *Saguenay* would follow when current refits were complete.

In Plymouth each ship got a 3-inch gun for anti-aircraft fire. Like the ships' single 2-pounder pom-pom guns from the Great War, it was aimed with open sights. Stuka divebombers had already taken a heavy toll of the RN. The same thing was happening day by day off France. As with the U-boats, peacetime complacency about the air threat had been shattered, but the technical answers just weren't there.

Every available hand plunged into the evacuation. Trainees were hauled off courses. Sub-Lieutenant Jack Pickford, RCNVR, led demolition parties ashore in Brest to destroy what they could ahead of the Germans. Sub-Lieutenant Bob Timbrell got his first command, one of the great ragtag armada ranging from destroyers to cross-Channel ferries to private motor cruisers that braved shellfire and strafing and Stukas to haul load after load of exhausted soldiers from the beaches to Britain. Timbrell won the Distinguished Service Cross.

The destroyers, racing out of sunny Plymouth, missed the main evacuation and plunged into hectic operations along the French coast. Now the job was to pluck out pockets of retreating soldiers – British, French, Polish, Dutch – as the German army raced southward. On 11 June *Restigouche* and *St. Laurent* took off wounded from St. Valery, near Dieppe. Lieutenant Desmond "Debby" Piers went ashore and found the general commanding the 51st Highland Division. But he was holding a flank and declined the invitation to embark. German guns moved in. Shells whistled close over the destroyers. They briskly hoisted their boats, returned fire, and zigzagged out between the splashes.

France surrendered to Hitler at Compeigne on 21 June 1940. Evacuations now centred at St. Jean de Luz near the Spanish border. *Fraser*, the senior Canadian ship under Commander Wallace Creery, plucked a party of fugitive diplomats from a sardine boat off the beleaguered coast, among them the British ambassador to France, the South African minister, and an old friend of Creery's, Lieutenant-Colonel Georges Vanier, Canadian minister to France who became Canada's Governor General. They were sent to the U.K. in an RN ship. *Fraser* and *Restigouche* went to work at St. Jean de Luz, marshalling the transports and patrolling for U-boats. They pulled out the better part of a Polish division. *Restigouche*'s Captain, Lieutenant Commander Horatio Nelson Lay, and three of his ship's company were later awarded the Polish Cross of Valour.

The destroyers headed north and joined the cruiser HMS *Calcutta*, flying the flag of a Royal Navy Rear Admiral. Their target was the Gironde River, lined with oil tanks and shipyard and port facilities of great value to the enemy. On the night of 24 June they headed in fast, bows cutting through mounting seas. It was dark and *Calcutta* signalled the ships to form single line ahead. As Nelson Lay records it, *Restigouche* was three miles off *Calcutta*'s starboard quarter. *Fraser*, with Commander Wallace Creery, was off in the dark on the cruiser's port bow. The ships had not been assigned sequence numbers by the Admiral and so it wasn't clear what order they should take in the line.

Creery turned *Fraser* inward to take station astern. Somehow she got right across *Calcutta*'s bow. The cruiser cut her clean in two, right below the bridge. *Calcutta* stopped briefly and dropped one boat. *Restigouche* was left to do the rescue work and sink what was left. Lay took his ship right alongside the after half, kept his own screws clear of damage, and ground against the broken hulk for ten long minutes plucking off survivors. The bow still floated with men aboard and he risked using lights and rescued more before it sank. Then he lay off while *Fraser*'s engineer officer and party went calmly back aboard the floating half to scuttle it.

At first light when *Restigouche* rejoined *Calcutta*, the cruiser's bow seemed turned up by the collision. But, incredibly, it was *Fraser*'s bridge sitting there.

It had been sheared clean off and deposited neatly on the cruiser's forecastle. The horrified Commander Creery and his bridge team had stepped down to safety while the two halves of their ship disappeared in the dark. Forty-seven Canadians and nineteen RN sailors lost their lives.

The toll could well have been much higher but for Nelson Lay. Dick Malin, one of his asdic operators, who frankly didn't like him, said, "He was one of the best guys to serve with when the shooting started. Coolness, nothing phased him . . . " And Malin remembered when a signal came to leave the scene that Lay said to the yeoman, "I won't read any messages for the next hour." How else can a man live up to being christened "Horatio Nelson"?

High-speed manoeuvring on a dark night at close quarters calls for skill, precise judgement, and quick response to rapid change. Ships had no radar and showed no lights, but that was standard. Their captains, all experienced officers, were on their bridges, but they had had very little sleep in ten days and nights of constant action. Reactions and judgement were overstretched, dulled inevitably by fatigue. There was no Board of Inquiry, no Court Martial.

Forty-five years later, long after retiring from a distinguished career, Rear Admiral Wallace Creery believed that if he had admitted his exhaustion to himself and turned over to his First Lieutenant, *Fraser* might have lived. Valid or not, it is an awesome load that a warship's Captain carries. The life of a ship and all her people hang time after time on that split second of judgement, decision, action. The feeling that your beloved ship and all your shipmates would still live "if only . . ." is a burden that many fine sea officers over centuries of war have carried to their graves. *Fraser*'s was a tragedy to be repeated in everybody's navy as the war ground on.

Now Hitler mustered the armies and the landing craft for Operation Sea Lion, that short step across the Channel that would conquer England and lay bare the world. Napoleon had mustered his army and thousands of craft, too, and Nelson and the Royal Navy stopped him. But now Hitler had aircraft and U-boats and bases for them from the northern tip of Norway to the south of France. Britain was encircled and alone, her army in tatters with its equipment left behind, her fleet hard hit and stretched too thin.

The Channel must be held. All England girded for invasion. The Canadian destroyers stayed. Lieutenant Commander Jimmy Hibbard in *Skeena* read the basic order: to fire to the last shell, then ram the landing craft to the bitter end. Marshal Goering's Luftwaffe flew wave after wave on Britain to destroy the RAF. But the Spitfires and Hurricanes held. Without a fleet to match the navy in the Channel and without controlling the air, Hitler could not command that twenty miles of intervening sea.

Sea Lion was called off but Britain was under siege. London and the Channel ports were bombed unmercifully, and the U-boats exploded from their brand new bases in France. Working with them, too, were the Kondors, long-range maritime patrol aircraft flying from Bordeaux. They spotted unopposed over the Channel and the route to the Mediterranean. Efficient bombers as well, the Kondors sank thirty ships in their first sixty days. Dönitz had forty operational boats, averaging eight on each of the shipping routes. They were his elite. They picked off independents and stragglers and made bold, single-handed attacks on convoys. The young aces called this their "Happy Time." They raced each other for tonnage and more tonnage. Returning to their massive concrete pens in Brest, St. Nazaire, Lorient, and La Pallice, they flew strings of pennants, each for the death of a ship. It was a hero's welcome: flowers and favours from the girls; an Iron Cross for the Captain. Then they would turn the boat over to a maintenance crew and go home for a month, or carouse in Paris with U-boat pay in the pocket and the elite U-boat badge as passport to untold delights.

WOLF PACKS AND THE WESTERN APPROACHES

In September of 1940 Dönitz ordered the wolf-pack attacks on the surface at night. A group would be positioned by U-boat headquarters on a patrol line at right angles across the expected route of a convoy. The boats were too far apart to talk to each other and used high-frequency wireless to report their positions to shore. When one boat sighted a convoy he reported and shadowed while headquarters directed the others in ahead of its track. They all reported by wireless and when they were effectively gathered headquarters released them to attack. They simply swamped the defence, picking their own opportunities to go in and attack and attack again till their torpedoes were gone. Their Achilles' heel was their heavy use of wireless. The transmissions could be fixed quite accurately by high-frequency direction finding or HF/DF stations ashore in the U.K. and then in Newfoundland and Canada.

Meanwhile, Hitler's "blitz" on London went on night after night to shatter its enormous port. The Channel was closed to shipping by October and all Atlantic convoys were re-routed north of Ireland to Liverpool and the Clyde. The key battle now was in the Western Approaches to Britain and the Canadian destroyers were all there. By mid-summer they had joined the Clyde Escort Force, covering outbound convoys beyond Ireland to 12 or 15° West and bringing another back in. When the U-boats raced in on the surface asdic couldn't detect them by pinging, though they could be heard on hydrophones at short range, and at night the low-profiled U-boat, which could pick its direction of attack, could always spot the bigger escort first. One by one the destroyers got the first seagoing RDF, Radio Direction Finder Type 286, or radar. It was a long wavelength set that could spot other ships at about three miles but could rarely detect a surfaced U-boat.

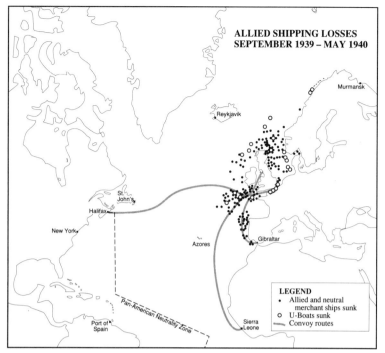

ALLIED SHIPPING LOSSES
SEPTEMBER 1939 – MAY 1940

LEGEND
• Allied and neutral
  merchant ships sunk
○ U-Boats sunk
—— Convoy routes

September, 1939 – May, 1940. Convoys had anti-submarine escorts only in the Western Approaches to the British Isles. But the U-boats didn't have to go far to find unescorted ships. Of 215 sunk only twenty-one were in convoy. Twenty-one U-boats were sunk.

It was a fierce fall and winter. The escorts were far too few, and the wolf packs had the upper hand. A fast convoy coming in from Halifax, HX 79, was loaded with munitions. Even with an especially heavy escort it lost thirteen out of forty-nine in a single night. Slow convoy SC 7 lost twenty sunk and two damaged out of thirty-four. Very few enemy were killed. Hundreds of oil-soaked survivors were fished from the icy seas. *St. Laurent*, still commanded by Harry DeWolf, rescued nearly 900 from *Arandora Star*. With the destroyer stopped and a sitting duck in those U-boat waters, the seamen in the boats and over the side on the scramble nets hauled in the survivors. Nearly all, as it turned out, were Germans and Italians, enemy aliens from Britain bound for internment in Canada. When DeWolf signalled the information to a circling RAF Sunderland, he flashed back, "How bloody funny" and flew off.

The RN, meanwhile, had found another destroyer to replace *Fraser*. She commissioned as HMCS *Margaree* and a lot of *Fraser*'s survivors joined her. They finished a refit in the worst of the blitz in London's Albert Dock. Every night the sirens howled; incendiaries showered down; high explosive bombs flung splinters. The dutymen ran out hoses, fought fires, dug people from the rubble. Ashore, the tube to Piccadilly Circus could get sailors to the light (inside the blackout curtains) and the music and laughter of the West End, to the Windmill Theatre with its famous nude tableaux where the decorative ladies were forbidden by the Lord Chancellor to move – even when the bombs fell close. The anti-aircraft guns in Hyde Park hammered away, fires raged, and rubble filled the streets. But the Windmill – as it still says proudly on its marquee – "Never Closed." Canadian sailors, making their way back to the wreckage of the docks through the tube stations crowded with night-sheltering Londoners, saw the cheerful, indomitable courage that kept Britain fighting and alive.

Margaree, on her first convoy in late October, was lost, cut in half by a merchant ship in poor visibility. The bow went down like a stone. *Port Fairy*, who had rammed her, came alongside the after part and took off some men. *Margaree*'s Captain (Commander Rouer Roy) and 140 men, many of whom had survived the sinking of *Fraser*, were lost.

Fraser survivors Lieutenant Bill Landymore, Surgeon Lieutenant Blair MacLean, and later arrival Sub-Lieutenant Bob Timbrell wrestled a carley float over the side and survived again.

The urgent dit-dit-dit, dit-dit-dit, dit-dit-dit "SSS" heard so often on the merchant ship frequency meant submarine attack. *Ottawa* and HMS *Harvester* raced to a call from the independent *Melrose Abbey* off Ireland. When they raised her there was the U-boat, an Italian in fact, blazing at her prey. The destroyers closed at full speed, opened fire, and the Italian boat submerged. Commander Rollo Mainguy in *Ottawa* was senior officer and the two ships searched systematically for five hours. Finally, they got solid asdic contact, and the ships took turns in co-ordinated attacks. *Harvester* lay off, holding contact; *Ottawa* ran in deliberately on the target's beam. The HSD, the Higher Submarine Detector Petty Officer, quietly called out the ranges and bearings. The U-boat was moving slowly, conserving batteries. Range, two hundred yards. Mainguy "threw-off," aiming the ship ahead to allow for the movement of the target while the charges sank.

"Target moving slowly right," from the HSD, and "Doppler slight high. Target coming towards." Yes. *Ottawa* would pass nicely ahead of the submarine. Then the HSD, "No echoes. Contact lost."

The asdic's pencil beam was passing right over the submarine. It was running deep. The depth-charge crews were ordered to make deep settings. From the Anti-Submarine Control Officer: "Fire by recorder." The rudimentary computer, a paper trace with a range mark for each asdic echo plotted against time, showed a sloping line. Projecting that ahead gave the zero range point and rang the fire buzzer.

Down aft the depth-charge crew dropped their pattern. After a long sinking time a jolting clang sounded in the engine room as each charge exploded.

Then *Ottawa* circled to regain contact. *Harvester* moved up and attacked, then circled back. And so the deadly game went on, drawing circles on the sea and blasting at the enemy below. The destroyers delivered nine careful depth-charge attacks between them. *Ottawa*, under-equipped still, had only the single rail aft and one thrower each side for firing five-charge patterns. *Harvester* was up to date and could fire the standard ten. After two of *Harvester*'s attacks they heard underwater explosions. In the morning there was an oil slick. Mainguy was convinced they had a kill. So was Captain (D), the officer responsible for escort vessels, in Liverpool. There was no wreckage, though, and Admiralty's U-boat Assessment Committee gave it "probably damaged."

Historians are always at it and over forty years later solid evidence pieced together the story of *Faa di Bruno*, actually sunk by *Ottawa* and *Harvester* on 6 November 1940. So *Ottawa* and Rollo Mainguy in fact got the RCN's first submarine kill of the war. It's a pity they didn't get the credit in his lifetime with the Distinguished Service Order for himself and likely the DSC for the asdic CO and Distinguished Service Medal for the HSD. Decorations went with a victory. In a good fighting ship every man, and especially those who received them, knew the "gongs" were for the whole team.

Soon the Italian navy struck back. On the night of 1 December *Saguenay* spotted a U-boat on the surface astern of her convoy. Almost at the same instant she was struck by a torpedo. Fire blazed fiercely forward and many were killed. The submarine, the Italian *Argo*, circled on the surface for another shot. Able Seaman Clifford McNaught, burned in the fire, dashed aft to supplement the depleted gun's crew by passing up shells. *Argo* was forced down by the gunfire and only then did Louis Audette, the Lieutenant in charge of the gun, see that McNaught was terribly burned on his face and hands. He was huddled now by the silent gun, sobbing quietly. Passing each shell with those mangled hands had been agony unimagined.

Up in the forecastle, skill and gut bravery finally controlled the flames. Flooding was limited in the pitch black bowels by shoring bulkheads with timbers. Lieutenant Commander Gus Miles got his ship under way on one engine, then, entering harbour, proud *Saguenay* was struck once more, this time by a German acoustic mine. But she was repaired to fight again, less twenty-one good seamen who had fought their last. Admiralty noted the fine seamanship of Miles and his company, as well as the speed of that after gun's crew that saved the ship and the convoy from further attack. But the war was taking a severe toll on the RCN.

Lieutenant Herbert Rayner took *St. Laurent* over from DeWolf after *Arandora Star*. It was Rayner's first command and in that dark and dirty December the Western Approaches gave him his due initiation. "Sally," as she was called ("Sally Rand" was her full *nom de guerre* after the famous fan dancer of the day), was detached from her convoy to support another under heavy night attack.

Pounding through heavy seas and swirling snow, Rayner found that four U–boats had sunk ten ships and crippled an armed merchant cruiser called *Forfar*. "Sally" gathered survivors and started escorting the cruiser eastward only to be called away again – another sinking, more survivors hauled on board. And there were U-boats everywhere. To confirm that unpalatable fact came the signal that *Forfar* was hit again and sinking.

Heading to the rescue through the murk, *St. Laurent* came upon a U-boat, a mile off and diving. She closed and picked it up on asdic. A U-boat! By the tail! But Herbie Rayner was a very careful, quietly systematic man. Coolly, he held the U-boat by asdic, circled round, holding his attack. He radioed for help. A single ship could easily lose a submarine. Running over it to drop depth charges, the ship's asdic always lost contact so she would then have to open to regain it, at which point the U-boat with a burst of speed could wriggle off. In addition, the depth charges churned the water up, giving cover and false echoes, and often the explosions knocked out power in the attacking ship. A second ship in the equation made a kill far more than twice as certain. *Forfar*'s survivors were in the water some miles off, but a Captain must make the hard decisions. The U-boats had killed too many this night, and this one must not escape to kill again. Rayner bided his time.

Soon the old RN escort destroyer *Viscount* arrived. She moved in and gained contact, too, and held it, then followed behind the U-boat slowly. Now it was co-ordinated attacks. "Sally" came in on the U-boat's beam to drop her ten-charge pattern while *Viscount* held contact. The deadly dance again, and again: eight patterns, eighty charges, over three hours. At last diesel oil spread on the surface and the contact faded. Both captains were confident they had a kill.

Next, *Forfar*'s survivors had to be found in the poor visibility and rising seas. Twenty still hung grimly to life and they were hauled aboard, stripped, warmed in the showers, cleaned of the terrible oil, their wounds tended, and tucked down wherever space could be found among so many others. "Sally" headed for the Clyde and in came another emergency call. Fifty miles away an independent merchantman had been torpedoed, which Rayner found crawling for home at five knots. Even worse weather now added its force to the U-boats. Towering seas threatened to overwhelm the crippled ship. Three days of struggle brought both exhausted vessels in to anchor in the haven of the Clyde.

St. Laurent landed her broken human cargo, and then began the work to get back in the fray: the clean-up of the oil and vomit and excrescence; the weather damage to be repaired; fuel and ammunition to be topped up; provisions and stores to be humped aboard. The ship's company would sleep – a little – and then take their turns for a run ashore in the blackout to the pubs of Greenock, or catch the train to Glasgow; for the officers there was the bar at the Bay Hotel in nearby Gourock. There might even be a girl, if a man was lucky, and perhaps a warm bed. Or else it was back aboard to the cold messdeck to crawl in the hammock or flake out on the locker tops and sleep. And then turn to in the early morning and it was back to sea. Out on the Western Approaches.

The certainty of the *St. Laurent/Viscount* kill was downed a bit to "probably sunk" by Admiralty's killjoys. But it was a higher rating, ironically, than *Ottawa*'s. Herbie Rayner won the DSC, and richly deserved it for those four days of fighting the U-boats and the sea. But "Sally's" U-boat, as evidence much later was to show, was a very tough nut. After the heavy pounding she actually had got home.

Of the few characters we have met so far, Lay, DeWolf, Creery, Hibbard, Piers, Landymore, MacLean, Mainguy, Rayner, Timbrell, and Pickford all became admirals in post-war years and Miles a commodore. Mainguy, DeWolf, and Rayner became, in that order, Chiefs of the Naval Staff. They learned their trade in a good hard school.

STRETCHED TOO THIN

By year's end the prospects were bleak. In twelve months the U-boats had sunk 400 ships – over 2 million tons. Only twenty-two U-boats had been killed and many more than that had been built. Since the war started over 5 million tons of shipping had been lost from all causes and only one-third of it replaced. Try as the escorts might, they were being beaten.

One overwhelming need was for more escorts. In late summer there had been a windfall. Fifty American Great War vintage flush-deck destroyers were turned over to the RN in the Churchill-Roosevelt destroyers-for-bases deal. Under heavy pressure from Admiralty the RCN took six and later a seventh, though manpower resources were far overstretched and the first corvettes were coming down the river.

By January, 1941, all six River-class destroyers and the four four-stackers not under repair – *Columbia*, *St. Francis*, *Niagara*, and *St. Clair* – were in the Clyde Escort Force. So, too, were ten corvettes. These were the ships, built to Admiralty's account, that had been brought down the St. Lawrence before freeze-up and ferried to Britain by skeleton RCN crews. They were barely outfitted and stored to the minimum in Canada. Some had even crossed the Atlantic with dummy wooden guns mounted bravely on their forecastles.

The RCN intended the Canadian scratch crews would form a small and badly needed manning pool at Greenock for replacing men in the destroyers. But things were so bad in the Western Approaches that the new corvettes were thrown willy-nilly into operations. The RN said they'd replace the Canadian crews but didn't. In Admiralty's view, the Western Approaches took priority over the RCN's need to man new ships at home. The Canadian position had been made completely clear when the barrel was scraped to man the four-stackers in September. There is no doubt that the RN still looked on the RCN as a convenient appendage there to do its bidding, rather than as an independent service. In retrospect, Canadian senior officers seemed too willing to comply. But these were desperate days.

Manning six four-stackers and ten corvettes quite unexpectedly in three months over and above planned commitments may not have loomed large in RN terms, but those 1,700 officers and men equalled the size of the whole of the RCN just one year before. Conjuring them up beyond the expansion already planned was squeezing blood out of a stone. Captain Harold Grant, the Director of Personnel, had done the squeezing. But four more corvettes were commissioned by the end of 1940, and nineteen more would need crews before the end of May, 1941, with thirty-one still to come and twenty-five minesweepers as well over the rest of 1941. And the RN would take none of them. So the RCN had to ram three years' emergency expansion into a chaotic two. To expect the men would be adequately trained and the ships properly equipped, tried and tested, worked up, and ready to fight at sea was beyond reality.

There was no doubt about the crisis in the Western Approaches. But escort vessels were useless without trained officers and men. That fall of 1940 Grant needed 7,000 more officers and men for the corvettes and minesweepers and the first of the Fairmile anti-submarine motor launches. He also had to provide people for the essential shoreside support. He needed 300 trained RCNVR officers by spring, and they had not even been entered. The training schools didn't exist. The experienced people needed to do the training were fighting the enemy at sea.

In short, the navy was already stretched far too thin. As late as May, 1941, RCN four-stackers and corvettes made poor showings in RN anti-submarine and communications exercises and two of the "British" corvettes that trained at HMS *Western Isles*, the RN's escort work-up base at Tobermory, were well below the RN par.

Operational training facilities like Tobermory and the experts to run them, the kind of things a major navy took for granted, the Canadians simply didn't have. Basic training geared up in 1940. On top of discipline and learning something about seamanship, nearly everyone needed specialized training, be it gunnery, asdic, electronics, torpedo, signals, wireless telegraphy, coding, engines, boilers, hull, plumbing, cooking, supply, pay and administration, medical aid, storekeeping. Every ship needed a great range of skills. Officers had to be versed in navigation and shiphandling and must understand signals, tactics, and weapons as well as administration, organization, naval discipline, and law. And they must demonstrate that essential, elusive quality, leadership. Schools were cobbled together, but equipment was short and the experts were at sea. Individual training lagged far behind.

Even a small warship was complex. Experienced people needed time to learn to handle a new one: to operate the engines and make ordered sense out of a myriad bells and buzzers and lamps, a tangle of voice-pipes and tele-phones, a forest of pipes and valves and shafts. It took time to shake down, just learning to get in and out of harbour safely.

Then the fighting teams needed practice on shoreside trainers like asdic teachers and gunnery battle trainers. They had to run their own equipment until they knew it blindfolded and upside down. Only then would they be ready for an experienced work-up team of officers and petty officers to oversee live exercises – firing at targets day and night; pinging on submarines; working with other ships, signalling and manoeuvring; sending boats away with boarding parties in rough weather; fighting fires and controlling action damage; the battle problems thrown at everyone from the Captain down; hashing over the mistakes and doing it again and again until it's right. All of this was necessary for proper training. Then a ship and her company could go to sea, trained but untried, to join an operational escort group or squadron.

But in the RCN the system just didn't exist. Harry DeWolf commanded *Skeena* through the Channel fray, was Staff Officer Operations in Halifax in late 1940 and then Director of Plans in Ottawa until he took command of his famous fighting destroyer HMCS *Haida* in 1943. He said, "We had no facilities really for training. As we found a crew for a corvette we'd send an officer to sea the first day with them to show them what to do. It was almost as simple as that."

An escort group, even of properly worked-up ships, needed time to work together, communicating under all conditions day and night, hunting target submarines, protecting dummy convoys, illuminating targets for each other, reviewing and remedying mistakes. The captains and their officers must thoroughly understand anti-submarine and convoy protection operations and know exactly what the Senior Officer expected of them. But the Cana-dian escort group that stayed together was an ideal hardly ever achieved. Ready or not, though, escorts were desperately needed with the convoys.

The Captain of a new corvette was likely a qualified merchant service officer with the rank of Lieutenant, RCNR. He was an experienced seaman and navigator who could get a ship safely about the ocean. He was likely the only officer on board capable, as a bare minimum, of avoiding marine disaster. But his knowledge of fighting a ship and defence of a convoy and his general experience in naval operations were minimal. He might have a junior RCNR officer as ship's navigator. The First Lieutenant, responsible for organizing the ship's company to work and fight, was an RCNVR officer who might possibly have had a few months at sea. The other two or three officers would be Sub-Lieutenants, RCNVR, straight from basic training. On the lower deck, a lucky corvette had half a dozen trained permanent force petty officers and leading seamen. That was how newly commissioned Canadian corvettes and sweepers went off to fight the sea and a professional enemy. They were terribly ill-prepared.

And most were dreadfully seasick. There was no cure for it other than toughing it out in tiny overcrowded, reeking ships that would "roll on wet grass," with chores and vital jobs that simply had to be done in any and all conditions however ghastly one might feel, weak from constantly vomiting such food as the truly miserable diet provided and exhausted from fighting the endlessly violent gyrations of the ship. The cold. The wet. The everlasting pounding and jarring and noise. These were the conditions that suddenly enveloped thousands of young men and boys who had spent only weeks in uniform. This was the navy. But they had volunteered, and tough it out they did. They learned by doing – on the job, at sea, where people died.

Percy Nelles, under pressure from the RN, forced conditions on his seagoing navy that the Royal Navy would never inflict on its own. As in the case of the ten corvettes, the RN was quite prepared to throw unreasonable demands at Canadians. That first scrambling, excessive expansion dogged Canada's navy through the war. As Harry DeWolf said, "We never caught up. We were always under pressure to man more ships." The essential conditions for attaining and maintaining operational efficiency eluded the RCN's escort forces until about the middle of 1943.

Until the spring of 1941, convoys steamed with no anti-submarine protection from flashing farewell to the local escort out of Halifax to meeting the Western Approaches escort west of Ireland. But the wolf packs reached further west to get at the merchant ships unopposed. In March Winston Churchill underlined the terrible danger out at sea when he declared "the Battle of the Atlantic." He appointed the first C-in-C Western Approaches, Admiral Sir Percy Noble, in charge of operations and training for all the escort force. In April the RN set up a base in Iceland. Now the convoys could be covered twice as far. In three attacks in the newly covered area that month, three U-boats were sunk. Then in May the wolf packs moved even further west, between Iceland and Newfoundland. They sank five ships in an eastbound convoy before it reached anti-submarine protection. Naked, the convoy dispersed and there were more losses. Complete transatlantic escort was the only answer, and in May of 1941 Admiralty asked the RCN to cover the western Atlantic. It would be a new escort force, mainly of RCN ships, based on St. John's, Newfoundland, and under Canadian command. Canada agreed.

THE NEWFOUNDLAND ESCORT FORCE

Now all ships except harbour defence and local escorts in Halifax and Sydney were committed to the Newfoundland Escort Force, the NEF. The destroyers and corvettes came back from the Western Approaches backed by some old RN destroyers of Great War vintage called "V's and W's" because their names began with these letters. Canadian escort groups were formed. Corvettes joined them as they commissioned. If the far-reaching U-boats made the through-escort plan essential, it was the rush of newly constructed corvettes from Canadian yards in the spring of 1941 that made it possible. Quantity was there – though it was never enough to provide proper rotation, training, and refit cycles or a reserve for inevitable action and weather damage – but quality, as we have seen, was not.

On top of that, the Canadian corvettes weren't really up to ocean work. Initial design was for a coastal escort, not for long, gruelling open-ocean passages. But now there was no choice. The RN, learning from early experience, was improving its own corvettes' seakeeping, capacity, and livability by extending their forecastles, enclosing the well-deck to make accommodation bigger and drier, and installing breakwaters. Ottawa knew this, but to modify Canadian construction would slow the flow. Then, because of overloaded shipyards it was mid-1943 through late 1944 before the first seventy Canadian-built corvettes were modified with extended forecastles. In that long interval Canadian corvettes fought on the ropes. With the best of crews their efficiency was impaired. And the creature comfort of their companies was rock bottom.

In 1941 most still carried minesweeping gear, which took up needed depth-charge space on their quarterdecks. They had only magnetic compasses, which were very unstable in rough weather and – most critically – while manoeuvring to attack. Gyro compasses were not manufactured in Canada. Most of the Canadian corvettes had no searchlights, carried no radio telephones, and were fitted with the rudimentary type 123A asdic, vintage 1920s. The RCN was at the back of the queue and everything had to come across a hazardous sea.

Initially an escort group had one destroyer and three or four corvettes. The senior of the officers in command, whether RN, RCN, or other Allied navy, automatically became the Senior Officer Escort (SOE) and in charge of defending the convoy in addition to handling his own ship. Usually he was in the destroyer, which was best equipped for the task.

A group would leave St. John's, take over from the local escort that had brought the convoy from Halifax or Sydney, slog northeastward until relieved by an RN group at the Mid Ocean Meeting Point (MOMP) south of Iceland, then steam into Hvalfjord for fuel. In that gale-plagued Iceland anchorage the RN provided bare subsistence: a depot ship for essential stores and emergency repair, ammunition ships, and tankers for fuel and water. On rare occasions there would be a dance ashore with some silent, icy, and well-defended blondes. Then it was out to pick up a westbound convoy, turn that over to the western local escort off the Grand Banks, and run back into "Newfyjohn."

Seven corvettes had arrived there on the 27th of May: *Agassiz, Alberni, Chambly, Cobalt, Collingwood, Orillia,* and *Wetaskiwin.* Their Senior Officer was Commander J.D. "Chummy" Prentice, CO of *Chambly* and also designated Senior Officer Canadian Corvettes. He had had the winter to work to some extent with these first corvettes around Halifax and they were far better manned and trained than those that followed.

LEADERS

Prentice was a Canadian who had joined the Royal Navy as a cadet in 1912 and retired in 1938. At the outbreak of war, like all the ex-RNs living in Canada, he was placed by Admiralty at the disposal of the RCN. He was the right kind of officer for building seagoing efficiency in such a ragtag force – energetic and dedicated with a fertile and innovative mind, a sense of humour, and a particularly colourful personality. He wore a rimless monocle in his right eye and could toss it in the air and catch it unerringly between bushy eyebrow and lower lid. He had a coffin-like box with a hinged lid built on his bridge so he could catch a little sleep between crises and it was said that even in there his monocle was always firmly in place. Legendary people are needed at times like these and Prentice filled the bill.

Commodore Leonard W. Murray, RCN, who had been Commander of Canadian Ships and Establishments in the United Kingdom, arrived to command the Newfoundland force in June. He was a Nova Scotian from Pictou County who had been a cadet in the Naval College class of 1912. He served with the RN in the Great War and periodically in peace. In 1919 he was a Sub-Lieutenant under Captain Dudley Pound, who by 1941 was First Sea Lord. Pound was influential in Murray's appointment to Newfoundland. It was very important that the RCN officer there should have the RN's confidence and, in fact, Murray was the best possible choice.

In an RN or ex-RN officer like Prentice, the distinctive accent and mannerisms running to handkerchiefs up the sleeve, boat-cloaks, and silver-knobbed canes roused no resentment among young Canadian officers and men. They served quite happily when, as was often the case, the CO of a Canadian ship or school was a Royal Navy officer on loan. Those officers were carefully selected and were intelligent enough to know that the class system so rigidly separating officers from men in Britain did not apply in Canada. They brought professionalism with them, which was the main thing, and their customs were just the way Brits were. But when an RCN officer brought such foibles back with him from his time with the RN or appeared to look down his nose at fellow Canadians, it was indeed resented.

Commodore Murray was not one of the latter, though his time with the Royal Navy had marked him somewhat and he was a bit remote, perhaps shy. He gave the impression of a rather portly stodginess. That was belied, though, by the hard-hitting brand of hockey he played whenever he could get on the ice. Right through his career he had a strong feeling for his men. Murray was a thoroughly competent officer and an able administrator. He was not the fire eater, the dashing leader. He did not have the flamboyance of Prentice or the presence of Admiral Percy Noble who, as Commander-in-Chief Western Approaches, was Murray's operational boss, or the ruthless toughness of Admiral Max Horton, who relieved Noble. But Murray inspired confidence, maintained a balanced view of what was possible, and coaxed rather than browbeat results from the extraordinarily limited resources he had at his disposal.

He had a well-earned reputation as a fine shiphandler. This might seem inconsequential for a shorebound senior officer, but shiphandling skill always carried a certain stamp of approval through any officer's career. It could strongly outweigh other shortcomings in a ship's Captain in the minds of his own people. Taking his ship alongside is the one time when the Captain's skill is on naked display to everyone from the admiral in his flagship and the other ships in harbour to the coxswain at the wheel and right below to the engine room crew working the throttles.

If, in his first command, an officer brought his ship alongside a jetty or up to a buoy, day and night in all kinds of weather, with precision and dash – and destroyers particularly had to be handled with dash – he had it made. The engine room staff would boast that their Old Man never used more than three engine movements to come alongside. The seamen would have all lines secured, be down out of the rain, dressed in their number ones, and off ashore before that other ham-fisted ship in the group had even got a headrope ashore. And their Old Man never so much as scratched the paintwork.

Good shiphandling, as much as in the days of sail, breeds admiration, confidence in the Captain, and pride in the ship. It has always been a real factor in reaching that most satisfyingly important state – a happy and efficient ship. And those two characteristics invariably go hand in hand. The often unfortunate corollary abides, however. A ship's company will growl and find it hard to forgive poor shiphandling.

The navy's memory of one distinguished career officer of otherwise Nelsonian cut who retired as a rear admiral is still dogged by his inept handling of one of the notoriously difficult four-stackers in 1941. The Halifax dockyard lies along the west side of the harbour and across a half-mile of water lies the city of Dartmouth. On a particularly cold and blustery day, after several attempts to get the ship alongside in the dockyard, Commander Hugh Pullen bellowed to the forecastle, "For God's sake, get a line ashore." An unidentified voice responded with equal frustration, "Which side? Dartmouth or Halifax?"

Commodore G.C. Jones was the Commanding Officer Atlantic Coast, situated in Halifax at that time. He was not in direct command of Murray, which was a good thing as the two were quite different in personality and never hit it off. Jones was a bright staff officer but not much of a seaman. Early in the war he ran his ship into a ferry, thus keeping her alongside for repairs when others were off fighting in the Channel. From then until he died the navy called him "Jetty" Jones.

On the other hand Murray, whose contemporaries remembered him forty years later as a consummate shiphandler, had the regard and confidence of the ones who counted most to him – those who served at sea. Both officers reported directly to NSHQ and Murray served the operational requirements of C-in-C Western Approaches. Otherwise Jones, as COAC, was in charge of everything on the east coast – operations, allocation of ships, the dockyard, the shore and sea training facilities and organization – such as they were, as well as the very important function of manning. So Murray to a very large extent had to depend on Jones for the tools – the ships and the people and the support facilities – to do his job. And he often considered he got short shrift.

They were in the same term at the Naval College but Jones was the senior by a hair, was promoted to Rear Admiral one day earlier, and in September, 1942, left Halifax to become Vice-Chief and then Chief of the Naval Staff in Ottawa. Murray succeeded him as Commanding Officer Atlantic Coast. He became Allied Commander-in-Chief Canadian Northwest Atlantic in April, 1943, and remained in that post until the war's end.

The shortage of trained people was chronic and as each new ship commissioned the situation got worse. Later in 1941 Murray and Jones had a major confrontation on the matter of manning ships. Murray knew how important it was that ships' companies stay together; it was the only way a fighting team got moulded. But when a Newfoundland Escort Force ship went to Halifax for maintenance or refit, experienced people would be yanked by Jones's manning commander to provide the core for a new corvette's crew. That, in fact, was the policy of NSHQ. In the Naval Board's view the operational fleet must suffer "temporary" inefficiency to get those new ships out to sea. Jones had to make the numbers and he was an ambitious man. Murray, who all his career thought of his people first, saw the results of that policy etched in the harrowed faces of his young ships' captains and in the terrible losses out at sea.

Command of the Newfoundland Escort Force was, operationally, the most daunting challenge ever put in the way of a Canadian naval officer. By the time Murray took command in June, 1941, the force consisted of six RCN and seven RN destroyers and twenty-one corvettes, all but four of them Canadian. There were forty corvettes by August, most of them terribly short on training and experience. Logistically, it was a nightmare of missing elements. For what became almost overnight the major naval operating base in the western Atlantic, St. John's, Newfoundland, had the leanest of facilities.

NEWFYJOHN

The entrance to St. John's harbour is a mere cleft in the massive wall of rock that faces the harsh Atlantic. Sailors for centuries have found it – or foundered near it – in fog and ice and gales and in those rare and lovely spells of fine, fish-curing "civil weather" that come in the late, brief summer. St. John's has seen centuries of war. Its harbour gives wonderful shelter in any weather, but it is rock-girt, steep-sided, and small – only 700 yards across and slightly over a mile long – and in wartime always overcrowded. Apart from its natural shelter and the friendship that Newfoundlanders always extend to men of the sea, it had little to offer the Escort Force. There were fuel tanks, one small drydock, some shaky jetties, and, at the beginning, no shore support facilities, no training equipment, no amenities of any kind – and the winter weather was almost as bleak as Iceland's.

For ships there were only the basics of fuel, water, ammunition, stores, provisions, and emergency repairs; for men, mail from home, a brief run ashore, beer or bootleg screech, a movie. There might be a dance in a church hall up the rain-lashed hill, a girl perhaps, or a welcome from a friendly family with a decent meal and a warm bed. While base facilities – to be called HMCS *Avalon* – were planned and built, support was afloat. HMS *Forth*, a submarine depot ship (without the submarines), provided running repairs and accommodation. Then an RN store ship and two oilers came, plus a Great Lakes steamer for a floating barracks called *Avalon II*. There were Free French, Belgian, Polish, and Norwegian corvettes, too. They were crewed by professionals who had escaped from their overrun countries and had been given little ships the RN couldn't man.

It was a major business starting from scratch to set up a naval operating base for some sixty ships. Anti-submarine defences, controlled minefields with detector loops, and anti-torpedo nets were installed. The nets were awkward to get around but well justified. A U-boat tried to fire torpedoes into the harbour mouth a year later. Over the next year wireless station, port war signal station, hospital, dockyard shops, new jetties and wharves, barracks and administration, stores, magazines, and fuel storage were completed. Admiralty paid the capital costs, the RCN carried operation and maintenance. While this was going on the U.S. Navy was fast building its own massive base facility at Argentia in Conception Bay.

That slit in the rock so often shrouded in fog got the first radar beacon in North America. It was installed in mid-1941 in the Cabot Tower, the site of Marconi's first transatlantic radio station high above the harbour entrance. A modified aircraft transponder gave an accurate bearing when triggered by the early ship's radar. It got many ships safely within sight of the surf at the entrance. From there the Captain had to zig around the net and line up with the green leading lights in the town. Then he was between the awesome cliffs with their fish houses and stages clinging to the rocks, then just as suddenly inside in the harbour's pool.

The physical limitations at St. John's were matched by ridiculously small staffs. Murray, as Commodore Commanding Newfoundland Force, a vital operational command, was charged as well with all naval administration in Newfoundland. He began with his secretary and one commander.

Responsible to Murray for the escorts' administration, training, efficiency, and readiness was Captain (D) (for "Destroyers"). During all of 1941 Captain (D) Newfoundland had one staff officer for gunnery and one for signals; he had no torpedo officer, whose expertise included ships' electrics and depth charges, until 1942, and no specialists in anti-submarine, radar, or engineering until 1943.

By any standard the suddenly burgeoning, vastly overstretched, under-equipped, and largely untrained Canadian navy was ill-prepared to fight at sea. It was up against the highly trained professionals of the U-boat fleet, who had Admiral Dönitz's large, skilled shoreside staffs and sophisticated support systems to back them up. And at sea the U-boats held tactical initiative. It is not surprising that in the first three years of war defeats for the RCN outweighed the victories. It is quite astonishing, in fact, that they managed as well as they did.

THE "PRINCES" AND THE WEST

How remarkably things had changed. Before the war the main threat to Canadian waters was seen as the surface raiders, roving heavy warships or armed merchant ships, and submarines that could lay mines. Hence the shape of the Canadian fleet that was planned but not built. As emergency counters to the merchant raiders the Royal Navy had earmarked a number of ocean liners to fit as armed merchant cruisers (AMCs) and they deposited some guns and equipment in Canada. At the start of the war they outfitted two such ships in Montreal. The RCN followed suit, collared the three "Prince" liners, and got what was left of the RN's stockpile. Each Canadian AMC got four single 6-inch guns dating from 1896, with no fire-control equipment, and a couple of 3-inchers – hardly formidable opposition for German cruisers and pocket battleships, but they would at least shoo an armed merchant ship away from a convoy.

During their year in conversion the pre-war view was turned on its ear. After the raiders' first flush came Norway, Dunkirk. The demand was for destroyers for the front line in the Channel, then for escorts and more escorts to counter the real threat, the U-boats. The mighty *Bismarck* wasn't destroyed until May, 1941, and big-gunned warships of the RN's 3rd Battle Squadron – battleships, cruisers, and some AMCs – still ran out of Halifax. But by the time the "Princes" got to sea the real threat from armed merchant raiders that they could handle was small. Compared to the U-boats it was nothing.

Prince Robert, fresh out of the shipyard in Vancouver in September, 1940, rushed south on operations. She was short on stores and, in the words of her CO, Commander Charles T. Beard, "in a very unready state" – distressingly similar to Commander Hose's *Rainbow* in 1914. However, she nabbed a merchant ship called *Weser*, which was the supply ship for a Pacific raider, sneaking out of Manzanillo, Mexico, and sailed her with a prize crew triumphantly to Esquimalt. Then she ranged the southwest Pacific under RN operational command, escorted the doomed Canadian army contingent to Hong Kong in November, 1941, and at year's end was part of the Esquimalt force.

Prince Henry commissioned in Montreal in December, 1940, and made for the Pacific, too. At the end of March, 1941, she intercepted a couple of German merchant ships that scuttled themselves off Peru. In January, 1942, she spent a short time as depot ship for the NEF in St. John's – the closest any of the "Princes" got to the heart of the navy's war. Then she joined the Esquimalt force.

Prince David commissioned in Halifax at the end of 1940 and had an uneventful year on the east coast and in the Caribbean covering convoys. Then she went to the west coast. By early 1942, then, with Japan and the U.S. in the war, the three AMCs with their ancient armament were Canada's defence for the west coast in the fast-exploding Pacific.

In June, 1942, the U.S. Pacific Fleet was still reeling from Pearl Harbor. Admiral Yamamoto mustered the whole power of the Japanese navy to seize bases at Midway Island and in the western Aleutians. The Aleutians were to be the northern anchors for the Japanese "ribbon defence" of the Pacific. At the same time Yamamoto intended to lure the far weaker American fleet to destruction. His light carriers bombed Dutch Harbour and amphibious forces took unoccupied Attu and Kiska. To the south, though, in the historic Battle of Midway, the U.S. fleet masterfully destroyed four Japanese strike carriers and turned the course of the Pacific war. The amazing American amphibious re-conquest of that vast ocean began. Their submarines started the campaign that actually achieved what the U-boats just failed to do in the Atlantic. They throttled Japan, destroying her trade and her power to go on waging war. And they had done it well before the huge carrier task forces heaved into view of the Japanese home islands. By 1942, although the Canadian government and the armed forces believed British Columbia very vulnerable to attack, the west coast was no longer even remotely threatened.

At the end of August the three "Princes," with corvettes *Dawson* and *Vancouver*, were assigned to U.S. Navy command for the brief campaign to dislodge the Japanese from Attu and Kiska. Their sole opposition was filthy weather, fog alternating with icy gales howling down from the Bering Sea and the sudden tearing winds of the well-known Alaskan "williwaws."

Apart from a single Japanese submarine lobbing some shells at remote Estevan Point Lighthouse on Vancouver Island in the summer of 1942, there was no other action on the west coast. The naval barracks, HMCS *Naden* in Esquimalt, trained many sailors. HMCS *Royal Roads*, situated on a lovely estate near Esquimalt, trained Volunteer Reserve sub-lieutenants. Then in 1942 it became the Royal Canadian Naval College and graduated midshipmen for the permanent force RCN and the RCNVR. West coast shipyards with their mild weather efficiently delivered corvettes, Bangors, and then frigates. All the corvettes went to the east coast in 1942, leaving some fifteen Bangor mine-sweepers to hold the fort along with the "Princes." Against the harshness of wartime Halifax and St. John's with their rough weather, grungy living, lack of decent recreation and entertainment, overstressed facilities, and reality of fighting a deadly enemy at the door, the west coast was lotus land.

In 1943 the three AMCs were converted in west coast yards for the new phase of the war – re-conquest of Europe. *Robert* was in action by the end of that year as an auxiliary anti-aircraft cruiser on West African and Mediterranean convoys. *Henry* and *David* became infantry landing ships. Their landing craft took first-wave assault troops to the beaches on D-Day, the 6th of June, 1944. Then they were in the landings on the south of France. In that rebirth they made their contribution to the war.

By then there were men in plenty, but in September, 1940, the navy scraped bottom to man six four-stackers. The 100 officers and 1,200 men slated for the "Princes" could have easily manned eight. When those first ten RN corvettes were landed in the navy's lap with hapless skeleton crews, the "Prince" crews could have fully manned fifteen with experienced officers and men left over for training staffs, work-up teams, repair parties, and manning pools to boot.

In the crucial, harrowing depths of the Battle of the Atlantic of 1941 and 1942, with the threat of surface raiders gone and the U-boats sinking, killing, inexorably winning, those men would have been manna from heaven to Leonard Murray, his embattled Newfoundland Escort Force, and the essential lifeline they were desperately trying to defend.

Admiral Nelles, in the face of all this, clung tenaciously to his idea of the "big ship" navy that he believed Canada should have. In that context, of course, the "Princes" were a joke. They provided sea billets for a number of senior officers and in Nelles's view perhaps they brought some prestige and credibility. As to the west coast, Nelles had always worried about it. But since

Ogdensburg in mid-1940, if Japan came in the Americans would be there. Priority had to be the Atlantic. Harsh reality had turned his navy into an escort force and it was being wrenched apart by shortages. But the Chief of Naval Staff looked on the embattled corvettes as stepping stones to his ideal navy. Percy Nelles was too far from the sea.

CHAPTER SIX

THE BATTLE OF THE ATLANTIC: THE TIDE TURNS

AT THE BEGINNING OF 1941 ADMIRALTY HAD TRIED TO CONJURE UP more escorts from nothing. They lowered the nominal speed of fast convoys so more ships sailed independently. That reduced the number of convoys and so beefed up their escort. But sinkings soared, mainly of independents, then dropped as sharply when the order was reversed. In the spring there were some heartening successes. Four U-boats were sunk in ten days, including Iron Cross aces Kretschmer, Shepke, and Prien. But the overall trend was as fatal as in 1917 – three merchant ships were sunk for every one replaced by new construction; eight new U-boats slipped into the sea for every one sunk. In March, when Winston Churchill dedicated full force to what he named the Battle of the Atlantic, it was being lost.

Then came an extraordinary stroke of luck. A U-boat was blown to the surface by RN escorts and briskly boarded. The Captain, Fritz Lemp, had mistakenly sunk *Athenia* on the first day of war. In his second blunder he failed to scuttle his brand new boat. The boarding party grabbed his Enigma cypher machine and all his code books and documents and shot him in the process.

Until then the Kriegsmarine's Hydra cypher had defied penetration. Now the shifting U-boat picture was available daily in Admiralty's submarine tracking room. Decrypted disposition signals combined with high-frequency direction finding (HF/DF) from the shore network in Britain, Iceland, Newfoundland, and Canada. Knowing accurately where the U-boats were positioned meant that evasive routing and warnings to convoys were exceptionally effective. Losses dropped sharply. This code-breaking operation, known only to a handful of people with "Ultra" clearance, remained completely secret. Dönitz's experts, certain their code was unbreakable, made no connection with the successful evasions and decreased sinkings. Only at year-end, when the new Triton cypher for U-boat traffic came in, did this great advantage disappear – until Triton, too, was penetrated at the end of 1942 through another U-boat capture and with the same happy result.

By the summer of 1941, thanks to the NEF, there was continuous surface escort right across the Atlantic. With Hudsons and Sunderlands based in Iceland, the convoys were routed far to the north to get under their air cover. From Newfoundland the RCAF's twelve Douglas Digbys, which could reach out about 350 miles, and five Catalina flying boats, which could patrol to 500 miles or more in the right conditions, were only useful in daylight. Their chances of sighting a U-boat, much less sinking one, were not great. But if a U-boat looking for a convoy or running to gain attack position spotted an aircraft it would have to dive. So air cover greatly increased the odds of a convoy getting through. There were no practical airfields in Greenland. And between the air cover radiating from Iceland and Newfoundland lay the awful area of ocean where the surface escorts had to fight the U-boats on their own. It was called the Black Pit.

In June, 1941, just a week after Murray took command, the NEF fought its first battle. HX 113, a fast convoy of fifty-eight ships, was escorted by HMCS *Ottawa*, Rollo Mainguy in command, with corvettes *Chambly*, *Collingwood*, and *Orillia*. From the first sinking Mainguy, a signals specialist himself, couldn't co-ordinate the defence because the ships at night could barely talk. The corvettes lacked radio telephones, their wireless equipment wasn't operating properly, and their visual signalling was terrible. The tiny blue flashing light, the only visual method allowed at night between escorts, was beyond the skill of a seasick neophyte signalman on the wing of a wildly heaving bridge. *Ottawa* had radar type 286 from her Western Approaches service. The corvettes had none. A strong reinforcement of RN ships from Iceland finally turned the scales in the battle. They sank two U-boats but not before HX 113 had lost six merchant ships.

That shaky start showed how badly training was needed. But facilities were almost nil. There was one asdic attack simulator in St. John's, no live submarine for training until late fall, no mock-up to exercise depth-charge or gun crews, and no sea training team to bring expertise to bear. By the end of August nearly fifty new Canadian corvettes were with the NEF. Prentice found they arrived from Halifax "inexperienced and almost completely untrained." He did the best he could but Captain (D), Captain E.B.K. Stevens, RN, wrote to Commodore Murray in the fall that "At present most escorts are equipped with one weapon of approximate precision – the ram."

When the Gulf of St. Lawrence was clear of ice the slow convoys out of Sydney could be routed past Cape Race at the southeasterly tip of Newfoundland, or up through the Gulf to reach the Atlantic through the Strait of Belle Isle. Slow convoys were for ships capable of speeds from 7.5 to 8.9 knots, mostly cranky old coal-burners who belched smoke and were far more

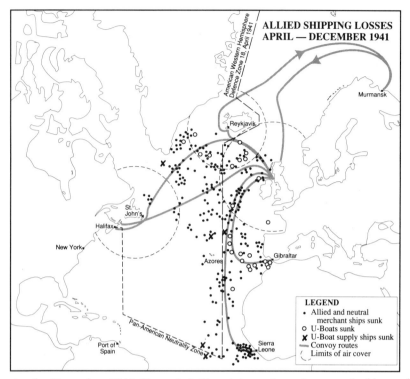

ALLIED SHIPPING LOSSES
APRIL — DECEMBER 1941

LEGEND
- Allied and neutral
  merchant ships sunk
- U-Boats sunk
- U-Boat supply ships sunk
— Convoy routes
— Limits of air cover

April – December, 1941. From their French bases the U-boats reached beyond the range of air cover for wolf-pack attacks on the convoys. The Newfoundland Escort Force made through anti-submarine escort possible. Breaking the U-boat code in May, 1941, saved even greater losses.

susceptible to breakdown and far less capable or amenable to convoy discipline than their more modern sisters. They straggled badly. With their low speed, effectively around six knots, they were a long time on passage. SCs were extremely vulnerable, but during that summer, with the Enigma breakthrough, evasive routing saved the day.

There were the fortunes of war, too, and the luck of the damned. SC 41, in late August, had the odds against it. The escort of one four-stacker and three corvettes was often down to one. Ships were scattered by icebergs, fog, and gales, there were incessant breakdowns, and an escort collided with a merchant ship that decided to leave the convoy. But with evasive routing, then help of air cover from Iceland and more than its fair share of luck, SC 41 staggered safely through.

THE BATTLE FOR SC 42

Behind it came SC 42 in early September and the luck ran out. There were sixty-four ships in the convoy when the 24th Escort Group took over south of Newfoundland. The SOE, Lieutenant Commander Jimmy Hibbard, and his destroyer *Skeena* were veterans of the Western Approaches. Corvettes *Orillia* and *Alberni* had worked with him on two convoys; *Kenogami* was completely new to the NEF. That was it.

Off Cape Farewell, the southern tip of Greenland, the convoy crept along at under five knots, badly scattered by heavy gales. The escorts pounded into heavy seas, pulling the ships back together, burning precious fuel. No air cover from Newfoundland could reach them now. Days in the Black Pit stretched ahead without hope of an aircraft out of Iceland. Weather almost stopped the convoy cold. Hibbard had to break radio silence to report they'd be late at the mid-ocean rendezvous. He didn't like doing that at all. His transmission could be intercepted and his plot already showed an ominous picture.

On 1 September the U-boat disposition signals were broken by communications intelligence at Bletchley Park in England. Marked up in Admiralty's submarine tracking room, they showed that Dönitz had placed fourteen U-boats in a group called Markgraf in a vast mid-Atlantic chessboard right across the path of SC 42. Out from Admiralty word flashed to Newfoundland, then was relayed to senior officers of escorts. Admiralty diverted all the mid-Atlantic convoys.

The feckless SC 41 was well to the east and out of trouble. SC 43, next behind Hibbard, was routed south. A troop convoy for Iceland and a fast convoy from Halifax were diverted south. Two westbound convoys made big diversions. All escaped the Markgraf net. But SC 42 was too far on to get clear to the south. On 8 September it was ordered due north to creep very close up the east coast of Greenland. It was an agonizingly ponderous end run around the wolf pack's northern flank. It was the right move, indeed the only move other than turning back, and the navy's watchword was "the safe and timely arrival of the convoy." Turning back meant defeat and that was unthinkable. The end run very nearly worked, but not far off Greenland a U-boat torpedoed a straggler. Then the convoy itself was spotted by the most northwesterly U-boat in Dönitz's masterly disposition.

Back to Germany flashed the contact report, with position, course, and speed. The shadower lay off, hull down, invisible in the heavy seas. Out went his amplifying reports. This was a ripe target, big, slow-moving, with only four escorts and no air cover. Dönitz was no man for half-measures. He had Hibbard cold and he hurled all fourteen U-boats of Markgraf at SC 42. His personal order was typical of the man. "This convoy must not pass. At them – Attack them – Sink them!"

Back in St. John's a short while earlier Chummy Prentice had pulled a training group of available corvettes together to try and work them up. Planning to take them to sea, he dropped in to Commodore Murray's operations room. There on the plot, plain to see, was Dönitz's giant convoy trap. Prentice instantly saw the danger. He also saw opportunity. With Murray's permission he took his group to sea to continue working up and also to act as a support group for SC 42 or the following SC 43, whichever became most threatened. This was good thinking, and support groups became a real winner later on when more forces were available.

With defects and other problems, Prentice's training group was down to his own *Chambly* and the corvette *Moose Jaw*, fresh from Halifax. *Moose Jaw*'s Captain, Lieutenant Freddie Grubb, was, most unusually for a corvette, a permanent force officer. He was somewhat withdrawn and RN–ishly inclined. His long cigarette holder and *Blackwood's Magazine* were rather out of place in a knock-about corvette. But Grubb knew his business, one of the few aboard who did. He reported later that most of his ship's company were laid out seasick for the better part of the operation.

It was lovely weather for U-boats – good visibility for spotting smoke and ships with strong winds from the eastward, where most of them were stationed. They could run downwind quickly and liked to attack that way: the same heavy sea that slowed the convoy helped the gathering pack into position and concealed them. A U-boat watch lashed in the conning tower to save being washed over by icy seas was no joke, and down below the crowding and the stench and the jarring of the seas and hammering of diesels were endlessly miserable, but they were superbly seaworthy, these U-boats. With no air cover to force them down they used their surface speed and were able to keep their batteries topped right up. They sent in their positions to Headquarters like clockwork. From their Admiral's disposition signals they could plot their friends' positions, see their whole trap closing in.

SC 42 plodded north at a miserable five knots. Greenland's mountains reared up to leeward, sheathed in ice. At night the northern lights leaped high and bright. The plot in *Skeena*'s charthouse, and the pack's transmissions chattering in his telegraphists' earphones, told Hibbard and his whole company they were in for real trouble. In the late afternoon of 9 September Hibbard flashed his request for a new convoy course to the Commodore, in the merchant ship at the head of the centre column. Near dusk the signal flags snapped at the Commodore's yardarm. They were repeated down every line.

As night fell SC 42 wheeled to starboard, northeast toward Iceland. Ships were darkened. The escorts roved the flanks to spot a tell-tale chink of light, then go in to berate the master through a megaphone. Over the side of each ship went the day's garbage. Ditching gash at random laid a trail like a paper chase. The watch below in the escorts drew their evening meal from the galleys, got it well doused with salt water on the way to the messdecks, clung to a bench or a stanchion, and shovelled down what they could. There was a stench here, too, of vomit and oil and unwashed bodies. The men didn't change their clothes. They didn't get out of them at all because, almost inevitably, that would be the time the action rattlers rang or the torpedo struck and there they would be, with their pants down. Pyjamas in the hammock? No fear. Just the seaboots off and lying ready to jump into. Up on the spray-lashed bridge there would be a mug of soup, corned beef sandwiches, and another mug of kye – that glutinous concoction fashioned of shavings from a hard block of pusser's cocoa, sugar, and condensed milk.

Soon after the moon rose, lighting the convoy from the south. The U-boats were off the leash now, and the night exploded. The first came from the dark side and torpedoed one ship. *Kenogami*, commanded by Lieutenant Commander R. "Cowboy" Jackson, RCNVR, was on the port wing. She spotted a surfaced U-boat but had no searchlight or starshell to illuminate. The 4-inch gun was ready, but RCN corvettes still had no outfit of flashless charges. The poorly drilled bridge crew was blinded by the flash and the enemy escaped. *Kenogami* swept with asdic but made no contact. *Skeena* joined her for a short sweep, then went ahead again, knowing there was plenty more to come.

The advantage was all with the enemy. They could pick their point of attack and see their targets. With their low profiles and no radar that could detect them, they could always spot the escorts first. They were faster on the surface than any but the one destroyer and were very hard to hit with gunfire. They had no need to attack in formation or worry about their consorts. Once the signal came they raced in independently, firing at will. If they got right into the grain of the convoy they were in prime position to strike and strike again. If forced down by an escort they were shrouded by the confusion of wakes. They could surface when the convoy had run over them and race up the flanks with their ten-knot margin for another attack, reloading torpedo tubes as they went.

Tracers lashed from the merchant ships. U-boats were right among them. *Skeena* raced down between the lanes. Lights flashed at the Commodore's masthead, and *Skeena* was caught as the ships turned. Great black shapes towered. Hibbard manoeuvred wildly to avoid being run down. He passed a surfaced U-boat on the opposite course so close his guns couldn't depress enough to fire. The merchant ships blazed away bravely with such ancient weapons as they had and sprayed tracers from machine guns. Two ships were torpedoed. Then, after two hours of deathly quiet, two more went down.

These nightmare battles in the northern dark were fraught with tenuous communications, garbled reports, no sensors but the naked eyes and ears, sudden cries of disaster and plaintive calls for help, the shock of depth charges and the sound and flash of gunfire, crisscrossing tracers, rockets flaring, starshell burning in the sky, and the underwater thumps and searing blaze that told of torpedoes striking home. No one had the whole picture.

Few had even a reasonably clear idea of what was going on. The SOE might, if he was well served with reports from all his consorts; if, standing on his spray-lashed bridge conning his own ship into an attack or avoiding collision with some looming merchant ship, he could develop enough of a picture in his head to devise intelligent plans. And if he could then speak reliably to the Commodore and to his group, who were spread over several pitch-black miles and seriously embattled themselves, he could then execute the proper action.

Depending on his knowledge, experience, and intelligence, an individual ship's Captain would more or less understand his own part in the overall action. Those around him – his plotting officer in the charthouse, his Yeoman of Signals beside him on the bridge – hopefully would as well. But otherwise the hundred or so men who steered, ran the engines, spun the asdic's handwheel, peered into the dark with binoculars, stood by their loaded weapons, tapped at a Morse key, or copied down code had only the sketchiest notion of what was going on.

Below in the magazines waiting to pass up high explosives, in the boiler rooms, at the switchboards, they could feel the ship responding to the sea and the helm. They could feel and hear that sinister thump of a torpedo in the convoy or the buckling clang of their own depth charges exploding. They could feel the engines race and slow down and – most ominous in a U-boat-infested sea – they could sometimes feel them stop. Mostly, though, they could only imagine what was out there. It was far better to concentrate on the job, listen for orders, and not let the mind run too wild or dwell on the others who were cindered already or struggling hopeless in that dreaded ice-cold sea.

No tugs or properly equipped rescue vessels ran with the convoys then. The last merchant ship in each column was simply detailed as rescue ship. But they were more than reluctant to do the job on a night like this. After the first attacks *Orillia* dropped astern to pick up survivors. Lieutenant Commander Ted Briggs, RCNR, was an experienced seaman. He stood by the damaged tanker *Tahchee* and when it was fairly certain she would stay afloat he got a line aboard, took her in tow, and set course for Iceland.

But *Orillia*'s brave, instinctively humanitarian action and fine seamanship had no place in the hard business of defending the rest of a convoy from U-boat attack. Hibbard, who didn't know for many hours, lost one of his precious corvettes for the rest of the battle. The other corvettes stopped for survivors, too, and were still astern when another U-boat got inside and another ship was hit.

Seven ships had been torpedoed when the cold dawn broke. Another ship went down in daylight. *Skeena*, ranging across the convoy's six-mile front, spotted a periscope, teamed with *Kenogami*, and dropped a ten-charge pattern on a solid submarine contact. There was a huge air bubble and a quantity of oil. Hibbard counted the U-boat sunk though in fact it wasn't. A single Catalina appeared briefly from Iceland during the afternoon and dropped flares to port of the convoy, indicating a U-boat. The pack was getting in position on the dark northern side for more night killing. In early evening they moved in. "U-boats on the surface," reported the convoy. Two more ships were sunk. *Skeena* pumped starshell out, illuminating an arc. The flares lit up nothing but they were spotted by Chummy Prentice's group, which was about to join the battle.

Prentice had made the right move with his little two-corvette support group, taking them ahead and to the dark side of the convoy where the pack would gather. His reward was a solid asdic contact and it was classified quickly by his asdic team as a positive submarine. *Chambly* was a well-trained ship and Prentice was a quick-thinking, experienced man. He ran in for a fast attack, planted a five-charge pattern. As he pulled away *U-501* bobbed to the surface.

Moose Jaw was close by. Freddie Grubb ran in to ram and glanced along the side of the damaged boat. As his stem ground past the U-boat's conning tower her Captain, quite extraordinarily, stepped dryshod onto *Moose Jaw*'s forecastle. Grubb pulled back, not ready with his weakened crew, as he said later, to stand off boarders! He rammed the U-boat once and raked her with machine-gun fire. Then Prentice took *Chambly* alongside. His boarding party under Lieutenant Ted Simmons, RCNVR, leaped aboard – no mean feat in the dark with a heavy sea running. Everyone knew that code books and cypher machines were the prize. But the U-boat crew had already opened the sea-cocks and *U-501* plunged to the bottom with eleven of her own and one Canadian sailor aboard.

It was a triumph for any ship to sink a U-boat and for rookies it was tremendous. This, as far as anyone knew at the time, was the RCN's first kill of the war and it was dead right that it should go to Prentice. As it turned out *U-501*, like *Moose Jaw*, was on her first patrol. An experienced U-boat skipper would never have submerged on spotting a corvette at night. He'd have tiptoed away and if sighted would have outraced her on the surface. Too, he was quite out of character for a U-boat man. He was a coward. His insistence that he climbed aboard *Moose Jaw* to surrender and save his crew didn't wash with the survivors. They would have no part of him. But triumph it still was, though the celebration was brief. The two newcomers were quickly added to Hibbard's screen. It now totalled five with *Orillia* off on her long tow, but within a few hours five more ships were lost from SC 42.

While veterans Hibbard and Prentice stayed up with the convoy, investigating contacts and trying to fend off attacks, the other three dropped astern to rescue survivors. Hibbard actually thought they were maintaining their screening stations, which speaks volumes on communications problems and on the lack of experience of the junior captains. The terrible irony was that their absence from the screen on rescue work was responsible for the loss of the last three ships that night.

The decimated convoy with sixteen ships gone – one-quarter of those that sailed – was met the next forenoon by RN reinforcements of five destroyers, two corvettes, and two sloops. And now the Iceland air support was overhead. Group Markgraf pulled away triumphant. The battle was over. Fourteen U-boats on one slow convoy, which had no air cover and mostly only three and at best five escorts, had overwhelmed it. An utterly exhausted Hibbard led his escort group into Hvalfjord for fuel. Secured alongside the tanker, he ordered "Finished with engines." His Engineer Officer called up to the bridge, "Finished with fuel." He had used the last drop.

Even after sixty hours of constant action without sleep, Hibbard called his key people into his cabin and spent the night putting together the narrative of the battle. This was not to make excuses for defeat; there were vital lessons to be learned. Then at 4 a.m. he led his group back out to sea to slog it out again if they must, taking a westbound convoy back to Newfoundland.

It was certainly a defeat, in fact, an overwhelming defeat, eased only by *Chambly* and *Moose Jaw*'s kill. But Jimmy Hibbard with his inadequate little force had done everything he possibly could. He had really fought a magnificent battle against overwhelming odds. Captain (D) wrote to Commodore Murray, "This is an appalling tale of disaster, but I feel that it is impossible to criticize any single action of the Senior Officer, Lieutenant Commander J.C. Hibbard, RCN; on the contrary I consider that he handled what must have appeared to be a hopeless situation with energy and initiative throughout, probably thereby averting worse disaster." The considered verdict of the historians, backed by neatly tabulated information, stands the same today.

Orillia, with the tanker tied to her like a drowning man, got her safely in. But Captain Stevens underlined Ted Briggs's "fine and successful feat of seamanship" as an "error of judgement," observing that it "deprived the surviving ships of the convoy of 25 per cent of their meagre escort." Perhaps Hibbard should have ordered him back. But not one man in the tanker *Tahchee* would forget the consummate seaman's skill and the dogged bravery of HMCS *Orillia* and the men whose lives were on the line with theirs. Whether he steeled himself to steam right by or succumbed to the wrenching dilemma, risking his own ship and others to stop to rescue fellow seamen, any Captain had endless lonely agonizing to face.

Every surviving ship's Master of convoy SC 42 signed a letter thanking Hibbard and his group for the battle fought on their behalf, and they made their appreciation known to Admiral Noble, the Commander-in-Chief, Western Approaches. Forty-eight years later the long-retired Rear Admiral Hibbard still treasures the letter and, even more, his men's reaction. When he received it a long time after the battle he cleared lower deck and read it to his whole ship's company. Then, among themselves they decided that the money they had saved in the canteen fund for their Christmas dance would go instead to decorating the ground-floor rooms of the Allied Merchant Seamen's Club in Halifax. That, to Jimmy Hibbard, far outweighed what any Admiral might have said about his battle. He was that kind of man.

The ten-ship escort that took SC 42 on the last leg to Britain was even reinforced for a time by three USN destroyers. It had air cover all the way. One U-boat was sighted by an aircraft fifteen miles ahead of the convoy and sunk by two of the destroyers. The U-boats couldn't press to get in, and only a single straggler was sunk. The lessons were simple and abundantly clear.

First: air cover. That meant much longer-range aircraft – the first of the Liberators, which had a radius of 800 miles, had just become operational in the U.K., carrying the brand new air-dropped depth charge – or escort aircraft carriers. The first of them, HMS *Audacity*, had fought a courageous action off Spain. She was converted from the fast German merchant ship that *Assiniboine* towed in to Jamaica in 1940. She sailed with a Gibraltar convoy on her first operation in September, carrying Martlet fighters to fend off the Kondor reconnaissance-bombers. The SOE had a big U-boat pack to deal with and he used the Martlets for visual sweeps. Without any anti-submarine weapons of their own, they kept the U-boats down and homed the escorts. *Audacity* herself went down but only one merchant ship was sunk and the escort killed four U-boats, and that was a victory. But the Black Pit had a long time to wait for air cover.

The second lesson: stronger escorts. Admiralty immediately asked the RCN to boost the size of each escort group to two destroyers and four corvettes, which was easier said than done. Corvettes were coming along in numbers if not quality, but there were no more destroyers and some of the old four-stackers were quite unfit for mid-ocean passage. The answer was to reduce the number of groups so that each one was a bit bigger. The ships just had to work harder.

But the convoys were being pushed further north for Iceland's air cover and fuel, which meant fouler weather, longer passages, more time at sea with each convoy. The cycle was inexorable but the ships must get through. Each NEF group was supposed to have twelve days in each cycle free for boiler cleaning, maintenance, cleaning ship, training, and some rest. But they didn't get it. Typically, *Chambly* spent twenty-six of each thirty days at sea in the last three months of the year. All of this took a terrible toll on ships and machines. And, finally, on men.

Captain Stevens warned Commodore Murray in mid-October that "a grave danger exists of breakdowns in health, morale and discipline." The same month Captain M.L. Deyo, a U.S. Navy destroyer squadron commander, warned Rear Admiral Bristol, USN, at Argentia that with their over-demanding cycle the RCN's Newfoundland force was on the verge of breaking down. The British acknowledged that the Canadians on their side of the ocean were working twice as hard as the RN in the Western Approaches. The USN deemed that one-third of an escort force should always be standing down. To the Canadians that simply could not apply . . . and there was a harsh winter to come.

No manning pool existed in St. John's. If a man went sick a ship did without and someone doubled up. Ships going to Halifax for maintenance were being robbed by Jones's Manning Commander to commission new corvettes. *Orillia*, with her hard-won skills, was stripped. Ted Briggs, her Captain, was her only qualified watchkeeping officer. Yet in October she slogged out twenty-eight days at sea. As Commodore Murray wrote in cold fury to Commodore Jones, "We are asking a lot of the morale of an inexperienced crew to expect them to be happy and remain in fighting trim and aggressive, in a ship in which they know their safety from marine accident, and not from any action of the enemy, depends upon the ability of their Captain to remain awake." How rock-bottom could a navy be!

In a one-night battle around SC 44 in mid-September the last of Group Markgraf sank four merchant ships and ripped the bow off HMCS *Levis*. *Mayflower* took her in tow but she sank with eighteen men. *Mayflower's* Nova Scotian captain, Lieutenant Commander George Stephen, RCNR, was an especially ebullient character who earned an Atlantic-wide reputation as a fine, intrepid seaman.

Going back out to that icy, raging sea in those wretchedly uncomfortable little ships for yet another thrashing, if not to be sunk, was becoming a horror. Commodore Murray, who tried defaulters for the more serious breaches of discipline, sent the guilty back to sea. He couldn't allow the blacklist to be the route to safety behind bars ashore. It was a real temptation for senior men to pad defect lists and get in for refit sooner, or worse, to create machinery problems. Some did. Everyone prayed for the chance to ram a U-boat. It was the honourable way to get a refit, some leave, a respite from the sea. Only bright lights of leadership – men like Stephen, Hibbard, Briggs – and Leonard Murray's rock-steady hand ashore staved off breakdown.

Sinkings went on and on in the wild months of autumn, 1941. A patched together Canadian/British/Free French group that hadn't worked together lost nine merchant ships from SC 48 and two RN escorts. Four U.S. Navy destroyers joined for support and USS *Kearney* was torpedoed. The only bonus in that debacle was that it brought the U.S. a long step toward the war. It couldn't happen soon enough. A huge new load had fallen on the RN. With the dark months beginning in October the Russian convoys began, and they had to have destroyers. So the Canadians on the North Atlantic had to carry an even bigger share.

THE U.S. NAVY IN THE BATTLE

The United States Navy had been involved in an undeclared war for nearly two years. First a U.S "neutrality patrol" warned belligerents away from fighting in Western Hemisphere waters. The Canada–U.S. agreement signed in August, 1940, at Ogdensburg, New York, by Mackenzie King and Franklin Roosevelt authorized the Permanent Joint Board on Defence. After the September, 1940, destroyers-for-bases deal, a major USN base and airfield were quickly built at Argentia, Newfoundland. In March, 1941, the Lend Lease Act was passed in Washington. Vital American cargoes had to be seen safely across the sea and the USN was inevitably involved. In May, two squadrons of destroyers were transferred from the Pacific along with three battleships and a carrier. In July, U.S. forces moved into Iceland escorted by their own ships and American destroyers began to work into the convoy system.

The Atlantic Charter signed by Churchill and Roosevelt in August, 1941, laid out the grand strategic plan for defeat of the Axis powers. The U.S. got strategic control and protection of shipping west of a line running between Iceland and Greenland and south through the Azores. With no reference to Canada at all, Jones's Atlantic Command and Murray's Newfoundland force came under strategic direction of the U.S. C–in–C Atlantic, Admiral Ernest J. King. Escort operations west of the Mid–Ocean Meeting Point became the responsibility of the USN's Support Force (later called Task Force 4, then 24).

USN destroyers began taking the fast convoys as far as Iceland in September. The RCN, with few destroyers and the slow corvettes, got the dirty end of the stick. Statistics showed what sailors knew all too well. Ships in slow convoys had a 30 per cent greater chance of being torpedoed. That month USS *Greer* and *U-652* exchanged depth charges and torpedoes. President Roosevelt ordered the USN to attack anything interfering with American shipping. American plans for actual war showed forty-eight destroyers allocated to the convoy routes. The RCN would give them eight destroyers and fifteen corvettes and provide local escorts. The rest of the Canadian ships would go to U.K. waters and the problem would be solved. Then, in October, came the *Kearney* torpedoing; the following day USS *Reuben James* was sunk with heavy loss. But the Americans weren't yet in. The RN had just pulled nearly all its destroyers east of Iceland while in the same breath urging the RCN to beef up their escort groups with non-existent destroyers. The NEF was on the ropes.

When Dönitz spotted weakness he went for it. At the end of October he threw twenty U-boats into Murray's backyard. One of them spotted SC 52, routed fifty miles off Cape Race. It had a large hodgepodge escort of two RN destroyers and seven corvettes, five of them Canadian. But the U-boat dispositions in Admiralty's tracking room showed all the portents of another SC 42. They turned the convoy north and ordered it back to Canada through the Strait of Belle Isle. Air cover was ineffective. Four ships were sunk by torpedoes and two ran aground in fog in the strait. In the whole course of the war this was the only Atlantic convoy turned back by U-boats alone. It was a bitter concession of defeat.

As it was, Canada's navy – locked in combat with the enemy day and night, month in and month out as the other forces were not – was on the very edge of collapse. Stripping experienced men from the salt-stained corvettes continued. Jones was carrying out the deliberate policy of Headquarters. NSHQ told Murray in December that temporary inefficiency was acceptable to make long-term gains in experienced, trained personnel. No policy was laid down for working up. Ottawa staff decisions (or non-decisions) were paid out in lives, not only in Canadian warships but in the hundreds of merchant ships that depended so utterly on them every day.

The destroyers stayed more stable around their initial solid core of officers, chiefs, and petty officers. They hung on to their experienced hands. The destroyers were more complex. An SOE needed advanced equipment and the destroyers got it first. Radar was one example. It was the technical innovation that had by far the biggest impact on tactics during the war. Chronically, as with all new equipment, Canada's navy lagged behind the RN, and the corvettes were astern of the destroyers. By the end of 1941 all RCN destroyers had a somewhat improved British type 286 radar, which still would rarely detect a submarine, and a quarter of the corvettes had a new Canadian set called SWIC or "Swick," which in most respects was a full generation behind the latest British radar, the type 271.

It was a sad tale. Canada's National Research Council had sent representatives to a British demonstration of radar, first devised to detect attacking aircraft, in March, 1939. Because the RCN had no kind of scientific liaison no one at NSHQ was more than dimly aware of radar until the destroyers were fitted in the U.K. in late 1940. Only then was NRC made responsible for naval research, development, and scientific liaison. RN policy was to fit all corvettes with radar, but in early 1941 they could barely meet their own needs, and Canada was on its own. A crash program got a prototype Swick to sea for testing in Prentice's *Chambly* in May, 1941. It was based on the same technology as type 286 but was such a leap ahead of no radar at all that it was rushed into production development. At the very same time as the *Chambly* tests, the RN was testing its new centimetric 271, which was a fine submarine detector. By year's end Canada was producing Swick and that is what the ships got.

Windflower, one of the first ten "Flowers" intended for the RN, had no radar at all when, on 7 December, 1941, she was run under in thick fog by a merchant ship. Icy sea water poured in, the boiler blew up, and the little ship sank with twenty-three men. That was the day Murray at last had enough ships to form one additional escort group so that everyone could rotate through a training period. But that same day the Japanese struck Pearl Harbor. The United States was in the war. In the long run it was the combination of

Allies that brought success. In the short haul the U.S. Navy was fighting for its life in the Pacific, and the American destroyers were pulled from escort service in the Atlantic. An even greater load fell on the fledgling Canadian escort force.

The fortunes and the tides of war aided the Allies in late 1941. In November Hitler, dead against Dönitz's advice, had had every U-boat pulled from the Atlantic to counter British moves in the Mediterranean. The sinkings stopped. The little ships had just the winter seas and bitter gales to fight. Murray's Newfoundland Escort Force held, remarkably, tenaciously together. Admiralty, until January, 1942, still had that priceless window into Dönitz's operations room via the broken Hydra code. Take away one of these twists of fate and defeat on the Atlantic could well have been total by the end of 1941.

THE BATTLE MOVES WEST

The U.S. Secretary of the Navy actually ordered Jones's and Murray's commands to go to war with Japan on the 7th of December. It was some days before Canada's cabinet made the decision. But things worked out in practice. Murray and the senior USN officers got along well, with tact and mutual professional respect. The USN was more than welcome aboard. They provided on request, up front, and with no red tape, just as they had in 1918.

But soon Commander Task Force 24 (Rear Admiral Arthur Bristol, then Vice Admiral R.M. Brainard after April, 1942) had only token escort forces. Just two groups of Coast Guard Treasury-class ships stayed on. They were about equal to the corvettes. There were a few destroyers, too, but Americans were very thin on the North Atlantic until May, 1943. They did give air support, though. Right away, U.S. Army B-17s flew from Gander and three squadrons of Catalinas from Argentia joined the patrols. They divided the ocean pie equitably with the still slender RCAF.

The USN got help in return. Its trade control and submarine intelligence networks were weak, so Eric Brand in NSHQ gave them a working link with the whole British worldwide organization. Ottawa in fact ran the submarine tracking and all the western Atlantic convoy routing for the first six months the U.S. was in the war – a fact yet to be acknowledged by British and American historians.

In the new year a new battle blazed. Admiral Dönitz pulled his boats from the Mediterranean, cut his force in the North Atlantic, and swung a scythe down the eastern seaboard of the U.S. He called it Paukenschlag, Operation Drumroll. There was no neutrality question now. There were no convoys south of Halifax either. Why do battle against escorts on the northern route when you could have a field day picking off independents? It was the old story and Dönitz was well rewarded. In the first month, from Newfoundland to

Cape Hatteras, fifty ships were sunk and not one of the thirteen U-boats on patrol was even touched. The carnage went on and on. Ships blazed like torches; men died in clear sight of the American shore.

Despite all the hideous lessons of the Great War and two and a half hard-fought years while the United States maintained neutrality during World War Two, the U.S. Navy was incredibly unready. Organization, forces, control of shipping – even of such basic things as regulating coastal radio traffic, navigation aids, and shore lighting – just weren't there. Three months went by with Miami providing a back-lit shooting gallery before the lights were doused. It was the tourist season, after all. Admiral King had the mindset of another Jellicoe and would not order convoy.

To the U-boat men this new killing orgy was their "Second Happy Time." All winter the small U-boat group in mid-ocean kept the pressure on. The 1941 year-end code change had blacked out communications intelligence. With only HF/DF for fixing U-boats, evasive routing didn't work nearly as well. In mid-February the convoy route was pulled straight to follow the shorter great circle well south of Iceland. At the same time the numbering system for groups changed to A, B, and C for American, British, Canadian. In practice, there were few American ships and a lot of mixing between the groups.

The mid-ocean groups of the Newfoundland force now picked up their convoys at Western Ocean Meeting Place, WESTOMP, east of Newfoundland. They went right across, turned over to the U.K. escort in sight of Ireland, and headed into Londonderry. It became the eastern terminal for all mid-ocean escorts and it was a wondrous change from Iceland. There were first-rate British and American dockyard and repair facilities there. More, there was the soft green of the countryside and warmth and welcome of the kind old town.

The storied "Newfy-Derry run" started with SC 47 and six Canadian corvettes. *Spikenard* was SOE. They steamed unscathed through fog and heavy weather until the night of 10 February. Then a tanker went up in flames and *Spikenard* was torpedoed. The other escorts, caught up chasing contacts, didn't know the corvette had gone until there was no answer from repeated calls by radio. A sweep astern in the morning found eight of her company, clinging half-frozen to a single carley float. The *Spikenard* memorial is a six-inch spike sunk in the ceiling of the Seagoing Officers Club, The Crowsnest, in St. John's. Her Captain, H.F. Shadforth, hammered it in there over a few drinks before he sailed. He signed it " 'Spikenard' his Spike." It is there today.

Along the American coast Operation Drumroll boomed. It was not a wolf-pack operation. There was no vast ocean area to "rake" for convoys, nor were there escorts to be swamped by pack attack. The traffic was plain to see, a stream of independents right along the coast. Cape Cod was a killing ground as it was in 1812 for the Nova Scotian privateers and in the Great War for the U-boats. As one area dried up they hit another.

To the Canadians and British it was unthinkable not to convoy, even with few escorts. But Admiral King was slow to take up Admiral Pound's offer in early February of twenty-four British anti-submarine trawlers. King had over 160 patrol aircraft and the whole route was close inshore, so ships gathered in convoy could have had full-time air cover. But as in the Great War, ships and planes were wasted in futile searching and patrol. The merchant ships kept going down.

Captain Brand went to New York in February to talk convoys with the Commander, Eastern Sea Frontiers. The first Boston-Halifax convoy sailed in mid-March. Its escort was Canadian. Losses on that leg stopped. The RN trawlers were in action by April and a patchwork coastal convoy system from Florida north started late that month. Ships sailed with escorts by day, sheltered in anchorages by night. They called it the Bucket Brigade. Sinkings slowed.

This left the Caribbean naked. Dönitz sent out "milch cow" submarines in May with fuel and torpedoes. The attack boats ranged right across the Gulf of Mexico and slaughtered tankers as far as Panama – 121 ships were lost in June, and nearly 500 were gone already in six months of paralysis in the American command.

And most of the ships going down now were tankers. It wasn't just cargoes going up in sheets of flame, but entire crews were being lost. And the tankers themselves were so terribly short. Canada's war-geared industry had to have Caribbean oil, so the navy pulled eight precious corvettes from mid-ocean and started Trinidad-Halifax tanker convoys in mid-May. Six more corvettes went later. The Canadian convoys came through without a single loss. Britain faced disaster without oil. They did the same, convoying their tankers from Aruba to the U.K. clear of the carnage on the American coast.

Now Canada had a whole new battleground. The Western Local Escort Force (WLEF) formed in Halifax in March under G.C. Jones. WESTOMP was now 700 miles from Halifax, so with the Boston leg Jones had a full third of the North Atlantic route. Murray had to send him sixteen corvettes. The RN sent twelve old short-range destroyers. Coastal traffic was under attack, too, even fishing vessels. More ships – properly equipped, well-trained, and worked-up ships – were needed. Things were stretched even more in September when New York replaced Halifax as the main western convoy terminus.

By mid-summer the USN finally had an interlocking convoy system. The special Canadian tanker convoys got absorbed in it and so did the corvettes. In the first three months of the convoys 1,400 ships sailed through the Caribbean and up the east coast; only eleven were lost.

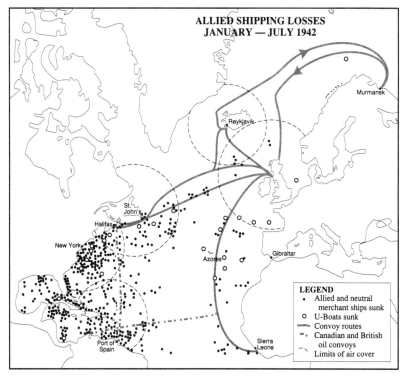

January – July, 1942. With the U.S. in the war and no convoy organization the U-boats moved west to slaughter 2½ million tons of unescorted shipping in independent attacks for very light losses. Hundreds of valuable tankers were sunk and Canada and Britain organized their own direct oil convoys.

Oakville was one of the corvettes. She started on the Triangle Run in March: Halifax, Boston, out to WESTOMP, and back to Halifax. In April she turned around in New York. Boston and New York were paradise to Canadian sailors. It was not just the cities, wonderful places for a run ashore in any man's navy, but the stark comparison with the bleakness of little St. John's and the dinginess of Halifax with its gross overcrowding and shocking lack of decent shore accommodation, recreation, and entertainment.

Americans may have been slow off the mark with convoys, but ashore they looked after servicemen with almost aggressive hospitality. There were lavish facilities, superb organization, and true generosity – girls, meals, Broadway shows, drinks on the house, dancing at the famous Stage Door Canteen to the big bands – Glen Miller, Benny Goodman, Tommy Dorsey. Movie stars dished up hamburgers. And here Canadian sailors were more than welcome.

As the sinkings moved south, *Oakville* sailed with the tankers from the gale-wracked North Atlantic to heavenly blue skies, azure seas, blessed warmth, and dolphins leaping and scuds of flying fish. Awnings spread over the bridge for shade. Solar topees, white uniforms with shorts and sandals, became shipboard wear, with dress whites for that rare run ashore. And there were beaches, rum punches, palm trees, and more girls. It was hard to believe war could visit such a charmed corner of the sea.

In August *Oakville* took her second tanker convoy back to Aruba and joined an escort from Trinidad to Key West. By now, with convoys and air cover, Dönitz had shifted his main attack back to mid-Atlantic. But there was still danger beneath the innocently beautiful seas. Twenty-nine ships northbound through the Caribbean from Trinidad had the destroyer USS *Lea* with three Canadian corvettes and one Dutch. South of Haiti, *U-94* slipped into position on the surface after dark. She was spotted by a U.S. aircraft. It attacked, put the U-boat down, and dropped a flare. *Oakville*, quick on the draw, ran in and dropped a five-charge pattern.

The boat surfaced. The corvette bore in, raked her with 0.5-inch machine gun and 20mm fire to keep her guns silent, hit her once with the 4-inch gun, rammed her twice in glancing blows. Then she dropped depth charges right under the U-boat's bow. One eyewitness swears that some of *Oakville*'s stokers bombarded the Germans at a range of twenty feet with the only weapons they had at hand – the empty Coke bottles stowed behind the funnel on the upper deck.

Lieutenant Commander Clarence King, DSC, RCNR, had won his Distinguished Service Cross in the Great War for sinking a U-boat, and he was no man for half-measures. A third ramming rolled the enemy under. Then he ordered a boarding party away and ran the ship alongside. Two figures leaped across before the vessels drew apart. They were Sub-Lieutenant Hal Lawrence, RCNVR, and Petty Officer A.J. Powell, each armed with a .45 pistol. They shot two aggressive Germans in their tracks. Powell controlled the rest. Lawrence dived down the hatch to close the flooding valves. In the dark and smoke he couldn't find them, or the code books. The U-boat sank. Both Canadians were picked up with the remnants of the U-boat's crew. Lawrence had been in *Moose Jaw* when she rammed *U-501* in September, 1941, and he knew the drill. This time he won his DSC. King got the DSO and Petty Officer Powell the Distinguished Service Medal.

Ramming and boarding smacked of an earlier swashbuckling age, but no one could guarantee to hold a U-boat with asdic. The depth charge wasn't very accurate and U-boats were incredibly tough. Trimmed down on the surface they were hard to hit with guns and they could outrun a corvette. Ramming might be primitive and it always damaged the rammer. But it was a sure thing.

Every escort had months and years of frustrating, exhausting, unglamorous work under her keel. No one who had been sunk, seen ships ablaze, fished oil-soaked survivors from the sea, or worse, been forced to leave them to die, would ever give up a chance. Staff experts ashore reasoned that a damaged escort was out of the battle. But what Captain would pass up a chance to ram? It was ferociously satisfying: guns blazing running in; the bellow, "Stand by the ram!"; the shuddering jolt; the grinding; the screech of rending steel. And, medals aside, his men would never forgive him if he sheered off. To top it all there was, most surely, that blessed, blessed refit.

Oakville's bottom was ripped out. Her asdic was gone and the after boiler room flooded. She was out of the battle and three ships were torpedoed that night. But she got to the American base at Guantanamo, Cuba, for temporary repairs. Then she steamed on her one boiler with a convoy to New York to be put back in fighting shape. And a refit in New York in 1942 surpassed a Canadian sailor's most opulent dreams.

THE BATTLE OF THE ST. LAWRENCE

The Gulf of St. Lawrence for centuries has rung to the sounds of battle: the privateers, the raiding squadrons, huge invasion armadas. It was the gateway to the heartland. From Confederation, defence planners saw it as the place where raiders, if unopposed, could cut the country's life, its main artery of trade. It is a substantial stretch of water. Without icebreakers, and that was the case in the war, navigation was stopped from December through to May.

Gaspé, where Jacques Cartier first claimed Canada for France, was the natural naval base. The first Canadian troop convoy of the Great War formed in its huge anchorage. Sombre British plans for a successful German invasion in 1940 marked Gaspé as an anchorage for the Royal Navy in exile. Re-conquest would start from Canada. Plans for defence of Gaspé were drawn up.

There was no point running convoys in the Gulf until the threat was actually there, and ships ran independently in steady stream between Montreal, Quebec City, and Sydney. In 1941 the basic needs of an escort base were built at Gaspé. With Drumroll, full development of the Gaspé base moved quickly – seaward defences, fuel tanks, jetties, magazine, maintenance shops, marine railway, communications, hangar and apron for flying boats, barracks. The new base commissioned on 1 May 1942. Escorts were so short everywhere there'd be none unless and until the enemy actually moved in.

In under two weeks he did. On 10 May an aircraft sighted a U-boat thirty miles off the famous Percé Rock and dropped depth bombs. It was, in fact, *U-553*. Two days later in the dark of the early morning the same boat – the only one in the Gulf – torpedoed a 5,000-ton freighter eight miles off the Gaspé Peninsula. Within hours it hit another. All the Naval Officer in Charge (NOIC) had was the small examination vessel. There was nothing he could do but tend to the survivors.

But the attack was on. Headlines across Canada screamed that U-boats were in the Gulf. Suddenly the war at sea was right at home, in sight of shore.

Questions were raised in the House of Commons. By the 1st of June five Bangor minesweepers, three Fairmile motor launches, and an armed yacht had been scraped into the Gulf Escort Force. It grew through the summer by seven corvettes and three more MLs to make a September total of nineteen.

There were some aircraft. Three Catalinas moved to Gaspé from Sydney and a detachment was set up at Mont Joli; 113 (BR) Squadron of Hudsons flew out of Chatham, New Brunswick. Summerside, P.E.I., had some operational aircraft and Charlottetown had a flying training and air navigation school. School aircraft, unarmed and with student crews, were deliberately flown over threatened areas to thicken up the air cover, reminiscent of the "Scare-crow" patrols flown by inexperienced pilots in British coastal areas during the Great War. If nothing else, they made the U-boats dive and reduced their mobility. The U-boats carried no radar, right to the end. But by now they had a radar search receiver. The airborne ASV radar and the shipborne Swick were both poor submarine detectors, but the squawk they made on the U-boats' search receivers kept their captains on guard and diving for cover a lot more than they really needed.

They were an adventurous lot, these U-boat men. That first one in, *U-553*, had found slim pickings outside around Newfoundland and Cape Breton. All ships were in convoy there and they had good air cover. So he had nosed up the Gulf. After scoring two off Gaspé he prowled about looking for targets in the fog. He was a bit early for heavy shipping and he left for better hunting on 21 May. That same day convoys began. His radioed report of an unready, unorganized area showed promise, though, so in mid-June Dönitz sent *U-132* straight in. His orders were to go after ships above Gaspé and scout the Belle Isle exit.

Crossing the Bay of Biscay *U-132* tangled with an RN ship, was damaged, but pressed on. Her Captain had no problem navigating Canadian waters. Lights and radio beacons were operating as in peace and he had his copy of the regular Canadian sailing directions. On 6 July he spotted a Quebec-Sydney convoy in bright moonlight a few miles off Cape Chat. He attacked on the surface and sank three ships in an hour and a half. The Bangor minesweeper *Drummondville* drove her under and shook her badly with depth charges. This added to the earlier damage, but *Drummondville* got no solid asdic contact.

U-132 was not too badly hit. He did his reconnaissance, then went back above Gaspé and spotted a convoy off Cap de la Madeleine. In a daylight periscope attack he sank one and got clear without being attacked. Back at base after sixty-eight days at sea, *U-132* had covered 10,000 nautical miles, about one-tenth of it submerged. Her score was five ships sunk (total 21,350 tons) for her full complement of twelve torpedoes. The patrol was counted "a fine success."

Now Commander Barry German became NOIC. He had been in the first RCN cadet class in CGS *Canada* in 1910. He had lost an arm in 1914 at the gunnery school in England but served through the Great War at sea and ashore. He was retired as medically unfit in 1919, but came back in the navy as soon as war began. The apocryphal tale that spread around Gaspé about his arm – "a moose got him" – seems typically Canadian and curiously un-nautical.

Dönitz was now shifting his weight north from the Caribbean and two well-commanded U-boats were already on the way from France. No sooner were they in the Strait of Belle Isle early on 27th August than *U-517* sank an American trooper bound for Greenland. *U-165* hit two more in a small convoy right behind. The escorts were U.S. Coast Guard cutters, which, according to the USN, were ill-fitted and ill-trained for the job.

Kapitanleutnant Paul Hartwig of *U-517* was an audacious and skilful U-boat commander and an inspiring leader. He was one of the best of the professionals from Karl Dönitz's school, a tough customer for the raw beginners in the Gulf Escort Force. Looking for something to torpedo, he crept right into Forteau Bay on the Labrador shore after dark and got within twenty metres of the jetty. He was chased out by what he took as a fast patrol craft, dived for the bottom, and heard asdic transmissions scratching at his hull. No depth charges were dropped, though Hartwig claimed that "the Canadian could not have failed to recognize that he was holding a U-boat at bay."

The next day he picked up a small convoy making for Goose Bay, Labrador. He didn't know it, but coming in the strait at the same time was a single ship escorted by the corvette *Weyburn*. Past midnight, as Hartwig fired on his first target, *Weyburn* appeared from nowhere. It was as much a jolt to Lieutenant Tom Golby on *Weyburn*'s bridge as it was to Hartwig.

Golby spotted the U-boat himself and went full ahead to ram. At the same time a ship in the convoy went up in flames. Hartwig went full ahead himself. The U-boat boiled along awash, her conning tower in plain view from *Weyburn* and very close ahead. One of the gun's crew said, "You could have hit her with a deck-scrubber." But they missed with their 4-inch.

Hartwig turned and dived. Golby ran right through the swirl and got away a couple of depth charges. *Weyburn* circled, but Leading Seaman Holloway at the asdic got no contact. Down below Hartwig braced for the attack. He was more than a little surprised when the corvette gave up the search. *Weyburn* had been SOE off Cap de la Madeleine when *U-132* got away with the daylight sinking.

Air sweeps from the following morning on were frequent. RCAF planes got in several attacks as *U-517* worked westward. Then a diversion came outside the Gulf. *U-513* crept silently into the Wabana iron mine anchorage at Bell Island, Newfoundland. Amazingly for such a loading port, there were no net defences, and the shore batteries didn't spot the surfaced submarine. At dawn she submerged and coolly torpedoed two deep-laden ships. In three minutes they plunged to the bottom with heavy loss of life and the U-boat slipped out unscathed. So close to the major base at St. John's, this brought more public furore.

Five days after Hartwig's brush with *Weyburn* his friend in *U-165* spotted a convoy off Father Point, the long-time river pilot station not far from Rimouski. There were eight ships with five escorts. Two were Fairmile MLs, one the little armed yacht *Raccoon*. *U-165* moved in before dawn and sank one ship five miles off Cape Chat. Some three hours later *Raccoon*, which had been screening on the convoy's offshore quarter, literally disappeared. She wasn't missed for some time, but *U-165* had torpedoed her and not a soul survived. Much later a life-ring and one decomposed body made up the only evidence of the death of one poor little vessel quite unsuited to this ferocious war.

Some ships by this time had broken ranks. With one reinforcement there were five escorts plus close aircraft cover for four in the convoy. Hartwig talked by wireless to Hoffman in *U-165* and waited in rain and mist. In late afternoon, eighteen miles off Cape Gaspé, he was in nice position for a periscope attack. The convoy moved toward him, right on track. One of the escort approached within 200 yards. It turned away without detecting him as he fired a salvo of four torpedoes. He got three ships. Half the convoy and one of the escorts were gone.

A Hudson from Chatham spotted *U-517*, photographed and machine-gunned her, then dropped a pattern after the boat submerged. Oil came up and the RCAF assessment was "probably sunk." In fact, there was no damage. Radio Berlin poured scorn on Canada's efforts that day:

> . . . the Canadian navy, which is nine-tenths composed of requisitioned fishing boats, coastal ships, and luxury yachts, is obliged to create an escort system with these third-class ships. This service comprises a third of the threatened maritime route between Canada and the British Isles.

There is a lot of waiting and watching in war. On these fine nights Hartwig would lie on the surface with the hatches open to the clean autumn air. It cleared the chronic U-boat stench a bit and gave his men a stretch of their legs on deck. Often they were close enough to shore to hear cowbells and smell woodsmoke from farmhouse stoves. Like the sailors in the corvettes, they would talk of home.

Four days later the corvette *Charlottetown* and Bangor-class *Clayoquot* were running on their own, a mile apart, not zigzagging. *Charlottetown* was struck aft by two torpedoes. She sank in four minutes. All but three got clear of the ship, but in the water many were killed or horribly ruptured by the ship's own depth charges. People ashore had seen a U-boat on the surface a very short time before. The marksman was Hartwig in *U-517*.

Next the U-boats spotted a convoy of twenty-one ships. The six escorts included the RN destroyer *Salisbury*, sent urgently from the WLEF. In periscope attacks the U-boats sank three, damaged two, and got clean away. Handled boldly as they were, these two seemed to have charmed lives. Often the escorts came within a few hundred yards but they weren't detected; counter-attacks thrown at them went wide; escorts couldn't hold contact; hunts weren't pursued. *Salisbury* believed the enemy must know about the atrocious asdic conditions west of Gaspé Passage because so many daylight sinkings occurred there with the U-boats just slipping away.

In fact, the water conditions right through the Gulf were very odd. Fresh water coming downriver caused tongues and layers of changing salt content and varied temperature. The asdic beam got severely bent trying to get from layer to layer, and consequently asdic most often got very poor results. The same state of affairs also cut the range of a U-boat's hydrophone and made it hard to keep the boat stable at steady depth.

The Bangor *Georgian* spotted a conning tower at 1,000 yards, made to ram, attacked the swirl, and continued deliberate attacks for two hours. As *Georgian* saw it the U-boat surfaced, then rolled on her side and sank. She was given a "probable" by Halifax. But Hartwig had slipped away again.

In late September the Hudsons were getting very close – 113 was the first RCAF squadron to use the new RAF Coastal Command tactics, flying higher than before, around 5,000 feet, and attacking in a steep dive. One attacker bracketed *U-165* with four charges; another scored very close aboard *U-517* on three separate strikes. Hartwig lay doggo. When he surfaced that night there was a depth bomb, firmly lodged in the submarine's foredeck.

Live or a dud? Hartwig went along himself to look, but there was no way to tell. He and his engineer worked carefully at it with crowbars. Slowly they pried it loose. Then he ordered full ahead and they flipped it over the side. Down it went and exploded impressively at its set depth. If it hadn't hit him in the first place it would likely have exploded right below him. Then his amazing luck had kept him from going below that depth when he dived to escape. A charmed life indeed!

Before he made for home, victorious and out of torpedoes, Hartwig reported a distinct change in the traffic. Very few ships were to be seen. In fact, on the 9th of September the Canadian war cabinet had made a momentous decision. They had closed the St. Lawrence to transatlantic traffic. Shipping in the Gulf was winding down. They made the decision after the fourteenth of the summer's twenty-two Gulf sinkings. Outcries in the press, of course, and questions in the Commons had scored the ability of Canada's forces to protect home waters. And home shores. A torpedo had actually hit the beach, exploded, and blown the windows out of a church near Cape Chat. In fact, the loss rate was not very high. One only need recall the hundreds of ships sunk in sight of Britain over the last three years. And the American coast and Caribbean had just seen thirty, forty times the sinkings. Canadians were fighting a war. Could they not expect a knock or two? There were no Churchills in Canada to bluntly put that kind of view.

But British shipping authorities faced losses overall that were terrible. If the extra thousand miles to Montreal could be eliminated it would economize on tonnage. They asked Canada to consider passing everything through east coast ports year-round. And for Admiral Nelles there was another strong compulsion. The First Sea Lord in August had asked him for escorts for a huge and highly secret operation. It was Torch, the coming seaborne assault on North Africa.

Admiral Pound had not talked numbers. Seventeen corvettes was NSHQ's target and they scratched around to find them. Nelles recommended support for Torch to cabinet and closing the Gulf to release the escorts. It could never be said that seventeen corvettes would make a significant difference to the massive North African landings. Mackenzie King said so and he worried that Canada might not get them back for home defence.

Seventeen corvettes, on the other hand, could have given NOIC Gaspé the means to fight it out until the ice did the closing in December, for the Gulf never had nearly that many all summer. Seventeen corvettes would have eased the terrible strain from New York right through to Londonderry. They could have eased training and refit and rotation problems. Dönitz was back in mid-ocean and the sinkings there were bad. Murray and Jones didn't even know where those seventeen ships were going. And they knew there was a very ugly winter yet to come.

The naval decision was made ultimately by Nelles. There was the old ingrained aye-aye to the RN; there was the urge to be a major player in a new campaign with the senior Allies; there was the immature show of "can-do" without really counting the cost to the ships and the men who were at sea. The quick cabinet decision to close the Gulf to through traffic suited NSHQ's book. It was a weak decision and, in naval and political terms, a poor one.

It meant a massive extra load of freight by rail to Halifax and Saint John; even great expansion of rail terminus and port facilities couldn't handle it all, and huge amounts went south to U.S. ports. A lot of money was spent, money going out of Canada, money for port facilities counter to the interests of Quebec. And money was the total muscle to fight the war. These matters were raised in the House of Commons and the press. They left real political sores.

There were more attacks to come. Coastal shipping still had to move. Off Métis on 9 October U-69 slipped into a Labrador convoy to sink a steamship in a night attack. That was a mere 173 miles from Quebec. On her way home, the same U-boat spotted the Sydney–Port aux Basques ferry SS *Caribou* in the Cabot Strait. *U-69* put a torpedo into the ferry at point-blank range. The Bangor sweeper *Grandmère* was the lone escort. She had no radar. She saw the surfaced boat and ran in to ram. With 150 yards to go the U-boat crash dived. *Grandmère* dropped a pattern of six charges.

Underwater, the U-boat Captain heard only one explode. He also heard the wracking sound of his target breaking up as she sank. He released an asdic decoy and got under the survivors to foil the escort's attack. Two hundred and thirty-seven people were aboard the ferry, and over half were lost, including fourteen out of fifteen children. It was a tragic blow. Cape Breton and New-foundland families lost many of their kin, and the incident said something to Canadians about the sinking and the dying that were the implacable daily diet out at sea.

Wabana was still disgracefully vulnerable. *U-518* ran in on the surface in early November to sink two ore carriers and damage a third. That closed the port until anti-torpedo nets were installed – in April, 1943.

U-518 was actually on her way to drop a secret agent near New Carlisle on Chaleur Bay. The Captain took the boat so close to shore that his conning tower was lit by headlights passing on the highway. The agent, Werner von Janowski, was an ill-trained and poorly briefed bumbler. He lugged his suitcase with a heavy radio transmitter to the local hotel. The proprietor first caught his pervasive U-boat stench, then noted his Belgian cigarettes, and finally his outdated, outsized two-dollar bills. He was nabbed by the RCMP and "turned," and his codes and call sign and radio sent a stream of misinfor-mation to Germany. Another agent landed by a U-boat near Saint John had deserted, spent his money on high living, and finally turned himself in in 1944. These were high-risk operations for U-boats but hardly true to the image of the diabolically clever German spy.

Still, the U-boats had won the Battle of the St. Lawrence. Hartwig got his Knight's Grand Cross, a promotion, and a riotous leave; he was renowned as a prodigious drinker when ashore. Heading out on his next patrol he was caught on the surface and captured. He spent the rest of his war in prison camp, ironically in Canada. And down the road to come was a distinguished second naval career in the West German navy and key NATO posts as a Rear Admiral. He had learned his naval business in a hard, efficient school with remarkable esprit. Those few U-boat men had scored a signal strategic victory for Germany. The Gulf of St. Lawrence stayed closed to transatlantic traffic until the spring of 1944.

MID-OCEAN ESCORT, 1942

Drumroll jarred Halifax right into the front line. Forty-four ships went down off Newfoundland and Nova Scotia from January to March. Most were stragglers or independents. In the Atlantic winter those who got clear of their sinking ships had little chance. Too often when a lifeboat was found it held only ice-sheathed corpses.

Out on mid-ocean, the Newfy-Derry run, there were eleven escort groups: one was nominally American; six were comprised of British and Allied ships, such as Free French and Norwegian; four were Canadian. In fact, there was a lot of mixing between groups. Whoever was the senior officer in the navy list took charge as SOE. The aim was to have two or three destroyers and five or six corvettes per group. Thus, with ships out for refits, repairs, maintenance, and training, a convoy would get six escorts. With around eighteen convoys sailing every month the escorts were on a treadmill.

Rolling everything together in mid-year – Mid-Ocean, Western Local, and Gaspe escort forces and the oil convoys – the navy needed over 200 escorts. It had 188 warships on paper but only thirteen destroyers, seventy corvettes, and thirty-four Bangors. That was almost 100 short. Ship training, therefore, nearly disappeared. Maintenance time dropped to near-suicide. To make it worse there were still far fewer skilled and experienced Canadians at sea than in either the British or American navies. And the Brits and Yanks got their one-third layoff and had far stronger shore support.

As well, the equipment gap was showing. The improved high-frequency direction finder was at sea in the RN. At least one destroyer in each British escort group had one. It wasn't complicated. The U-boats talked a lot on high-frequency radio. With a huff-duff the escort could snap a bearing of a U-boat's transmissions and get a shrewd idea of near or far. Two HF/DF ships spread a few miles apart could get a good fix. In addition, without having to know their code, the ships could tell by some German procedure signals if the U-boat had sighted them or was in contact.

The only RCN ship to get HF/DF before late 1942 was *Restigouche*, and she only had it because her captain, Lieutenant Commander Debby Piers, scrounged a set quite illegally from the U.S. Navy base in Londonderry. Staff in Ottawa hadn't understood what HF/DF was about. The Director of Communications, Commander Sam Worth, said it wasn't properly proven and put it off. He should have listened to the men at sea. Piers's intelligent use of his HF/DF was to save a convoy from heavy loss in June. His Petty Officer Telegraphist "Snakey" Ellis intercepted U-boats sighting transmissions time and again. The escorts ran out on the bearings, drove them off, and damaged two for the loss of only one ship. Luckily, the rescue ships that now sailed with most convoys had a set.

As for radar, RN ships had type 271, which could detect surfaced submarines. The Canadians still suffered with type 286 or Swick, which rarely could, and those sets could be heard by the U-boats; the 271s could not. Britain said Canada must depend on North American supply, but the U.S.

couldn't provide and Canada was to take until 1944 to get a centimetric type like 271 produced and out at sea. In August the RN rationed Canada to ten sets per month and fitted the remaining old Flowers. The seventeen corvettes that went to Torch got 271, too, but that was no help on the Atlantic.

There was a new weapon in the RN called Hedgehog. It fired a pattern of explosive bombs ahead so the ship could strike at the submarine while still holding asdic contact. This was a great advance, and Hedgehog got its first kill in February, 1942, but the RCN was way behind the RN in getting it. As well, only ten RCN corvettes had the extended forecastles. Virtually all RN ships had them, plus gyro compasses, improved asdic, better bridge layout. The RCN was always at the rear of the queue, and thus the Canadian ships were the obsolete ones in the battle. Their officers and men knew it, and they saw ships and friends die because of it.

History remembers the convoys that met action, the sinking and the killing. But the percentage attacked was small. Safe and timely arrival was what counted. Each of the unsung convoys that got through by skilful evasion, good convoy discipline, dogged seamanship, endless, wet, frozen days, and plain sailors' luck was a victory in itself. Win or lose, each passage got rehashed from The Crowsnest in St. John's to the pubs in Derry.

In spite of all the problems, that summer of 1942 had a good share of Canadian success. *St. Croix* of the Second Canadian Escort Group, Lieutenant Commander A.H. Dobson in command, cracked *U-90* open in four solo attacks. Then the third Canadian group, under Commander D.C. Wallace in *Saguenay*, fought a tremendous battle for westbound ONS 115 with no air cover, no HF/DF, no efficient radar. Lieutenant Commander Kenneth Dyer in *Skeena* directed closely co-ordinated attacks with Lieutenant Commander Guy Windeyer's *Wetaskiwin* on *U-588* for five hours and finished her off. Later Lieutenant Alan Easton's *Sackville* flushed three U-boats on the surface in fog and dark, blew one half out of the water with depth charges, and hit the next point blank with 4-inch shells. Neither sank but both were out of the battle. ONS 115 was a victory. Only two merchant ships were lost.

Assiniboine, running through fog patches off Newfoundland in August, 1942, used radar to keep station on convoy SC 94. But Lieutenant Commander John Stubbs had no warning of the U-boat that popped suddenly out of the fog. It turned away and Stubbs followed. A wildly weaving chase went on for an hour, in and out of fog banks, catching a glimpse now, then losing sight. The radar was no help – it was the old 286. At last Stubbs got close enough to rake the enemy with 20mm and half-inch machine guns. He got so close the big guns couldn't depress to get in a shot. There was plenty of fight in *U-210* and she riddled *Assiniboine*'s bridge with 20mm shells. One caught the upper-deck gasoline stowage and a fire burst out right beside the bridge. First Lieutenant Ralph Hennessy swung the firefighters into action. The

Coxswain, CPO Max Bernays, coolly kept full control in the wheelhouse as the fire raged. The U-boat could turn tighter than the destroyer, but Stubbs was a master shiphandler. Up on the bridge with the flames and smoke, he harried so closely the U-boat couldn't dive. Still ablaze, the destroyer finally rammed, pulled back, and rammed again. As *U-210* went to the bottom the joyful cry of "Refit! Refit!" rang through the ship. Her asdic was torn out. She turned back to St. John's with her prisoners, her wounds, and her wounded. In January, 1943, she was back in action. With *Assiniboine* gone from SC 94, the 271 radars in the two RN corvettes in C1 group were a big factor in countering the attacks. HMS *Dianthus* rammed another U-boat. Two killed for eleven merchant ships sunk was a respectable rate of exchange.

The slow convoys had the rough times, and during the summer of 1942 by pure chance the brunt of the action fell to the Canadian escort groups. They had the losses but also the kills. Including *Oakville*'s Caribbean victory, the RCN had sunk four U-boats in a month to *Dianthus*'s single for the RN. The Canadian escorts' tails were up. (They'd have been even higher had they known that *Morden* had sunk *U-756* with three smartly delivered depth-charge attacks in early December while defending SC 97. It took till 1987, but that singlehanded kill was definitely credited to the Canadian corvette.) But now, with the eastern seaboard and Caribbean under convoy, Dönitz's hammer fell back on the mid-Atlantic.

Thirteen U-boats lay across the path of ON 127 in the Black Pit in mid-September. *Ottawa* made a second destroyer with *St. Croix* in C4 (the fourth Canadian escort group), along with four corvettes. HMS *Celandine* again had the only 271 radar but it was out of commission at some of the worst times. No one had HF/DF.

One of *Ottawa*'s seamen came down with acute appendicitis. There could be no turning back, of course, so Surgeon Lieutenant George Hendry had to operate. The First Lieutenant, Tom Pullen, had a strong stomach and helped. In the heaving ship the job was neatly done. Then in the Black Pit came the U-boats. Day and night they sank seven ships and damaged four. *Ottawa* picked up survivors. One of them had a rivet blown deep into his gut and the doctor set up surgery again on the Captain's dining table. Pullen, with his experience, helped. It took four hours and things looked good. But on 13 September the poor man died. They buried him at sea at sunset with proper seaman's honours.

In a few hours *Ottawa* was ten miles ahead of the convoy to meet a relief destroyer from St. John's. Suddenly a torpedo tore her bow right off. Tommy Pullen went down to inspect the damage in what was left of the fore lower messdeck. "It was a scene of carnage and shambles. We were scrambling around there in the wreckage and you could see the sea straight ahead where the bow used to be and I had that awful feeling if there was one torpedo there could be another. When the second torpedo hit, the ship started to break up. Larry Rutherford and I were the last two on the bridge and we walked down the side of the ship and jumped in the sea. The extraordinary thing was to observe men simply giving up and letting go of the carley floats and drifting off into the night . . . they were uninjured . . . I think probably shock and not being mentally geared to a catastrophe. We lost a hundred and thirteen officers and men and about sixty-five survived. The survivors of the ship we had picked up a few days earlier, we lost most of them."

And they lost Doctor Hendry . . . and his appendicitis case . . . and Larry Rutherford, the Captain, who gave his lifebelt to a rating and his own life with it. *Ottawa* had run right into the U-boats gathering ahead to attack the convoy. If she'd had a huff-duff or a 271 radar it could have been a very different story.

Live or die. Win or lose. In every battle there were hard lessons, and reports had to be made – part of the paper war. These were assessed up the line with Admiralty printing final judgement in Monthly Anti-Submarine Reports. Not all the staff officers' vitriol reached the light of day, but more and more the finger was pointed at the RCN. RN staffs, too, were very critical of the staffs led by Rear Admiral Murray and Captain Rollo Mainguy, who was now Captain (D) Newfoundland. In fact, they had hardly any staff officers and were too harried putting out fires.

The strain was too great for some. A corvette Captain who took refuge in drink had to be forcibly pulled right after one convoy. He was not the only one. Admiral Brainard said bluntly that Canadian maintenance, "appreciably below the standards demanded of experienced regulars," cut the size of the fleet to a "dangerous and unacceptable figure." Always open-handed, he offered USN engineering officers for the Canadian corvettes. By custom, though, the engine room departments of corvettes were headed by CPOs and the offer was declined.

The criticisms – and their sources – might be hard to take. But the facts were there and the battle was now. Nearly forty U-boats were at sea – the highest total ever deployed. Most were on the North Atlantic and the new German Triton cypher still had not been cracked. Pushing the expansion snowball up the steep hill for so long, Murray could see it was about to roll right back. He warned Headquarters that heavy losses were in store for convoys escorted by the weak Canadian groups. He remembered Jimmy Hibbard's SC 42.

Scouting U-boats near Newfoundland spotted convoy SC 107 before it rounded Cape Race. They knew it was coming because the Germans had broken its routing signal. The main patrol line of seventeen boats – Group Veilchen, it was called – had been carefully placed further east, right across the convoy's track. C4 had Debby Piers in *Restigouche* as SOE with a hastily scraped-together group of four corvettes. An RCAF Digby sank one shadower but the air effort wasn't enough to shake them all off.

The U-boats' sighting reports cackled on Piers's HF/DF. *Stockport*, the rescue ship, had HF/DF, too. Piers's plot showed where the U-boats were. But his was the lone destroyer – he couldn't chase them all off. And now they were in the Black Pit with no aircraft for days. Just then HMS *Celandine*, C4's most useful corvette, lost her precious radar for four critical days.

That night the pack stormed in. Snowflake rockets from the merchant ships lit the sky. The escorts could only dash to each disaster, snap-shoot at quick glimpses of the enemy, and take brief swipes at asdic contacts. This was the pack attack par excellence. It swamped the escort. Three got through and sank eight ships. An ammunition ship went up with such a gigantic blast that sailors in engine rooms miles away thought they'd been torpedoed themselves.

At first light Piers had to regroup. *Stockport* was crammed with survivors. She was way astern and needed screening. Stragglers had to be rounded up and the convoy shoved back into shape. All that thinned the tiny screen and a daylight attacker sank one ship. A bonus came that night, though, when an RN destroyer joined from a nearby convoy, a fast one that was slipping by untouched.

The following morning *Amherst* chased a surfaced U-boat ahead of the convoy. Her new Captain was Lieutenant "Uncle Louis" Audette. (You got to be "Uncle" if you were over thirty; Piers was twenty-five.) Audette conned the ship and spotted his gunfire from the crowsnest. As he put his target down another stole past the screen and sank a ship. Later, two U-boats got in for another night of carnage, of sinking ships and brushes with the escorts.

Next night *Amherst* closed on a torpedoed ship and asdic reported a solid echo, classified submarine. Audette lined up to attack and turned toward, closing the range. A depth-charge pattern was ready, and then, right ahead, the sea was dotted with tiny lights – survivors, in the water and very close to the U-boat. There was no question about it, the devil was right below those blinking lights. Drop the charges and the men would die a ghastly death; sheer off and a U-boat would live to sink again. Forty lives against the embattled convoy. Only the Captain could decide.

The First Lieutenant: "Good God, sir, are you going to attack?"

Audette, his agonized decision made, answered "Yes."

The range closed and the asdic pings came shorter and faster, like a quickening heartbeat, nearing the moment to fire. Men's shouts came faintly through the dark, seeing rescue overcoming death. Then, the power to the asdic failed. Precision gone, Audette ordered "No attack." The wheel over, he skirted the survivors, heard their cries of anger and despair from the icy water as he drew away. The power came back but the U-boat was gone.

While the rescue vessel picked up the survivors, *Amherst* circled the blazing hulk of SS *Daleby*, which they'd abandoned. Three men still on board screamed for help and Audette broke his own and every standing order in the book to stop his ship with U-boats near and send a boat. When he asked for volunteers there was a rush to man it. Pitch dark and high seas; cold courage and fine seamanship – and all three men were rescued. The Coxswain, Petty Officer Taylor, won the British Empire Medal. Louis Audette had the most wrenching night of his life.

The next day strong reinforcements arrived: ships and very-long-range (VLR) Liberators that had begun to fly from Iceland, shrinking the air gap, closing up the Black Pit. They got *Restigouche*'s HF/DF bearings from her by radio, ran out, and forced the U-boats down. Dönitz preferred odds in his own favour and called off the pack.

The five-day battle bought him a stunning victory – fifteen ships out of forty-two. The Germans lost one U-boat, though the Canadians didn't know. *U-132*, Hartwig's fellow killer in the St. Lawrence, just disappeared. Likely he was too close when he torpedoed the ammunition ship that exploded with such gigantic force.

Piers had fought a tremendous battle against seventeen U-boats with a wretchedly inferior escort. C-in-C Western Approaches couldn't find much to criticize but his youth and inexperience. He was young, yes – twenty-five years old – but Piers was experienced for the North Atlantic. He'd been out there for three years.

The devastation to SC 107 was a hard blow at a time of rising threat. Operation Torch had a big bearing. The corvettes taken for Torch robbed the Mid-Ocean Escort Force. The main assault convoy for Torch was in fact crossing the Atlantic well to the south and quite unmolested at the very time the U-boats were ripping up SC 107. The campaign caused a massive deflection of shipping and the materials of war and necessities of life away from Britain. So every cargo on that North Atlantic route was even more critical to her survival. Africa had to be supplied, but on the grand strategic scale the North Atlantic was the key to Allied success or failure. It had to hold.

BITTER PILL

At Western Approaches Headquarters the tough new C-in-C was Admiral Max Horton. Like Karl Dönitz, he was a submariner. Escort groups couldn't be conjured from thin air. Horton focused on efficiency. He aimed to make each ship and each group better and put the first team into the most crucial, toughest areas. The British groups on the record were doing better. The Canadian groups had the majority of the vulnerable slow convoys, and the straight luck of the game had brought more of theirs under attack.

These survivors are among the lucky ones, comfortable enough in well-equipped lifeboats and spotted by a destroyer that was able to stop. Destroyers had medical officers; smaller ships did not. In the near boat the medical party lashes an injured man into a stretcher to be hoisted aboard. In some of the worst battles smaller escorts became so loaded with survivors they became dangerously unstable. (*Maritime Command Museum*)

Ice, formed by freezing spray in the worst cold of winter, coated everything on the upper deck. It was an endless chore with axes and steam hoses to keep guns, depth charges, and vital equipment clear. As well, if it was allowed to build up, the weight could affect the ship's stability to the point of actually turning turtle. (*Maritime Command Museum. Source: Parks Canada, Halifax*)

In Halifax dockyard, 1940. Left to right: Commodore H.E. Rastus Reid, Navy Minister Angus L. Macdonald, and Chief of Naval Staff Vice Admiral Percy Nelles. Reid was naval attaché in Washington, Vice Chief of Naval Staff, then Flag Officer Newfoundland in September, 1942. Nelles, CNS from 1934 to 1944, was pushed upstairs by Macdonald after the crisis of confidence in 1943. (*Imperial War Museum*)

U-94 leaves her French base. This U-boat, a Type VIIC, sank four ships in the spring of 1942, then was sunk that August by *Oakville* in the Caribbean. (*Department of National Defence. Source: Bibliothekfur Zeitgeschichte, Stuttgart*)

U-boat killers on board *Chambly* in August, 1942. Left to right: Rear Admiral
Leonard W. Murray; Vice Admiral Sir Humphrey Walwyn, RN, Governor of New-
foundland; Commander J.D. Prentice, DSO, who has just been decorated by Admiral
Walwyn for sinking *U-501* during the battle for convoy SC 42, and Mrs. Prentice.
Behind, the officer with the beard is Lieutenant Commander Guy Windyer, who
earlier had sunk *U-588* in *Wetaskiwin* along with *Skeena*. The tall officer is Captain
Rollo Mainguy, Captain (D) St. John's. He actually scored the RCN's first kill of the
war in *Ottawa* in 1940. (*National Archives of Canada*)

Fairmile motor launches in the Gulf of St. Lawrence. Eighty of these 112-foot, 20-
knot craft were built in Canada. Each carried a fixed-beam asdic, depth charges, and
3-pounder or 20mm guns. Supported by mother ships *Preserver* and *Provider*, they
escorted convoys in the Gulf and in the Caribbean and patrolled from Bermuda and
St. John's. They were no match for a U-boat but they did useful chores like harbour
approach patrols and coastal rescue that freed bigger escorts for ocean work.
(*National Archives of Canada*)

A Wren operates a high-frequency direction finder at HMCS *Coverdale* near Moncton, N.B. The shore-based, Atlantic-wide radio direction-finding net was a major player in the Battle. Bearings of U-boat transmissions, combined with "Ultra" communications intelligence (which was sporadically available), meant that convoys could be evasively routed, reinforced, or at least warned of U-boat dispositions. (*National Archives of Canada*)

Restigouche, picking up survivors from a sunken U-boat in 1943. For their escort role most of these River-class destroyers lost their after 4.7-inch gun and one set of quadruple torpedo tubes to reduce topweight as equipment was added and to make room for more depth charges. The first RCN ship to get HF/DF, *Restigouche* "scrounged" hers in Londonderry in 1941. It is in the box behind the aft funnel. (*Imperial War Museum*)

A VLR Liberator over an Atlantic convoy. This American bomber, converted for ASW and with added endurance, was the best aircraft available for the job (once enough of them were diverted from the bomber role). The convoy is four miles across. On the far side two little escorts can be seen. The nearest ship is committing the worst convoy daylight crime, belching smoke. (*National Archives of Canada*)

Corvette *Sackville* after her forecastle was extended in May, 1944, in Galveston, Texas. Her 271 radar antenna is in the plexiglass "tower" above the bridge; her new Hedgehog is hidden by the 4-inch gun mounting. *Sackville* fought many hard battles. After thirty years as a survey and acoustic research vessel she was faithfully restored in 1985 by old navy hands and can be visited in Halifax today in her 1944 fighting trim. (*National Archives of Canada*)

Tribal-class destroyers *Haida* and *Athabaskan*, seen from sister ship *Huron*, in the English Channel in the spring of 1944. They were designed for surface gun-fighting – short-ranged, 2,000 tons, 377 feet long, 36 knots with three twin 4.7-inch gun mounts plus a twin 4-inch for starshell and high-angle anti-aircraft fire, four torpedo tubes, and a crew of 260. *Haida*, saved from the wrecker by naval veterans in 1964, is preserved at Ontario Place in Toronto with the lighter armament she carried in the Korean War. (*National Archives of Canada*)

Swansea, one of the early frigates, commissioned at Yarrow's shipyard in Esquimalt in October, 1943, rides North Atlantic seas. British-designed, these were fine ships and twice the corvette – twin screws, 1,445 tons, and 301 feet long, with a crew of 140, Hedgehog, and a twin 4-inch gun (or in the early ones, one 4-inch and one twelve-pounder). Their range was double – 7,200 miles at 12 knots with 19 knots top speed. *Swansea* sank four U-boats – all in 1944 – and was the RCN champion. For three of them Commander Clarence King was her Captain. He had four personally (equalling Prentice), plus one in the Great War. *Swansea* was converted in 1957 as an ocean escort and served until 1966. (*National Archives of Canada*)

Prince Henry, seen here with some of her eight assault landing craft loaded with troops heading for the beach. *Prince Henry* and *Prince David* were converted from armed merchant cruisers to infantry landing ships and were in the first wave in the D-Day assault. (*National Archives of Canada*)

Chaudière alongside an oiler on 21 August 1944 after sinking *U-678* and *U-984* with *Ottawa* and *Kootenay* (*Kootenay* is on the right). She had already taken part in sinking *U-744*, so the painter is adding the second of three swastikas. In the euphoria of success no one cares that he has them backwards. All the RCN's escort destroyers were RN-built in the thirties for fleet work at around 1,400 tons, 330 feet long, and 31 knots. (*National Archives of Canada*)

Algonquin comes alongside *Nabob*, well down by the stern and struggling to stay afloat, to take off excess crew members. *Nabob* was torpedoed in August, 1944, during operations against the battleship *Tirpitz* but was saved by intrepid damage control and courageous flying. *Algonquin* and *Sioux* weren't Tribals. They were wartime-construction RN fleet V-class destroyers – 1,700 tons, 362 feet, 36 knots, with four 4.7-inch guns and eight torpedo tubes. (*Imperial War Museum*)

U-744 in her final throes, her conning tower riddled with shell-holes, boarded by Canadian sailors in March, 1944. *Chilliwack*'s boarding party, a few lengths ahead of *St. Catharines*', draped a White Ensign over the conning tower, held the crew at gunpoint to prevent scuttling, and recovered the U-boat's key cypher machines and code books. In the heavy seas the boats overturned and the important capture was lost. (*National Archives of Canada*)

But equipment, training, experience, group stability, maintenance standards all came into the naked light. The RN's jaded view of the Canadians as enthusiastic amateurs surfaced. "Temporary inefficiency" for long-term gain hadn't worked. Public scorn over the Gulf of St. Lawrence defeat still echoed. Just then *Saguenay* collided with a merchant ship. Her own depth charges blew her stern off and she retired from the war to be a training ship. But the catalytic disaster was SC 107. Something had to be done.

Vice Admiral Nelles appealed to old friends at Admiralty. The RN would help with equipment, but it would take time. Winston Churchill right at that point was deeply worried about a breakdown of merchant service morale. Everywhere their losses were terrible, and their rewards were nil. Inner collapse could finish what the U-boats had nearly achieved. The North Atlantic must have – and must be seen by the merchant mariners to have – the best escort force that could possibly be mustered. Mackenzie King received a message:

> A careful analysis of our transatlantic convoys has clearly shown that in those cases where heavy losses have occurred, lack of training of the escorts, both individually and as a team, has largely been responsible for these disasters.
>
> I appreciate the grand contribution of the Royal Canadian Navy to the Battle of the Atlantic, but the expansion of the RCN has created a training problem which must take time to resolve.
>
> Winston Churchill, 17th December 1942

The proposal was not to strengthen the Canadian groups with more well-equipped RN destroyers. It was to pull them right off the mid-ocean and put them on the easier U.K.-Gibraltar route under good air cover. This was deeply resented by Nelles and his staff. They said equipment was the difference. Commander Pelham Bliss, RN, agreed. He was the anti-submarine specialist who had worked so hard in Newfoundland since the early days of the NEF. But right on the heels of that came convoy ONS 154.

ONS 154 was the Christmas convoy of 1942. Lieutenant Commander Guy Windeyer in *St. Laurent* was new to the ship and to C1 group. Like Chummy Prentice, he was a retired RN officer living in Canada prior to the war. He was not inexperienced in escort work – in *Wetaskiwin* he had shared a U-boat with *Skeena* – but he was not a Prentice. There was a two-week layover in Ireland. All five corvettes got 271 radar and "Sally" got her long-awaited HF/DF. However, C1's second destroyer, HMS *Burwell*, was laid up with defects and there was no relief; pre-sailing exercises were aborted; the priceless new huff-duff was not calibrated prior to sailing; and for his own insufficient reasons, the SOE didn't call a pre-sailing conference of his captains.

They were routed south past the Azores since some ships had to detach from the convoy and head for the South Atlantic. Besides, the weather would be far better. It was much longer than the northern route but – something quite new – a tanker went along to fuel the escorts. The longer route also meant maximum time in the Black Pit. (Portugal didn't let the Allies use airfields in the Azores until October, 1943.) Another breakthrough had just been made in the U-boat code but new positions hadn't been plotted. Quite unwittingly, ONS 154 was routed just to the south of two U-boat groups containing twenty boats. One made contact and the pack closed in.

On the night of 26 December *U-356* raced through the convoy twice and hit four ships. *St. Laurent* caught him on the surface and put him down with a hail of 20mm and 4.7-inch fire, followed by a shallow blast of depth charges, then a deliberate ten-charge pattern. An eleventh explosion convinced Windeyer he had a kill, but there was no credit given until German records after the war showed *U-356* was lost that night.

The next day while *Chilliwack* was fuelling astern of the convoy the tanker was torpedoed. It survived but had to make for home, so the escorts had no filling station. HF/DF in the rescue vessel *Toward* and the fleet auxiliary HMS *Fidelity* provided ample bearings to chase but Windeyer didn't move out boldly to put them down. His own set, remember, wasn't calibrated. His was the only destroyer and he couldn't get more fuel.

St. Laurent's First Lieutenant, Fred Frewer, recounted the mounting horror: "We could see submarines on both flanks of the convoy, on the surface, just out of gun range, oh, six-seven miles away and perfectly visible, but haring at full speed on the surface, reloading torpedoes and charging their batteries and getting ready for the dusk attack again. This happened two days running and I remember very vividly how unprotected the convoy must have felt and we felt inadequate watching these bloody submarines. . . . It was a terrible nightmare that one."

Chilliwack that night had a fierce fight with a U-boat but with no score. *Fidelity* carried two seaplanes and lowered one to put down the lurking U-boats. It crashed on take-off. As "Sally" was fishing the pilot out, *Battleford* was fighting off four U-boats on the other flank. But Windeyer had failed to tell *Battleford* he was going to alter convoy course after dark. So the corvette was agonizingly out of the battle for the second night's mêlée. The long-coveted 271 radars were new and teething. *Battleford*'s went blank with the first 4-inch round she fired at her four attacking U-boats.

Five U-boats got through. In two chaotic hours nine ships went down. It was "a holocaust" to *Napanee*'s Captain, Lieutenant Stuart Henderson, RCNR. "All ships appeared to be firing snowflakes, and tracers crisscrossed in all directions, escorts firing starshells. The sea was dotted with lights from boats and rafts and two burning wrecks which had hauled out to starboard helped the illumination."

That night the battle was out of hand. Windeyer had quite clearly broken down. He was put under the doctor's care and Frewer took command. Next day the U-boats picked off the derelicts astern and sank *Fidelity*. She had dropped back with engine trouble and no escort. She lost over 300 men. Two RN destroyers joined for a while and chased off shadowers. The grim reckoning was fourteen sunk for one U-boat damaged, though in fact it was on the bottom.

Back in St. John's Windeyer was taken to hospital, not to return to sea. He had done well before and he killed two U-boats, which few other men can say. But the constant, grinding strain of command, physical pounding from the sea, days on end with hundreds of lives hanging on those snap decisions, the barest of sleep, and the dead hand of utter fatigue had all taken their toll. It took far more than an ordinary man to be an escort group commander – and a near superman to be a good one.

Shorebound and peacetime tacticians with their easy hindsight notwithstanding, leadership had failed. ONS 154 took the steam out of NSHQ's resistance. Nelles gave in. The Canadian groups would be yanked. They were pulled off their own North Atlantic battleground and watched from the bench while the great issue was decided in those wild months of winter and spring 1943. It was resolved in the main by reorganizing RN escort groups, with reinforcements from the battle fleet, to form "support groups." They could move to help the most threatened convoy. Also, air cover improved. A few RAF Liberators at last patrolled the Black Pit gap, and in March the first escort carrier, USS *Bogue*, was in action in mid-Atlantic.

It was a fact that 80 per cent of all ships torpedoed in transatlantic convoys in the last two months of 1942 were hit while being escorted by Canadian groups. They were the ones Max Horton's new broom reached first. It was also a fact pointed out in the January Monthly Anti-Submarine Report that "The Canadians have had to bear the brunt of the U-boat attack in the North Atlantic for the last six months, that is to say of about half the German U-boats operating at sea."

The RCN's time had yet to come.

COMBINED OPERATIONS

Good men step up when there's a chance of some special adventure. The call for navy volunteers for "specially hazardous duty" in late 1941 was oversubscribed. It was for Combined Operations. Since 1940, when Britain still feared invasion, small Commando units had been running vicious throat-slitting raids along the French coast. They were great for morale but were really only pinpricks. Sooner or later Britain and her Commonwealth allies would have to storm Europe, and that would mean amphibious assault on a huge scale.

Raids and landings had been the navy's business for centuries. Special training and first-rate co-ordination spelled success at Louisbourg and Quebec. The Gallipoli landings in the Great War were disastrous. Throwing men on a beach in the face of a determined, entrenched enemy with machine guns was suicidal. Now there was airpower and a whole new range of weapons. Combined Operations had to develop the equipment, the know-how, and the special forces for the job. And try them out. By late 1941 Admiral Lord Louis Mountbatten was in command. He added his special touch and Combined Ops had the aura of a rather glamorous game.

Three hundred and fifty RCNVR volunteers arrived for training in January, 1942, raw crews for six landing craft flotillas. Some of them were quickly into a night raid on Bruneval that captured radar equipment. Next, at St. Nazaire, a destroyer filled with explosives was rammed into a drydock gate and blown up. In August sixty of them manned craft for the doomed landing at Dieppe. Some were killed and wounded. Some were captured with the Canadian soldiers who suffered such a terrible defeat.

Whatever the reasoning for Dieppe, it re-taught old lessons that never should have been unlearned and raised some new ones. No major landing could be made without heavy advance air bombardment; heavy gunfire support from ships was vital during and after the landing; special craft and equipment were needed to breach defences; a defended port was too tough a nut to crack by direct seaborne assault. That last point led to the great Mulberry prefabricated harbours that were towed to the Normandy beaches. They filled the bill amazingly well until seaports like Le Havre and Cherbourg were taken.

The lessons came at a high price. Around 5,000 Canadians sailed for Dieppe. Close to 1,000 were killed, another 2,000 taken prisoner. For the men in Combined Ops, Dieppe stood as a very sobering first lesson. By October the Canadians were formed in their own flotillas of small landing craft, trained up, and ready for a major show. They didn't know the destination but it was Operation Torch.

OPERATION TORCH

The seventeen Canadian corvettes that left Canada in the fall of 1942 didn't know where they were going either. The first of them left about the time *Ottawa* was sunk. In her group there wasn't a single operating 271 radar. Yet the Torch corvettes got theirs in the U.K. right away, plus their first 20mm guns. Then off they went to join in the North African assault.

The landings caught the Germans off balance. U-boats were disposed elsewhere. South off Africa, which had been stripped of escorts for Torch, they had a field day. In the North Atlantic they ripped into *Restigouche*'s SC 107. One Torch armada sailed from the U.S. aimed straight at Casablanca in French Morocco. The other from the U.K., with the first of the Canadian corvettes, made for Oran and Algiers inside the Mediterranean. For these two greatest armadas of the war to date not a U-boat pack was in place.

Near Algiers on 8 November the Canadian assault craft took in first-wave troops. Vichy French shore batteries and warships were there, but after a sputter of fire the massive landing went in unopposed. It was the same on all the beaches. Now, for the navies, it was just a matter of resupply, and a huge task it was. The Canadian landing craft ferried mountains of stores ashore. The corvettes got on with the business of escort.

Dönitz had told the German High Command that the North Atlantic was the crucial win-or-lose area for his U-boats, but Hitler, who took his advice on naval strategy from Grosadmiral Erich Raeder, a surface navy man, ordered him into the Mediterranean anyway. It was too late and the convoys were far too well defended. Seven U-boats were sunk in a single week.

This was a very different game for the Canadian corvettes. It was a small sea and the enemy was close. The RN had been fighting air attack here for years and it was part of the scene. The Med was far softer than the brutal North Atlantic. The U-boats operated singly rather than in packs. The hauls were short and the escorts much stronger, and air cover was first rate. Easier weather gave full range to the 271 radars. Asdic operating conditions were much better. Also, some of the submarines were Italian and they lacked the Dönitz brand of iron.

There was plenty of action. In mid-January *Ville de Québec*, Lieutenant Commander A.R.E. Coleman, RCNR, killed a U-boat in ten minutes from first asdic contact to ramming her under – something of a record. *Port Arthur* got an Italian. Ted Simmons was Captain and it was his second submarine. He had jumped aboard *U-501* when *Chambly* and *Moose Jaw* sank her in the battle for SC 42 back in 1941.

In early February *Louisburg* was with a big escort of fifteen corvettes when in swept Italian aircraft. A torpedo caught her. She sank in four minutes and half her company died, including most of the engine-room crew. The depth charges exploded at depth and added to the toll. Then, within six days, *Regina* got a night contact on radar. It disappeared: a "sinker." After asdic sweep, depth charges, and a fierce point-blank gunbattle another Italian went down.

The pendulum swung back late in the month. Since *Weyburn* first met the enemy in the Gulf of St. Lawrence the previous summer she had become a taut, efficient ship. Four months in the Med had brought plenty of action with

U-boats, aircraft, and fast torpedo boats. The RN group they were with had downed two Heinkels.

Leaving Gibraltar for a U.K.-bound convoy, *Weyburn* struck a mine. The engine room filled with a lethal rush and the ship settled low in the water. The RN destroyer *Wivern* came alongside to take off wounded. Remembering their friends who died in *Charlottetown*, the depth-charge crew quickly pulled the primers. Two charges buckled by the explosion defied disarming. Suddenly the bow reared high and *Weyburn* sank in seconds, taking her Captain, Tom Golby, and others with her. Able Seaman Tom Clark, suffering a head wound, had swum clear. Clinging to a splinter mat 200 yards off, he watched the ship sink. Then came two huge, crushing explosions. Two friends with him were terribly ruptured inside and one died later. Clark was half on the mat with his stomach out of the water and that saved him.

Wivern, with her load of survivors, was hit heavily by the explosion and her own wounded added to *Weyburn*'s. The destroyer's medical officer, Surgeon Lieutenant P.R. Evans, had both ankles broken. In intense pain himself, he directed operations in the blood-drenched wardroom. It was akin to the battles of 1812. *Weyburn*'s First Lieutenant, "Hip" Garrard, had a mangled ankle but refused treatment until all the others were looked after. Then, with a cheerful "Hack away, boys," he endured the agony of amputation. As in those bygone battles his only anaesthetic was a generous tot of rum.

SICILY

The landing craft flotillas had meantime returned to England to regroup. The glamour was off Combined Operations. It was too like the army they served, with not much of the derring-do and a great deal of marking time. A major landing took a long time to get in gear. In mid-March they loaded their assault craft into transports and sailed as the 55th and 61st LCA flotillas. In a later convoy came the 80th and 81st LCM flotillas with larger craft for landing vehicles.

They had no idea of their target but they steamed due south and got plenty of sun. The convoys sailed clear around Cape Horn and came north through the Suez Canal to Port Said. They trained and rehearsed in the eastern Mediterranean and at last, on 5 July, they hoisted their craft at the landing ships' davits and sailed west. Sixteen convoys of transports from Africa, the U.K., and the U.S. gathered at the rendezvous south of Malta. Add a heavy covering force of carriers, battleships, cruisers, destroyers, and minesweepers and it was a massive armada. Over 2,700 vessels sorted and regrouped in two great forces and made for Sicily.

The climactic battles of the North Atlantic had taken place in the spring of 1943 while the landing craft men had been journeying around Africa. The U-boats in the Mediterranean had been beaten. Now Africa was firmly held. The unsinkable Malta airfields, fifty miles from Sicily, and the carriers gave air cover.

The American Seventh Army landed along the southwest coast of Sicily. The British Eighth Army beaches were around the corner of Cape Passero on the southeast coast. The First Canadian Division and First Canadian Army Tank Brigade were part of it. Other than the foray to France in 1940 and the tragedies of Hong Kong and Dieppe, this was the Canadian Army's first action. The Canadian flotillas, though, were in a different sector.

In the pre-dawn hours of 10 July the sea was rough as the LCAs dropped down from their davits. Assault troops swarmed down the nettings and each craft embarked its one platoon. It was a seven-mile run to shore in pitch black and sharp sea, which reduced the soldiers to heaps of seasick misery. Otherwise, opposition ran from nil to light. Most craft beached safely. The beachheads were quickly secured. By dawn the heavy transport ships moved in. Unloading them was the job of the LCMs. The vehicles and the tanks moved ashore.

At that point the Luftwaffe intervened. Breaking through the fighter cover, they strafed and bombed the beaches. Two British craft were destroyed right beside the Canadian LCMs. Enemy airfields were by no means out of action. Over the next two days there were twenty-three raids. In the anchorage five merchantmen and a hospital ship went down.

Every vehicle, every shell and gallon of gasoline, every ration box had to go over the beaches. The LCMs stayed on the job, moving up the east coast as the army advanced. There were no parent ships. With an open LCM as home, the crews lived off the land, scrounging as resourceful sailors will. Then, on the 5th of August, they pulled out for Malta. In less than a month the twenty-four LCMs had landed close to 9,000 vehicles, 40,000 men, and 40,000 tons of stores.

In September, repaired and in top shape again, the 80th LCM Flotilla was back in Sicily near Messina, looking across the six-mile strait at the Italian mainland. Their cargo this time was all Canadian – the Royal 22nd from Quebec, the West Nova Scotians, and the Carleton and Yorks – and this was the assault wave. At dawn on 3 September they headed out under an enormous barrage. Shells howled overhead from artillery on the Sicilian side. The 15-inch guns of the RN battleships *Warspite* and *Valiant* thundered; their shells sounded like express trains. Opposition along the beach was light, casualties in the flotilla and their assault troops nil.

On 8 September Italy surrendered, then in mid-month declared war on Germany. The LCMs grinding jobs were done. The two LCA flotillas had gone back to the U.K. directly after the first assault. By fall all the Canadian Combined Ops units were back in the U.K. to regroup, re-equip, train, and fret and wait for the next assault. It was to be in seven months, 6 June 1944, on the beaches of Normandy.

THE WORST OF WINTERS

Weather on the North Atlantic through the winter of 1942-43 was the worst for thirty years. A third of the escorts were knocked out with weather damage. In one month eight merchant ships were sunk by monstrous seas. A rescue vessel turned turtle from the weight of ice and sank. A convoy commodore's ship opened up in a gale and went down with every soul on board. The Captain and First Lieutenant of an RN destroyer were killed when the bridge was smashed by a monstrous wave.

Sailors in the little ships lived in physical misery. Wet and cold, in the same clothes for weeks, they got what rest they could between watches in leaking, reeking messdecks. They subsisted on scratch meals. And always, day and night, they had to cling physically to a heaving, pitching, pounding ship, hammered by the waves in an eternal sea of noise. Foul weather scattered the convoys, put vital equipment out of action, cloaked the movements of the enemy, badly cut the air cover. The mounting number of U-boats faced the same abominable blinding, debilitating weather, but overall it worked in their favour.

Admiral Dönitz now had 382 U-boats – more than he had first told Hitler he needed to win the war. Their losses had climbed: thirty-four in the last three months of 1942. But 1942 was the worst year yet for the merchant ships and their indomitable crews. Over 6 million tons, 1,000 ships, went down.

The serious shortage was long-range aircraft. Stripped of its armour, with the heavy self-sealing tanks replaced, the VLR version of the American Liberator bomber was the answer. Only in late 1942, though, did Admiralty and Coastal Command modify more than a handful of their small allocation to VLR. They hoped to reap an easy harvest close to home by patrolling the Bay of Biscay, but the return was very small. The place to kill U-boats was around the convoys, but in November the RCAF pleaded in vain for VLRs to fly from Newfoundland. The Black Pit was as black as ever. The light at the end of the tunnel was North American shipbuilding. The net loss in merchant ships was halved from the year before. But statistics were cold comfort on the convoy lanes. In this most monumental of battles, ships and sailors were dying as never before in the history of war.

Now, as the crisis grew, the Canadian groups were cycled out of the MOEF. C1 with Dobson in *St. Croix* was in the U.K. and the eastern Atlantic from January until April and got in top shape – mind, body, and soul. In spite of Nelles's resistance it was a badly needed break. In the U.K. they had all the support that fighting ships needed, which barely existed in Canada. Dockyard repairs, new equipment, alterations and additions brought them up to date. They got their tired ships back in shape and took leave in England in turns. Then they plunged into team training – gunnery, signals, asdic, depth-charge crews, damage control, and firefighting. The equipment was there with expert instructors. Captains and officers and signalmen learned to out-smart U-boats at the Western Approaches Tactical Unit in Liverpool.

In mid-February the whole group went through the fire and brimstone of a week at *Western Isles*, the work-up base in Tobermory, Scotland. Commodore G. Stephenson, RN, "the Terror of Tobermory," and his staff had a fearsome reputation for diabolic cunning and superhuman demands. They brewed up battle problems and special manoeuvres and harried the crew to do them better, faster, in the pitch dark. When things started going right they'd knock the power off, fill the ship with smoke and thunderflashes, cause a steering breakdown, kill off the Captain and the senior hands. Anchored at night for a few hours' rest, the unwary ship would be mined by frogmen, boarded by saboteurs.

On his first inspection of one Canadian corvette the Commodore stepped aboard, flung his cap on deck, and snapped, "That's an incendiary bomb. Get on with it." The young bosun's mate coolly kicked it over the side. Then he piped, "Away sea boat's crew. Recover the Commodore's cap." It is said to be the only time Commodore Stephenson was ever seen nonplussed. His cap sank, the corvette had a double working-over from his staff, and the bosun's mate was marked by the Captain for early promotion. In short order, though, the Tobermory team culled out the worst and brought out the best in a ship's company from top to bottom.

In late February, with its ships and people in top shape and morale high, C1 sailed with a Torch convoy. Off Portugal German aircraft spotted them. Three U-boats closed in. One penetrated the screen for a sinking but another was caught and held by *Shediac*. In came *St. Croix* and between them they sent *U-87* to the bottom. It was the second U-boat for Dobson and *St. Croix*, the first for *Shediac*. Next *Prescott* chased a contact on her new 271 radar, put a U-boat down, and pounded her hard. Another late reassessment awarded her the destruction of *U-163*.

It put a rousing cap on the weeks of hard work by all hands in escort group C1. C2 and C4 followed the same route but didn't graduate with a U-boat.

At this point Hitler grasped that only the U-boats could win. He swept Raeder aside and gave Dönitz command of the entire Kriegsmarine. The U-boat fleet got top priority and it mounted its most gigantic offensive of the war. On the mid-ocean the Canadians didn't completely disappear. C3, with RN additions, stayed flogging it out. So did the American group with its majority of RCN corvettes. But the British groups took the brunt and in the first months they did no better on the score sheet than the Canadians.

Admiral Horton, however, instead of flaying the escorts for their failures, used their poor results as ammunition to form support groups. In March, Horton cut into the sixteen Western Approaches escort groups, begged four destroyers from the Home Fleet, and formed five support groups.

But none was yet on task when ON 166 sailed from Britain in mid-February. *Trillium* was one of four Canadian corvettes in the American group under Commander Paul Heineman in USS *Campbell*. Sixty-three ships hammered westward into fierce gales and a patrol line of U-boats. Thirteen ships turned back to the U.K. crippled by the weather. Twelve were torpedoed. Between weather and U-boats, less than half of that convoy got to its destination.

As for the escorts, *Campbell* rammed and sank a U-boat, then had to make for port. *Trillium* picked up 160 survivors. She was one of the first seventy Canadian corvettes still without her extended forecastle, and now she was loaded with three times her regular complement. Sick and wounded crammed every sheltered corner. Men huddled on the upper deck in sodden blankets. Down to the nub in food and fuel, she fought three U-boat actions through ghastly weather. In St. John's at last, *Trillium* and her mates, brutally mangled as they were, had forty-eight hours to turn around before heading east into yet another vicious battle.

This, too, was fought in heavy gales. Twenty-seven U-boats sank thirteen merchant ships without a single loss. They had the momentum now. In mid-March two convoys with British groups lost twenty-one ships to a pack of thirty-three. If these huge packs made contact out in the Black Pit it was certain death for ships and men. In three weeks in March, ninety-seven ships went down in mid-Atlantic. One in five that sailed in convoy was sunk. The code-cracking war had a major hand in this. The German cryptographers had broken the British convoy code in February, so until early summer they could lay their patrol lines right on target. Then in late March, with slaughter at its height, the British broke into Triton again and ended the blackout.

The facts shouted out. These disasters couldn't be put down to the Canadians. Even the best-trained ships, powerful groups with the latest equipment, couldn't beat the U-boats out there in the air gap with close escort alone. Without support groups to send to threatened convoys, extended land-based air cover, and carrier aircraft out with the convoys, the Battle of the Atlantic would be lost.

EMERALD ISLE

For RCN ships, Londonderry's American and British dockyards were saviours. For sailors coming in off the mid-ocean this blessed corner of Ireland was heaven indeed. The lasting recollection of Lieutenant Jack Pickford, Captain of the corvette *Rimouski*, was of "how tired everybody became because of this constant hanging on and constant pounding. And of course the ship was wet. Very often these passages would take three weeks and the euphoria that we all felt when we arrived at our destination, I think, had to be experienced to be understood.

"At the Londonderry end we would first go to the tankers at Moville to top up with fuel. And suddenly the ship was still and quiet for the first time in weeks, and it was a remarkable feeling. Mail would come aboard and there would be a tremendously happy atmosphere reigning in the ship. On completion of fuelling we would go up the River Foyle to Londonderry and it was a lovely passage and you would pass between the fields that were so green and you could smell the land. Everything was so quiet and you could hear the cowbells on the cattle in the fields. Then as we approached Londonderry . . . every ship – or many ships in those days – had theme songs and *Rimouski*'s was "Paper Doll" and just a few miles downriver from Londonderry was a large country house called Broome Hall, the residence of the Wrens working in Londonderry. So we would always have "Paper Doll" blaring merrily on our upper-deck speakers as we passed Broome Hall and it was kind of fun to see the windows being thrown open and everything waved from handkerchiefs to bedsheets in welcome . . . . "

And Londonderry, cramped little town that it was, had cheerful pubs and Guinness on draft and dances with the pretty Irish girls. And with the Wrens. They, as well, were so good at their jobs and fresh and cheerful and they warmed a sailor's heart. There was the lovely green countryside and you could hide your cap, stay wrapped in a burberry, and go quite illegally across the border to Eire and lush little inns with unlimited Irish whisky and fabulous food. It's what a sailor needed to survive.

TURNING POINT

In late March, five support groups deployed in the North Atlantic. One of them formed around the escort carrier HMS *Biter*. The Biscay air offensive still burned up thousands of aircraft hours for slight result (in April: ninety-four U-boats sighted, sixty-four attacked, one sunk). But now forty Liberators swung into the mid-ocean battle. By May, Liberators the RCAF had been pleading for since November were flying out of Newfoundland. On the other side, the U-boats had lost heavily. They were going to sea with less experienced captains and crews. With the escorts it was the reverse. A final factor – the one that must always be counted in sea warfare – was the weather. As it got better, so the advantage swung to the surface and air.

With the support groups at sea, the April convoys fared well. The Americans had left MOEF and the Canadian groups were back. But they were all on close escort and the support groups of RN ships got the action. They kept the U-boats away and harried them. With no convoy of their own to worry about they stuck with their contacts till they killed them.

In May the convoy cycle stepped up. The battle was finally starting to work as it should for the Allies. Ultra intelligence gave safer routes. Escort carriers HMS *Biter* and USS *Bogue* were out in the air gap. The support groups had the

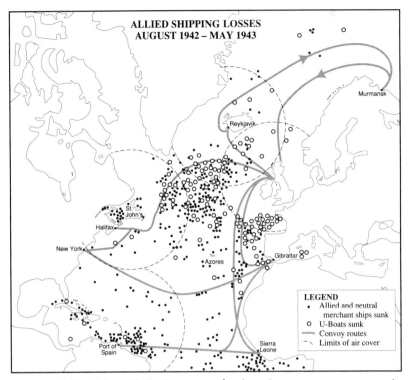

*August, 1942 – May, 1943. As soon as the American convoy system was in place the
U-boats moved closer to home for wolf-pack attacks in mid-Atlantic. The St. Lawrence
was closed in September. Losses were very heavy but stronger escorts, support groups,
extended air cover, and escort carriers finally turned the tide.*

offensive. At the beginning of the month came the climactic convoy battle of
the war – ONS 5 (the series was renumbered after ONS 171) – and it was as
close as any battle can be. It was fought by B7, led by Commander Peter
Gretton, RN, one of the top anti-submarine warfare professionals of the war.
His strong, finely honed group was backed up by the Third support group
and, later in the battle, by the First. Against him were two packs totalling no
less than forty U-boats.

The convoy of slow ships crawled westward in ballast into heavy gales. It
was badly scattered. Few escorts were able to fuel. The SO was running so low
he had to leave for St. John's before the main action was joined. Bad weather
meant spotty air cover, though an RCAF Canso from Newfoundland caught
U-630 on the surface and sank her. The escort was down to three destroyers
and four corvettes. Heavy weather helped shroud the German movements
and the U-boats overran the close escort and in two days torpedoed eleven
ships.

Another disastrous defeat was in prospect. But in every battle there is an
element of luck; this time it was the weather. On the 6th of May came a

dramatic change – calm seas and heavy fog. The U-boats were now gathered for the kill. But they had no radar or search receivers that could detect the escorts. They groped blindly for the convoy and talked on their radios. The escorts, with modern radar and HF/DF, could hear and see the U-boats, and suddenly they were in control. That night alone they attacked fifteen confirmed submarine contacts, chased four off on the surface, rammed two with damage, and sank four. Only one more merchant ship was sunk. At battle's end it was twelve merchant ships for six U-boats. For once it was a slaughter in the enemy's camp.

British and Canadian groups took their next convoys through a heavy concentration untouched. There were three escort carriers now. The support groups in the area sank eight U-boats. C2's convoy lost three ships but sank three U-boats. *Drumheller* shared *U-89* with two RN ships. February's total had been nineteen U-boat kills, March's fifteen, April's eighteen. In May, 1943, forty-seven U-boats were sunk and Grosadmiral Dönitz's own son was lost among them.

Now the statistics highlighted not merchant ships sunk but U-boats killed. In summer the VLR Liberators closed the North Atlantic gap. The U-boats tried to get at the American–Mediterranean convoys further south but were crushed by the four USN carrier support groups that had finally been formed. North America could move the outpourings of her mighty arsenal across the Atlantic unassailed. The Battle of the Atlantic was turned. Fortress Europe would yet fall.

CHAPTER SEVEN
POLITICS AND WAR

IN THE WARDROOMS AND THE MESSDECKS OF THE CANADIAN ESCORTS IN Derry, Halifax, and St. John's it was a hollow celebration. Only *Drumheller* with her one-third of a kill had a sniff of the enemy in the smashing climax. These young seamen, for better or for worse, in success and failure, life and death, had doggedly fought the toughest battle of the war for three and a half years. For months on end they had carried it on their own. Without the Canadians and their ill-equipped little ships the battle would certainly have long since been lost. And now their glasses were raised to their RN colleagues, not themselves.

Where were the facilities and the shore support, the pools of trained people so the ships could get efficient and stay there? Where were the right kind of radar, the huff-duffs, the gyro compasses, the improved corvettes? With the same equipment as the RN they could have been in the van instead of on the sidelines. There had indeed been failure at the top. Agonizing changes and upheavals were to come. But the steel was there and there was a great navy being forged. In 1943 the Royal Canadian Navy came of age. This was the rite of passage.

THE NORTH ATLANTIC COMMAND

While the struggle at sea moved to a climax, a different sort of battle was being fought between Ottawa, Washington, and Whitehall over command in the North Atlantic. It was light years from the day-to-day slogging on the convoy lanes but it profoundly changed the basic military relationship between Canada and her Allies and it has lasted to this day.

There were a lot of players in the control and defence of shipping in the northwest Atlantic. The American Commander Task Force 24, Vice Admiral Brainard in Argentia, was in charge. He reported to the C-in-C U.S. Atlantic

Fleet. He had his substantial operating base, few escorts, but a strong air element. Sea operations were run by his two Canadian sub-commanders, Flag Officer Newfoundland Force – now Commodore H.E. "Rastus" Reid – and the Commanding Officer Atlantic Coast, Rear Admiral Leonard Murray in Halifax. On the Canadian air side, Eastern Air Command answered to Air Force HQ in Ottawa. So did Number 1 Group RCAF, which had the maritime aircraft. It was pretty hard to tell who had the ball.

Admiralty in their turn didn't like handing a convoy over in mid-ocean and mid-battle and they felt there were too many American blunders. In January, 1942, they had pushed for Western Approaches to control all the convoys all the way. Admiral King said no. The U.S. Navy had strategic control of the western Atlantic and that included the trade routes. NSHQ wasn't even asked.

After the eastern seaboard shambles of 1942, however, two RCN staff officers began to stir the pot. Acting Captains Horatio Nelson Lay (Director of Operations) and Harry DeWolf (Director of Plans), with destroyer commands under their belts, knew what went on at sea. Lay began to pile up ammunition for the RCN to take charge.

In the meantime, in July, 1942, the Canadian Joint Staff set up shop in Washington under the Canada-U.S. Permanent Joint Board on Defence. The Americans didn't want smaller Allies to clutter the stage with military missions. The USN viewed the RCN rather as an auxiliary to the Royal Navy and chose to deal with the British Admiralty delegation and have them deal with NSHQ. That was fine by the British. But the first naval member of the Joint Staff would have none of it.

He was Rear Admiral Victor G. Brodeur, a prickly character, a fierce nationalist, and a thoroughly dedicated naval officer. Brodeur admired Britain's navy but, unlike most of the older RCN, he heartily mistrusted RN senior officers. He was no diplomat, but for a tough task at a hard time he was the right man for the RCN and Canada. Writing to Nelles, he reached back into the history he learned so well from his father: ". . . regardless of all decisions reached at previous Colonial and Imperial Conferences, the Admiralty still looks upon the RCN as the naval child to be seen and heard when no outsider is looking in or listening in."

Then the USN, with RN support, wanted to issue all the U-boat dispositions. The RCN had good shore HF/DF and very efficient U-boat tracking. Information was always fed to the USN anyway. But the extra link would mean delay. Such vital stuff had to get to the escorts at sea while it was hot. Admiral Nelles fired back at Admiral King. Canada provided 48 per cent of the escorts on the Atlantic, the USN 2 per cent; Canada was doing her best for the Allies, pitching in on the eastern seaboard and Torch, for example. But Canada was her own boss and her navy wouldn't be pushed around. Nelson Lay was the driving force at NSHQ on this. He drafted Nelles's letter to

Admiral King and urged that Canada take over all convoys and escorts in the western Atlantic. He pushed for a three-way conference to resolve it.

Percy Nelles was not a great leader. He'd not had much sea time, and it was far in the past. He had inherited a tiny RCN in 1936. A competent bureaucrat running a small show in Ottawa, he was out of touch with the events at sea. Originality was not his forte. He was a small terrier, though, and he got this particular bone between his teeth and worried it until finally Admiral King agreed.

The Atlantic Convoy Conference opened in Washington on 1 March. The redoubtable Victor Brodeur said loud and clear that all Canadian armed forces were under control of the Canadian government and if everyone "will remember that important factor, a great deal of time will be saved and many misunderstandings avoided."

These were the darkest days of the bloodletting on the Atlantic. The Conference made immediate major decisions: U.S. escort carriers to support the battle; VLR Liberators in strength, including the RCAF in Newfoundland; and the matter of command. The RCN won it because its share of the battle was there to see. Now, north of latitude 40, ocean convoys and the U-boat battle came under the British and Canadians. The pie was divided at longitude 47 west. Admiralty and C-in-C Western Approaches took the eastern half. The new C-in-C Canadian North Atlantic under NSHQ had direction of all anti-submarine surface and air forces to the west. Admiral Brainard hauled down his flag. On the 30th of April Rear Admiral Leonard Murray became the new Commander-in-Chief.

Murray was the only Canadian officer to command an Allied theatre in the war. It was won for him and for Canada by the escort fleet that he had been forced to drive beyond the reasonable limits of endeavour. That fleet may, in its own eyes, have failed at the crux of the battle, but it had held the line against defeat and in fact won a victory of long-term consequence for Canada.

Angus L. Macdonald, Minister of National Defence, the Prime Minister, and his war cabinet watched all this from the sidelines. It was a milestone in Canada's history – the clear assertion of the country's authority over its own military affairs. It was a remarkable achievement. Without a yea or nay from the highest levels of the land, the navy did it on its own.

HARD FACTS

High command was one thing, fighting at sea another. The young veteran Captain of *Restigouche*, Acting Lieutenant Commander Debby Piers, knew that junior officers, even very experienced ones, got no thanks for criticizing their seniors. Still, he put the bitterness of the mid-ocean Canadians on paper and sent it up the line in June. His points: RCN ships were twelve to eighteen months astern of the RN in anti-submarine equipment; Admiral Horton's staff weren't happy with Canadian performance; Commodore (D) Londonderry, the helpful and friendly "Shrimp" Simpson, agreed they were poorly equipped; flogging between St. John's and Londonderry the C groups were the worst off for support facilities, home leave, and regular mail; work-up periods were too short; pulling people from ships destroyed efficiency; there were too many gaps in reserve officers' training.

From Newfoundland, Commodore Reid hit out again, especially on equipment. Admiral Murray had been fighting the same kind of problems there eighteen months before. On the plus side four refurbished RN destroyers had just commissioned into the RCN. Two more were due later. The first of seventy new frigates building in Canadian yards was delivered in June. These were real ocean escorts, much more effective than corvettes. The Mid-Ocean Escort Force was much better for the refurbishing and training that had taken place that winter. Training in Halifax was much improved under Murray's Captain (D), Chummy Prentice.

As well, Commander Jimmy Hibbard, in from sea knowing all about the shocks and alarms of night action on the convoy lanes, had made an important contribution. He had built an action trainer in Halifax. It was a mock-up of a ship's bridge and key compartments and it gave a ship's team a very realistic workout, right to buckets of salt water in the face at crucial times. With asdic, communications, radar, and plotting added, it was the first realistic ship-action simulator in anyone's navy. Wrens made up most of the operating crew. It worked well, trained thousands in ships' fighting teams, and was copied by other navies. A huge training base, HMCS *Cornwallis*, was growing fast at Deep Brook, Nova Scotia. The signal school at St. Hyacinthe, Quebec, was getting into gear. The RN had lent some fine specialists to these facilities, and trained, skilled sailors were coming out in big numbers at last.

Regarding seagoing equipment, Murray agreed with Debby Piers – the ships were just getting in decent shape to fight the battles of a year before. By this time, though, the call was for support groups, escort carriers, advanced detection and weapon systems, electronics – controlled precision rather than valiant blundering. His report arrived in a Headquarters that was as poorly equipped for the battles of 1943 as were the ships at sea.

Planning – or the lack of it – was the problem. The Staff had built helter-skelter from a tiny professional core. It coped with emergencies, put out fires. But now the fire on the North Atlantic was under control. Other eyes, professional and political, were cast over the state of the RCN. The Atlantic Convoy Conference had set up the Allied Anti-Submarine Survey Board. It was a tight professional team topped by Rear Admirals Kauffman and Mansfield, American and British, respectively, with Canadian navy and air force observers. They moved quickly, looking hard at operations, training, and maintenance.

Among the Board's conclusions were that the RCN and RCAF must work more closely and that the worst training snag was lack of practice submarines. The biggest issue, though, was that of maintaining and modernizing the fleet: dockyards in Halifax and St. John's were vastly overloaded; the small Maritime shipyards needed 6,000 men; new construction and merchant ship repairs took up too much effort; the number of escorts overdue for refit was unacceptable. New construction, the Board said, should be cut to get the fleet in shape. U.K. dockyards should fit RCN ships with the latest equipment.

Engineer Rear Admiral George Stephens, the RCN's Chief of Naval Engineering and Construction, agreed with the Survey Board. But operations had had top priority. As he said, "while we have been keeping our ships running and providing escorts, Admiralty have kept their ships home and modified them." Also, the RCN depended on U.K. for plans, drawings, and specifications and a lot of equipment. Admiralty was slow to deliver and looked to their own needs first. Likely the result of naive faith, until mid-1943 only one rather junior RCN technical liaison officer was in London.

The U.K. was still building Tribal-class destroyers for Canada. Back in 1941 naval staff had discussed building more in Canada. They were short-range, heavy-gunned ships for a big-ship permanent navy of the future; they had nothing to do with winning the Battle of the Atlantic. Admiral Stephens was against the expense, the tooling, and the special steel needed for such a short run. Worse, he said it would drain too much strength from the main battle. But Navy Minister Angus Macdonald saw his own Nova Scotia short-changed in war material contracts.* The Tribals were an industrial plum. Nelles seized the chance to fulfil his post-war dream and four of them were laid down in Halifax in September, 1942. The result was just as Stephens predicted. They were the wrong ships for the wrong reasons and not one of them was finished until after the war.

Peacetime policy had given Canada's navy no base on which to build. Now it was near collapse from the weight of its own enormous wartime expansion. In this atmosphere of unease and pending crisis, chance, personalities, and unorthodox means come to play.

THE QUESTION OF LEADERSHIP

Captain William Strange, Director of Naval Information in Naval Headquarters, made a trip to the U.K. in July, 1943, and crossed in HMS *Duncan* with Commander Peter Gretton, RN. Gretton knew anti-submarine warfare as well as anyone afloat. He admired the Canadians and deplored their crippling

---

*That was certainly true. The policies of C.D. Howe, Minister of Munitions and Supply, had concentrated industrial development in central Canada. Most shipbuilding was up the river and in the Great Lakes and little had been done to strengthen Maritime yards.

lack of equipment. Strange wasn't a seagoing or technical naval officer; his job was dealing with the news media. But he kept his ears open and Gretton's words matched the growls he'd heard in Canadian wardrooms. Then, in Londonderry, he called on Shrimp Simpson, who treated him to his searing views.

Heading home in *Assiniboine*, Strange got Commander Kenneth Adams to help him write a memorandum. Adams, just back at sea in command, pitched in and sent his own report to Captain (D) Newfoundland. He made the clinching point that in his own group he had to use the RN ships as his striking arm. Strange sent his memo, not to the Chief of Naval Staff – as properly he should have – but privately and directly to the Minister of the Navy.

The timing was dramatic. It arrived in Macdonald's hands at the Quebec Conference in early August where Mackenzie King was hosting Churchill and Roosevelt. Admiral Pound, the First Sea Lord, was there with the Anti-Submarine Survey Board's report fresh in mind. Mackenzie King was look-ing for some recognition of Canada's war effort. All politicians needed victories. Canada had had none. Other than the First Division's foray in France in 1940 and Hong Kong and Dieppe, the army had spent three years training in England until Sicily in July. And they landed there as part of a British formation. The navy had made a tremendous contribution but Chur-chill didn't seem aware of it.

Macdonald pondered. The previous fall the Gulf had closed down. At the turn of the year, when Churchill had underscored lack of training, Nelles asserted it was mainly equipment. When the slaughter of the U-boats came, the Canadians had been out of sight. Now, according to men at sea, that was because of equipment that still wasn't there. Why not?

Macdonald kept Strange's memo in his drawer but used it to ask Nelles some tough questions. Why, for instance, were only two Canadian corvettes fitted with gyro compasses and Hedgehog when only five RN corvettes lacked them? What equipment did RCN escorts actually have on the North Atlantic, compared to that carried by escorts of the Royal Navy? And what about other matters, such as RCN representation in Londonderry? And disci-pline (the reflection of morale) in Britain? Nelles didn't give the hard answers. In fact, in NSHQ there was no systematic record of which ship had what equipment.

Macdonald had never taken the high ground of leadership. He had heard all the problems at Naval Board meetings but never took much of a hand. His abiding concern was his political flanks. He suspected a cover-up and went right behind Nelles's back. He sent his executive assistant, John J. Connolly, to the U.K. Simpson and Horton filled Connolly in and he brought back an anonymous memo, including a lot of the Survey Board's points and a basket-ful of criticism of NSHQ's staff work, planning, and decisions.

The confidence that must exist between Minister and Chief of Staff had gone. In December, Macdonald concluded what anyone at sea could have told him: "Our ships were putting to sea inadequately equipped as compared to British ships . . . over an unduly long period of time." Macdonald's deviousness had taken over four months to resolve a critical matter of leadership at a crucial point in the war. Nelles was finished. In January, 1944, he went to England as Senior RCN Officer. Vice Admiral G.C. Jones became CNS. A year later Percy Nelles retired, promoted to full Admiral, the first in Canada's history.

Certainly under Nelles the navy didn't have modern, capable ships in the Battle of the Atlantic at the crucial time. They didn't have the right equipment, proper support, or enough trained people. Because there was no proper training base, hundreds of early volunteers were sent to the U.K., and they gave fine service to the RN as radar specialists, in aviation, coastal forces, submarines, combined operations – in every corner of the fleet. Most were lost to Canada's navy. Nelles certainly failed to say "no" to excessive demands from across the Atlantic, but in the early days Britain and the Commonwealth stood alone and faced imminent defeat.

Perhaps his greatest blunder was to agree to close the Gulf in 1942 while giving ships to Torch for the sake of prestige. Nelles, like most of his naval generation, looked on the ragtag little escorts as the stepping stones to the big-ship navy that Canada should one day have. He clung to the three armed merchant cruisers. He started the Tribals in Canada. With its naive good faith in the RN, the Royal Canadian Navy didn't look out for itself with technical staffs in London and Londonderry. Poor early decisions on modifying corvettes, on radar and HF/DF, let the fleet down. As head of the most highly technical of services, Nelles was, as the navy's first scientific adviser said, "a most untechnical man."

Probably even a brilliant, experienced, and dynamic leader could not have pulled it off, and Nelles was not of that calibre. He had next to nothing to work with at the outbreak of war, and that was the product of Canada's lack of naval policy. So it is fair to say that Percy Nelles fell too far short in his failure to achieve the unachievable.

On the other hand, under Nelles – dedicated and hard-working as he was – the RCN multiplied by fifty and put a large escort fleet to sea in an incredibly short time. Ill-trained, ill-equipped, and terribly overstretched as it was, through the desperate battles of 1940-42 it hung on and held the line. And that was decisive. Without Canada's navy the Battle of the Atlantic – and so the war – would very likely have been lost. The men out at sea who were given so little and gave so much achieved the unbelievable.

THE CANADIAN ATLANTIC

Through the summer of 1943 the U-boats were harassed and sunk in the Bay of Biscay by support groups and Coastal Command. Across the southern routes and east of the Azores the USN's escort carrier groups killed sixteen U-boats, including most of their valuable "milch cows." The Americans concentrated on the U.S.-Mediterranean route but their carrier groups quite often backed the northern convoys.

While Nelles and the Minister were fencing in Ottawa, Canada's navy got truly in its stride. *Ottawa* (the second of the name) headed a new escort group, C5. The Canadian Support Group (later the 6th Support Group) formed with five corvettes and two RN frigates. *Calgary*, *Snowberry*, and HMS *Nene* got the group's first kill in November while supporting a convoy some 500 miles west of Cape Finisterre.

By August, 1943, with the air gap closed, the convoys sailed the shorter great circle route. They got much bigger and so got fewer, which sprung escorts for more support groups. A four-ship support group of four-stackers formed with the Western Escort Force out of Halifax. The galling word "Local" had been dropped from the WEF. Another group, EG 9 (*St. Croix*, *St. Francis*, *Chambly*, *Morden*, and *Sackville* and the RN frigate *Itchen*), went to work in the eastern Atlantic.

In late September they were setting out for a Biscay offensive patrol when they were sent racing off to support two west-bound convoys. It was a tricky situation. The fast convoy, ON 202, was overtaking the slow ONS 18, and they were heading straight into a big U-boat concentration. As the submarines moved in the convoys joined and the close escorts, C2 and an RN group, combined. In the convoy was a MAC ship – a merchant ship with a regular cargo and a rudimentary flight deck – carrying three Swordfish. It was a powerful defence.

But the U-boats were in force. Thirty were back on the Atlantic with their steel-hard morale intact and new equipment. They had search receivers to detect airborne 10cm radar, and new radar decoy balloons. They also carried a dangerous new weapon in their tubes. The U-boats swarmed in and punched through the escorts to the convoy. HMS *Lagan* was hit aft and knocked out of the battle. Then EG 9 raced in through the shifting fog banks. In a series of wild encounters, attacks, and counterattacks, they fought the U-boats off.

Battle-hardened *St. Croix* was just short of three years in commission with two U-boats to her credit. She was hit by two torpedoes and went down with heavy loss. Lieutenant Commander Dobson, DSC, went with her. In the surge of the battle it was thirteen hours before the RN frigate *Itchen* and corvette *Polyanthus* went back for survivors. *Polyanthus* was torpedoed on the way. *Itchen* picked up one survivor and called for help. *Sackville*, Lieutenant Gus Rankin commanding, went back to join.

They reached *St. Croix*'s survivors after dark. As *Sackville* stopped for the rescue *Itchen* signalled: "My asdic's broken down. You screen. I'll pick up."

Sackville had to turn away from old friends shouting weakly from the water. *Itchen* picked up eighty-one. It was a fateful switch.

Back near the convoy at midnight they joined *Morden* in chasing a surfaced U-boat. The three ships were quite close together when Rankin, on *Sackville*'s bridge, saw *Itchen* go up in a blinding explosion. In no more than a minute she disappeared. Nothing was left but some chunks of metal that fell on the two Canadian ships. And there were three survivors – one from *Itchen*, one from *Polyanthus*, one from *St. Croix*. Three escort ships torpedoed and sunk, plus *Lagan* hit, all in a matter of hours. Something new and very dangerous was going on.

These were, in fact, the first sinkings with the U-boats' new acoustic homing torpedo. Once launched it zeroed in on the ship's propellers. Before, the U-boats always tried to dodge the escorts and sink the merchant ships. Now they were setting out to sink the escorts to cut the defences, then go for the fat targets. It was a whole new game.

The next morning *Sackville* went back through the fog to search again. She found no survivors but got a U-boat on radar. Running in close she hammered away with the 4-inch. The U-boat dived and Rankin got in a depth-charge attack. He turned and ran in again. As the first of his pattern exploded there was a colossal underwater blast. It heaved the ship bodily upward, started rivets in the hull, and cracked a boiler. Rankin was sure it was a torpedo, very close to striking, detonated by his depth charges. *Sackville*'s U-boat slipped away.

In the rage of the whole battle six merchant ships sank, three escorts were gone with only three survivors. Another was finished. The price was high, but three U-boats were destroyed. The defence had held like iron against a formidable new and unknown weapon, and against new U-boat tactics. Now the fighting was toe-to-toe.

The reports from sea and intelligence sources put things together. The new torpedo was quickly dubbed the "Gnat." Amazingly, it was only weeks before counters were devised, built, and out at sea. They were noisemakers towed behind the ship to attract the torpedo away from the propellers. The RN's was called "Foxer." A simpler gadget called "Cat" (for Canadian Anti-Torpedo) was produced in Halifax. Nothing in war is infallible, though. With the Gnat in the U-boats, life in the escorts was a much more perilous proposition.

THE ATLANTIC SECURED

The battle of ONS 18 and ON 202 saw the last great pack attack of the North Atlantic war. In October, Portugal allowed Britain to fly from the Azores and another big slice of the Atlantic was covered. Convoy after convoy steamed across in safety. New escorts came in service; by the end of 1943, for example, sixteen Canadian frigates were in commission. Statistics for 1943 told the drama in hard figures. Losses to U-boats were down to 800,000 tons, some 160 ships for the year. The cost to the enemy was 237 boats. The U-boat men were lucky to live for three patrols. As well, this was the peak year for building merchant ships – new construction topped losses from all causes by 10 million gross tons.

Dönitz was beaten but he wouldn't quit. He pulled his forces back in a great semi-circle from the Faeroes to Brest to catch the convoys on their last legs in. He was holding on, taking what toll he could till his new high-performance boats, Types 21 and 23, came off the line. And all his existing boats in turn got the revolutionary air-breathing device, the "Schnorkel." The snorkel or snort, as it was called, went to sea in February, 1944. The boat could now run on its diesels at periscope depth keeping batteries charged. Speed was lower than on the surface but the snort really cut the chances of being spotted by radar or eye. Life below was pretty uncomfortable. The engines stank out the boats. They gulped air, too, and when the snort dipped in a wave there was an agonizing vacuum. With a stroke, however, the U-boat was far more mobile and elusive, far more dangerous.

There were no more big battles, but determined forays that winter would have seen plenty of sinkings without the better-equipped and professionally handled Canadian escorts. And they had steady success. *Camrose* shared a kill with HMS *Bayntun*. Then *Waskesiu*, the first Canadian-built frigate, sank one solo on one of the last slow convoys.

The next Canadian action, on 5-6 March, was a classic of its kind. Convoy HX 280 had C2, a very strong escort group of three destroyers, *Gatineau*, *Chaudière*, and HMS *Icarus*, a frigate, *St. Catharines*, and corvettes *Chilliwack* and *Fennel*. Also, there was an RN support group nearby for back-up.

It started when *Gatineau* caught a U-boat in mid-morning well ahead of the convoy. It went very deep. *St. Catharines*, with the Senior Officer of C2, joined and called in *Chaudière*, *Chilliwack*, and *Fennel*. The five ships ran a series of co-ordinated, creeping attacks. Soon, however, *Gatineau* had to leave for Londonderry with engine trouble, and U-boat transmissions ahead warned of a threat to the convoy. The other two destroyers rushed back to defend while the frigate and corvettes held contact. A new RN Castle-class, the big improved corvette, joined from the support group for eighteen hours. Watches changed. The hands went quietly to supper. But soon, inevitably, someone was going to die.

As night fell, the ships burned dimmed running lights to guard against collision. Radar men were glued even tighter to their scans; asdics pinged endlessly. Six more deliberate, precise attacks were made, and by early the next morning, with the convoy out of danger, the destroyers came back.

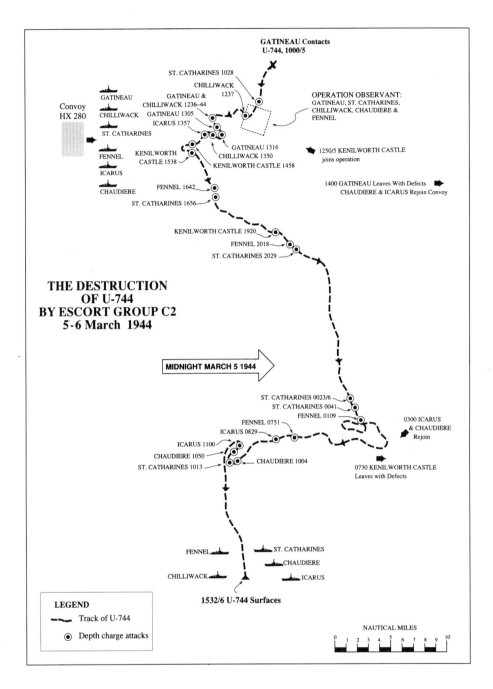

GATINEAU Contacts
U-744, 1000/5

ST. CATHARINES 1028

CHILLIWACK
1237

GATINEAU &
CHILLIWACK 1236–44

OPERATION OBSERVANT:
GATINEAU, ST. CATHARINES,
CHILLIWACK, CHAUDIERE &
FENNEL

GATINEAU
CHILLIWACK
ST. CATHARINES

Convoy
HX 280

GATINEAU 1305
ICARUS 1357

FENNEL
ICARUS
CHAUDIERE

GATINEAU 1316
CHILLIWACK 1350
KENILWORTH CASTLE 1458

KENILWORTH
CASTLE 1538

1250/5 KENILWORTH CASTLE
joins operation

1400 GATINEAU Leaves With Defects
CHAUDIERE & ICARUS Rejoin Convoy

FENNEL 1642
ST. CATHARINES 1656

KENILWORTH CASTLE 1920
FENNEL 2018
ST. CATHARINES 2029

THE DESTRUCTION
OF U-744
BY ESCORT GROUP C2
5-6 March 1944

MIDNIGHT MARCH 5 1944

ST. CATHARINES 0023/6
ST. CATHARINES 0041
FENNEL 0109

0300 ICARUS
& CHAUDIERE
Rejoin

FENNEL 0751
ICARUS 0829

ICARUS 1100
CHAUDIERE 1050
ST. CATHARINES 1013

CHAUDIERE 1004

0730 KENILWORTH CASTLE
Leaves with Defects

FENNEL
ST. CATHARINES
CHAUDIERE
CHILLIWACK
ICARUS

1532/6 U-744 Surfaces

LEGEND
Track of U-744
Depth charge attacks

NAUTICAL MILES
0 1 2 3 4 5 6 7 8 9 10

There is no dashing about. This is calm, steady, dogged killers' work with a
deadly enemy below. Down at 200 metres the crewmen of *U-744* lie flat on the
cold plates, not talking, saving every precious breath of oxygen, moving only
for a whispered order. Everything is by feel, or the quick glimmer of a
flashlight. Every light bulb has long since gone – 200 depth charges have
smashed them all. And jarred and crashed and started leaks and cracked pipes

and broken gauges and shattered glands . . . and brought men to the edge. But still the engines, on waning batteries, turn dead slow. It has been over twenty-four nerve-snapping hours since that first attack, and the reek of feces and urine and vomit adds to the sickening stench of every U-boat on patrol.

Sounds: the scratch of the asdics, like gravel flung along the U-boat's length; the whisper of the hydrophone operator to the Captain; an escort moves steadily closer, closer; it can be heard overhead; the Captain's murmur to the hydroplanes; the sudden horrifying creak of the hull squeezed in the ocean's giant hand. The Captain has gone deeper. He guesses charges are coming down. He's clever and experienced and he's got no nerves.

A tremendous hammer on the hull . . . another and another. The submarine shakes and shudders, again and again, as yet another ten-charge pattern comes down, yet somehow the men are still alive and counting. The engines pick up, draining the battery for a burst of speed, trying to break contact behind the massive boils of those underwater blasts.

Up top contact is lost. Did the charges get him this time? No wreckage. No contact. The Senior Officer re-orders ships, combs the area. Perimeter patrols move quietly, probing with asdic. They keep the U-boat in a box. The black pennant flutters close up at a yardarm – contact regained.

After six more creep attacks the group just holds. Both sides learned long since there is no quarter in this deadly game. But even this incredibly tough, brave one will have to surface soon or die with no oxygen or battery power. Lose him now, though, and he could surface after dark and tiptoe off. But in late afternoon the asdic operators get a new sound in their headphones. He's blowing tanks. He's coming up. Word sweeps through each ship like an electric current. He's coming up! All eyes sweep the surface. All guns at the ready.

The U-boat bursts for the surface. With just enough compressed air to blow, his men three parts dead and his battery gone, the Captain has no choice but one last fight. His boat leaps and settles and he's up the ladder and out the hatch. His men scramble to their guns. He's ringed in by four Canadians, one British. He smells the clean air, feels salt spray, and sees the light of day one brief last time. Then 4-inch shells and 20mm tracers arc in and he dies a fighting man on his own conning tower.

St. Catharines and *Chilliwack* have whalers away with boarding parties in double time. *Chilliwack* wins. They hoist the White Ensign, plunge into the foul, gas-filled, pitch-black boat, grabbing a precious haul of code and signal books and the cypher machine. But in the heavy sea both ships' boats capsize. The equipment is lost. Canadians and Germans are fished from the sea and finally *Icarus* fires the *coup de grâce*, a torpedo into the guts of a tough, tenacious foe. It took the second longest hunt to exhaustion of the war – thirty-two hours, seven ships, twenty-three attacks, 291 depth charges, a rain of shells, and a torpedo – to dispose of *U-744*. The spirit of Grosadmiral Dönitz's U-boat men still burned with an incredible flame.

In a few days *St. Laurent*, now under Lieutenant Commander George Stephen, RCNR, teamed with *Owen Sound, Swansea*, and HMS *Forester* to blow *U-845* to the surface, then smashed her with point-blank gunfire. Two days after "Sally's" kill, Canadian frigate *Prince Rupert*, with two U.S. destroyers and U.S. and British aircraft, sank *U-575*. All the right elements were out on the Atlantic now. People knew the game and they were playing it right. The new era in anti-submarine warfare had begun. In April *Swansea*, screening an escort carrier, scored again, then teamed with *Matane* for another kill. That made a lifetime five for Commander Clarence King. On top of his Great War kill he had scored with *Oakville* in the Caribbean in 1942 and got an assist with *St. Laurent*.

In May, 1944, only one Allied ship was sunk in the North Atlantic, the Canadian frigate *Valleyfield*. C1, like many groups, now carried a Senior Officer in one of the ships over and above the Captain. ASW tactics were complex. Like a mini-admiral, he could make the big decisions for the group while the Captain handled the ship itself. *Valleyfield*, with the Senior Officer, had five corvettes in line abreast two miles apart. They'd left their convoy and were heading in for St. John's eager for a run ashore.

Lieutenant Ian Tate on *Valleyfield*'s bridge found the Canadian-built 10cm RX/C radar "unreliable as ever." Luckily, there was a bright moon to help him dodge the icebergs and growlers. The ice also cluttered the operating radars and let *U-548* get in undetected. He was running on the surface when he spotted the group from ahead. He slipped into good position, submerged, let them close, and fired a Gnat at 1,500 yards. It took *Valleyfield* in the boiler room and literally tore her in half. Less than a third of the ship's company got clear and into the choking oil and ice-cold water. Reaction from the other ships was slow. Asdic sweeps caught nothing.

Forty-three oil-soaked wretches were pulled from the water. They had been in as much as ninety minutes and five were already dead. Lieutenant Jake Warren remembers being dumped on deck and moving just enough to be spotted as alive. Someone got some rum into him, which confirmed it. Once ashore he spent days in hospital packed in ice-cubes having his body temperature and circulation gradually restored. One hundred and twenty-five died.

The build-up for the great assault on Normandy rolled on. The MOEF destroyers formed EG 11 with Captain Prentice in command and EG 12 under Commander A.M. McKillop, RN. At last, with the invasion in sight, the RCN escort fleet had a real striking arm out to kill U-boats. New frigates commissioned with plenty of experience among their crews. By the spring of 1944 the whole of the North Atlantic route from New York to the north of Ireland was in the hands of escorts of the RCN.

Convoys got bigger and bigger. The largest of the war, HXS 300, sailed from New York on 17 July. There were 167 ships, including four MAC ships, and it covered thirty square miles of ocean. Close escort was one frigate and six corvettes of the RCN. After a seventeen-day passage it delivered over a million tons of cargo. Only one ship straggled and there was not a single loss. People had the hang of things, all right.

THE SOMERS ISLES

During the winter of 1943 work-up training had moved to Bermuda. The weather and the water conditions for asdic, in fact for all training, were immeasurably better than Halifax. In mid-summer a fully staffed work-up base was commissioned at St. George's called HMCS *Somers Isles*, the historic name for Bermuda. Captain Ken Adams set up a kind of all-Canadian Tobermory in more salubrious clime. It was what the RCN should have had from the start. By war's end Chummy Prentice was in command of *Somers Isles*. It was fitting that he should be there. The role for *Somers Isles* by then was preparing frigates for the Pacific war.

Things run full cycle. In 1944 Louis Audette was bringing his new frigate *Coaticook* in through the coral-lined channel when he spotted a submarine coming out on opposite course. As they drew abreast he recognized her and barely controlled the urge to put the wheel hard over to ram. It was the Italian *Argo*. Audette had last seen her from the torpedoed, blazing *Saguenay* in 1940. But by this time, of course, the Italians had long since left the Axis, and their submarines were finding good use as asdic targets.

NEW DIRECTION

By mid-1943 Allied escort-building was being cut back. The USN had built over 400 destroyer escorts that year and there were now enough. Nelles and his contemporaries had viewed escorts all along as stepping stones to the balanced fleet; they had met the emergency but a navy's first purpose, after all, was defence of the nation. War was the great chance to build the kind of fleet they had dreamed of since 1910 and still to serve the Allied cause.

The RCN had already raised its sights from 50,000 to 100,000 to man more escorts. The government's motive for building ships from the start was to have Canada profit from the war – and it did. Yet, Canadian yards (except Halifax, where the Tribals were on the ways) could build nothing more complex than escorts and men were pouring through a well-organized training stream with no ships coming on. Britain, on the other hand, was producing cruisers, carriers, and destroyers its navy couldn't man, precisely the sorts of ships RCN senior officers looked to for their balanced fleet.

CHAPTER EIGHT
BIG SHIPS AND LITTLE SHIPS

THE ESCORT FLEET WAS WITHOUT DOUBT CANADA'S MOST IMPORTANT contribution to the war, despite being beset with crippling shortages of resources and key manpower until mid-1943. During this time, as we have seen, four Tribal-class destroyers were built in Britain for Canada. These were commissioned between November, 1942, and summer, 1943. Well over 1,000 officers and men were involved and they were the pick of the navy in long service and experience. They would have been a godsend to the escort fleet but the Naval Board's vision of the future blurred its view of the hard vital job the navy was struggling to get in hand.

To sailors locked in the tedious, comfortless, and mostly unrewarding work on the convoy lanes, fighting in destroyers with the RN looked glamorous and exciting, and by comparison it certainly was. Men selected for the Tribals got away from dreary cheerless Halifax and limited St. John's. Britain, wartime shortages or no, was exciting. People were hospitable. Doors opened. There were girls to be met. The pubs were filled with laughter and song and the fellowship of dangers shared. London was a mecca for a weekend or leave during refit. And at sea you were running with the big boys.

There were disadvantages, to be sure. The bigger the ship the more formal the routine, and more eagle-eyed senior officers looked on. They were sticklers for routine and appearance and exact ceremonial. Canadians were far less amenable than RN sailors when the fine line between justifiable smartness and irksome petty restriction was crossed. They'd get on with the job with the best, if they understood why and if it made sense. Moulding Canadian sailors into a first-class destroyer's company took informed, alert leadership. When the combination was right they were the best anywhere. But sometimes leadership failed.

THE DESTROYER WAR

Iroquois, with Commander W.B. Holms, commissioned in November, 1942, and did trials and a winter work-up at bleak, gale-swept Scapa Flow. Hull problems and weather damage kept her pretty well out of action until summer. Recreational facilities at Scapa for the gigantic Home Fleet consisted of a cinema and a cheerless canteen with harsh lights and a concrete floor. On a short winter afternoon, if it wasn't blowing too hard, it was just possible for a soccer or rugger team to get ashore in the duty lighter and let off steam on one of the stony, undulating playing fields. There were no changing rooms or showers. The two squash courts and a golf course, per British social structure, were used only by officers. A small officers' club was a two-mile walk from the squash courts. It was a dreary time in a dismal place.

That summer *Iroquois* got into action. On a Gibraltar convoy two heavy-laden troopships were sunk by German bombers and she picked up over 600 survivors. On the way back to Plymouth she picked up three survivors of a sunken U-boat from an RN ship. While their oily clothes were being scrubbed some unknown person filched the U-boat badge from one of the jackets. The owner demanded it back. The Captain saw an infraction of the Geneva Convention in this and a reflection on his own ship's discipline. When the badge didn't show up he stopped the leave of the whole ship's company.

Holms was a rigid type, autocratic and harsh. His heavy-handed methods hadn't gone down well from the start and he didn't have the confidence of his officers, CPOs, and petty officers. Unhappiness had been brewing for some time and this capped it. The ship simmered in Plymouth, then, on the morning she was due to sail on operations, all the men below leading hand shut themselves in the messdecks and refused to fall in. It was mutiny, nothing less, and in time of war. When Holms heard the news he had a heart attack and was taken straight to hospital and the First Lieutenant was put in command. The men got on with their duties without a murmur and the ship sailed that evening to cover support groups in the Bay of Biscay. Ten days later Commander Jimmy Hibbard, DSC, arrived to take over. *Iroquois* went on to play her full role with spirit and élan.

The ship's company had taken aim at one man alone – their Captain. His leadership had failed and he never had another sea command. No one, in fact, was brought to task. The solution at the time, with Holms's heart attack, had been fortuitous and quick, and the whole disgraceful matter was downplayed as an "incident." This wasn't an isolated case, though the circumstances gave it special prominence. The RN, the USN, and other Canadian ships had similar incidents. But *Iroquois*'s was an altogether bad precedent and it was not to be forgotten.

Athabaskan was next to commission. In August she was covering the Canadian 6th Escort Group in an anti-U-boat sweep off northwest Spain when twenty-one Dorniers and Junkers 88s roared in to attack. The guns blazed away. The sky puffed with shell bursts. Down plunged the Junkers' bombs, throwing up towering columns of water. The ships dodged, weaved, and bucked through the splashes. Then the Dorniers circled curiously and launched something quite new. Missiles with wings glided down and actually changed course to zero in on their targets. In fact, they were radio-controlled, visually guided "glider bombs." As with the Gnat a few months later, the Canadians were in on the launching of a new and ugly weapon.

"Chase-me-Charlie" didn't draw blood that day but it was clear enough what it was. The way to handle it was to fire at the mother plane with the heavy guns and try to hit the bomb with close-range fire. But the Tribals' three twin 4.7-inch mounts wouldn't elevate enough to hit a high target. Their only fully effective long-range anti-aircraft gun was the twin 4-inch.

As at Dunkirk, British gunnery was still far behind the air threat. The gunnery control computers in these most modern of destroyers were designed to hit aircraft flying straight and level – something they rarely did when attacking ships. Radar helped, but the Royal Navy hadn't caught up to either enemies or Allies. If Canada had taken Winston Churchill's advice early on and bought Fletcher-class destroyers from the U.S. instead of Tribals, far better gunnery systems would have come with them.

For close-range weapons the British pom-pom wasn't a patch on the Swedish 40mm Bofors. The Swiss 20mm Oerlikon was better than anything the British or Americans had developed in that class. Both were built in Britain and the United States under licence. In 1943, though, aiming the close-range guns was just changing over from open sights, by-guess-and-good-luck to a U.S.-developed gyro gunsight.

Two days after the glider bomb's debut the Dorniers were back, and they had sharpened their technique. One completely destroyed the RN sloop *Egret*. Another hit *Athabaskan* up forward. A tremendous explosion racked her and set her ablaze. But Captain Gus Miles had seen this before. He'd brought *Saguenay* safely in after her torpedoing in 1940. All hands worked round the clock battling fires, shoring bulkheads, restoring power. She was a sitting duck for air attack and U-boats, but she limped the long haul back to Plymouth under her own steam.

By December *Athabaskan* was repaired and up to Scapa Flow to join her three sisters. Lieutenant Commander John Stubbs, who had duelled his U-boat in *Assiniboine*, was her new Captain. Sweeps in northern waters and fighting Russian convoys through were the hard business of that winter, but all the captains were top hands. *Huron*, with Lieutenant Commander Herbie Rayner in command, did three round trips to Murmansk; *Haida*, with Commander Harry DeWolf, the senior of the four, did two; Jimmy Hibbard's *Iroquois* and Stubbs's *Athabaskan* one each.

In these far northern latitudes they laboured through pitch black, bitter cold, howling gales. Harry DeWolf would have preferred it otherwise. He was seasick all his career and carried his own bucket with him in heavy weather. It was not much consolation that Admiral Nelson had had the same affliction. Air attack was less of a worry in the winter dark but U-boats were on the attack. The biggest threat, though, lay hidden in the Norwegian fjords.

Over Christmas, 1943, *Haida*, *Iroquois*, and *Huron* were hammering their way northward with convoy JW 55B when the powerful German battleship *Scharnhorst* slipped out and made straight for them. The Tribals, with only four torpedoes each, were ordered to stay as close escort. The big, solid echo on their radars bored steadily in. They got set for a last-ditch defence while the cruisers made spirited thrusts at the menacing giant. Twice *Scharnhorst* turned away. Then, fought off by the terriers, she ran south. The Tribals stayed with the convoy as they were told. The cruisers shadowed *Scharnhorst*. Meantime, the battleship *Duke of York*, with more cruisers and destroyers, was neatly positioned to intercept and closed the trap. She detected the lone enemy on radar at thirty-three miles. Her ten 14-inch guns and her consorts' torpedoes hammered *Scharnhorst* to death. There were thirty-six survivors.

Tirpitz still lay in hiding along the Norwegian coast, but with *Scharnhorst* sunk the Tribals were released from the Russian run and joined the 10th Destroyer Flotilla in Plymouth. The job: to secure the western flank of the invasion against the German surface ships based in the French ports. To do it the RN pulled together the heaviest destroyers they could find.

THE FIGHTING TENTH

Royal Navy Tribals had been in the thick of the action since war began. Losses had been heavy. The war-toughened survivors were *Tartar* (the leader), *Eskimo, Ashanti,* and *Nubian*. Now came *Haida*, *Huron*, and *Athabaskan*. *Iroquois* joined from refit in June. Meanwhile *Javelin*, a lighter version with one less gun mounting, joined, plus two Polish ships, *Blyskawika* and *Piorun*. The destroyers were backed by the 5.25-inch-gunned cruisers *Bellona* and *Black Prince*. It was a powerful small-ship fighting force, under command of Admiral Leatham, C-in-C Plymouth.

The first objective was to clear the Channel of German destroyers. There were two basic plans, always carried out at night. Operation Tunnel meant offensive patrol along the French coast to disrupt the German convoys; Operation Hostile covered the fast minelayers that raced across to enemy harbour approaches and focal points. Either one gave a good chance of meeting enemy destroyers, probably under the guns of their own shore batteries and in close waters laced with minefields.

The Channel coast of France conjures up centuries of blockade and battle. The coast runs its weather-lashed way west from Cherbourg, past the

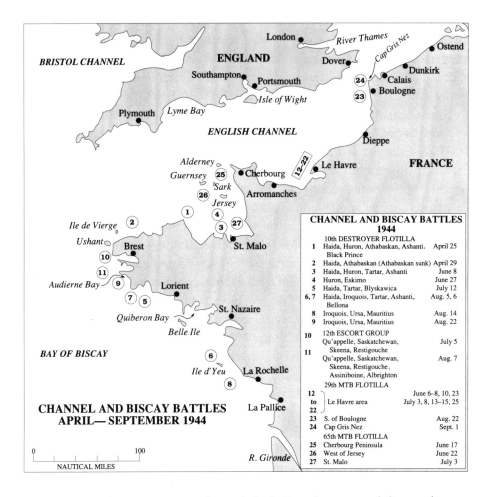

CHANNEL AND BISCAY BATTLES 1944		
10th DESTROYER FLOTILLA		
1	Haida, Huron, Athabaskan, Ashanti, Black Prince	April 25
2	Haida, Athabaskan (Athabaskan sunk)	April 29
3	Haida, Huron, Tartar, Ashanti	June 8
4	Huron, Eskimo	June 27
5	Haida, Tartar, Blyskawica	July 12
6, 7	Haida, Iroquois, Tartar, Ashanti, Bellona	Aug. 5, 6
8	Iroquois, Ursa, Mauritius	Aug. 14
9	Iroquois, Ursa, Mauritius	Aug. 22
10	12th ESCORT GROUP Qu'appelle, Saskatchewan, Skeena, Restigouche	July 5
11	Qu'appelle, Saskatchewan, Skeena, Restigouche, Assiniboine, Albrighton	Aug. 7
	29th MTB FLOTILLA	
12 to 22	Le Havre area	June 6–8, 10, 23 July 3, 8, 13–15, 25
23	S. of Boulogne	Aug. 22
24	Cap Gris Nez	Sept. 1
	65th MTB FLOTILLA	
25	Cherbourg Peninsula	June 17
26	West of Jersey	June 22
27	St. Malo	July 3

**CHANNEL AND BISCAY BATTLES
APRIL— SEPTEMBER 1944**

Channel Islands, ancient St. Malo, and Ile de Bas, then around the northwestern extremity of France, with Ile de Vierge and Ushant laying off, then down past Brest. It is rock-bound and tide swept, a constant challenge to the seaman. There are countless islets, rocks, shoals, and inlets. Brest itself is tucked well back, guarded to the north by Ushant and a ring of saw-toothed islets called the Black Stones. To the south lies a rocky shoal, The Saints. Further south is another deep gash, Audierne Bay, then the stretch to Lorient and down past Ile d'Yeu to La Pallice. To the natural hazards and hiding-holes for E-boats – the fast motor torpedo boats – add the minefields, the shore radar and the coastal batteries, and the enemy on his own home ground. This was no place for the faint-hearted.

The flotilla ran its first operation in January. Harry DeWolf, the senior Canadian, said it was lucky they didn't meet the enemy. The ships needed a lot more training together in night encounters. In early March they missed the enemy twice. Admiral Leatham was a man for brisk action, and he put in a new

Flotilla Captain (D), Commander Basil Jones, RN. Jones was an experienced destroyer man and he got on well with his COs. In his view the Canadian ships and their captains were "highly efficient and full of aggressive spirit."

The enemy forces hidden in the French ports were powerful Narvik-class destroyers mounting five 5.9-inch guns and eight torpedoes and smaller Elbings with four 4.1-inch and eight torpedoes. As well, high-speed E-boats could be expected to dart out with their dangerous armament of four torpedoes. The close escorts for the German convoys were small but heavily gunned flack-ships, trawlers, and minesweepers. Shore batteries had radar. The break of dawn would bring the air strikes unless fighter cover was at hand. From Ushant back to Plymouth is 120 miles – four hours as the Tribals steamed.

Plotting the tactical situation had come a long way with radar and HF/DF and better radio. The ships had efficient little action information centres. But all the sensors were "aids." Human eyes and ears were basic, and the Captain fought his ship from the open bridge. His razor-edged decisions and the zip of a finely trained ship's company were the margin between win and lose, life and death. And cold, clear decisions must come as the ship shuddered, the guns roared, the tracers came arcing in, and the white-hot metal flew.

It was a strange interlude. The core of Plymouth, levelled in the blitz, was acres of rubble crisscrossed by tidily bulldozed streets. The pubs, the dance halls, the hostels, the hotels, the grassy Hoe where Drake played bowls – that was always a place for lovers. And that sunny spring, with its lovely green and peaceful fields, sunken lanes, and rolling hills, its country inns and hideaways, Devon was a place for life, not death. All of this just hours from the crash of gunfire.

The flotilla fought in divisions, usually four ships. By late April *Haida* had completed nineteen night missions. Clear of the swept channel, they ran across at speed and turned along the French coast, radar sweeping to pick up the enemy, then out of it by daylight because of German aircraft. As Harry DeWolf said: "If you were unlucky ten times, on the eleventh time you might meet them." On 25 April they did. *Tartar* was in refit. *Haida, Huron, Athabaskan*, and *Ashanti* were backed by *Black Prince*. At two in the morning they ran head on into three Elbing-class destroyers. According to plan *Black Prince* lay back and lit with starshell. The Germans turned away through their own smoke screens, hit by the Tribals and hit again. One turned back, fired torpedoes at *Black Prince*, and escaped. Another, *T29*, was stopped by *Haida* and *Athabaskan*'s gunfire. They blasted her to a blazing wreck and down she went. In the mêlée all four Tribals fired torpedoes without one hit. The flotilla had more confidence in their guns than their torpedoes from then on. On the way back to Plymouth *Ashanti* collided with *Huron*, lightly but enough to put them both out of action for a while.

The next two nights *Haida* and *Athabaskan* covered a large pre-invasion exercise called Operation Tiger. After the Tribals were called away, E-boats swarmed in among the landing craft, lashing out with their torpedoes and guns; 400 American soldiers drowned. On the 29th of April the same pair were in mid-Channel when coastal radar in Britain got a very-long-range contact near the French coast. In they went. Likely it was *T24* and *T27*, which they had hit four nights before running from St. Malo to Brest for repairs.

Action crews closed up; doors and hatches were dogged down; damage control crews settled in position. The "Y" operators scanned radio frequencies, strained on their headsets for German voices. Eyes glued to radar scans. Lookouts swept the black line of the horizon, focusing a little above it because at night the eye picks up off-centre objects better. Every man wore his life jacket, clean clothes in case of wounds, anti-flash hoods and gloves for burns; all on deck wore steel helmets.

A final test of gun circuits, ammunition at the ready. The Captain takes the mike. "Captain speaking. Plymouth radar's got two contacts and . . ." Every man hangs on the words. Guns' crews coil down, sheltered from the spray.

Four a.m. Radar contact. Two ships, running south for Brest. All hands alert. Gunnery radar has them now. Starshell ready. All guns load, load, load. DeWolf sends a quick message on voice radio. The wheels go over, the ships lean sharply, turn toward, increase speed.

"Illuminate." Up go the 4-inch starshell. They burst in clear white, falling light. There they are. Two Elbings, all right. The director tower has them, selects one, reports: "Director, target."

"Engage" – crisply from the Captain. Six 4.7s thunder. Gun-blasts sweep the bridge again and again and stun the ears. *Athabaskan* is firing, too. The Germans turn away. "Hard a-starboard." The Canadians alter 30 degrees to sidestep torpedoes. They're still turning and *Athabaskan* reports: "I'm hit and losing power."

DeWolf goes hard over and lays smoke to cover his consort. It's one on two now. He drives *Haida* full speed after them, guns blazing. Astern there's fire in *Athabaskan*, the flash of an explosion. Ahead the enemy splits. They're firing back with after guns, their tracers curving in. If they turn on him together. . . . *Haida* concentrates on *T27*, the hits making small, bright orange flashes. The enemy's afire now, weaving, runs hard ashore, a blazing, battered wreck. The other has a big lead now. DeWolf looks at the sky. It's getting on for dawn. He turns *Haida* back to the rescue.

Athabaskan, hit by a torpedo, had quickly settled aft. Fires broke out and in minutes there was another explosion. Some thought it was shore batteries, others were certain an E-boat got them. Reports reached the bridge that the main engines were finished. She was settling quickly, and Stubbs knew she was done. He passed the wrenching words: "Abandon ship."

Haida got back in the breaking dawn. Lifejacket lights blinked and bobbed. *Haida* stopped among them, slipped all her boats and floats. Scramble nets dropped down her side. Men climbed down and pulled up forty-two oil-soaked men. *Haida* lay just five miles from the enemy coast, in easy range of shore batteries. Aircraft could be overhead any time. The tide was setting, moving the ship, and there were mines.

John Stubbs called up to DeWolf from the water: "Get away. Get clear." It was DeWolf's decision. He had to give priority to the safety of his own ship. It was 5:15 a.m. Twenty minutes more. Then there was no choice. He had to leave good friends in the water.

Haida's motor cutter was left behind. Leading Stoker Bill MacLure had picked up Able Seaman Jack Hannam and Ordnance Artificer Fraser Murray, who had been swept off the scramble nets while fishing men from the water. They rescued eight *Athabaskans* who weren't in the carley floats, then headed north. Just in time. German minesweepers were on their way to collect prisoners. They made it all the way to England in their twenty-seven-foot boat. Eighty-three officers and men ended up in prison camp; one hundred and twenty-eight of *Athabaskan*'s company were lost, including Lieutenant Commander John Hamilton Stubbs, DSO.

Three Narviks and two Elbings remained in the French ports. The sweeps went on through the nights of May but they didn't show their noses. Then on D-Day, 6 June 1944, the whole 10th Flotilla was waiting for them on the western flank as the mighty assault armada sailed for the Normandy beaches. At dusk on 8 June air reconnaissance spotted four destroyers leaving Brest. They were making north toward Cherbourg. Eight ships of the flotilla raced across the Channel and met the four straight on.

It was a blazing, close-in mêlée. The experienced ships did the scoring. *Tartar* and *Ashanti* sank a powerful ex-Dutch destroyer, then damaged a Narvik, but *Tartar* took four shells in her bridge. Boiler room damage slowed her. *Haida* and *Huron* chased old adversary *T24* and Narvik *Z24*. They hit both hard but had to skirt a minefield and the two got back to Brest. Back to the fight, they nailed Narvik *Z32*, hit before by *Tartar*. For three hours they chased her, hitting again and again, and drove her ashore on Isle de Bas, a flaming wreck. Two destroyed and two heavily damaged. That finished the German destroyers as a threat to Operation Neptune. The Fighting 10th had done its job.

Nor did the U-boats get at the invasion fleet. Only two actually penetrated the area and one landing ship was sunk. In two weeks in June, Coastal Command aircraft sank six and damaged seven in the Channel. Ships sank four, one of these shared by *Eskimo* and *Haida* under Harry DeWolf. "Hard-over Harry," Commander Basil Jones said, "was an outstanding officer, not only in skill but in aggressive spirit. Furthermore, he had that priceless gift of fortune . . . of there always being a target in whatever area he was told to operate.''

Three nights later *Huron* and *Eskimo* caught a minesweeper and three trawlers. *Huron*, with the quiet, imperturbable Herbie Rayner in command, sank the sweeper and a trawler. In the enemy's smoke screen *Eskimo* got very close to another trawler. It bravely fired back with everything it had – 20mm shells bursting in the engine room knocked out power to her guns and radar. *Huron* ran interference while *Eskimo* recovered her faculties and her dignity, and the incident pointed out some sharp lessons: destroyers had very thin skins; the more sophisticated a ship, the more vulnerable it became to a minor blow; and the Kriegsmarine hadn't lost its fighting spirit. It didn't pay to get too close.

On the lst of July Harry DeWolf was promoted to Captain. If he'd been an RN officer he'd have had command of the flotilla, and Basil Jones would have been the last to say he didn't deserve it. Admiral Leatham, though, underlined to both of them that Jones was in command. DeWolf never said a word, but other Canadians, with justification, took it as a slap in the face and another piece of that old RN superiority. Still, the mutual regard of men who fought so hard together made things work. Later, Jones was made an Acting Captain, which didn't answer the basic question but it did look better.

On the night of 12 July, *Haida*, *Tartar*, and *Blyskawika* steamed close under the shore batteries near Lorient. In an hour they sank two merchant ships and a trawler. *Haida* hammered away at another darkened vessel, which stopped but wouldn't sink. She moved in for the kill. Hilariously, it turned out to be a gunnery practice target.

The U-boats had left the French ports for Norway by August but the garrisons stayed. The countryside swarmed with Maquis guerrillas, who hit road and rail transport so hard that German coastal convoys were stepped up. On 5 August, *Haida*, *Iroquois*, *Tartar*, and *Ashanti*, with the cruiser *Bellona* as back-up, had a busy night. They caught a formation off Ile d'Yeu and in twelve minutes sank seven vessels. *Haida* sank her first in four minutes but a charge at the after gun mount exploded, killing two, wounding eight, and knocking the gun out of action. But she didn't miss a beat, and they hit a second convoy right under the noses of the shore batteries.

Iroquois had come back from refit too late for the invasion, but she caught up. With RN cruiser *Mauritius* and destroyer *Ursa* she hit three convoys in a week, two in Audierne Bay. They sank seven ships and drove five ashore in flames, including an Elbing. Jimmy Hibbard marked some up for the ships he'd seen go down in convoy SC 42 three years back.

In late September Operation Neptune ended. The Channel coast was quiet, the war in Europe on the way to being won. The 10th Flotilla had piled up a remarkable record: thirty-three enemy ships and one U-boat sunk in three months of furious fighting, to a loss of one of their own. These blistering, brilliant actions proved an important point in a way that the shrouded, groping battles on the convoy lanes could not. They showed the RN, the public, and the navy itself that Canadian sailors could fight with the very best.

There was another message, too. Canadians reacted strongly against routine and rote they didn't understand. But, given common sense and strong leadership of the kind that understood them, they would rise to the heights. In the Tribals in that spring and summer of 1944 it was all there.

Of all the farewell signals they received on leaving Plymouth, the top of the list was flashed to them by the Wrens in the Signal Station who had seen them so often come and go. It's final verse:

We hope we'll always see you thus with ensigns flying free
For the Fighting Tenth's a lovely sight when coming in from sea.

DESTROYERS WITH THE FLEET

In February, 1944, two RN V-class fleet destroyers commissioned into the RCN as HMCS *Algonquin* and *Sioux* and joined the Home Fleet's 26th Flotilla. Their captains, Lieutenant Commanders Debby Piers and Eric Boak, and most of their companies had a lot of North Atlantic experience. But it was a far cry from Senior Officer of Escort on slow convoys to small cog in a huge, high-speed striking fleet.

At the end of March they joined a massive *Tirpitz* strike with two fleet carriers and four escort carriers. More strikes followed along the Norwegian coast, then they joined the great Neptune armada, two of the seventy-eight fleet destroyers that pounded special targets on D-Day. Then it was back to Scapa Flow, screening carriers – mostly dull business.

In early November, *Algonquin* joined cruisers *Kent* and *Bellona* and three other destroyers on a Norwegian coastal sweep. Near Egersund, through a gap in the screen of inshore islands, they caught an eleven-ship convoy. The cruisers pumped out starshell. The destroyers raced in with guns and torpedoes. *Algonquin* hit an escort with her first broadside and in minutes six of the enemy were ablaze. Shore batteries lit the attackers with starshell and big shells plunged close aboard, but the destroyers chased their quarries right in, sank eight, and drove one aground.

On a bitterly cold New Year's 1944-45 they both fought mountainous seas and U-boats on their way to Russia. Their only casualty was Canadian pride. In their layover in Murmansk *Algonquin*'s hockey team trounced *Sioux*'s but then lost to the Murmansk all-stars. The tournament, played "with Russian equipment and Russian rules," was a foretaste of international hockey to come. There were more Russian convoys, then both ships went back to

Halifax to get set for the Pacific war. *Algonquin* had reached Alexandria, heading east, when Japan surrendered.

LITTLE SHIPS IN NARROW SEAS

Many of the new Reserve officers who went to England for training in 1940 found their way to Coastal Forces. The high-speed motor torpedo boats and motor gun boats fought in the narrow seas and they were night birds. Running out of Channel and east coast ports, they snapped constantly at the enemy. They hit his convoys, defended their own from German E-boats; they landed and backed up raiding parties, attacked transiting U-boats and surface ships. There were countless fierce lightning-fast engagements. Casualties were high; succession to command was often very quick.

Some went to the Mediterranean. One of them was Lieutenant Tom Fuller, RCNVR, a profane, colourful, two-fisted character from the construction business. Close along the African shore as the desert battle seesawed, then with the Sicilian landings, the Italian operations, in the Aegean and the Adriatic, Fuller had a charmed life. He counted 105 gun and torpedo actions, plus another thirty operations without a fight. He wrote off thirteen boats along the way. When he was working with Tito's Yugoslavian partisans, a journalist dubbed him "the Pirate of the Adriatic."

MTBs called for quick thinking, innovation, and a special individual leadership. It took all kinds. Lieutenant Tony Law, RCNVR, was dead opposite of Fuller. He was a small, soft-spoken, and thoughtful man, an established artist before the war. He commanded an RN boat that went in to attack *Scharnhorst* and *Gneisenau* when they broke through the English Channel in February, 1942. Later, while waiting for the Canadian flotillas to form, he went off as an official war artist and put some fine naval canvases into Canada's national collection. He was also an artist in running MTBs.

In late 1943 the RN had offered to provide boats if the RCN would man them. Law was promoted to Lieutenant Commander and given command of the 29th Canadian MTB Flotilla. There were eight of the G-type Short boats – seventy-two feet long, forty-knot speed, two 18-inch torpedoes, a 6-pounder, and twin 20mm guns. They carried three officers and fourteen men. Lieutenant Commander J.R.H. Kirkpatrick, RCNVR, another shoot-from-the-hip type like Fuller, commanded the 65th Flotilla. He had ten 115-foot D-type boats with a speed of thirty knots and twice the armament – four torpedoes, two 6-pounders, and two twin 20mm –and twice the number of men.

The German E-boats were much better vessels. They were more heavily armed and made forty-eight knots on supercharged diesel engines. British craft ran on 100-octane gasoline and it caused some terrible casualties. However, the RN boats had much better radar. They were directed into battle rather like fighter aircraft by a skilfully run radar system from their headquarters ashore.

For D-Day Kirkpatrick's 65th was in the armada's western flank. The Tribals had done such a thorough job there that the MTBs quickly turned to striking coastal convoys inside the Channel Islands. They were wild shoot-outs – destroyer battles in miniature but at twice the speed, one-tenth the range, and a far higher rate of killed and wounded.

Le Havre, just a few miles east of the beachhead, harboured a nest of E-boats, some slower, more powerful R-boats, and two Elbing destroyers. They were the business of Tony Law's 29th. The open, storm-tossed invasion anchorage was busy around the clock. At night starshell lit the sky and MTB tracers crisscrossed with the enemy's in fierce actions along the flank. At daylight the little boats off-loaded casualties, got reliefs if they could, fuelled, and repaired. In the time left they snatched some rest tethered to a frigate's stern.

In early July, Lieutenant David Killam's MTB 460 was demolished by a mine. The only survivors were the gunners in their life jackets and bulletproof vests. Law's 459 was hit by a shore battery off Cap La Havre, and 463 (Lieutenant D.G. Creba, RCNVR) was blown up by a pressure mine. The constant close-range gunfights pushed casualties for the flotilla close to 30 per cent.

The action moved west with the land battle as the First Canadian Army drove through Belgium and Holland during the summer and fall. Convoys ran from the Thames to Antwerp, and MTB bases were set up in liberated ports. On 14 February 1945 the 29th was tucked into the inner basin in Ostend along with several RN flotillas. There had been trouble with water in the fuel. Tanks had to be pumped and 100-octane gasoline lingered on the surface. Suddenly, in mid-afternoon, the gasoline went up in a tremendous sheet of flame. It was a holocaust – boats blew up; men were thrown like blazing dolls into the fiery water. Five of the 29th and seven RN boats were destroyed. Twenty-six Canadian and thirty-five British sailors died in the searing flames.

Tony Law was in Felixstowe with his second boat for radar repairs when he heard of his flotilla's tragic fate and the loss of so many hard-fighting friends. Death in battle was the luck of the game. MTB sailors lived with it every night. But now accident had done what the enemy could not. The 29th flotilla was finished. The 65th fought on to the end of the European war. Then they turned their boats back to the RN in June, 1945, and went home.

CHAPTER NINE
THE END OF
THE U-BOAT WAR

OPERATION NEPTUNE

IN AMONG THE MAMMOTH ALLIED FORCES INVADING THE NORMANDY coast on 6 June 1944, the U-boats could have dealt out havoc on a grand scale. They were much tougher to handle by then, with their Gnats and snorkels. That they did not impede the invasion was testimony to the ultimate success of earlier Allied actions – along the North American coast, on the Atlantic convoy routes, in the Channel and around the coasts of Europe. Now they could deploy huge, efficient anti-submarine forces. But Grosadmiral Dönitz's U-boat fleet remained a lurking, dangerous presence to the end.

Overlord, the invasion of fortress Europe, mounted the greatest seaborne assault of all time. Operation Neptune, the naval side, mustered a vast armada of 5,300 ships and landing craft. They had to land 150,000 men and 1,500 tanks over a fifty-mile span of Normandy beaches in the vital first forty-eight hours. Then, over a million men and millions of tons of material must move in. They would land over the beaches and the portable Mulberry harbours until regular ports were taken by the armies. The Mulberries were a stroke of genius and, remarkably, were kept completely secret. So convinced was the German General Staff that the Allies must take major harbours right away that their army was caught off balance. It was a key factor in the failure of their plan of defence.

Channels through the minefields had to be cleared and the whole armada protected from surface, submarine, and air incursion. Shore defences, beaches, and batteries had to be neutralized by air and warship bombardment during the critical run-in and landing when the army had little firepower of its own. Units fighting their way inland had to have naval gunfire on call until their own artillery arms were fully deployed.

To Operation Neptune, Canada sent sixty-one ships, sixteen MTBs, and thirty LCI(L) – landing craft infantry (large). The Tribals and the 29th and 65th MTB flotillas were closely engaged before and during the invasion, as we have seen. Nine escort destroyers of the 11th and 12th escort groups and eleven frigates of the 6th and 9th escort groups joined the anti-submarine campaign. The two fleet destroyers were in the bombardment force. Nineteen corvettes assigned to Western Approaches ran close escort to the endless stream of shipping heading to and from the beachhead.

THE MINESWEEPERS

Mostly, minesweeping was an unglamorous, unsung, and dreary job. In an assault, though, the battleships, destroyers, and landing ships stood back and gave the humble sweepers pride of place. They were essential. They were expendable. They led the way. Slow and steady, close along a hostile shore with mines below and the barrels of the shore batteries looking down – this was a job for steadiness, precision, and iron nerve.

Sixteen Bangor minesweepers were pulled from their Canadian east coast convoy escort duties and sent to the U.K. in late February, 1944. They had to be re-equipped and trained from scratch because this was a role they had virtually never filled. Ten of them formed the 31st Canadian Minesweeping Flotilla under Commander A.H.G. Storrs, RCNR, in HMCS *Caraquet*. The other six joined the RN's 4th, 14th, and 16th flotillas. Ten flotillas in all were assigned and each had one channel to sweep.

The great day approached. The troop convoys and tanks rumbled through the choked-up English roads. Invasion ports right across southern England were chock-a-block with landing ships and craft. Troops, tanks, vehicles streamed endlessly aboard. Then the weather went sour.

Surf along the beaches could kill an assault that guns couldn't. Landing craft skippers sniffed the wind, peered anxiously at the sky. They were the ones, the sub-lieutenants and the leading seamen, who had to put those first platoons safely on the beach. They were expendable, like the sweepers. In fact, the cold-blooded planners had already written off the whole first wave of assault craft. Delay D-Day? The juggernaut was rolling. How long before the Germans knew, and more, guessed where it was headed? Weather, time, and tide . . . the Admiral could advise, but only the Supreme Commander could make the decision. A one-day delay and General Eisenhower said, "Go."

On D minus One, 5 June, at 5:30 p.m., the sweepers headed south for the French coast. Each flotilla was in staggered sweep formation. Seven swept. Three stayed in their wake ready to take over if one blew up. Trawlers followed close behind, stacked with dan-buoys. They marked the safe channel for the main force following behind. All of this required pin-point navigation. The sweepers had the most advanced radio fixing system akin to later Decca and Loran. Running right to the minute and down to the last few yards was crucial to success. Night fell. Tides shifted. Courses were adjusted. There could be no light but the dim glow of the compass repeaters on the sweepers' bridges leading in.

The coast loomed, dark, forbidding. Lookouts strained for E-boats, destroyers, flak ships. Could they get away with this? Knocking right on Europe's door? At three a.m., right on schedule, the 31st had cleared channel number 3. They stood nakedly alone, one and a half miles off the line of surf on Omaha Beach where the Americans would land at dawn. The moon broke from the clouds. Tony Storrs turned his flotilla and methodically combed his transport anchorage, then the fire support lane the bombarding ships would use. Efficiently, precisely, the sweepers had earned their front-row seats.

At 5:15 a.m. they saw the first of the assault ships come in through their swept waters, heard the anchor cables roar and rattle. Out of the pre-dawn loomed the big-gunned battleships, USS *Texas* and *Arkansas*, cruisers, and destroyers. Overhead the drone of aircraft gathered volume. Planeloads of paratroops, transports towing troop gliders, headed for their targets. Right across the front through all ten swept channels the armada was moving in.

The sweepers' plodding work – widening channels, clearing new areas, sweeping for fresh-sown mines – would go on for weeks, scarcely noticed. But 100 minesweepers had quietly and efficiently led the way to the fortress door.

THE ASSAULT

Ten lines of ships streamed in. Well to the east of the 31st, in the British-Canadian sector, *Prince Henry* followed *Algonquin* through Lane 7, *Prince David* followed *Sioux* through Lane 8. They anchored seven miles offshore. On board each were over 400 first-wave troops, mostly of the Third Canadian Division. *Prince David*'s were Le Régiment de la Chaudière and a Royal Marine assault party. *Prince Henry*'s were Canadian Scottish Regiment.

Now it was all by the clock. Out swung the davits. Down went the scramble nets. Eight forty-one foot LCAs in each ship slipped smoothly down into the choppy sea. Engines, finely tuned, barked alive. Each craft, its thirty-man platoon embarked, slipped and headed in. The first wave was away. Toward the beach and whatever lay in store the assault wave crawled in a great wrinkled line across the entire massive front. Right on time the bigger craft came in behind them straight from the U.K. They carried tanks, special breaching vehicles, and guns. In the assault craft that rough hour-long, seasick-making, heart-in-mouth run to the beach was for the soldiers the most miserable D-Day memory of them all.

With daylight to see their targets, the ships' big guns opened up. Shells by the thousands roared over the heads of the landing craft. Ahead of them, bucking and pitching, could be seen the flashes and the bursts all along the shore. *Algonquin* and *Sioux*'s targets were gun batteries that could rake the beaches. They knocked them out, shifted to other buildings that could hide defenders. The amphibious tanks – marginally seaworthy with collapsible canvas bulwarks – were delayed because of rough seas. But the lighter destroyers close inshore and the gun-carrying and rocket-firing landing craft blasted the beaches with their fire.

Just before touch-down the thunderous bombardment stopped. Except for the sounds of engines and the sea there was an awesome silence. Then, suddenly, the hush was broken. The enemy, battered and stunned but not out, fired back with everything he had.

It was rough along the beaches – the surf was heavy; jagged obstacles were as thick as a picket fence; mines were everywhere. Two of *Prince Henry*'s LCAs charging in to Red Mike beach struck obstacles and broached sideways in the surf, but all her craft made it in. Within five minutes their soldiers were racing for the sand dunes. To the east *Prince David*'s craft had trouble. Machine-gun bullets laced the beaches. Mortar bombs plunged down among the craft and the attacking troops. Only one craft reached the beach undamaged but they all got their soldiers ashore. All along the beaches lay stranded and broken craft, overturned tanks. Bodies mixed with swimmers struggling in the surf. In many places casualties were heavy. Surviving craft brought wounded out to the anchorages. But the assault troops were ashore. They were fighting their way in, making their objectives.

Over *Algonquin*'s radio came a call for fire. Three German 88s two miles inland were holding up Le Régiment de la Chaudière. Piers and his men couldn't see them but the Forward Observation Officer – the artilleryman ashore with the infantry – could and he passed the map co-ordinates. After quick position plotting, measured range, and bearing, the ship fired two single guns for ranging. The observation officer radioed corrections. The third salvo was dead on. Then the ship shook to three full broadsides of four guns each. They were right on target, the enemy was silenced, and the Chaudières moved on.

Whatever the planners had said, one craft returned to *Prince David* and all save one of *Prince Henry*'s survived. Follow-up troops went in on tank landing craft that had unloaded and hauled themselves off the beach on the rising tide. That afternoon both "Princes" sailed for England with their loads of wounded. Then they brought reinforcements to the beaches for the steady massive build-up to break out of the hard-won bridgehead.

Meantime, the second wave had moved in directly from the U.K. in the larger landing craft, along with tanks, vehicles, and guns. The 260th and 262nd Canadian flotillas were hit heavily by mine explosions, mortar, and machine-gun fire. The lucky 264th had a clear run in. They beached in heavy surf on beach Jig Red in perfect formation. All their troops ran ashore intact. The three Canadian flotillas put 4,600 men ashore on D-Day. Only a few Canadian sailors were wounded in the operation and not a single one was killed. Most damaged craft were salvaged from the beach to fight another day.

The Canadian corvettes brought in all sorts of vessels. They navigated for landing craft, escorted transports, herded barges. They brought in blockships – tired old vessels to be sunk as breakwaters. They trudged back and forth for days on end, brought in the great concrete Mulberries with their heavy cranes and cargo-handling gear to be flooded down on the beach at Arromanches.

Operation Neptune was superbly planned and near-flawlessly carried out. Canadian sailors in 107 varied vessels played their parts and played them well. No small part of the honours went to the anti-submarine forces that had so badly mauled the U-boats and at the crucial time kept them well and truly at bay.

THE CANADIAN SUPPORT GROUPS

The Royal Canadian Navy's MOEF destroyers, formed into two support groups, had trained at Londonderry and then joined the great pre-invasion U-boat hunt. In Neptune they were part of the blanket of anti-submarine force that virtually smothered U-boat opposition.

Escort Group 12 had *Qu'Appelle*, commissioned in February, *Saskatchewan*, and hoary North Atlantic veterans *Skeena* and *Restigouche*. In one go at a U-boat they battered away for twenty hours, drew no less than seven Gnats, raised tons of fish with their Hedgehogs and depth charges, but got no kill. The foe was still wily and tough. Then in early July they had their turn at the classic destroyer role – surface action.

Fitted as escorts, they had long since traded guns and torpedoes for more depth charges and Hedgehogs. *Saskatchewan* had three of her 4.7-inch guns left, the others had only two. All were down to four torpedoes. Their companies had seen many a scrambling fight with U-boats, but for most of them tangling with a surface foe was something new.

Operation Dredger was, in fact, a special anti-submarine operation. U-boats were being heavily escorted in and out of Brest and the idea was for a strike force to knock out the escorts so an anti-submarine group could have a clear run. On the night of 5-6 July EG 12 had its turn. They ran well to seaward off Ushant to avoid radar detection, then headed in toward The Saints, the rocky cluster a little south of Brest. The rock-girt coast painted on the radar scans as they closed. At about midnight, new echoes appeared, just outside the harbour minefield. Ships, but what kind? Destroyers? U-boats? Minesweepers? The M-class sweepers were slow but they carried two 5-inch guns, a match for two 4.7s, and they had plenty of close-range firepower.

Commander A.M. McKillop, RN, the Senior Officer in *Qu'Appelle*, led the group right inshore, then turned north, curving toward the targets. The plots in the ops rooms developed fast: to the northwest, the harbour of Brest; the channel buoys could be seen on radar. Four ships were running out in line ahead, and the notorious Black Stones were just beyond. With a burst of speed, *Qu'Appelle* swung westward parallel to the enemy's line. The others followed tight in the wake of the next ahead. It was a beautiful manoeuvre. They'd come up right behind the enemy, cut him off from harbour, and trapped him against the Black Stones. At 4,000 yards up went the starshell: four M-class heading to sea, and two U-boats. The destroyers stormed past, blazing away at the sweepers one-on-one, loosing torpedoes as they went by. The enemy fought back with everything he had.

Alan Easton, *Saskatchewan*'s Captain, had fought U-boats in *Sackville*. But now he saw the tracers lacing both ways "like streams of liquid fire," felt the hammering of shellfire and the waves of heat and gunsmoke, saw his own shells hit home and the enemy's fire coming straight back. The leader turned to reverse course and Easton followed around as they drove straight in the enemy's teeth once more.

Qu'Appelle and *Saskatchewan* cut right through the enemy line. Standing a mere half-mile off the Black Stones, they blazed away at four hundred yards range. The rear destroyers were hard at it, too. Three of the enemy were wiped out in a few short minutes. The fourth, and possibly the two submarines, turned back into Brest.

But as in *Huron* and *Eskimo*'s party ten days before, EG 12 paid the price of close action. *Qu'Appelle's* steering was knocked out, her bridge was riddled with 20mm, her Captain and several others badly wounded. Pat Russell in *Skeena* also had some wounded. He took over as SO. David Groos's *Restigouche* got off lightly. Easton's *Saskatchewan*, radar knocked out, had one dead and seven wounded. The medical officer had to amputate a man's arm as the ship sped back to Plymouth.

A month later EG 12 had a turn at the Tribals' game. Commander J.D. Birch, RNR, had replaced the wounded McKillop in *Qu'Appelle*. *Assiniboine*, with Lieutenant Commander Bob Welland, had joined the group, as had HMS *Albrighton*. They found no convoy but between Brest and Lorient they caught three trawlers and drove them ashore in flames. To Alan Easton this kind of crashing action was far preferable to the gnawing, drawn-out anxiety with the convoys in the U-boat war. And if you were hurt here you could get home in a few hours. There was hardly a man who didn't feel the same.

Escort Group 11, on the other hand, got no run at the gunfighting but fared much better with the U-boats. Chummy Prentice had left his acting rank as Captain (D) Halifax to go back to sea as Senior Officer in *Ottawa*. Just as EG 12 was coming in from its first night of action, *Ottawa* and *Kootenay* joined the RN frigate *Statice*, which was holding a contact in the Channel.

This area had all the anti-submarine snags and pitfalls: poor asdic conditions, shoals of fish, strong and changeable currents, continuous heavy traffic, a bottom strewn with the wrecks of centuries. To sort U-boats from the wrecks the navigational echo sounder was a very useful gadget. If a ship steered right over something on the bottom the paper trace would show a neat graphic outline. This particular object had, distinctly, a hull and conning tower.

Prentice had a team of top hands. His Staff Officer Anti-Submarine, Lieutenant Bob Timbrell (DSC from Dunkirk, sunk in *Margaree*), was one of the three fully qualified "Long A/S" specialists in the navy. Bob Welland and Pat Russell, both driving destroyers in EG 12, were the others.

This U-boat, however, had all the tricks in the book. They'd caught her with their first Hedgehog attack and confirmed her with the echo sounder. But with the tide running the charges and Hedgehog bombs were swept aside and they couldn't open her up. Then came some sailors' resourcefulness. They armed a depth charge with an electric detonator and lowered it over the side on a wire with a grappling hook attached, then steamed slowly over the bottomed U-boat, dragging the charge along the bottom. The grapnel caught the U-boat. The gunner on deck saw the wire tighten, triggered the charge, and it cracked her open like an egg. The grisly evidence bubbling to the surface showed it was *U-678*. In mid-August on a Biscay patrol, *Ottawa*, *Kootenay*, and *Chaudière* methodically destroyed two more. That made a wartime four U-boats for Chummy Prentice and three each for Lieutenant Commander Pat Nixon of *Chaudière* and Lieutenant Commander Bill Willson of *Kootenay*.

The frigates of EG 6 and EG 9 had some hard luck on Neptune. *Teme* was rammed and cut nearly in half by an escort carrier. She was repaired and back with the group by February. But in a few weeks she was torpedoed. With sixty feet of stern gone, her career was over. *Matane* was hit by a glider bomb but lived to fight again. Corvettes *Regina* and *Alberni* went down like stones to torpedoes with heavy losses. Success came to EG 9 at last on 31 August. *Saint John* and *Swansea* caught a U-boat off Land's End. It took them twenty-four hours but finally up came the wreckage. Among it was a certificate marking the ten-millionth engine revolution of *U-257*. On the record at the time, this was *Swansea*'s third kill. In fact, it was her fourth.

In September, Operation Neptune wound to an end. There was hard fighting to come before Europe was liberated. The Russian convoys still must be fought through and there could be no let up on the Atlantic convoy lanes. But the weight of the Royal Navy was shifting to the support of the U.S. Pacific Fleet. Plans were afoot for the RCN to join them.

THE MEDITERRANEAN

After Neptune the big landing craft were turned back to the USN for the Pacific war, and the three flotillas disbanded. But the landing ships *Prince David* and *Prince Henry* were off in late July for Naples. This time it was Operation Dragoon, General Patton's invasion of the south of France, planned for the 15th of August east of Toulon.

Shore batteries on three islands and one shore flank commanded the landing area. In the pitch dark, hours before the landings, the two Canadian ships moved close inshore to send in Commandoes. All of them reached their targets. There was some sharp fighting and every battery was knocked out. But this was no Normandy. The main landings met little opposition and Patton's tanks swept north.

In September the German occupation of Greece was being challenged by guerrillas of differing political stripes. Yugoslavia, too, was on the boil. The "Princes" ran troops about the Adriatic and Aegean, then lifted the Greek Prime Minister-designate, M. Papandreou, and supporting troops to Piraeus, the port of Athens. The reception was very uncertain. The ships anchored off while Canadian landing craft made a cautious advance probe into the harbour. But they were met with wild enthusiasm as liberators. The ships then pitched in, repatriating prisoners of war and refugees. *Henry* moved 4,400 of these poor unfortunates, plus all their baggage and uncounted sheep, goats, and chickens.

Admiralty wanted both ships in Southeast Asia, but the Canadian government didn't want to be identified with restoring colonial regimes so both ships were transferred to the RN. *Prince Robert*, in the meantime, had put in solid service as an anti-aircraft cruiser with convoys from the U.K. into the Mediterranean – seventeen in all. By now she was back in Esquimalt refitting for the Pacific.

THE LAST OF THE U-BOATS

Losing their French bases put the U-boats off their stride but it didn't knock them out. North Germany and Norway served as bases and Dönitz sent his boats far and wide. It was a long-standing principle of his to stretch and dilute his enemy's force. Hit and run by lone roving boats scored no great tonnage but it made the Allies stick to convoys. Even if the U-boats were beaten – which Dönitz would never admit to his men even though he did to himself – they still tied down a huge effort. His staff estimated over half a million Allied personnel were tied up in escorting, supporting, patrolling, organizing, and maintaining the whole convoy effort.

The U-boats had made real technical advances: snorkels were better and more widely fitted; Gnats had improved; radar search detectors covered the 10cm band; radar itself was being fitted for the first time; improved batteries

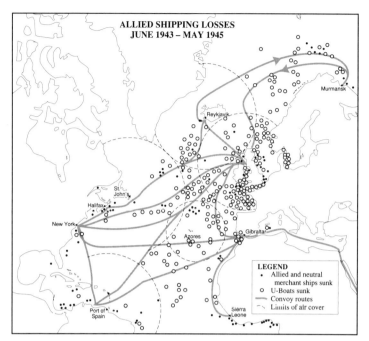

ALLIED SHIPPING LOSSES
JUNE 1943 – MAY 1945

LEGEND
• Allied and neutral
  merchant ships sunk
○ U-Boats sunk
— Convoy routes
- - Limits of air cover

June, 1943 – May, 1945. The U-boats were beaten on the Atlantic but they fought back with new weapons and equipment. After D-Day they concentrated around Britain, though some still ranged far afield to stretch Allied resources. With the loss of their French bases they fought to the end from Norway and the Baltic.

boosted submerged endurance. Now there was the prospect of the high-performance Type XXI. Offsetting all that, their shattering losses meant experienced hands were critically short.

They tried mining again, that cheap and potent way for an inferior navy to tie up its enemy. *U-119* had laid sixty-six moored mines off Halifax harbour in June, 1943, and a similar field was planted off St. John's that October. Their toll then was small – one ship sunk and one damaged – but they delayed sailings and drew a big effort away from anti-submarine work. Another try in July, 1944, was nipped when two boats were sunk by the groups of USN carriers *Card* and *Bogue*. By fall, however, there were five U-boats in Canadian waters.

Since the disastrous summer of 1942 the Gulf of St. Lawrence had been closed except for local traffic. The only incursions had been two bizarre and very risky tries at snatching escaped U-boat POWs from shore. One didn't come off. The other was a real thriller. It showed to what lengths Admiral Dönitz would go to bolster the U-boat man's morale.

Prisoners in a camp near Belleville, Ontario, included the legendary ace Otto Kretschmer, captured in 1942. They talked to U-boat headquarters by mail passed through the Red Cross using a memorized code. It took a year, but finally a rendezvous was set in Baie des Chaleurs. A mass escape from the camp via a tunnel was foiled but Kapitanleutnant Wolfgang Heyda slipped away and made it to the rendezvous by train. However, the plan had been uncovered by searching mail and a party under the ubiquitous Lieutenant Commander Debby Piers was waiting on the spot, complete with radio, portable radar, and a cordon of ten ships flung across the bay. The aim was to capture the rescue boat.

U-536 slipped in and quietly waited off the appointed spot right on time. Heyda was hauled in by Piers's party from the beach but the U-boat twigged to the ship activity and crept away. Had Dönitz got one of his men back to Germany, Kretschmer especially, it would have been a remarkable coup.

From spring, 1944, joiners for ocean convoys ran to and from Quebec again. All was peaceful in the Gulf until September. Then the corvette *Norsyd* put a U-boat down off Anticosti and drew a Gnat in return. It missed. The frigate *Magog* with a convoy well up the river mouth was hit and lost sixty feet of her stern. In early November, when traffic had dwindled, a grain ship was torpedoed in the same area. The Gulf asdic conditions still had the escorts baffled.

At the end of November the corvette *Shawinigan*, with USCG *Sassafrass*, escorted the routine run by the ferry *Burgeo* from Sydney to Port aux Basques. The *Caribou* tragedy of 1942 was a very live memory and U-boats were certainly about. But NOIC Sydney detached the U.S. ship without relief, leaving the lone corvette for the ferry's return run. Then *Shawinigan* went off on an independent patrol, planning to meet the ferry in the morning. That was the second mistake. If she did run into a U-boat singlehanded she'd be no match.

In the morning *Burgeo* left Port aux Basques on schedule, but in the fog outside she found no escort waiting. Mistake three, by the Master: he ignored standing instructions and headed for Sydney unescorted. Mistake four, by the Master again: he kept radio silence and didn't report *Shawinigan* as "not met." Only when he got to Sydney at 6 p.m. did the navy know the corvette was missing. Eight hours of precious daylight search time were lost. Over the next three days searchers combing the icy waters found carley floats, flotsam, and finally six bodies. *Shawinigan* had been hit in clear moonlight by a Gnat fired at 3,000 yards from *U-1228*. All eighty-five of her company died, victims of a train of blunders.

In the meantime there was running warfare along the convoy lanes. On 10 September a Liberator of RCAF 423 Squadron got a contact south of the Hebrides. C5 ships *Hespeler* and *Dunver* moved in and sank *U-484*. Then the frigate *Chebogue*, on a convoy in mid-Atlantic, was completely crippled by a Gnat. In mid-October the frigate *Annan*, patrolling with EG 6 near the Faeroe Islands, got a solid submarine contact and dropped a pattern. The group searched but lost their quarry. *Annan* was RN-built, commissioned into the

RCN in June, and fresh from work-up at Tobermory. Leaving the area after dark she got a radar contact astern, turned, and chased back.

Annan was by herself. The echo was, in fact, *U-1006*, damaged by the earlier depth charges, making off on the surface. Tactical instructions said it was deadly dangerous for a single ship to approach a U-boat now that they had the Gnat. Also, it was important to "step aside" with a big alteration of course to avoid the vicious weapon. But Lieutenant Commander C.P. Balfry raced straight in, fired illuminating rockets, spotted the enemy, and opened fire with all guns. A blistering return fire knocked out his radar but he pressed in and fired depth charges right alongside the surfaced boat. One actually bounced off the casing. Up she went, then down. The group arrived in time to pick up forty-six prisoners. *Annan* got sole credit for the kill. The decision that wins a battle can hardly be considered wrong.

Six frigates of EG 9 did a Russia convoy in December and were back with the return run to Greenock on the Clyde for Christmas. Greenock had been a familiar and friendly place to the Canadians since 1940. HMCS *Niobe*, the navy's manning and accounting depot, had been there from late 1941 in a gloomy and drafty old mental institution. Parts of industrial Clydebank and nearby Glasgow were very tough indeed, but Scots by and large were friendly to Canadians. Ships could book ice at the arena in Paisley for a hockey game. Eggs, milk, and cream could be found at farms. In nearby Gourock the Bay Hotel escaped the bombs. It was run by a warm-hearted and steady-handed lady named Jean Cook who will always be remembered as a generous friend of the RCN. It seemed that Miss Cook had some secret line to Admiralty and Western Approaches because she always knew who was in what ship and what ship was where.

Christmas, 1944, was a time for optimism and high hopes. But the war wasn't over. On 21 December a merchant ship was torpedoed right in the Halifax approaches and a trooper was due to sail on Christmas Eve. There was a major step-up in patrols. Among many others, Lieutenant Commander Craig Campbell and the ship's company of his Bangor sweeper *Clayoquot* were called back from Christmas leave.

At mid-day on Christmas Eve, *Clayoquot*, another Bangor, *Transcona*, and the frigate *Kirkland Lake* with Commander N.V. Clark, RCNR, in command were sweeping about three miles from Sambro Light Vessel. Just as the off-watch hands mustered in *Clayoquot*'s forward messdeck for grog a torpedo hit her aft. It was a Gnat fired by *U-806*, the same boat that had hit the merchant ship three days before. *Clayoquot* went down like a stone. The search force grew quickly to fourteen escorts and seven MLs. Captain W.L. Puxley, RN, Captain (D) Halifax, ordered Clark in *Kirkland Lake* to take tactical command on the scene (as, in fact, he already had in the time-honoured way). But four hours later Puxley sent out the shore-based Staff Officer AS Training, an RN officer senior to Clark, to take over. It was the kind of RN assumption of superiority that really galled.

The massive search expanded systematically, assuming the U-boat was making for deep water. In fact, *U-806* lay doggo and dead quiet on the bottom in shallow water right by the shipping channel between Halifax harbour and the point where *Clayoquot* went down. Her Captain had short U-boat experience but he was a cool customer. Hour after hour he lay with everything shut down and his men dead still in the fetid air. He listened to the "circular-saw" noises of the searchers' Cats. He heard the gravel-scrape of their asdics along his hull. Finally, near midnight, he tiptoed away from the scene. He didn't even show his snorkel for twenty more hours. His crew had their first breath of fresh air forty hours after submerging. Then with batteries topped up and the boat aired out, *U-806* settled on the bottom and celebrated Christmas one day late.

Three modern Type IX C boats were in Nova Scotia waters to read the New Year's signal from Admiral Commanding U-boats: "Our watchword remains the same! Attack, let 'em have it, sink ships. Sieg Heil." Grosadmiral Dönitz added, "The striking power of our Service will be strengthened in the New Year by new Boats."

This was no idle talk. Snorkel-fitted U-boats were very hard to find. In British waters there were over 400 escort vessels and close to 400 Coastal Command aircraft; Murray had around ninety ships and Eastern Air Command had ninety-four aircraft. It was taking an enormous force to keep things even.

The German construction was taking a beating from the RAF. Nonetheless, intelligence said they would very soon have seventy boats on patrol, including twenty-five of the Type XXI. These new boats ran sixteen knots submerged with great endurance. They would put a whole new complexion on the battle. The First Sea Lord warned of a devastating campaign that could cut seriously into supplies for the land battle in Europe. There was a deadly sting in the U-boat force's tail.

Early in the New Year *U-1232* sank two ships out of three in a convoy off Egg Island, twenty miles from Halifax. A major hunt geared up, but her Captain slipped in just two miles east of Sambro Light and caught a Boston-Halifax convoy strung out in single line, coming in the channel like ducks in a shooting gallery. He torpedoed three ships in thirteen minutes.

The frigate *Ettrick* sowed a string of depth charges in the right neighbourhood, and in fact, ran right over the U-boat and actually ripped off the forward net guard with her Cat. She didn't know it at the time, but the U-boat did. A massive search proved fruitless. Six merchant ships and one escort in half as many weeks with no loss in return was good pickings. U-boat headquarters planned a massive campaign. The action heated up.

In February the frigate *Saint John* killed her second U-boat in Moray Firth on the northeast coast of Scotland. Then *Trentonian* was sunk off Falmouth. Next *La Hulloise*, *Strathadam*, and *Thetford Mines* of EG 25, with Lieutenant Commander Jeffry Brock, RCNVR, as Senior Officer, got a kill. In March *New Glasgow* rammed a U-boat outside Lough Foyle. The others in EG 26 joined in but Lieutenant Commander Ross Hanbury, RCNVR, of *New Glasgow* properly got the credit.

The Senior Officer of EG 26 was Commander Ted Simmons, RCNVR, in *Beacon Hill*. He had started his U-boat killing with Prentice in *Chambly* in 1941 and got another in the Mediterranean. Of the eight frigates in these two actions, six were commanded by officers of the RCNVR. Five years of hard experience had turned the Saturday night sailors into highly competent sea-going officers. These frigates were up-to-date, well manned, well trained; they were first-class fighting ships.

In February and March a dozen U-boats made for the eastern seaboard and either passed through or operated in Canadian waters. Group Seawolf of six boats went out for the last pack attacks on the convoys. Two U.S. carriers and twenty destroyers got four of them in a week. Through the late winter months U-boat reports and contacts soared in Murray's command. Two frigate groups now worked out of Halifax and put in a lot of chasing, but without any luck.

Early on 16 April the Bangor *Esquimalt* was on anti-submarine patrol in the Halifax approaches. She was due to meet a sister ship, *Sarnia*, on independent patrol in another sector, at 7 a.m. It was calm and clear and she had switched off her old radar; it wouldn't detect a U-boat periscope or snorkel anyway. She pinged away with her even older asdic. It was only a slight improvement over the first sets that went to sea under wraps in the 1920s. Like all her sister minesweepers, even with a top crew and the best will in the world, *Esquimalt* on her own was absolutely no match for a U-boat.

Close to Sambro Light Vessel at 6:20 that morning she ran right smack into one. *U-190* was lying quietly in the favoured spot waiting for a juicy target when *Esquimalt*'s asdic came scratching along her hull. It was like stepping on a coiled snake. The U-boat Captain took a quick cut with his periscope at an escort coming right at him. He snapped off a Gnat; it went straight home. The ship's asdic operator reported nothing. No one sent a radio message or even fired a flare. The stricken ship went down in four minutes almost within hail of the Light Vessel. Two of six carley float releases stuck fast because they hadn't been looked after.

PO Writer Terrence Manuel, just off watch at the depth-charge throwers, had stripped to his shorts and stretched out in his mess for some shut-eye. Somehow he popped out through a wall of water. He got to a floating kit bag, helped a shipmate cling to it. As it slowly sank, PO Motor Mechanic Carl

Jacques spotted them from a carley float. He knew his messmate, Manuel, couldn't swim. He called, "Hold on, Scribe," swam over, got them back to the float. The effort in the bitter cold was just too much. Jacques died. His friend lived.

Like Manuel, most men were in light clothing, the Chief Bosun's Mate in red pyjamas, the Navigating Officer in shirt and shorts. Few had life jackets handy. The lessons of the North Atlantic weren't taken to heart here. But the sea was smooth, the shore near, Sambro Light Vessel not far off. Rescue must be at hand.

The sun rose, bright and clear. Aircraft overflew, but they thought the carley floats were fishermen. They didn't even circle. The light vessel crew, surely they'd seen the sinking and radioed in. But they must have been asleep. Then two minesweepers approached. Cheers, shouts, frantic waving. The sweepers' officers of the watch and lookouts must have been asleep, too. In horrified disbelief the survivors watched them pass within two miles, then fade away. Spirits then sank as deep as their own lost ship – the water was like ice; cold crept deep into the bones; men drifted off, and died.

It was seven hours before *Sarnia* came across the survivors and radioed the first word on the sinking. Forty-four out of seventy perished with home and safety a few short miles away, most during those fateful, unbelievable seven hours.

This sinking had its deadly train of errors. *Esquimalt* wasn't zigzagging. Neither had she streamed her Cat – though, in any event, she wouldn't have had time to trip it. She was by herself. Why, with the harsh lessons of *Shawinigan*, *Clayoquot*, and a multitude more, were any ships, much less those ill-equipped Bangors, still sent out singly on patrol? The Board of Inquiry didn't put that tough question to Captain (D) or his Admiral. Neither did it find out what happened to *Sarnia*'s radio report made when *Esquimalt* didn't show up at the rendezvous. Did it get lost? Or did Operations ashore just shrug it off? Some link in the chain failed, fatally. But there was no Court Martial to reveal it.

Keeping an ill-equipped ship on her toes is doubly hard when doing dull chores on your own doorstep, seemingly a long way from the action. On that sunlit April morning, too, the war seemed all but over. *Esquimalt*'s Captain, Lieutenant Robert MacMillan, RCNVR, was experienced. He had won a DSC and his promotion to Lieutenant Commander was on its way through. But the U-boats were still out there, deadly to the end, and his ship wasn't in top gear. Neither were communications and operational control in the Atlantic Command.

The search that followed the sinking, with every ship available, concentrated along the hundred-fathom line. But *U-190*'s Captain did exactly what his forerunner on the Sambro shooting range had done – bottomed in shallow water and waited it out. Admiral Murray got a USN group to help with the search. No one caught U-190 but destroyers USS *Buckley* and *Reuben James II* – familiar names on the North Atlantic – did sink U-879. The USN by now deployed a huge anti-submarine force. Down the eastern seaboard the curtain closed. It was the twilight of the U-boats' war.

Esquimalt was the Royal Canadian Navy's last loss. In three weeks came Germany's final surrender, and with it events in Halifax that would submerge all else. Headquarters found the Board of Inquiry's report "inconclusive" and the file was closed. But wrapped up in *Esquimalt* and the men who died needlessly that day were all the navy's problems: equipment, manning, training, maintenance. Going right back to lack of pre-war policy, the navy began the war with far too little. Then it had taken on too much, and after the long years of war it was still too thinly spread.

RECKONING

The U-boats' homeland was in flames behind them. The north German bases and the building yards at Hamburg, Kiel, Wilhelmshaven, Lubeck were smashed to rubble by the RAF ahead of the advancing armies. The U-boat pens were too thick with reinforced concrete for the RAF's Blockbusters, but the cities were completely shattered.

In early May the Germans scuttled over a hundred U-boats in home waters. Dönitz cancelled the order but still more were sunk by their own crews. Out at sea they "fought like lions," as Grosadmiral Dönitz said of his own, until the very end. It was on his order that they surfaced at last with black flags of surrender flying. The deadly U-190 was brought into Bay Bulls south of St. John's and U-889 to Shelburne under the White Ensign of Canada's navy. The Battle of the Atlantic was won.

Surrender came with no answer to the remarkable new submarines. Had Hitler understood his navy better, given more to his U-boats before the war, paid less heed to Raeder and more to Dönitz earlier, and allocated resources sooner for the new types, Karl Dönitz and his superbly fashioned U-boat force could well have won Germany the war.

They started with fifty-seven operational boats, built well over 1,000; in January, 1944, the fleet reached its peak of 445. Among them they sank 2,603 merchant ships – 13.5 million tons – and 175 Allied warships. They killed over 50,000 people. Five thousand U-boatmen were taken prisoner, and the submarine war cost Germany 632 U-boats and 28,000 men lost at sea. Thus, 70 per cent of the 40,000 who went to sea in U-boats died fighting. No other major formation in any war of modern record, anywhere, has suffered such a ghastly toll. To fight to the end amid such carnage was a truly awesome feat of arms. Their own numbers were comparatively small – a bad day's casualties in one battle on the Russian front. But their battle was the lynchpin of the war, and they came within a hair of winning.

The RN and USN, too, had badly undercalled the U-boat threat and overestimated their ability to handle it. The right ships and equipment weren't there when the war started. Then there were serious failures in high-level decision-making: the agonizing American delay in starting convoys in 1942; low priority on long-range aircraft for the North Atlantic; spending air effort on Biscay sweeps instead of concentrating it around the convoys; delays in getting escort carriers into the Battle of the Atlantic.

This was the sole battle of the Second World War that ran its full five and a half years. There were blunders in Naval Headquarters. Blunders in command. Blunders out at sea. But Canada's navy, starting off with next to nothing, learned to fight out there on the convoy lanes against the toughest and the best. And they learned their hard trade more than passing well.

CHAPTER TEN

BEGINNINGS AND ENDINGS

THE BEGINNING OF CANADIAN NAVAL AVIATION

THE ROYAL CANADIAN NAVAL AIR SERVICE OF 1918 WAS STILLBORN. ADMIral Lord Jellicoe included aircraft carriers in his 1920 proposals for Canada's postwar fleet, but the navy barely survived and could dream of nothing so ambitious as its own aviation. The RCAF was responsible for shore-based maritime air, as was the RAF. At the start of the war it was even less ready. Organizing, training, and equipping to fight the U-boats took time and travail, just as it did in the navy. Co-ordination between the two left a lot to be desired.

Seaborne aviation was crucial to controlling the sea. The Royal Navy hadn't really grasped this and lagged behind Japanese and U.S. naval aviation in peacetime and paid for it severely. But by 1942 the naval air lessons were legion: defeat off Norway; the key roll of the Fleet Air Arm in the Mediterranean in beating the Italian fleet and fighting convoys through; *Bismarck* caught by some intrepid little Swordfish; Pearl Harbor; the sinking of *Repulse* and *Prince of Wales* off Malaya; Midway and the mounting series of American amphibious assaults. Then – right in the Canadian navy's line of business – the proven power of shipborne aircraft out with the convoys in the battle against the U-boats.

Land-based air was vital, of course, and British experience had proved that whatever uniform the air crew wore, they must be under naval operational control. But distance and weather cut effectiveness. Every naval air expedient had proved its worth against the U-boats: the CAM ships – merchant ships with catapults that launched a lone single-mission fighter to shoot down the Kondor reconnaisance-bombers; the MAC ships – cargo-carrying merchant ships with lash-up flight decks and a clutch of creaking old Swordfish; the first escort carrier, HMS *Audacity*, using fighters to put down U-boats in 1941.

Wherever naval shipborne aircraft came to bear, the balance tipped against the submarine.

But naval aviation was vastly expensive and complex, and a very high-skill, hard-risk business. Combat flying in the 1940s was tough enough. For naval pilots, add the sad fact that most British naval aircraft were ludicrously inadequate. Then throw in the problems of navigating with a plotting board on one knee over the weather-plagued ocean to find pinpoint targets. Press in your attack, then get back to your carrier that's been dodging the enemy unpredictably in the meantime. Pitch in the vagaries of weather and lack of alternate airfields. Cap it off by landing on a ridiculously small, violently heaving deck offering no room for error. Naval aviators, at any stage of advancing technology, always have to be the very best. In any navy in those war years their skill, bravery, ingenuity, *joie de vivre*, insouciance even, were extremely high. They had to be, because so many died.

Early in the war a few adventurous Canadians had found their way into the Fleet Air Arm. Ted Edwards joined the RCNVR and worked up to command. He led his RN squadron of Wildcats and Swordfish against the super battle-ship *Tirpitz* lying in a Norwegian fjord in April, 1944. In the same operation Lieutenant Commander Digby Cosh, RCNVR, commanded a squadron of Wildcats, four other Canadians flew fighters and bombers, and two were fighter direction officers in the fleet carriers.

In December, 1942, Admiralty, suffering the manpower shortage that had so much effect on the shape of the RCN, asked for more Canadians to train as Fleet Air Arm air crew but stay in the RCNVR, i.e., be paid by Canada. In NSHQ, Acting Captains Nelson Lay (Director of Operations) and Harry DeWolf (Director of Plans) jumped in. These two forward thinkers were Vice Admiral Nelles's operational advisers and they pushed hard to send people for advance experience in RN escort carriers and get four "Woolworths" – escort carriers cheaply built with merchant ship hulls – one for each of the Canadian groups on the MOEF.

In the spring of 1943 Captain Lay went off for familiarization and fact-finding in the States and the U.K. At the end of August, with DeWolf gone to command *Haida*, Lay made a one-man report to the Naval Board. He recommended a Royal Canadian Naval Air Service modelled on the RN's Fleet Air Arm. That was pretty well pre-ordained. It struck no one as strange that Lay had spent only two weeks with the USN compared to two months with the RN. The navy was too RN-aligned to think otherwise. Technical matters and subjects like whose aircraft to use didn't enter seriously in the matter, and Lay had had no air engineer or pilot to advise him.

He recommended that two escort carriers be procured and manned by the RCN and shore-based maritime air be left to the RCAF. The air force agreed to provide the shore support in Canada and that made for trouble after the war. Adopting U.S. Navy pattern aviation from the start, which included shore-based maritime air, would have shaped a very different future for Canada's navy. Had Lay made a pitch for it the RCAF would certainly have fought. Also, he wouldn't have had much support from Admirals Murray or Jones, the operational commanders. They weren't at all air-minded. At the time, too, the task of getting the carrier end going loomed quite large enough in the sights of the overstretched Naval Staff.

Things moved quickly. At the Quebec Conference of August, 1943, it was clear the U-boat was under control. Production of escort vessels was cut. Now the Allies' aim, beyond the invasion of Europe, was on the Pacific. Canadian navy recruiting and training were in full gear and Admiral Pound wanted manpower. Escort carriers were needed for both oceans. Nelles and the Naval Staff were determined to finish the war with a lot more than a small-ship navy, and a balanced big-ship fleet certainly would want naval aviation. It was as good as done.

Two escort carriers, *Nabob* and *Puncher*, built for the RN in Seattle, commissioned in September, 1943, and February, 1944. The RN constructors didn't accept the American practice in things like watertight subdivisions, so the ships moved to Vancouver for conversion. The RCN wanted anti-submarine carriers but these were fitted for the strike role. The RN owned them and there was no changing that. So that Canada wouldn't be accepting Lend-Lease aid, both ships stayed on the British books as "HMS."

The RN provided the entire aviation component. Shore support came from the RN on the eastern side of the Atlantic and from the RCAF on the west. Captain Nelson Lay, the only senior RCN officer who had had even a few weeks' exposure to modern carrier operations, took command of *Nabob*. Captain Roger Bidwell took *Puncher*.

Nabob picked up the RN's 852 Squadron with their Avenger torpedo-bombers in San Francisco in January, 1944, and headed east through Panama. She had an unhappy start. In carriers the aviators and sailors work different and often conflicting routines. In the best-ordered ships it's not easy to keep them hauling together. With some 300 RN air people, 500 inexperienced Canadians doing the seamen's chores, and the engine room manned substantially by British merchant seamen on special RN engagements, this ship's company was a real dog's breakfast.

As well, RN rates of pay were a lot lower than those of the Canadians. So was the daily victualling allowance. RN standard prevailed and the food was terrible. On the very first takeoff the aircraft ditched. A mutiny by a few men was nipped in the bud when the ship fortuitously went to action stations in the Caribbean. When she got to Norfolk, Virginia, there were deserters, mostly young new entries who apparently hadn't bargained on going overseas. Lay had a problem on his hands and wouldn't take his ship to sea until he had things sorted out. He flew to Ottawa himself and got Canadian victualling scales all-round and RCN rates of pay for RN personnel other than the air arm.

When *Nabob* got active in U.K. waters, things shook down. By July she joined Home Fleet strikes on Norway. *Tirpitz* had been hit in the April strikes and then she was attacked by midget submarines. But she was still a menace. By mid-August the whole of the Home Fleet that hadn't gone to the Indian Ocean and the Pacific sallied from Scapa Flow on Operation Goodwood. It wasn't a patch on the scale of American carrier task forces in the Pacific but it was the biggest air operation ever planned by the RN. The core of the attack, Force 1, had three fleet carriers with a battleship, three cruisers, and thirteen destroyers, including *Algonquin* and *Sioux*. Force 2 was *Nabob* and sister ship *Trumpeter*. With their stately maximum of eighteen knots they were escorted by five frigates.

They steamed north of the Arctic Circle through the summer's constant daylight into the Barents Sea. *Nabob*'s four Wildcats flew combat air patrols; her Avengers flew anti-submarine. This was U-boat country and the risk was high. Weather fouled the operation but three squadrons of Barracudas from the big carriers scored several hits on *Tirpitz*. Eleven of the sluggish planes were lost. Preparing for the second round, the escort carriers pulled westward to fuel the destroyers.

It was smooth and clear as *Nabob* laid out her fuelling hose, and without warning she was torpedoed. None of the escorts got a sniff of a submarine. Eight minutes later, HMS *Bickerton*, the senior officer on the screen, was hit. *Nabob*'s torpedo, from *U-345*, had ripped a fifty-foot hole below her waterline, starboard side aft. Her stern quickly sank by fifteen feet. Power went off the board. The electric engine-room fans stopped. The temperature soared to 150 degrees and main engines had to be shut down. The ship wallowed, a sitting duck. Up on deck boats and floats were slipped, ready to abandon ship. But far down in the dark and flooded recesses the damage control parties under Lieutenant Denny Forrester and the engine and boiler-room crews worked furiously to save their ship. There might be another torpedo. Or she could take an instant plunge. They would go with her if she did.

Groping in the dark, they gradually regained control. Emergency diesel generators came on line. Power leads snaked to auxiliary switchboards. Portable pumps were wrestled into place. Pumping mains were patched and began to draw. Flooding was limited and held down. But the key engine-room bulkheads bulged ominously inward from the enormous pressure of the sea that had rushed in through the huge underwater wound. With every roll of the ship they worked and creaked, ever nearer to bursting. Chief Shipwright

J.R. Ball coolly directed a complex timber-shoring operation to hold them firm. He'd got his practice salvaging damaged ships in St. John's.

Reports reached Lay on the bridge. Power restored, fans running again, steam on the turbines. *Nabob* began to move. But now she had no boats or floats. The injured and some 200 more were taken off by destroyer. The rest worked furiously, ditching heavy gear or working it forward to improve the trim. Gradually, Lay worked his crippled ship up to ten knots.

Early the next morning an HF/DF bearing, then a surface radar contact, said a U-boat was moving in. Two Avengers, their pilots' luck stretched to the limit, catapulted off the sloping deck. For three and a half hours they kept the intruder down. That gave *Nabob* a safe lead. But landing with the carrier moving at only ten knots and a sharp upwards slope to her deck called for inspired flying. One made it; one crashed and smashed six others in the deck-park. Live depth charges careened around the heaving deck. They were coralled before they rolled, perhaps fatally, over the side. But the Avengers had done their job.

More men were taken off by *Algonquin*, then a fierce gale blew in that pounded the crippled carrier for eleven hours. The toil below was ceaseless. Ball's classic shoring job, using every piece of timber in the ship, held firm. At last, five days and 1,100 miles since being hit, *Nabob* entered Scapa Flow under her own steam. She got a hero's welcome.

Right at the start of the war the fleet carrier *Courageous* had gone down quickly, victim of a single torpedo. Sound damage control likely could have saved her. But it had been treated in a lot of peacetime ships as a rather tiresome and grubby hobby of the engine-room department rather than a responsibility of all hands. Harsh wartime experience brought in proper control of watertight doors and hatches, training in fire-fighting and emergency operation, pumping and flooding and providing auxiliary power. *Nabob*'s team had learned their business well.

Later, in drydock in Rosyth, bodies of fourteen of the twenty-one dead and missing had to be recovered from the bowels of the ship. They had been down there a month. Dockyard mateys refused the job so ship's officers, fortified with stiff belts of rum, manhandled the wretched remains of their lost shipmates up deck by deck by deck.

Nelson Lay could be proud indeed of the mixed bag of a ship's company he had led through such a testing time. Seamanship and damage control and airmanship saved the ship. The sad irony after such a monumental struggle was that U.K. ship repair facilities were overtaxed. *Nabob*'s damage was judged too heavy for worthwhile repair. Her brief and gallant war was over.

In the meantime, in April, 1944, *Puncher* got to sea. She spent irksome months ferrying aircraft and passengers across the Atlantic. Not until early February, 1945, did she at last take on an operational load: fourteen Wildcats of RN 881 Squadron and four Barracudas of 821. Then for the next two months she was suddenly and fully in the war with five major operations off the Norwegian coast. First she flew air cover for an inshore surface striking force. Then she covered surface minelayers and flew fighter escort for mine-laying Avengers from *Premier*, her RN sister ship. Ten days later the two escort carriers were back covering minesweepers and launching Barracudas to drop mines. There were more strikes in March, and in early April another four-carrier operation aimed at the U-boat base in Kilbotn, Norway. But gales and huge seas north of the Arctic Circle knocked it out.

That was the end of *Puncher's* short, sharp operational life. The RN didn't need her in the Pacific and after V-E Day she had a quick conversion to a troopship. Bunks were welded in the hangar and until year-end she shuttled Canadian troops from the Clyde to Halifax. In January, 1946, Bidwell took her to Norfolk and turned her back to the USN, to whom, under Lend-Lease, she actually belonged.

Canada's two wartime carriers had proud, if brief, records. They were too late and in fact wrongly fitted to play the part DeWolf and Lay had planned for them with the Canadian escort groups in the North Atlantic. But they got Canadian sailor's feet wet in the complex, demanding business of running carriers. *Nabob* and *Puncher* wrote the introduction to modern Canadian naval aviation, a most important part of the navy's story. On one of *Puncher's* eastbound runs in October, 1945, she carried stores and a draft of men for the ship's company of HMCS *Warrior*. With that new light fleet carrier the story of Canada's own naval aviation would begin.

THE WRENS

The Women's Royal Naval Service was a strong organization in Britain in the Great War. WRNS of course right away became "Wrens" and it always seemed to characterize the brisk and cheerful way that Jenny Wren got about the job. Britain got women's services going again before World War Two broke out. Senior officers in Canada saw no place for women – other than as nurses, of course, who had proved themselves with armies in former wars.

Then in the spring of 1941 the RAF proposed sending some of its Women's Auxiliary Air Force to their training units in Canada. That did it. The RCAF and the army started women's services and began recruiting in the fall. NSHQ said all they needed was twenty women as motor transport drivers. In the turmoil of navy expansion women looked more like a problem than a solution. So the navy was a year behind the others. Only in January of 1942 was a Director of Women's Services appointed – a male, Captain Eustace Brock, RCNVR. Three WRNS officers borrowed from the RN did a fine job getting things going. Recruiting began with a selection committee of Captain Brock and Superintendent Joan Carpenter, WRNS. Her rank was equivalent to Captain.

The WRNS was an auxiliary service but the WRCNS was part of the navy so its people had regular naval ranks. Canadian female officers, however, wore blue stripes on their sleeves like the British; gold remained a male prerogative. In March, 1943, one of the original WRNS officers, Chief Officer (Commander) Dorothy Isherwood, took over from Captain Brock. That September the top post was taken over by Canadian Commander Adelaide Sinclair, who had been getting experience in the U.K.

At the outset 2,000 applications were on file. Sixty-seven were taken in for a month's training in Ottawa. A third of these became officers, the others Leading Wrens, and that was the start. Young women across Canada, eighteen to thirty-five, were urged to join the Wrens to release a man for sea service. There were plenty of volunteers.

Their basic training centre in Galt, Ontario, was a requisitioned correctional institute called the Grandview School for Girls. The first new entries started training in October under Dorothy Isherwood. HMCS *Conestoga* commissioned officially on 1 June 1943 under command of Lieutenant Commander Isobel Macncill, WRCNS, one of the original class. She was the only woman in the Commonwealth to command an independent naval establishment. *Conestoga*'s origins provided steel bars for the windows and an oppressive atmosphere. Tradition provided the names "Drake," "Nelson," "Collingwood," and "Beatty" for the buildings. A strange urge to give young women a salty edge to their talk gave everything shipboard names and levied punishment for failure to use them. Thus the bus that shuttled Wrens between "ship" and town became the "liberty boat." The kitchen was the "galley," the bathroom the "heads," dormitory rooms were "cabins," floors "decks," stairs "ladders," corridors "gangways." Doing one's laundry was "dhobeying," nightly cocoa was "kye." The lounge was the "fo'c'sle" and a wooden platform beside the parade ground was called the "quarterdeck" and demanded a salute on passing. When fire struck a dormitory block the occupants were turned out by the cry "Abandon ship!"

To learn one of some forty specialist ratings, Wrens went to the main naval schools. To the general astonishment of the average man of the day, they proved every bit as good, and often more efficient in the same position, as the men. Soon Wrens were not a burden but a very welcome addition. Nearly 7,000 joined. Five hundred of them served in the U.K., many more in Newfoundland, and some in the U.S. They did what their branch of the navy set out to do – release men for service at sea – and they did it extraordinarily well.

Wrens were an adventurous lot, but in today's terms they were often treated more as schoolgirls than as responsible young women. They suffered some gallingly Victorian restrictions. They were not, of course, allowed in the wet canteen in *Stadacona*, about the only place in Halifax where a sailor could buy a glass of beer. But in their undaunted and high-spirited way they learned to find their way around such things. And their very presence made life more pleasant for the men.

Sailors lives are womanless for long periods at the best of times. Ashore they quite naturally look for girls. In overcrowded, woman-shy wartime ports like Halifax, St. John's, and Londonderry, a dance to the Sally Ann juke box, sharing a Coke, then walking a Wren home to the barracks gate gave a man a lift. The cheerful girl's voice on the radio circuit, or a neatly turned-out Wren clambering aboard a corvette to take short-hand evidence at a Captain's investigation could lighten a forenoon's work. There was no official statement that an objective of Canadian women's services was to improve male morale, but the Wrens very definitely did. A more enlightened and realistic outlook would have produced more Wrens earlier – it would have done a lot for shoreside efficiency and for morale.

MEET THE NAVY

Some Wrens and sailors who had been in show business, and many who had not, joined the company of the unique and highly successful wartime stage musical *Meet the Navy*. It was the brainchild of Captain Joseph Connolly, RCNVR, Director of Special Services. With the help of Hollywood director John Farrow, a Volunteer Reserve officer, he reached Hollywood and Broadway for a top professional producer and a choreographer. There was no shortage of volunteers and the cast topped 200.

It was wonderfully fast-moving, zestful, tuneful, and funny – a smash hit from opening night in September, 1943. No one who heard John Pratt singing "You'll Get Used to It" in his peanut-sized cap and baggy stoker's coverall could take life in the navy too seriously again. After a year touring Canada, they went to the U.K. Through V-2 rocket attacks *Meet the Navy* played to packed houses at the London Hippodrome. They played for the King and Queen and after V-E Day entertained Allied troops across Europe. After a two-year commission the liveliest, best-looking, and undoubtedly the most unorthodox ship's company in the navy's history paid off.

Meet the Navy brought light and laughter to Canadian sailors – badly needed commodities in six years of war. Had some of that brand of creative energy been applied earlier at the roots of morale, the service could have been happier and, by definition, more efficient. As it was there were serious shortages, especially in Halifax, of the things that would have eased a sailor's life: recreational facilities; pleasant places to have a drink without the stony-faced Shore Patrol looking over the sailors' shoulders; clean rooms to have a comfortable night away from an overcrowded messdeck; reasonable, respectable rental accommodation so a man could have his wife and family near; many more restaurants.

Halifax had suffered badly in the depression. It was run down and poor and suddenly it was grossly overcrowded. Good-hearted citizens and volunteer organizations did everything they could, but very little was done by any level of government or by the navy itself to relieve the basic situation, to provide amenities. The very name of Halifax – "Slackers," as it was called – brought on a sailor's scorn. The attitude grew, unhappily. By war's end it had grown to the point of serious explosion.

THE MERCHANT MEN

"The Battle of the Atlantic was not won by any Navy or Air Force, it was won by the courage, fortitude and determination of the British and Allied Merchant Navy." So, at the end of the war, said Rear Admiral Leonard Murray, Commander-in-Chief Canadian North Atlantic

Canada herself, worldwide trading nation that she was, had allowed her peacetime merchant fleet to erode to a mere forty-one ocean-going ships. It was as small a token as her navy. In the first months of war Britain's coastal fleet was hard hit and Canada sent twenty-five lakers that could squeeze down the Lachine Canal. Six were at the beaches of Dunkirk; only nine survived the war. Later, others left the lakes to serve around the world and wartime building swelled the ocean-going ranks.

But Murray had his finger right on it. Had those embattled, rust-streaked ships not kept sailing through the terrible years of loneliness, misery, and loss after loss, the war itself would have been lost; all the vast effort, the blood, the technology and skill thrown against the U-boats would have been to no avail. Statistics were one thing. They told their ruinous, implacable tale. But what of the will to continue? At the end of 1942 Winston Churchill himself had seen sure death to the Allied cause, not so much in the struggle between the escorts, aircraft, and U-boats, as in the simple human loss of heart of the merchant seamen. It was his action to put the best of the escort groups on the Mid-Atlantic that had pushed the RCN aside.

As to organizing shipping, the RCN's Naval Control Service was ready at the start under Commander Eric Brand in Ottawa and in the key ports, and it stood the test. In Halifax, Commander Richard Oland, the Naval Control Service Officer, sailed the first convoy on 16 September 1939, ran things extraordinarily well, and died of endless overwork two years later just after promotion to Captain and winning the OBE.

Ships even in convoy needed some self-defence, if only for their own morale. A few pieces of old cannonry had been stored in Canada by Admiralty and there was an embryo organization called Defensively Equipped Merchant Ships or DEMS in Halifax to fit them and provide men to match. At first a ship would be lucky to have a turn-of-the-century 4-inch gun, a few shells, a stripped Lewis machine gun, and a single navy DEMS gunner. Even-

Day and night, in the tower high above the narrow entrance to St. John's, Wren signallers handled huge volumes of traffic. Some 7,000 young women learned a legion of naval trades to release men for sea duty. (*National Archives of Canada*)

Five of the eight motor torpedo boats of the 29th Canadian MTB Flotilla race across the Channel at their full 39 knots. These "G" type boats were 72 feet long with a crew of 17. They carried a 6-pounder gun forward, two 20mm, and two torpedoes. Here, though, for the invasion, their torpedo tubes have been replaced by depth charges for attacking submarines and manned torpedoes. (*National Archives of Canada*)

Kapuskasing, an Algerine minesweeper fitted for escort duty, fuels from a tanker in one of the last convoys of the war. Escorts' fuel was always a problem but underway fuelling was only introduced in the convoys in 1942. This astern method was slow but safer for merchant ships and the less powerful and less responsive escorts than was the alongside method familiar with fleet units. *Vancouver* is on the right. The photo was taken from *Barrie*'s bridge. (*National Archives of Canada*)

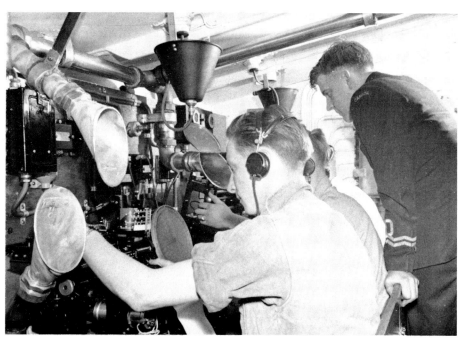

The asdic hut wedged in forward of the open bridge in corvette *Cobourg* is a tight squeeze. *Cobourg* was one of the twenty-seven corvettes commissioned in Canada in 1943 and 1944 with increased endurance and extended forecastle, mostly with gyro compasses and considerably better asdic than the originals. (*National Archives of Canada*)

V-E Day, 8 May 1945, in Halifax a day of shame. This scene on Barrington Street, at first glance, looks high-spirited enough for an old naval town with a couple of centuries of scuffles. But the rampage by servicemen and civilians was destructive. The breach between the navy and the city took many years to heal. (*Maritime Command Museum, N.D. Brodeur Collection*)

HMCS *Uganda* (*Quebec* from 1952 to 1956) runs with Task Force 57, the fast carriers and heavy ships of the British Pacific Fleet, in the summer of 1945. *Uganda* was designed at 8,800 tons, 555 feet, 30 knots speed, with nine 6-inch guns, four twin 4-inch anti-aircraft mountings, and a crew of 730. (*National Archives of Canada*)

The deck landing control officer or batsman in *Warrior* in late 1946. The job took experience and a fine pilot's eye. This human link in the hazardous business of landing on a carrier's deck was only eliminated by the RN invention of the mirror landing aid, and the angled flight-deck of the early fifties. (*National Archives of Canada*)

Wave-off! This Sea Fury, hook down to catch the arrester wires stretched across *Magnificent*'s flight deck, comes in too low, to be waved off by the batsman to try again. The batsman and his assistant are diving for the safety net, lower right. The British-built Fury's engine was very powerful but not designed for the rapid throttle changes needed by carrier aircraft. (*National Archives of Canada*)

Haida in Korean waters, her heavy armament turned in for two twin 4-inch mounts and a Canadian-built twin 3-inch 50-calibre aft for anti-aircraft use, new radar, and Squid for anti-submarine. (*National Archives of Canada*)

Vice Admiral Harold Grant, the Chief of Naval Staff, on *Cayuga*'s quarterdeck with her Captain (and Commander Canadian Destroyers Pacific), Captain Jeffry Brock, alongside in Toyko in October, 1950. This was Admiral Grant's farewell tour to the Korean War theatre before turning over as CNS to Vice Admiral Mainguy. (*Department of National Defence, courtesy Mrs. H.T. Grant*)

Grumman Avengers, fitted for ASW, fly over HMCS *Magnificent* in October, 1950. In "Maggie's" wake is *Huron*, who will move out to the port quarter as "plane guard" during flying on or off the deck. (*National Archives of Canada*)

The backwash of war. A junk, loaded with refugees and flying the Republic of Korea flag, works its way out of Chinnampo. Smoke rises from the fires set by gunfire from *Cayuga*, HMAS *Bataan*, and USS *Forrest Royal*, under Captain Brock's command. Such craft were a constant problem as they could sow mines and carry infiltrators. The great number of genuine refugees were helped whenever possible by the ships with food and medical aid. (*National Archives of Canada*)

Dirty North Atlantic weather, summer, 1953. *Magnificent*'s Avengers are lashed down and flying suspended in weather beyond the limit for safety. (*National Archives of Canada*)

HMCS *Bonaventure* enters Grand Harbour, Malta, in late 1958 during NATO exercises in the Mediterranean. She had commissioned in 1957. Her flight deck, only 700 by 80 feet, and top speed of 22 knots would have daunted less determined aviators. The angled flight deck, mirror landing aid, and steam catapult made it possible to fly the Banshee fighters, but for this exercise they were left behind in favour of a full complement of anti-submarine Trackers and HO4S helicopters (*National Archives of Canada*)

St. Laurent in 1957. The first of the distinctive breed of Canadian-designed warships of the 1950s and 1960s, she rides heavy seas with the ease and stability built into her to handle the worst of North Atlantic weather. Commissioned in 1955, she was converted to carry a helicopter and variable depth sonar in 1963 and finally paid off in 1974. (*Department of National Defence*)

Chaleur, Thunder, and *Fundy* snug in St. John's harbour below the Marconi Tower in 1961. They were among the twenty 390-ton wooden-hulled minesweepers designed and built in Canada in the early fifties. (*Department of National Defence*)

tually they carried quite a range of simple armament and a nucleus of DEMS sailors to look after it and train the crew for action. Some 1,600 Canadians served in DEMS.

How effective were they? Independent ships sometimes staved off attackers or at least made them spend torpedoes. In convoy they sometimes put a U-boat off its mark. Shells and flying tracer could point to an enemy or pepper a friend. Always, though, gunfire did the heart some good. The oiler or the fireman in the tanker's bowels had a dog's chance if torpedoed. At least he could feel some satisfaction in the whump and shudder of his own ship's gun, whether it hit anything or not.

The vital thing was the merchant seaman's spirit, and the Germans knew it. They used radio broadcasts. Agents swarmed in neutral ports, especially in the U.S., at dockside bars and seamen's hangouts. They tilled a fertile field. The merchant seaman's life was mostly wretched and ill-paid through the depression years. Now it was almost unrelieved misery. The "Merchant Navy" wasn't a navy. Only elite lines like Cunard had esprit, uniform, pride of service, organized man-management, and scope for initiative or ambition. The vast majority simply ground on at the job because there was nowhere else to go, or it was less odious to them than the army.

Men under foreign flags whose lands were overrun lived without families and homes and without hope. They heard the endless Axis chant that the British would fight to the last Greek, Dutchman, Norwegian, Dane, French-man, Belgian, or Pole. The lascars, East Indian and African hands serving their outcast nomad's life under British flags, had thin prospect of ever seeing their homes. Ashore, the merchant seaman had few of the amenities of the uniformed services and none of their panache. They too often drew contempt because they weren't in uniform. A cheap little lapel badge with MN on it didn't impress.

Heap on this the weakness of the escorts, the nightmare of being herded into convoys only to be killed, seeing the next in line vanish in a sheet of flame, friends dying in the oil-layered, icy sea. They shared a cheerless forecastle with men twice or thrice torpedoed, reached harbour to face a single certainty – going out again. Nobody looked out for the merchant seaman. So long as their ships lined up with the convoys, kept in station, refrained from making smoke or pumping bilges, showed no lights outboard, and weren't torpe-doed, nobody cared. And even when they were torpedoed, how often did the navy stop to pick them up?

By mid-summer of 1940 Eric Brand's Trade Division had recorded eighty-seven ships that missed their convoy sailing in Halifax. There was a growing shortage of alongside berths, dockside labour, bunker fuel, loading equip-ment, and, of course, ship repair. Better late than never, a new Controller of Ship Construction and Repairs was set up with the legislative teeth to get things on a war footing. But there was another factor, far more difficult – "crew trouble." Ships were being delayed by sit-down strikes (mutinies, by their proper name), deliberate damage to engines, desertion, refusal of duty. Then Admiralty warned that time-fuzed explosives could be planted in ships by enemy agents in American ports. In Halifax Commander Oland set up a Naval Boarding Service to examine cargo manifests and search for explosives and saboteurs.

By great good fortune all of the few involved were bright, sensitive to human factors, practical, and energetic. The navy ratings chosen had had pre-war merchant service. Very quickly, in getting about their ship searches, they began to hear the gripes and groans of the merchant seamen and their genuine concerns. The senior hand, Able Seaman Allan Oxner, put his CO, Lieutenant Frederick Watt, RCNVR, into the picture. Watt's steady hand won the confidence of ships' officers, the co-operation of the sound ones, and the respect of all. His friendly, efficient, smartly dressed sailors – always with gleaming boots, blancoed belts and gaiters, and bayonets at the hip – solved many a problem on the spot. Some they handled with their fists. Over cigarettes and mugs of tea they became a respected and friendly finger on the pulse. In Halifax the merchant seaman's grievances found the light and didn't fester in the f'o'csle.

Information, problems, insights came via Oxner to Watt: a malcontent, an agitator, a heavy drinker or a brutal officer, a thieving steward or an utterly incompetent cook, a chronically leaking crew compartment, undermaintained or undermanned machinery. Watt then dealt directly with ships' captains and officers. If necessary he took problems to his boss. Commander Oland had earned the confidence of ships' masters right at the start of the war. Problems were quickly aired and adroitly handled. Eric Brand, now a Captain, saw the value of this quite unorthodox network. He brought Ted Watt to conferences on North America-wide naval control matters.

Volunteer groups led by the Navy League sent warm clothing and comforts to merchant seamen as well as to the navy. The Boarding Service discovered filching by some ships' stewards so they took over distribution. Halifax women bundled hundreds of thousands of magazines and the Boarding Service delivered them in their launches, too. The same with 78,000 ditty bags and four million cigarettes and special Christmas cheer. The system spread to other Canadian ports. The Boarding Service became the friends of the merchant men where before they had none. The link to the navy strengthened. New warmth seeped through the battered, seaworn ships. In Canadian ports someone listened, someone cared.

In 1941 Eric Brand got major reforms rolling. Manning pools in the main ports provided decent accommodation and recreation, medical services, and pay between ships for all Allied merchant seamen. They made life far more pleasant and also made it easier for shipowners to muster crews. Under a new Merchant Seaman Order a Boarding Service officer with an RCMP officer could hold any crew member they believed might delay a ship's sailing. Now they could back ships' masters or deal with them smartly if they were the problem themselves. Time and again this cleared the decks for sailing.

Word reached Britain, where Admiral Noble was grappling with these very problems. He had Ted Watt brief him, and he listened well. Watt had come across for familiarization with Oxner and Stoker First Class "Rocky" Wolfe. Wolfe was an experienced union man, and Watt took him to meet Charles Jarman, secretary of Britain's National Union of Seamen. Like Admiral Noble, Jarman recognized experience, competence, and results. He threw his influence into getting co-operation from his huge membership in the merchant ships.

One RCNVR Lieutenant, a few sailors, and Canadian initiative had a large hand in beating that truly menacing and nearly fatal undercurrent of the war at sea. Ted Watt, OBE, was the right person in the right place and time. So was Able Seaman, later Chief Petty Officer Al Oxner, British Empire Medal. And so, too, was their immediate boss, Richard Oland, and Captain Eric Brand, who won his OBE for the superb job he did in Trade.

Trade, when you got right down to it, was at the heart and core. Canada built over 400 merchant ships for the Allies, including 150 run by Park Steamship Company, a Canadian crown corporation, All told, 210 ocean-going merchant ships sailed in the war at sea under Canada's Red Ensign. Thirty were lost, and with them went 1,064 Canadian merchant seamen. It is a poor epitaph to their gallant, dogged war that the Canadian Merchant Marine died from failure of government policy after it was over. Sixty per cent of the nation's trade – its lifeblood in war or peace – must move by sea, yet the Canadian Merchant Marine of those fighting days has never been revived.

HERO'S FAREWELL

On 7 May 1945 Germany surrendered. The 8th of May was officially V-E Day. In every city and town and village, every ship and unit, every service mess and canteen throughout the Allied world, celebration was the order of the day. In naval ports like Portsmouth tens of thousands, service and civilian, surged happily through the streets, singing, filling the pubs and themselves to overflowing. There were impromptu bonfires. Here and there were broken windows and broken heads. There was isolated excess. But it was happy. Delirious. A true celebration.

In Halifax it was an ugly outburst of all the pent-up frustrations and resentments that had grown between the sailors and the city – their enforced home for nearly six years. Without doubt the Command did too little to prepare. So did the city. Movie houses in Halifax and Dartmouth had refused the Mayor's request to stay open. Of the fifty-five eating places in the whole area, only sixteen were open on the 7th of May and six on V-E Day. The provincial liquor stores were shut tight on both.

At HMCS *Stadacona*, the naval barracks, there was nothing to do but go to the wet canteen, the only drinking place for sailors in the entire city. No senior officer had had the foresight to organize any form of entertainment, attraction, or celebration in the barracks or the dockyard. The "gangway was open," that is, men could come and go as they pleased. When the canteen closed at 9 p.m. on the 7th there was a general movement downtown. Some streetcars were smashed en route. Three liquor stores were ransacked.

The following day it was "open gangway" again. The only event organized was a huge gathering on the Garrison Grounds and a parade with Rear Admiral Murray and the other service chiefs taking the salute. The time-honoured signal, "Splice the main brace," flew at the Admiral's yardarm in the dockyard. In the ships men drew their daily rum plus the extra tot for all hands. Most celebrated on board. But up at *Stadacona* the wet canteen ran out of beer at one in the afternoon. Sailors joined soldiers, airmen, and civilians milling around in the city with nothing to do, smashing windows and brewing trouble.

The liquor stores were attacked again. Civilians cheered sailors on, then looted the stocks far more systematically. In one of the saner moves of the day, Colonel Sydney Oland, the head of the old brewing family, joined his warehouse staff and gave a case of beer and his personal thanks to each sailor until he ran out. Along Barrington Street boisterous skylarking turned ugly. The crowd became a mob. Civilians in serious numbers came to steal. Window-breaking turned to looting. Police and Naval Shore Patrol had lost control. The centre of Halifax was torn apart.

In the morning armed soldiers moved in from out of town. Mayor Allan Butler broadcast on the radio: "I speak to the solemn protests of the citizens against the Canadian navy. It will be a long time before the people of Halifax forget this great crime." In fact, when the dust had settled it was generally agreed that while sailors took the lead in smashing windows and breaking into liquor stores, civilians did most of the looting. Pictures in the papers confirmed it.

But it was a day of shame, a day of disgrace. And for such days heads must roll, and fast. The government appointed a one-man commission in Mr. Justice Roy Kellock of the Supreme Court. The police blotter showed 152 arrested for simple drunkenness, and nineteen airmen, thirty-four naval ratings, forty-one soldiers, and 117 civilians charged with various disorders. The judge's summation: the Naval Command had failed to plan, hadn't kept their people off the streets, and hadn't stamped out disorders early enough or with enough energy and force. No finger was pointed at the other services – Halifax was a navy town.

Admiral Murray faced the civic officials' accusations squarely. It was the civilian population that had done most of the damage and looting. Whether he hadn't given the right personal direction or was let down by his officers, he didn't argue. For what the navy had or hadn't done he took full responsibility on himself. All Canada was shocked by the Halifax riots. The navy, certainly not blameless but by no means alone, was seen as the scapegoat for the whole unhappy event. In the glorious moment of victory it drew damnation for the day rather than paeans of praise for those finest fighting years.

Yet, the Judge hadn't put his finger on the real underlying cause. The guilt for that was far more widely spread. Halifax was a city swollen beyond all reasonable bounds. The Atlantic provinces had been far behind the rest of Canada economically for fifty years. The depression had widened the gap. There were rotten slums in Halifax, verging on the dockyard. Young men and women coming from elsewhere found the core of the city dingy, unpainted, run down. Its population of 65,000 very nearly doubled during the war. There were few enough amenities for its own population and not enough resilience or entrepreneurial spirit to expand. Federal policies, deliberately focusing industrial development in Ontario and Quebec, had done next to nothing for Atlantic Canada.

Apart from barracks blocks, between 1939 and 1943 only 776 dwelling units were added to the city. The influx reached 55,000. In spite of a booming Canadian economy no money, federal or provincial, was put into housing. In fairness, Haligonians suffered from the overcrowding, too. Among them lived a generous share of very warm-hearted people. But a lot of landlords gouged and gouged deep. A navy man who brought his young family down at great expense on his meagre pay counted himself lucky to find a single room. Unlike England, it was a long expensive train ride home, only possible if a man had a rare long leave.

Living in their crowded, spartan little ships or in the bleak barracks block, the men lacked welcome and comfort ashore. They queued up in the rain to get into the Green Lantern or one of the other two sizable restaurants. None of them was licensed. The only place they could get a glass of beer was the cavernous wet canteen at *Stadacona* under the baleful eyes of the Shore Patrol. No girls were allowed there, not even the Wrens. Beer and spirits otherwise had to be bought at the provincial liquor store or from bootleggers at outrageous cost. And, unless a man had a room ashore, he drank it in an alley and polished it off because he couldn't take it back aboard. From 1941 the liquor stores were closed on Saturdays.

Private funds and volunteer energy opened hostels. The Ajax Club was a pleasant place with comfortable rooms, a library, and a garden behind where a sailor could relax over magazines and a beer. But the outlook of some Haligo-nians was as narrow as Nova Scotia's liquor laws. The club was shut down on complaint by the thin-lipped vestry of the neighbouring church. The Ajax group then arranged hospitality in private homes. There were hostels – YMCA, Salvation Army, Knights of Columbus, Merchant Seamen's Club – but not nearly enough to go around, and hardly anywhere could one get a clean comfortable bed for a night's or weekend's break from the ship.

Straight numbers, and prejudice, too, made it hard for a sailor to meet a decent girl. Prostitutes trooped into town. They paid the rents that a sailor who wanted to bring his family down to Halifax couldn't afford. The whores' trademarks became white galoshes in the gloom of rain-lashed streets, stand-up sex in alleyways, and a sky-high rate of venereal disease.

Officers had much readier social access and more money, but not much. An acting Lieutenant Commander, Captain of a destroyer and group senior officer to boot, got $5 a day! Officers had their own comfortable club-like messes ashore and afloat, however, with liquor and a good standard of food. Stemming from the RN heritage, built on British society, they were better off than their men by a very big margin. Probably they didn't feel the squeeze enough.

In this whole sea of conditions of service, the old RN chart wasn't right for Canada. The traditional divisional system, where a ship's officer saw to the performance, discipline, advancement, and welfare of his men, was basically sound. But wartime officers were short on training themselves. In the turmoil of war the system badly needed support by proper social and welfare services ashore. The Canadian, generally with a higher standard of living, didn't have the RN sailor's stoic acceptance of harsh conditions. On the other hand, he lacked the well-developed British gift for making do and drumming up amusement of his own. For sport and recreation, Halifax was nearly as bereft as Scapa Flow. The one quite inadequate gymnasium was turned into living space early in the war. The *Stadacona* recreation centre, with pool, gym, squash courts, and bowling alleys, didn't open until 1944. And at that it was only adequate for a navy one-fifth the size.

In June, 1943, as Debby Piers had reported from sea, the sailor on the Newfy-Derry run had little to look forward to at either end. Not until 1944 was a Special Service Officer appointed to Londonderry and a recreation camp set up. It had taken Captain Rollo Mainguy's personal efforts as Captain (D) St. John's to organize a camp there earlier. It was Mainguy, too, plus the generosity of businessman Leonard Outerbridge (later Lieutenant-Governor of the province), who started the Seagoing Officers' Club. The Crowsnest, up a teetering flight of wind-lashed steps in a warehouse attic, was famed the breadth of the Atlantic and written in naval posterity as a tight little haven for relaxation – rowdy or restful as the choice might be.

In St. John's, in Londonderry, in Boston, in Argentia, wherever Americans went, what they did for their own showed how poorly the RCN provided for theirs. By reasonable North American mid-twentieth-century standards, Canada's navy looked after its people very badly indeed. The senior officers, reared in the Royal Navy, sought to shape young Canadians to its mould. It was an uneasy and often painful fit. But war was no time to cast a new mould. That would have to wait.

Attitudes breed attitudes. To the great majority right through the wartime navy, "Slackers" was the place you didn't want to be. And, sad to relate, when word flashed around the Fleet that "Slackers had got it," there was a boisterous, bitter cheer. It was the only Canadian city that had really been in the war's front line, had seen its ravages firsthand: haggard survivors and the shrouded dead; wounded ships staggering in for repairs to fight again; gunfire and explosions that meant death. Of all cities, Halifax should have seen rejoicing at war's end. But it finished there in anger and bitterness and left a deep and lasting scar.

And Rear Admiral Leonard Murray, who had steadily, implacably fought the U-boats, who had led the fighting navy through the most terrible of times, who more than anyone had shaped a real and potent fighting force, went down in disgrace. The politicians must have a scalp. No one stood on his behalf. From the Chief of Naval Staff and long-time rival, Vice Admiral G.C. Jones, Leonard Murray got no real support. An officer and gentleman, he took the whole load and buttoned his lip. He retired early, in September, 1945, left the country of his birth for good and all, and went to live in England. A fine career of dedicated service was unalterably wrecked.

Leonard Murray, from Pictou County, Nova Scotia, the first Commander of the Canadian North Atlantic, was deeply and deservedly respected by the seagoing navy. He was neither colourful nor brilliant, yet he was a hero, a dogged hero, though Canadians resist that word. His name should never be forgotten. The irony of his life was that his downfall came the very day his arch-enemies, the U-boats, surfaced to surrender.

PACIFIC WAR

There was still Japan to fight. Pearl Harbor, then the loss of Singapore in March, 1942, and the American collapse in the Philippines had taken Allied fortunes to the depths. From the Battle of Midway in June, 1942, however, the Americans were on the offensive. Marines landed in Guadalcanal in the Solomon Islands that August. By July, 1944, the greatest seaborne campaign of all history had taken the mounting might of America across the Pacific island stepping stones to the conquest of Saipan. By that time the ceaseless and skilful USN submarine war against Japan's merchant fleet had all but choked the country off from Southeast Asia and its essential sources of supply.

Japan started the war with some 6 million tons of merchant shipping. They increased to 10 million by capture and new construction but ended up with less than 2 million tons, mostly small wooden coasters. They lost over 2,100 vessels and submarines accounted for 60 per cent. With a far smaller fleet than Dönitz's and less than 10 per cent of his losses, the Americans actually did to Japan what the U-boats had so nearly done to Britain.

Canada's projected Pacific naval force was to be 13,000 men and some sixty ships: two light fleet carriers, two cruisers, a flotilla of fleet destroyers, thirty-six frigates, and eight Castle-class corvettes. Six more destroyers, including the three unfinished Canadian-built Tribals, and two dozen escorts were earmarked as operational reserve. It was to be a sizable contribution. This was no escort fleet any more; it was the big-ship kind of navy, the balanced fleet so long the aim of Canada's admirals.

The first to head for the Pacific was the 6-inch cruiser HMCS *Uganda*. She was taken over from the RN while refitting in Charleston, South Carolina, and commissioned on 21 October 1944. Her first Captain was Rollo Mainguy. Apart from him, his Executive Officer, Commander Hugh Francis Pullen, and a handful of officers and senior hands, most had served in nothing larger than a corvette. An old sailors' superstition against changing a ship's name is the only apparent reason for keeping the British-colonial identity rather than making her Canadian.

Mainguy took her to Halifax for stores, to Scapa Flow for work-ups, then east via Suez and on to Sydney, Australia. There, on 1 March 1945, she joined the Fourth Cruiser Squadron of the British Pacific Fleet. Events were moving fast. Two weeks before, U.S. Marines had landed on Iwo Jima, then on Okinawa, 340 miles south of Japan itself – though it would take eleven weeks of bitter fighting to subdue it.

For the Canadians this was a new kind of war. The submarine threat was minor and random. A huge fleet of transports, landing ships, and special craft to move the armies had been formed. The carrier task force was the mighty weapon to control the sea. Battleships, cruisers, and destroyers ringed the carriers, defending them from air and surface attack. Alternately, they backed the landing forces and bombarded for them.

Another vital element was the Fleet Train. The Pacific Fleet had to live at sea many miles from established bases. Its fuel, its ammunition, its supplies and provisions, its spare parts, its replacement aircraft all went forward with it. Repair ships and floating drydocks, store ships and hospitals, moved with the surge of war. Everything was afloat. Atolls with their protecting reefs became naval bases overnight. The RN had forgotten some of its time-honoured principles and become base-bound in the nineteenth century. It was still so minded well into World War Two and they had plenty to learn from the U.S. Navy.

Uganda left Australia in late March and joined Task Force 57. This was the bulk of the British Pacific Fleet – four fleet carriers, two 14-inch-gun battleships, six cruisers, including *Uganda*, and two flotillas of destroyers. Their job was to stop enemy aircraft from getting through to Okinawa. Day after day, strike after strike flew off to hit the staging airfields on the Shakashima Islands and Formosa. The enemy struck back with kamikazes.

On 1 May the battleships and cruisers moved in to blast airfields in the Shakashimas. While that was going on two of the carriers were hit. Then right on the heels of a returning air strike, the Japanese flew in a massive attack. The heavy ships formed around the carriers in the "iron ring." Up went an enormous barrage, a sky pocked with airbursts, crisscrossed with tracers. Kamikaze pilots flew in to their death. They hit both *Victorious* and *Formidable*. But the British carriers shrugged them off. In half an hour the fires were out, decks cleared away, and both were flying off again. Their armoured steel flight decks were far tougher than the U.S. carriers' wood.

By mid-July, the whole might of the combined U.S. and British forces, under Admiral "Bull" Halsey, moved on the southern Japanese home island of Honshu. Aircraft smashed at ships, naval bases, airfields, and the industries around the Inland Sea, then at Tokyo itself. Lieutenant R.H. "Hammy" Gray, RCNVR, leading a strike from *Formidable*, was heavily hit by gunfire but pressed in to sink a Japanese destroyer and was killed. Already gazetted for the DSC, his last courageous flight won him Canada's only naval Victoria Cross of the war.

On 28 July, the British Task Force pulled back to the replenishment area. When she'd topped up, instead of going back to the battle, HMCS *Uganda* headed for Esquimalt. She did so in silence and without cheers, the only ship in recorded naval history whose own company had actually voted her out of a war.

This stain on the navy's history stemmed from a politically self-serving decision made by the Canadian government three months before. Prior to that, in November, 1944, reinforcements for the hard-fighting Canadian army in Europe were so badly needed that Mackenzie King withdrew his dead-set opposition to sending conscripts overseas. By spring an election was in the offing and King announced in the House of Commons on 4 April that it was "not intended to detail men for service in the Pacific." Those in formations directed against Japan would be "chosen from those who elect to serve in the Pacific Theatre."

The Prime Minister did this against the unequivocal advice of all the service heads. Now each man in every service had to sign an official form. If he volunteered to serve in the Pacific he got thirty days' special home leave before he went; if he didn't he stayed in line to be released, to go home and get first crack at civvie life and a job.

Captain Wallace Creery, in command of the auxiliary anti-aircraft cruiser *Prince Robert* now on the west coast, was getting her ready for the Pacific. He knew each man had to make a tough decision, the married ones especially. He pointed out to his company that *Prince Robert* had escorted the original Canadian contingent to Hong Kong. Were they going to leave them there in the prison camps or do their damnedest to get them out? Eighty-five per cent said they'd go.

But *Prince Robert* was getting ready to go. *Uganda* was already there. Her crew had last seen Canada nine months before. No one liked being crowded and uncomfortable, and RN-designed ships were low on comfort: ventilation was bad and the ship was a great steel oven; the engine room ran up to 159 degrees Fahrenheit; boilers had to be cleaned at anchor at 120 degrees; fresh water was always short. Food, from RN victualling, was poor. Hardly a man had set foot ashore since the ship left Sydney in March. Actions had been sharp but few against monotonous months of steaming. Canadian sailors weren't alone in their discomfort. Most had endured tough years at sea, growled, and got on with it. They'd signed on to fight. If they were told to go somewhere, they'd go. But give anyone in any fleet the choice of the Pacific war or going home . . .

As Captain of a ship of war operating against the enemy, Rollo Mainguy was required by Ottawa to ask his whole ship's company if they were prepared to fight the Japanese or not and to sign accordingly on the dotted line. At anchor in the forward base of Manus in June the democratic process was observed. Three ballot boxes were set up on the quarterdeck. One was for the federal general election, the second for Ontario residents for an election there, the third for the Pacific volunteer election forms. Of 900 officers and men, 600 elected not to serve. It was clearly a vote to leave the war.

The whole dreadful business divided the ship into two bitterly opposing camps. While she was on the July strikes, doing what the majority had voted not to do, the matter of sending out 600 replacements was mulled over in Ottawa. And what about the 300 volunteers on board? They were due thirty days of home leave. The only decision was to call the ship back to Esquimalt, her tail between her legs. Four days before she arrived, on 6 August 1944, the historic atom bomb obliterated Hiroshima. On the 9th, Nagasaki was destroyed. There would be no bloody landings now. On 14 August Japan surrendered unconditionally.

The second cruiser, *Ontario*, arrived too late for the fighting. Her Captain, Harold Grant, had commanded the RN cruiser *Enterprise* and won a DSO for a resounding victory against eleven German destroyers off Biscay. After a variety of tasks in Manila, Hong Kong, and Japan she went home to

Esquimalt. On the same day that *Uganda* got home *Prince Robert* arrived in Sydney to join the British Pacific Fleet. On 31 August she entered Hong Kong. Captain Wallace Creery, whose ship *Fraser* was the RCN's first loss of the war, represented Canada at the official Japanese surrender there in mid-September. He and his company of Pacific volunteers returned proudly to Esquimalt in late October loaded with Canadian prisoners from the Hong Kong camps. Sadly, the political craft of Mackenzie King had clouded Canada's pride in the solidly efficient and effective job done by HMCS *Uganda* in the Pacific war.

WAR'S END

Halifax on V-J Day was relatively subdued. As Wren Fiddy Greer observed: "... this time 'Stadacona' was ready, the solution to any possibility of a recurrence of the V-E Day 'celebrations' so simple as to be ludicrous. The Drill Shed opened its doors to all and there appeared to be an unlimited supply of beer, hamburgers sizzling on stoves brought in for the occasion and dozens of officers to serve them all day and far into the night. The 'Stadacona' band played for hours while we danced and ate and drank. There was no need to go into town to celebrate ... everything was right there at home. And it was all free! ... For one glorious day there were no rules or regulations. It was a wonderful party."

The party was really over, though, on the 28th of May. At one minute past midnight all the ships at sea – the merchant ships still in convoy after six long years; the faithful escorts still busy in their screening stations; the aircraft on their lonely sweeps and carrier patrols – switched on their running lights. The U-boat war, the longest, hardest, most bitter and costly battle in the naval annals of the world, the one that very nearly brought Adolf Hitler's Third Reich to world domination "for a thousand years," had come to its end.

It was the campaign that brought Canada's own navy to real stature. Twenty-four ships went down and nearly 1,800 gave their lives. All but four of the ships were lost in the U-boat war. In return the navy sank thirty-one of the U-boats and disposed of forty-two surface ships. In the give and take the little ships saw 25,000 merchant voyages across the Atlantic, 180 million tons of vital trade. And that was Canada's most decisive contribution, not just to the war at sea, but to the war itself.

With all its agonies, its shortcomings and mistakes, Canada had forged a navy from virtually nothing. A generation of young shore-bound Canadians had turned to face the sea. They had shown themselves, if not the world, that they could fight there as well as any and a good deal better than most. That war, too, laid a base of hard experience on which a navy to meet the country's future needs could well be built.

If the country did not turn its back once more, and if its will was there.

CHAPTER ELEVEN
THE SICKLY SEASON

DOLDRUMS

CLOSE TO 100,000 MEN AND WOMEN WHO HAD VOLUNTEERED FOR WAR service in the Royal Canadian Navy couldn't get out soon enough. Veterans' preference gave them their old jobs back if they wanted, and there were plenty of new ones in a buoyant economy, as well as free university courses and vocational training. Social programs begun in the war, such as unemployment insurance and family allowances, stayed in place. Labour hung tough and pushed hard, and wages rose. Canada had had a profitable six years of war; by 1947, the country had passed the wartime economic peak despite drastic cutbacks in all the armed services.

The great escort fleet the navy had built with such agony and ultimate success was scrapped. Government authorized a peacetime force at first of two aircraft carriers, two cruisers, twelve destroyers, and 10,000 all ranks. The Wrens were dismissed as a wartime anomaly. The two light fleet carriers, *Warrior* and *Magnificent*, were coming forward in British yards. The other ships were in commission or, in the case of the Canadian-built Tribals, near completion in Halifax. A handful of frigates and sweepers was kept in reserve. It was a dizzy descent from the wartime high but, compared to 1939, a substantial force. And it was what the admirals had been looking for – a "big ship" navy, not an escort force.

Finding 10,000 people for the post-war fleet meant fleshing it out with Reserves, appealing to war-trained people to join the permanent force, and attracting new recruits. But who wanted armed forces now that the war was over, much less be in them? Family separations had gone on quite long enough. Who, indeed, would choose to stay at sea and sling a hammock in a creaking messdeck? Things were great outside and that's where the money was. Besides, where was the motive? Canada was active in forming the

United Nations in 1945. Then, guided by Mackenzie King, the country turned away from Europe's tensions as it had in the 1920s. Canadians scarcely heeded Winston Churchill's icy warning that "An iron curtain has descended across the continent." That was in March, 1946, the same month Canada pulled its occupation troops out of Germany.

THE COLD WAR

The country was no longer bound to Britain. Continental defence, as the very junior partner of the United States, seemed more to the point, and in 1947 Canada agreed its forces would use U.S. weapons, communications, and methods. Stalin, using German technology, was building a strong fleet of submarines, but Prime Minister King and his cabinet saw the combined American and British fleets as vastly superior to the Soviets. There seemed no point to an expensive navy for Canada.

Indeed, after the atomic bomb seared into the world's psyche, there seemed little purpose at all for a navy. A convoy or fighting force would surely be snuffed out by a single bomb. In mid-1946 Captain Nelson Lay led the RCN observers at Operation Crossroads, the awesome tests of atomic airburst and underwater blasts on a huge sacrificial fleet anchored inside the reef at Bikini Atoll. Measurement dispelled myth. There was no heavy damage to ships outside 1,000 yards from air or underwater burst. Aircraft on deck were damaged at 2,000 yards, so loss could be limited to one ship by keeping them 2,000 yards apart. New ships, it was clear, must survive heavy underwater blasts, and radioactivity was obviously a major problem. Ships must some-how deal with fallout and contamination. But proper construction and the right tactical dispositions would cope with the Bomb at sea.

In the U.S. fear of subversion and spying within the nuclear fraternity verged on hysteria. In September of 1946 a Soviet cypher clerk, Igor Gouzenko, defected from his embassy in Ottawa with evidence that Soviet spies were gleaning allied atomic secrets. In Europe, meanwhile, the tension rose between East and West. Yesterday's ally, the Soviet Union, seemed poised to move. But in January, 1947, the year columnist Walter Lippmann called it the "Cold War," Canadian defence spending was cut 25 per cent; the navy's manpower ceiling dropped to 7,500. By the end of that year the fleet stood at the carrier *Warrior*, one operative cruiser and one in maintenance, five destroyers, and two Algerines.

Then in February, 1948, came the Communist takeover in Czechoslovakia. Europe, shaken and fearful, closed ranks. Britain, France, Belgium, the Netherlands, and Luxembourg formed a military alignment called Western Union. In weeks the Soviets slammed a blockade on Berlin. American strength in Europe was down to one weak division, but President Truman brought back the draft and the U.S. still had the monopoly of the Bomb. U.S. aircraft joined in the inspired airlift that kept the German city virtually alive. Prime Minister King, with his horror of the European vortex, wouldn't let the RCAF take part.

King, with his isolationist fears, retired later that year. The new Liberal leader and Prime Minister, Louis St. Laurent, had clear, broad views of Canada as a nation in the world. So did his Minister at External Affairs, Lester Pearson. In continental terms, Canada's eyes were turned to the potential polar battleground. *Warrior*, with *Haida* and *Nootka*, exercised during the summer of 1948 in Hudson Bay. The RN-designed carrier was no northern ship; in fact, she had to spend her only Canadian winter on the west coast. She was swapped for *Magnificent*, which at least had steam heat and some cold-weather engineering. That same year there was money in the Estimates for an Arctic patrol vessel.

In 1949, when the Soviets produced their own atomic bomb, Western Union became nothing without the Americans. Canada, uneasy in the lop-sided North American alliance, joined the drive to pull the U.S. back to Europe. On 4 April 1949, Canada, with the original Western Union plus the United States, Denmark, Iceland, Italy, Norway, and Portugal, signed the North Atlantic Treaty. It tied Europe and North America together in mutual defence against the Soviet bloc. And it was something quite new in treaties. It required not just response to actual aggression, but each member – except Iceland, whose assets were airfields and geography – must maintain forces pre-committed to the alliance.

This march of world events and time of national growth had, for the navy, been four years of drift. Vice Admiral G.C. Jones died in harness just after the war. His relief, Rastus Reid, spent one reluctant year heading the navy, then went fishing on the west coast. Vice Admiral Harold Grant then became Chief of Naval Staff. During the war Grant had been Chief of Personnel and Captain (D) Newfoundland. Then he was Captain of HMS *Enterprise*, won his DSO battling German destroyers, was wounded in the Normandy invasion, and later became Captain of the brand new *Ontario*. Harold Grant was blunt, arbitrary, a firm decision-maker, and a sea-dog to the core.

Recruiting improved in 1948 with a rose-coloured campaign offering a good job, a skill, and security, but the valuable older hands weren't signing on again because of conditions. And for mid-twentieth-century Canada they were bad: pay and allowances were low; food was poor; the time spent at sea was very high, especially in critical skilled trades like the engine room; there was too little slack to allow for thorough training; and moves between ships were too frequent, especially for over-taxed key men. As well, there wasn't enough housing for families in Halifax and Victoria – except for a few senior officers, no one had married quarters. A leading seaman trying to support a family on $120 a month was forced to moonlight, and when he went to sea his family had real hardship. Often they had to go home to live and marriages suffered. Some ships' captains unofficially rotated men ashore so they could earn enough to keep their families together. For the single man, barracks were bleak and lacked privacy. Recreational facilities were poor. Young men thinking about their future saw little chance of a satisfactory family life. Requests for release or transfer to the RCAF with its stable station life were epidemic.

Those at the top didn't seem to be grasping the point or making it with government. Pay, housing, and food were marginally improved through a series of niggardly budgets, from a Parliament that didn't much care representing a country that didn't want to know. But the basic problems went deep. There was a malaise in the navy and it took mutiny to bring it to the surface.

MUTINY AND THE MAINGUY REPORT

Mutiny is an ugly word. It smells of anarchy, violence, and death. These Canadian mutinies weren't violent. No one swung from the yardarm. But, as in *Iroquois* in 1943, they all involved collective insubordination. And mutinies they were.

On 22 August 1947, HMCS *Ontario* was on a shake-down cruise anchored off Nanoose, Vancouver Island. Captain Jimmy Hibbard had been in command for six weeks. Commander Jeffry Brock was Executive Officer and had been there a year. Hibbard was old navy, Brock, pre-war RCNVR, with most of his sea service on loan to the RN. Both had fine war records.

After dinner that day some fifty junior men locked themselves in a messdeck intending not to answer the routine pipe for "hands fall in." Word got out and the pipe wasn't made. Technically, that avoided the actual crime. The Captain cleared lower deck, spoke to the ship's company, and all hands turned to. He found that there were petty complaints against having to wear night uniform, aggravations over unsettled ship's routine. A general disgruntled feeling centred on the Executive Officer.

Commander Brock was pulled from the ship by the Flag Officer Pacific Coast, Rear Admiral Rollo Mainguy. The men, as in *Iroquois* in 1943, gained their ends; they got rid of one officer, in this case their XO. There was no formal investigation, and no charges were laid. Brock carried the blame personally though not officially. He was seen as an ex-Reserve lacking the experience to manage a big ship. Brock was an intelligent man, brilliant even, and supremely confident at higher staff levels. But his arrogance outweighed his understanding. He kept distant from his subordinates and had little feel for the lower deck. He hadn't built the confidence and support an XO needs from his officers.

The new Commander, Patrick Budge, DSC, had an altogether different cut to his jib. He was a hands-on man, a firm and fair disciplinarian who set clear standards and insisted that all hands toe the mark. Pat Budge was already a legendary character. He came up the hard way from Boy Seaman on the pre-war lower deck, had served on the North Atlantic, and was First Lieutenant of *Huron* in the Channel. He was a great hand at getting up ships' choirs and concert parties, and co-composed "Roll Along Wavy Navy," the classic signature song of the RCNVR. His unusual hobby at sea was doing intricate needlepoint. Everything in Budgie's book – from getting on his knees to show an ordinary seaman how to scrub a deck to chasing destroyers into their screening stations – was done with gusto and good humour, and, as he called it, "a seamanlike manner." Later he put his hallmark on new entry and leadership training at HMCS *Cornwallis*.

The *Ontario* episode seemed isolated. Then, a year and a half later, in February and March of 1949 there were three more. *Athabaskan* (the built-in-Halifax successor to the "Atha-b" sunk in the Channel) was fuelling in Manzanillo, Mexico, when the junior hands refused to turn to. The next came a couple of weeks later in the destroyer *Crescent* in Nanking. She was in the Chinese Nationalist capital guarding the interests of Canadian citizens as the Communist army advanced. Roughly the same thing happened there.

In the meantime, *Athabaskan* had gone through the Panama Canal to join the carrier *Magnificent* in the Caribbean. The ships' companies met ashore in Colon so talk of the destroyer's mutiny was rife. Out at sea after flying stations early Sunday morning, thirty-two of *Magnificent*'s aircraft handlers stayed in their messdeck rather than falling in after breakfast. Captain Gus Miles interviewed them all, and there were no charges.

All cases were pretty much the same: only junior hands were involved, and they got on with their work after their captains spoke to them, and no one was punished. The immediate complaints were mainly about upset routines. All three incidents were short-lived, and in each case the target was the Executive Officer, the one responsible for the day-to-day running of the ship.

The three destroyers' XOs lacked experience, though *Magnificent*'s was Commander Debby Piers, an officer with plenty of hard-fighting seatime in command. A carrier is a complex organism, very different from a destroyer – it needs a lot of intricate co-ordination and co-operation between aviators, operations staff, seamen, engineers. An XO's job is different from that of a Captain. Piers's leadership was the arbitrary kind.

Three mutinies in three weeks sent out shock waves, but even the journalists called them "incidents." Punishment in the law for mutiny, reaching back centuries, was death – death for all in a mutiny with violence; death for ringleaders without violence, and life imprisonment for all the rest. So everyone was careful to avoid the dreaded word.

Another dread was abroad in those days, the fear of communism. Three mutinies in three weeks raised spectres of a navy rife with subversion, about to mutiny en masse, to fly apart. The Minister, Brooke Claxton, quickly appointed a commission to investigate. It was not to take disciplinary action –

the time for that was gone – but rather to record what happened and make proposals "to improve conditions of service, the relations between officers and men, the machinery for the ventilation of grievances and . . . the training of naval personnel." The result was a searching inquiry into conditions in the navy.

Claxton chose the commissioners wisely. The chairman was Rear Admiral Rollo Mainguy. Consideration for his people was written in his record. As Captain (D) in St. John's he started the recreation camp for men and the Crowsnest Seagoing Officers' Club; as Captain of *Uganda* in the Pacific he held direct talks with the ship's company en masse. This he called "Town Hall," and it took a fair-minded, well-informed, and respected man to carry it off. Mainguy's fairness showed in the Report's statement that pulling Commander Brock from *Ontario* "without a complete investigation, appears neither completely wise nor completely fair." That decision had been Mainguy's own.

Another commissioner was ex-RCNVR officer L.C. Audette. "Uncle Louis" was torpedoed in *Saguenay*, commanded *Amherst* in convoy battles – including SC 107 under Debby Piers – and the frigate *Coaticook*. A lawyer by peacetime profession and a member of the Maritime Commission, Audette was a perceptive, objective, and broadly educated professional. The third member, Leonard Brockington, was a lawyer who became first chairman of the CBC, then a wartime special adviser to the Prime Minister. His resonant voice was familiar to Canadians through his radio commentaries on major issues.

Over 200 witnesses, from the Chief of Naval Staff to new entry sailors, were interviewed in camera. Each was promised immunity. The commissioners found that men from the *Ontario* and *Iroquois* mutinies were scattered through the affected ships. The modus operandi and its previous success were well known, and though there was no collusion or subversion, one successful mutiny certainly fuelled the next. There were as well some strong common threads. Routines were unsettled and disruptive. The XOs concerned were highly arbitrary or inexperienced or both, and they didn't have the confidence of their officers, chiefs, or petty officers. Out of their control, however, were changes in ships' companies which were far too frequent. Leonard Murray had fought that problem in the first half of the war. As young Captain Horatio Nelson had written in 1783: "The disgust of Seamen to the Navy is all owing to the infernal plan of turning them over from ship to ship so that men cannot be attached to their officers or the officers care twopence about them." The "Nelson tradition" is too often scoffed at as barnacle-bound prejudice, pageantry, and polished brass in lieu of leadership. There was a certain amount of that in the navy, to be sure, but that great sea officer left all the navies of the world a legacy of enlightened humanity in a harsh age, of leading by example and rock-solid professional ability.

In the RCN, communications up and down the line between officers, chiefs, and petty officers and the junior men weren't working. Neither was the divisional system that grouped men under an officer responsible for their work, advancement, and welfare. Nearly two years before, Headquarters had realized all wasn't well. A group of chiefs and petty officers had told Lieutenant Commander Bill Landymore – a man they implicitly trusted – about unhappiness and unrest on the lower deck. Landymore reported personally to Rear Admiral Frank Houghton, the Vice Chief of Naval Staff, and Commodore Adrian Hope was sent off to investigate. A lot of problems boiled down to money, but a big one was that people didn't think they were being heard.

A month prior to *Ontario*'s mutiny, a general message ordered all ships and establishments to set up standing welfare committees, to be chaired by the ship's Executive Officer and to provide "free discussion between officers and men of items of welfare and general amenities within the ship." Many tradition-bound officers found it hard to accept, a threat to the established way. Running a ship by committee (though, of course, this was not intended) was not for them. They knew sailors and ships and they knew how to run them.

In fact, *Athabaskan*'s committee hadn't met during that cruise, and during *Crescent*'s lonely duty in China several welfare committee proposals were quashed by the Captain, David Groos, or XO out of hand. *Magnificent* had no welfare committee at all – the XO had read the order but didn't believe it was the right thing and ignored it. Worse, neither Captain nor Flag Officer saw to it that the clear Headquarters order was obeyed in the navy's biggest ship. There could be no justification here for a Nelsonian blind eye. Disregard of orders on the quarterdeck was an invitation to disobedience by the lower deck.

The commission found throughout the service an artificial distance between officers and men – people who in Canadian society could well have gone to the same high school. No one objected to officers having privileges but when officers didn't deliver on their basic responsibilities, resentment replaced respect. Discipline – the right kind – had broken down. The report put it thus: "The only discipline which in the final analysis is worth while, is one based upon pride in a great service, a belief in essential justice, and the willing obedience that is given to superior character, skill, education and knowledge. Any other form of discipline is bound to break down under stress."

It boiled down to the quality of officers. The timeless nub of the naval profession was summed up in the report's quotation of Admiral John Paul Jones, who said in 1776: "The naval officer should be the soul of tact, patience, justice, firmness, charity and understanding. No meritorious act of a subordinate should escape his attention or be left to pass without reward, even if the reward be only one word of approval. He should not be blind to a single fault in any subordinate; at the same time he should be quick to distinguish error from malice, thoughtlessness for incompetency and well-meant shortcoming from heedless and stupid blunder. As he should be universal and impartial in his rewards and approval of merit, so should he be judicial and unbending in his punishment or reproof of misconduct."

Though they might have good hands-on junior training, officers in the RCN were not very well educated. They fell far behind the USN. Too, most of the wartime entry officers had had the sketchiest of training. The navy was also behind the RCAF, which pre-war had set university degrees as a requirement for career officers. As in the Royal Navy, leadership wasn't actually taught. The assumption was that this most vital attribute of all went along with social class or would somehow be acquired by osmosis as the young gentleman advanced. The inspirational side of leadership wasn't easily defined, but the RN, and thus the RCN, had no manual on leadership. The U.S. Navy did, and it was well worth the study.

Many aspects of navy life, such as decent accommodation, pay, food, and social services, lagged behind the other Canadian services and compared very badly with the USN. Discipline in the U.S. Navy was far harder, but the facilities and services on their bases filled the RCN with envy. Also – an old RCN story – there were too few people for too many tasks. All these things could be fixed with money, and the report was prime ammunition.

But another frustration could be fixed for nothing. The feeling came mostly from the lower deck and it was the simple urge to be "Canadian." The RN label had stuck to the RCN and that stuck in a young Canadian's craw. Without question the RCN inherited much of deep and lasting value, above all a great sea-fighting tradition. But time was overdue for the RCN to keep what was worthwhile, throw what wasn't over the side, and be its Canadian self. This wasn't a rejection of naval smartness, ritual, and ceremony. The traditional flourishes had evolved since men first flew flags at sea and would always have their time-honoured place in ships' and sailors' lives. Every navy worth its salt has its own treasured version and guards it well. But restoring the wartime Maple Leaf on the funnel was obvious and simple. How easy it would have been to give Canadian names to *Warrior* and *Magnificent*. It was easy to sew on "Canada" badges, and designing more livable ships and feeding men properly would come. Moulding a navy to fit Canadian social values, traditions, and character went deeper and would take a good deal longer.

The Mainguy Report was a watershed in the navy's history. Mutiny, shameful as it was, had triggered a much-needed self-examination. It was a catharsis. And like it or not, events in the world at large soon meant Canada's navy had to stand firmly on its own.

CRACKING SHOW

Through this uncertain time Canadian naval aviation was taking shape. Back in 1943 those Headquarters mainstays, Acting Captains Nelson Lay and Harry DeWolf, had gone hard after aircraft carriers, one for each escort group. Lay manoeuvred a directive straight from the Minister to go look at aviation in the USN and RN and report to the Naval Board.

Lay's report, given his imbalanced examination of the British and Americans, predictably recommended that the Canadian navy's air service be modelled on the RN's Fleet Air Arm. Without a doubt, the RCAF would have fought against an American model, which would have meant more control of aviation, including shore-based patrol aircraft, in naval hands. But the truth was that the U.S. had the superior carriers, planes, and techniques for naval aviation. Going the U.S. route would have meant a stronger navy and a different future for Canada's armed forces, but old ties, not long-term logic, cast the die.

Nabob's fighting record under Lay's command strengthened the navy's hand in getting an air arm. So, perhaps, did family bonds. Nelson Lay's widowed father had married Mackenzie King's sister in 1907 and he'd always called King "Uncle Willie." The war against Japan was the clincher. Britain was building the ships; Canada had the men. In April, 1945, Uncle Willie's war cabinet approved two RN-built light fleet carriers for the Pacific war. Four Canadian squadrons were formed from old Fleet Air Arm hands plus the cream of some 500 RCAF-trained pilots who had joined the RNVR for a chance to fly in the Pacific. The war ended before they got their chance.

No modern navy was complete without naval air. For Canada after the war, one carrier and two squadrons were the limit. Even at that, enthusiasm was once again taking on too much with too little. *Warrior* commissioned in January, 1946; in March her two squadrons, 803 with Seafire fighters and 825 with Firefly fighter-reconnaisance planes, flew aboard off Spithead and the ship made for Halifax. Canadian naval aviation was in business. With the training done by the RN, the carrier on loan, aircraft with replacements and stores, and destroyers *Crescent* and *Crusader* tossed in, Canada paid no more than $10 million – a bargain-basement price.

But even without an enemy and wartime pressures, naval aviation was a high-risk business. An efficient warship needs a fine-tuned team and equipment; a carrier has to have the ultimate. RN aircraft weren't good, while the U.S. Navy's were. In the British Pacific Fleet, where Canadian pilots like Lieutenant Dickie Bird had flown in action, they beached the Seafires for American Corsairs. The USN's reliable old fighter, the Hellcat, also outclassed the Seafire in the air and on the deck. The RN Barracuda strike plane was a menace, and the Firefly couldn't compete with the proven American Avenger.

This went right back to the RN losing control of its Air Arm in 1918. It was still stuck with adaptations of RAF planes. The legendary Spitfire's landing gear, fine on grass flying fields, was too narrow and far too fragile for carriers, and the Seafire inherited it. The Firefly's wasn't much tougher. The U.S. Navy, by contrast, had complete control of its own aircraft, designed them from scratch for deck operations and, among other things, built in twice the undercarriage strength.

True to the old-boy network, key naval air posts in Ottawa were filled by RN officers until the mid-fifties. Other important slots, such as Commander (Air) in the carrier and at the air station, were filled by RN officers in the early days, too. There were some fine officers among them but the RN didn't generally send its best. And Admiralty dearly wanted to sell planes. Acting Captain Hank Rotheram, RN, Director of Naval Aviation in Ottawa from 1946 until 1949, knew, for example, where his final loyalties lay. Just as a new batch of Seafires was going to be purchased, he shot down a USN offer of fifty surplus Hellcats, all in top shape, for under $3,000 each. It was a steal. But as he wrote in his memoirs (characteristically called *It's Really Quite Safe*), he was afraid accepting the U.S. offer over the Seafires would prejudice the Canadian order for the new RN Sea Fury. The Furies were running late but enough were diverted from the first RN delivery to equip an RCN squadron. So the inexperienced Canadians, with their small, slow carrier, got the hot new RN aircraft in 1947 complete with its development bugs. It had serious problems and good men died.

In addition, the new Firefly MK V ASW aircraft from the RN was hard to maintain and fell far short in all-weather performance. Like the earlier Fireflies and the Seafire, exhaust flames interfered with the pilot's vision in the carrier circuit at night. Four of them cracked up on *Magnificent*'s flight deck off Bermuda the first time the squadron tried night deck landings.

There were problems at the top, too. Admiral Jones certainly was not air-minded. His successor as CNS, Vice Admiral Reid, observed that "naval aircraft are merely weapons like torpedoes or guns." That hardly made for confidence among the rising generation that aviation was properly understood. The Chief of the Air Staff, Air Marshal R. Leckie, had started his career as a sub-lieutenant in the Royal Naval Air Service, transferred to the RAF in 1918, and joined the RCAF in 1940. He'd seen the disastrous rundown in British naval aviation and maritime air between wars and was determined that the RCAF would hold all the post-war aviation cards. A priority of Leckie's was developing a corps of well-educated, well-trained staff officers, and in the tough infighting for budget dollars the RCAF beat the simple sailors hands down. It wasn't until September, 1948, that the RCAF's Dartmouth air station was commissioned as HMCS *Shearwater*.

Carriers were new territory to most Canadian sailors, and they didn't take kindly to weird routines to accommodate the "flyboys." The early COs – Captain Frank Houghton and Commodores Harry DeWolf, Gus Miles, Gus Boulton, and Ken Adams – had plenty of experience in small ships and were determined to make naval aviation go, but they had to pick up carrier operations as they went along. The same was true of their executive officers. The wartime ground crew had gone quickly to prime jobs in civilian aviation or comfortable shore billets in the RCAF, so there wasn't enough skill to go around. Short of flyable aircraft, pilots were lucky to get four hours in the air per month, which was dangerously low. Even in 1948 Lieutenant Commander Pop Fotheringham, an Air Group Commander, was getting under seven hours. It wasn't until 1950 that pilots got a reasonable twenty hours a month.

In fairness, the RCN wasn't alone in its accidents and casualties. But the early years were too expensive in aircraft and, what is worse, in good people. Carrier aviation had grown up in wartime hazard. One didn't dwell on the death of a squadron mate but laughed it off – risk be damned. Surviving the dangers of the sea and the violence of the enemy in the faithful old Stringbag bred a cavalier, press-on-regardless outlook. Amazing deeds went with ludicrous aircraft. This rubbed off easily on the Canadians, an ebullient lot themselves.

Now these young aviators were trying to prove themselves in a navy that understood little about the air. They tried to do too much with an oversized can-do approach. Thinking of safety, as Air Group Commander Ray Creery said later, was looked on as a sign of cold feet.

An accident required the pilot to make out a report on a form "A 25." Wartime had produced the classic Air Arm song:

They say in the Air Force the landing's okay,
If the pilot gets out and can still walk away.
But in the Fleet Air Arm the chances are slim,
If the landing is poor and the pilot can't swim.
Cracking show!
I'm alive!
But I still have to render my A-twenty-five.

The song lived on with many ribald and cheerfully insulting Canadian verses added. The naval aviators were an insouciant, irrepressible lot who worked as hard as they played. But poor aircraft, marginal maintenance, and too little flying practice equalled too many killed. Major accidents were running at five, six, seven per 10,000 flying hours, which was unacceptably high. In the six months from October, 1948, to March, 1949, seven aircrew lost their lives.

There was talk of suspending flying. Operations were set aside for basic measures like tighter training, more attention to safety, upgrading of instrument flying standards. Challenge would always be part of the game, but it was a game for professionals. The dashing aviator with the white scarf and the cracking-show syndrome had to go.

At last Canadian naval aviation looked to North America for aircraft and for attitude. It had been through a bad time, as had the navy as a whole. "A bloody war or a sickly season" has been the toast drunk on Thursday night in naval messes for generations. In the dark old days, it took gunfire or an epidemic to make room for promotion. From war's end to 1950, Canada's navy had been through its own sickly season. Now, new prescriptions had been written and new cleansing winds began to stir.

NATO was calling for commitment. Concepts for ships designed and built in Canada were taking shape. The coming years would see new ships, new aircraft, new people, new drives, energy, thrust, and, above all, a new, proud, and quite distinctly Canadian naval identity. And suddenly there was a war to fight along the way.

CHAPTER TWELVE
KOREA

THE OPENING GUNS

ABLE SEAMAN GEORGE BROWN, A STEWARD IN HMCS *ATHABASKAN* ALONG-
side in Esquimalt, was working in the wardroom pantry on a fine June
morning in 1950 when a messmate called down, "Hey, war just broke out in
Korea." Brown said, "Oh, where's Korea?"

He and his shipmates found out quickly enough. In ten days *Athabaskan*,
Cayuga, and *Sioux* were topped up with ammunition, stores, and all the extra
men and spare parts they could filch from other ships in Esquimalt and were
on their way to join the United Nations force in the Korean War.

Few Canadians knew any more about Korea than Brown. At the end of
World War Two an Asian equivalent of Europe's Iron Curtain had drawn
across the Korean peninsula at the 38th parallel. North Korea was firmly in
the Communist Chinese orbit. South Korea emerged as a somewhat shaky
democracy. Nearby, Japan was garrisoned by the Allied occupation forces –
mostly U.S. troops – under General Douglas MacArthur.

The United Nations Commission on Korea watched uneasily as tensions
between the two small states rose. At dawn on Sunday, 25 June 1950, North
Korean troops and tanks burst across the border. The United Nations Security
Council call to withdraw was ignored. Two days later the United States put a
resolution to the Security Council asking all members to help the Republic of
Korea repel the attack and restore peace and security. The U.S.S.R. had only just
withdrawn from the Security Council. It couldn't exercise its veto and the
resolution passed. President Truman had already ordered U.S. forces to help
South Korea and neutralize Formosa. Now he had the legal stamp.

In four days Britain turned her ships in the Far East over to the UN under
General MacArthur. Australia and New Zealand followed. The next day, on
30 June, the House of Commons in Ottawa rallied unanimously behind Louis

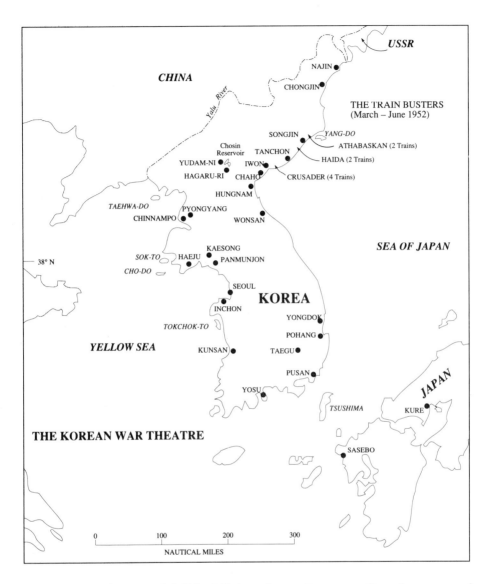

St. Laurent and External Affairs Minister Lester Pearson – Canada supported the UN. Only the navy could provide a fighting force for immediate service; hence, on the 5th of July the three destroyers sailed. In command was Captain Jeffry Brock in *Cayuga*.

THE NAVY'S ROLE

As the Canadian ships island-hopped across the Pacific, North Korean infantry swept through the Republic of Korea (ROK) forces and some hastily mustered U.S. troops. The USN rushed fresh troops from Japan to Pusan at the southern tip of the peninsula. By the time the Canadian ships arrived in Sasebo, Japan, on 30 July, the Pusan bridgehead was surrounded by North Koreans and defeat was very close.

There were a lot of old hands in the destroyers, and green ones like young George Brown. None of them knew what to expect. What kind of enemy were they up against? Submarines? Aircraft? Torpedo boats? Were the Russians coming in? What about atomic bombs? The answer was, be ready for anything. They started right away, escorting troopships to Pusan and taking oilers around to the west coast for the naval force already there. For the third war in a row the navy was the first in action. On 15 August, with fierce fighting going on ashore, *Cayuga* opened fire on port installations at Yosu, the first of 130,000 rounds hurled at the enemy ashore by Canadian ships over the next three years.

In September, General MacArthur launched a full-scale amphibious landing at Inchon on the west coast, spearheaded by U.S. Marines, and suddenly the situation was turned around. The enemy besieging Pusan cracked and ran north in disorder. The ROK and U.S. forces followed. The UN navy battered at their flanks and flew strike after strike from the carriers. The North Koreans retreated across the 38th parallel, then crossed the Yalu River with the 6th ROK Division at their heels. The river was the border with Communist China, and there the Allies stopped.

The UN navy's role was the historic one of projecting land power. It could deliver men and material across the ocean, put forces ashore when and where it chose, evacuate them when it had to. It could support the land battle with air strikes anywhere on the peninsula and gunfire on the seaward flanks. Overwhelming power at sea held the whole of it in a tight blockade against infiltration and support, except of course overland from the north, from Communist China, and that was immune. The war must finally be decided on land, but without control of the sea the UN would have been powerless to pursue it.

The American 7th Fleet was strongly reinforced and provided the fast carriers, Task Force 77. It operated in the Sea of Japan, east of Korea. The RN had a light fleet carrier, HMS *Triumph*, three cruisers, and four destroyers, and Australia and the Netherlands each contributed a destroyer. Including the Canadians, the total UN force by October, 1950, counted eight carriers, a battleship, nine cruisers, fifty-four destroyers, six submarines, sixteen minecraft, over 100 amphibious force vessels, and seventy-five transports. There was also a sizable swarm of ROK small craft for the close, inshore work.

Some North Korean gunboats were knocked out early on and there was no sign of more naval opposition, no sign of Soviet submarines. Commonwealth naval forces worked mainly on the western, Yellow Sea side. A brush with the Chinese or Soviet light forces was more likely there, and such an encounter would be less explosive than if American ships were involved. The North Koreans had few aircraft to worry about, though that could change at any time. The hazards at the moment were shore batteries and mines.

INSHORE OPERATIONS

Through the Inchon landings and the North Korean retreat all ships ran flat out. The west coast is difficult, shallow, heavily indented, and studded with small islands, rocks, and shoals. Tides range to thirty feet and run strong. Channels shift and change. There are few good harbors but countless villages, fishing coves, and landing places – ideal for enemy small craft to slip in, land raiding parties, and sow mines. Navigation is taxing and tricky. Mines laid on the bottom – acoustic, pressure, and magnetic types – were a constant hazard. So were drifting mines sown by small craft.

Athabaskan, commanded by an experienced destroyer man, Commander Robert Welland, worked non-stop like all the others. In a single patrol she co-ordinated landings with ROK forces, sent parties of her own ashore, bombarded enemy enclaves, illuminated night operations with starshell, intercepted junks and other small craft, destroyed a radio station with demolitions, and gave medical treatment to ROK and civilian casualties. George Brown's regular duty as a steward was serving meals and tending to the wardroom. But he was often at his action station at B gun. Also, he'd had some first-aid courses and volunteered his services to the medical officer, which meant sometimes going ashore to help evacuate wounded soldiers and civilians.

Mines took endless vigilance. Sonar could often detect them, but in these tight waters there were close calls. *Athabaskan* had a real problem with moored mines in her area. She couldn't reach them with 40mm gunfire when they were floating at low water, but at high water they were an invisible menace. This called for ingenuity. Commissioned Gunner David Hurl took in the motor cutter with the ship's little sailing dinghy in tow.

He closed on the first mine in the dinghy. The trick was for the oarsman very delicately to keep it just far enough from the mine to avoid a fatal explosion but close enough for Hurl and his helper to reach over the bow and attach a TNT charge. Then the oarsman backed off and rowed away like mad, and up went a spectacular explosion. The team scored four mines by the turn of the tide. Next day HMAS *Bataan* learned the Canadian trick and joined in.

OPERATION COMEBACK

The wretched plight of the Koreans living in the war-torn islands, washed over by the tides of war, had made a deep impression on the Canadians. They had done what they could where they could but it was a daunting task and winter was coming on. Back in Sasebo for maintenance in September, Captain Brock put a plan to Vice Admiral Andrewes, RN, to get the inhabitants back on their feet. The idea was to clear out pockets of North Koreans and sympathizers, establish law and order, set up guarded fishing sanctuaries, and provide food and medical aid. Andrewes heartily approved and told off two of the Canadian destroyers and some ROK vessels for Operation Comeback, under Brock's command. After Inchon, with the enemy pushed north, the destroyers weren't needed for cover so the ROKs did the job themselves.

The UN advance to the Yalu River in October had the messdecks buzzing that it would all be over by Christmas. Forces on patrol were reduced. The Canadian ships were given a spell in Hong Kong. On the way they rode out a typhoon. To George Brown in *Athabaskan* his first tropical storm was awesome. A man was swept over the side but rescued by Welland's skilful shiphandling. The new sailor's unspoken fears that no ship could survive such monstrous seas were dispelled by the sight of a forty-foot sailing junk bobbing along safe as a cork.

The ships all had weather damage to repair in the RN's Hong Kong dockyard as well as getting up on their maintenance backlogs. Hong Kong always had entrepreneurial working parties, mostly Chinese women, who contracted with the First Lieutenant to do all manner of ship's work, such as chipping, scraping, and painting the side and upper deck. Their "pay" was the privilege of taking the food the ship would otherwise throw away – something to give well-fed Canadians cause to reflect. Hong Kong has always been a legendary leave-port, so for the men their spell of leave ashore for the first time in four months was one to remember.

CHINNAMPO

In late November Captain Brock took over the west coast blockade with the three Canadian destroyers, two Australians, an American, and three small ROKs. Suddenly, the news that many feared flashed in – the Chinese army had come into the land battle, and in force. It was a whole new war. On the eastern front the Tenth Corps pulled back with heavy casualties but stayed intact. On the west the front crumbled. Chinese troops lanced through, and the Eighth Army broke in full retreat.

Another sea withdrawal loomed. Chinnampo, the port for the North Korean capital of Pyongyang, was the place and transports were on the way. Brock disposed his force to cover the transports to the harbour approaches and give gunfire support to the army retreating south. On 4 December, with Chinnampo bulging with refugees, troops, and stores, the senior USN officer there signalled, "The local situation may reach emergency basis (tomorrow) forenoon." Offshore in *Cayuga*, Brock had to make the tough decisions.

The passage up Daido-ko estuary to Chinnampo was a tortuous twenty miles through a maze of low islands and shifting mudflats. On a clear day with the right tide it was difficult enough. Added to the natural hazards were hundreds of mines planted by the North Koreans when they had pulled north. A swept channel 500 yards wide was marked by unlit dan-buoys, but with the current and the tide their positions were shaky at best, and navigation marks were suspect. No UN ship had ever tried the passage at night. It was likely, too, that floating mines would be released from the myriad small craft about. Altogether, Chinnampo was an unappetizing proposition, especially as the destroyers couldn't get there before nightfall.

But the enemy was nearly at the gates. The transports there would need destroyers' guns to get them clear. Waiting until morning could very well mean that the destroyers would be too late. Captain Brock made his decision, and at 8:30 that night he took the lead in *Cayuga* and headed in. It was, said Bob Welland, following in *Athabaskan*, "one of the blackest nights I have ever seen."

All the Canadian ships had the new Sperry radar. It could detect very small targets like snorkels, even dan-buoys. It was outstanding in precision work at short ranges and better in that bracket than anything the other Allies had. Equipment, of course, is only as good as the people using it, but the Canadians' skill at spotting tiny targets and using their radar to navigate in very close waters was already proved.

HMAS *Warramunga*, running behind, grounded and dropped downstream to check for damage. *Sioux*, with Commander Paul Taylor, grounded lightly, backed off the mudbank, and her screw fouled a dan-buoy wire that had drifted into the channel. She, too, had to drop back. In *Cayuga*'s operations room, the Navigator, Lieutenant Andy Collier, used the Sperry radar and fixed the ship's position with consummate skill every two minutes for the four-hour blind passage. On the bridge Brock conned the ship through the inky dark. *Athabaskan*, *Bataan*, and *Forrest Royal* followed and the four anchored before dawn off Chinnampo. As Captain Brock ordered, "Ring off main engines," the harbour looked to him "a blaze of lights and all peaceful and serene."

Serene was hardly the word for the day that dawned. A Chinese breakthrough was reported by the Eighth Army twenty miles north. Refugees swarmed, trying desperately to get south in junks, sampans, anything that floated. Vast quantities of war materiel had to be loaded into the LSTs and transports or demolished, and loaded ships had to finish their outward passages before night fell – a ship aground could plug escape for the rest.

Demolition and fire parties were detailed to destroy what couldn't be loaded. They, too, would pull out at dusk. Ships' gunfire would wreak the final destruction after the docks were cleared. Targets were identified and allocated to each ship's gunners. The day raced on. Explosions shattered rail lines, boxcars, workshops, warehouses, factories. Smoke rose in columns.

Athabaskan moved to seaward to hold a protected anchorage halfway down. It was intended for the destroyers when their job was done and for any other ships that couldn't make the open sea by dark. Steward Brown was at his gun station as the ship slipped along with the procession of sampans and junks. Armed sailors in the ship's boats searched native craft for mines; sonar probed; lookouts kept eyes peeled for floaters. Along the bank lay a string of concrete pillboxes, empty now but waiting occupation by the enemy. Welland passed the word to knock them out. Brown and his mates passed ammunition, and the 4-inch guns blasted away point blank, shattering pillboxes one by one.

Back at Chinnampo there was still no sign of the enemy. As darkness fell the last shore parties put the torch to the dockside and pulled out. The fires lit the scene enough for the gunners to spot their targets. Three destroyers opened fire. With the first broadsides they started fresh blazes. The whole waterfront lit up – an oil tank flung a huge shower of molten metal, then another; giant fireballs merged into a pall of thick black smoke. The guns hammered away through the night, brewing a monstrous inferno of destruction. From *Athabaskan*'s anchorage, Chinnampo looked to George Brown "like the Fourth of July."

At first light the destroyers weighed anchor and shepherded the last of the LSTs downstream. All ships were clear of the channel by mid-forenoon. It had been an impeccable operation in a tense, action-packed thirty-six hours. In the words of Admiral Andrewes, it was "a fine feat of seamanship on the part of all concerned, and its bold execution was worthy of the finest traditions of the Naval Service." Decorations were awarded, in part at least, for Chinnampo. Captain Brock got the Distinguished Service Order to add to his World War Two DSC, Commander Welland a bar to his DSC, Lieutenant Collier the DSC; the British Empire Medal went to Chief Petty Officer D. J. Pearson, *Cayuga*'s Coxswain. He'd been in charge of the wheelhouse and at the wheel himself during those faultless river passages.

But this was a retreat and not a victory. The report of an enemy breakthrough had in fact been wrong, but the Eighth Army was badly shattered and confusion reigned ashore. On the eastern front the Tenth Corps pulled out by sea to Pusan. Inchon was now the west coast evacuation port. The destroyers ran and ran, topping up with fuel and ammunition from replenishment ships offshore, going in for more shooting, trading gunfire as the enemy moved south. The army pulled out of Inchon and in early January it was abandoned.

CREATURE COMFORTS

The destroyers rotated to Sasebo for maintenance and a rest. When *Cayuga* got in she'd been on patrol, including Chinnampo, for a full fifty days. Christmas was livened as always by the youngest man in the ship becoming Captain for the day. *Athabaskan*'s "Captain," resplendent in Commander Welland's bemedalled blues, ordered away his motor boat and called on Vice Admiral Dewey Struble, USN, flying his flag in the battleship *Missouri*. The Admiral, with due courtesy, entertained the young "Captain" in his splendid cabin in "Mighty

Mo," gave him a glass of medicinal brandy and a large cigar, and saw he was properly piped back over the side.

At the UN bases new sailors like Brown saw the three navies side by side. The Commonwealth base at Kure, near Hiroshima in the lush and lovely Inland Sea, was much less to their liking than the main U.S. base at Sasebo. The British had the right kinds of ammunition and machinery spares for the Canadian ships, but ashore there wasn't much for sailors and British provisions were terrible. Canadian ration scales were much better than RN now, but in Kure they mostly got tough mutton. It was supplied, per RN custom, by the carcass. From the Americans in Sasebo there was first-rate beef, neatly butchered, trimmed, and ready to cook. Steaks, the great U.S. Navy staple, came right from the package to the grill. Ice cream, milk, fresh fruit and vegetables, and such magic as frozen French fries came in abundance and packed with ships in mind.

The young fellows were getting to be seasoned fighting sailors. The destroyers' operations rooms, weapons, equipment, and communications had been improved, and both men and equipment got better with use – and they had plenty of that. This was a gunnery war and the tradition of the fighting Tribals was very much alive. Living conditions, though, were mostly as of yore. *Sioux* had been fitted with bunks and a central cafeteria as an experiment a few months before she went to Korea; but even the Halifax-built destroyers, laid down in wartime, had followed RN plans.

In *Athabaskan*, George Brown and eleven others lived, ate their food, and slung their hammocks like sardines in the stewards' mess. It was about the size of an average home's kitchen. Sailors were issued with two hammocks, a thin mattress, two mattress covers, two blankets – no sheets, no pillow or pillowcase. A man who harboured notions of hygiene and comfort bought his own.

The faithful and time-worn hammock, which every old sailor remembers with wry affection, was a relic of sailing men-of-war. Seamen then slung them in the open 'tween-decks over the guns. A dozen men formed a mess, rigged a portable table, and that's where they lived, prepared and ate their food, and slept. With a leading hand in charge, the "mess" was the social unit of the ship. The USN had turned hammocks in for bunks long since, as Canadians who served in the horrendously rolling four-stackers well remembered. Also, their men fed in separate mess-rooms. It was far more efficient and sanitary and food was served to each man direct from the galley, piping hot. The RN had stuck firmly to the old concept that men, their hammocks, lockers, living, and feeding arrangements fitted in where weapons weren't.

Officers in RN ships lived in relative style in a club-like wardroom fitted with comfortable (but inflammable) mahogany and leather. They could spend pleasant leisure hours there and entertain themselves and their guests with a drink – at modest expense because liquor was duty free. Sometimes the

George Browns served at some pretty boisterous parties. Wartime, though, had ingrained a general "no drinking when under way" dictum in the wardroom.

Canadian ships and customs still followed the RN suit. There was a separate officers' galley with specially trained cooks who were adept at getting the best cuts from the carcass. Dinner in the wardroom in harbour on special occasions was an elegant affair with polished table, gleaming silver, and sparkling crystal filled with good wines. In Sasebo, Kure, or a quiet isolated anchorage, such a dinner was a chance to extend hospitality, celebrate an event, entertain a distinguished visitor, or just enjoy good fellowship. It preserved a certain island of civility in harsh and grinding times.

In USN ships the men were far better off but officers' wardrooms were rather spartan places, mainly for eating with little added comfort. That pushed officers back to their own staterooms, where they worked endlessly on correspondence courses and as like as not kept a bottle for a surreptitious drink. The ship wasn't their home as it was in the British tradition – in harbour they got ashore as fast as they could to the officers' club or a restaurant or a bar. Overall, the USN's modern ships combined far better creature comfort for the majority in conjunction with heavier armament.

As always, the bar in the Canadian wardroom and rum in the messdecks were magnets to the USN. Officer or man, the reciprocal hospitality of American steaks and ice cream with a first-run movie to follow were doubly enjoyed in the hot, humid Sasebo summer. USN ships had been air-conditioned for years. The RCN's old Rolls-Royce destroyers had led the RN with steam heat by some twenty years, but air-conditioning was still to come.

Not long before George Brown joined the navy, it had taken a leaf from the USN book and issued all men with dungarees for everyday working dress. Before that, World War Two included, only stokers and artisans had boiler suits. Everyone else worked in his blue serge or tropical white shorts and kept one suit clean and "tiddly" for Sunday Divisions and going ashore. Another USN lead put officers, chiefs, and petty officers into khaki uniform for summer weather. In American navy stores dungarees and khakis were top quality and dirt cheap. George Brown noted the USN sailor changed his dungarees every day and sent them to the ship's laundry. Canadians changed theirs once a week and put them in the washing machine they'd bought with their own canteen funds. The British sailors changed theirs once a month and washed them in a bucket.

Ashore the Americans had ship's exchanges with every imaginable goodie at rock-bottom prices. There were recreation facilities, USO shows with top stars, leave centres in Tokyo and Japanese resorts – and a Shore Patrol that used nightsticks first and asked questions after. The Sasebo hotels had lush hot baths fed by volcanic springs.

ARMY AND AIR FORCE

The first of the Canadian Brigade Group, the 2nd Battalion Princess Patricia's Light Infantry, had arrived in Pusan on 18 December. They finished their training there and joined the British Commonwealth Brigade at the end of February, 1951. After seven months the destroyer men weren't the only Canadians on the front line in the Korean War.

In the meantime an RCAF transport squadron was plugging efficiently away on the Pacific airlift. No Canadian air fighting units went to the Korean War. RCN airmen made a determined bid to get *Magnificent* out there, but the carrier was needed in the Atlantic for NATO. Later, nudged through the personal net, the RN asked for a Canadian Sea Fury squadron to fly from their Korean carrier. It was working up for the job when the war ended. Lieutenant J.J. MacBrien, on exchange with a USN squadron flying Panther jets, spent six months off Korea in USS *Oriskany*. He flew sixty-six combat missions, mostly ground attack, and was the first Canadian to win the U.S. Navy's Distinguished Flying Cross.

DARK NEW YEAR

At the end of 1950 the whole of North Korea was firmly in enemy hands. Withdrawals continued; General MacArthur's headquarters was in disarray; morale had shrivelled. Talk was that the UN would soon be right out of the whole peninsula. At the United Nations the General Assembly set up a Cease-fire Committee. But the Chinese were implacable. There would be no compromise and no end to the fighting.

The beaten, dispirited American Eighth Army was whipped into fighting shape by General Matthew Ridgway, the new ground forces commander who arrived in late December. The Chinese took Seoul but the defence held south of the Han River. Revived units moved up from Pusan; fighting spirit was restored. The UN, including the Princess Pat's, attacked in the harsh winter weather. Hard fighting forced the enemy out of Seoul. The ships, coping with cold, pan ice, and blinding snowstorms, hammered away with their guns along the flanks. By April, all South Korea was back in UN hands. The workhorse destroyers had fired 60,000 shells at the enemy, a fair share of those from Canadian guns. They had also taken relief food and supplies to a great number of destitute and suffering Koreans.

Nootka had left Halifax in November, arrived in Sasebo in mid-January, and the next day *Sioux* sailed for home. *Huron*, from Halifax, would spell off *Cayuga* in March and *Sioux* would come back to spell *Athabaskan* in May. From then on the rotation kept each ship away from her home port for about a year.

THE YELLOW SEA FUELLING STAKES

The carriers ran day in, day out through that winter, flying strikes, reconnaissance, and bombardment spotting sorties. The Canadians spent a lot of time off the west coast screening the duty carrier and rotating on plane guard. It meant high-speed steaming and topping up with fuel from a carrier or fleet oiler every couple of days. Mostly it was dull work.

But whatever the manoeuvre, doing it precisely right, smartly, and faster than the next is the mark of a good ship, and every sailor worth his salt works his butt off to make sure his ship is the top. That way even a chore like fuelling at sea can liven up a long patrol. To do it right calls for polished skill and split-second timing by the whole team: finely judged shiphandling by the Captain or Officer of the Watch; instant response by the helmsman and the engine room and boiler room crews; skilful line throwing and handling on the upper deck; dexterity with tools – all on a moving deck in whatever weather God provides. It doesn't *have* to be done faster than the next ship, but sailors are always sailors.

The record in the Commonwealth ships, from the moment the first line was thrown across until pumping started, was eight minutes; the tanker always did the timing. *Sioux*, at her first crack Canadian-style, knocked it down to 4:46. *Cayuga* beat that by a minute. Then, during a long spell of carrier screening in March, *Athabaskan* and *Nootka* polished their skills, whittling away at the record. Finally, they were assigned to fuel in succession from the oiler *Wave Knight*. The RN tanker had a sporting Captain and an agile Chinese crew.

Nootka ran in fast and close. Up went the "pumping started" signal in an amazing two minutes and twelve seconds. To beat it meant the narrowest possible gap between ships. With the whole ship's company on the upper deck to cheer their fuelling team, Commander Welland took *Athabaskan* in himself, scant feet from the oiler. The first line was over, the hose hauled across and coupled on, and pumping begun in an incredible one minute and forty seconds.

That was it. For safety's sake, the Canadians called the competition off and let that record stand. No one else in the entire multi-nation UN navy ever touched it. Replenishment at sea has been refined over the years and Canada's navy has taken a lead in developing gear and techniques. But the basic principles still apply and seamanship wins. Topping the fuelling stakes is a Canadian navy tradition to this day.

Soon after, *Athabaskan* took the short great circle route home via the Aleutians. Getting alongside the exposed fuelling jetty in Adack in a gale-driven snowstorm, ship's legend had it that Welland came in at twenty-five knots. It wasn't that fast, of course, but George Brown swore the American sailors on the jetty ran for their lives. One precisely timed "Half astern" on the engines and the ship nudged so gently alongside she wouldn't crack an egg. Their Captain's shiphandling was as much a point of pride in the stewards' mess as on the upper deck. Brown's other lasting memory was the fresh, clean scent of evergreens that wafted out to greet the ship as she closed the lush forest of the B.C. coast. The perfumes of the Orient had their allure, though. He volunteered for *Athabaskan*'s second tour.

THE SEAWARD FLANKS

By spring the blockade and escort force, Task Force 95, had eighty-five ships – carriers, cruisers, and destroyers – clamped around the peninsula. Mostly, the Canadians worked the west coast. Shore raiding parties with ship's gunfire kept the enemy off balance, worried always about another big amphibious assault. Destroyer guns backed ROK landing parties and they seized the islands in the approaches to Inchon and Chinnampo. The blockade spread north right to the Yalu River to stop everything that moved. Even Chinese fishing boats were targets because they were landing their catches in North Korea. *Nootka* caught a Chinese fishing fleet in dense fog. Off went the motor cutter with an armed party, and the ship guided them with radar and radio as they rounded up the whole fleet.

In late May *Nootka* joined in hitting the railway and roads on the east coast. The east side of Korea is quite different from the west. Shores are steep, almost unbroken, and backed by mountains. The water is deep inshore and the rise and fall of tide is slight – good conditions for moored mines. The prevailing current is north to south so floating mines were always a threat, too. The main railway line hugged the coast, ducking through tunnels and crossing trestles. It was the main supply line for the North Koreans and a prime target for naval bombardment.

Nootka's first target was a bridge near Songjin spanning a gully between two tunnels. There'd been some doubt that the enemy was actually using the line and as *Nootka* moved in there was no sign of life. On the principle that well-placed explosives are more certain than gunfire for such jobs, Commander Fraser Fraser-Harris decided on an armed landing party and demolition crew in the motor cutter, with Lieutenant Tony Slater in charge. At this point fog moved in. The ship couldn't back them with gunfire now but they could get inshore unseen.

The cutter chugged steadily in. Along the shrouded shore nothing moved. There was little surf and the cutter crunched up on the rocky beach. Out popped North Korean soldiers from the tunnels above and laid down a blistering fire. Slater's crew fired steadily back. He'd been told not to stay and do battle and pulled out in good order. A little more patience by the North Koreans and the foray could have had an ugly end. From then on *Nootka* stuck to gunfire. But Fraser-Harris came from the "cracking-show" school of naval aviators. He had been a squadron commander with the RN and the first pilot to land a Seafire on a carrier and had the DSC and bar. He added some ingenious twists.

Next he drew a specially stubborn target that the whole force had dubbed "The Rubber Bridge." It was a trestle that shrugged off shells. Any damage was repaired at night and the trains kept rolling. Fraser-Harris, with the naval aviator's light regard for gunners, saw he must get in really close. There was high risk of mines along the shore, however, and there were no sweepers about, so *Nootka* provided her own. Two motor cutters towed a wire between them and swept a channel. *Nootka* followed in, searching with sonar for mines and firing Squid bombs ahead as an extra counter. Cautiously, they moved right in. The cutters' wire snagged nothing. They got inside 1,300 yards from shore.

Suddenly soldiers poured from the tunnels. *Nootka* levelled her 4-inch guns, firing right over her own boats at near point-blank range. The 40mms joined in. The enemy scuttled for cover. *Nootka* then turned her guns on the trestle as USS *Stickell* followed her wake, joining the party with her 5-inch guns. The Rubber Bridge was reduced to splinters. Resource and that ever-ready willingness of the Canadians to work the small ship close inshore did what hundreds of heavy shells hadn't. *Nootka* won a cutter-load of fresh fish for her trouble, killed by the Squid bombs. The North Koreans at great expense of time and labour restored the rail line by filling in the gully.

TRUCE TALKS

By mid-June the Chinese and North Koreans were badly battered. They made overtures and truce talks began on 10 July 1951 at Kaesong. But it was a holding device and talks went on sporadically for two years. There was no more major land offensive but there were fierce actions with limited objectives. They cost the UN another 100,000 casualties.

Naval and air forces could keep pressure on the enemy with less risk so the truce was even busier for the ships in many ways. The west coast islands were a shifting, dangerous battleground. Both sides wanted them because they controlled harbour approaches and communications and were used to gather intelligence. The enemy wanted them for mining bases. The ships worked hand in glove with ROK units and guerrilla groups ashore.

Lieutenant Donald Saxon was an anti-submarine specialist but this was a war without submarines, so he became liaison officer with the ROK units. Living ashore with the South Koreans, he joined in planning and organizing raids and counterattacks and supporting guerrilla actions. They used fleets of small boats, junks, and sampans. Saxon organized support by the ships: supplies and medical help; gunfire; starshell when needed. For his outstanding services in this phase of the war he won the DSC. There were some fierce skirmishes and the ships' medical parties tended a lot of the wounded, many of them ashore in difficult situations.

THE GREAT IMPOSTOR

Around this time *Cayuga*'s medical officer, Surgeon Lieutenant Joseph Cyr, drew a lot of attention in the hero-hungry press in Canada for some spectacular medical feats and operations on wounded Koreans under fire in primitive conditions ashore.

But "Dr. Cyr" was actually Ferdinand Waldo Demara, an American with a strange psychosis who made his bizarre way through life filling fantasy roles. He had served a hitch as a medical corpsman in the U.S. Navy and so knew the medical jargon. A real Dr. Joseph Cyr practised medicine in rural New Brunswick and was also licensed in the state of Maine. Demara had called on Dr. Cyr, introduced himself as an American physician interested in the same kind of practice from the U.S. side. He borrowed Dr. Cyr's medical documents, saying they'd help him with his application, and presented himself, documents and all, at the Naval Division in Saint John as a volunteer for active service.

With the war on, doctors were badly needed and he got a quick commission as a Surgeon Lieutenant. In Halifax he blended affably into the wardroom officers' mess. He genially carried out routine medical duties in the naval hospital and even took over as resident psychiatrist when the regular well-qualified practitioner went away on a course. Off to Korea in *Cayuga* on her second tour, his exploits – real or apocryphal – were his undoing. In October, 1951, when Demara had been a seagoing medical officer for five months, the real Dr. Cyr spotted a newspaper account of amazing deeds by the brave New Brunswick doctor. He'd seen the face in the photo before, and he blew the whistle.

Demara was rushed back to Canada, released by an embarrassed navy, and deported. He basked in the limelight and perhaps some wealth for a time as consultant on a Hollywood film about himself called *The Great Impostor*. His strange mental quirk took him into more weird situations; none, though, could match the sheer gall of posing as a ship's medical officer in a war zone. He actually had extracted Commander Jamie Plomer's wisdom teeth – and neatly and efficiently, at that. It was lucky for the ship's company that they were the most critical thing he had to remove. No one ever knew how many Korean lives might in fact have been saved had Ferdinand Demara been a genuine MD.

ANOTHER YEAR

New Year's in the navy is traditionally rung in by sixteen strokes on the ship's bell. *Cayuga* welcomed 1952 with sixteen salvoes fired at enemy positions on the stroke of midnight. Enemy aircraft were appearing now, from airfields beyond the Yalu River in Manchuria or China. They hit ground targets in the islands so when the destroyers were working inshore away from the carrier, they had their own Combat Air Patrol (CAP) flying overhead for defence.

The price of staying the UN advance in June had come home to roost. The Communist forces had dug in with enormous strength and firepower all along the truce line. The chances of taking them by storm or forcing a reasonable settlement were gone. Another amphibious assault behind enemy lines was out because of the total forces they could muster.

Ships lived off the fleet train and rotated for major storing and maintenance in Japan and rest and recreation in Hong Kong. The UN navy was endlessly busy around the islands off the west coast. Along the east coast there were railway and road targets and gunfire support of the army's flanks. And the enemy gun batteries on the east coast were getting far more accurate. They hit over a dozen ships. *Nootka* got close into an eight-gun battery and took some near ones that raked the upper deck. She had to do some fast manoeuvring. In October, *Iroquois* was on a "railway package" bombardment when she was hit by a shore battery. One officer and two men were killed and ten wounded. The dead and badly wounded were transferred to an oiler, the damage patched, and the ship back on task, barely missing a beat. The Captain, Commander Bill Landymore, had seen plenty of action before.

The east coast railway got endless pounding from air and sea but it stubbornly stayed in business. Ships' gunners now zeroed in on the trains themselves. A USN ship destroyed two on a single patrol in July, 1952, and the great game now for every ship was to get a bona fide membership in the "Trainbusters Club." It wasn't that easy. The tunnels along the line gave solid shelter, and if a train was stopped with gunfire the engine often was uncoupled and shunted to safety. The club rule was that you had to get the engine itself to score a complete train.

Crusader, who relieved *Iroquois* in the fall, smashed boxcars in one train and hit all the cars and demolished the engine of another. *Haida*, fresh in from Halifax, stopped a train and destroyed the cars but the engine chuffed into a tunnel. On her last Korean patrol in May, 1953, she scored a clean kill and then a second.

With all this opposition the trains usually ran at night. An alert ship's lookout could spot sparks from the fire-box and from the wheels when the engine braked. Then up went the starshell and the guns would swing into action.

Crusader's 4.5-inch guns proved deadly again in April, 1953. Her Gunnery Officer, Lieutenant Fred Copas, spotted a southbound train on a dark night. All guns swung into action and quickly knocked it off the tracks. In the morning the ship lay off and deliberately smashed the wreckage, one shot at a time. Then in late afternoon another train was spotted on an inland spur. Lieutenant Commander John Bovey took his ship in to the very edge of the swept channel. The range was still 14,000 yards – seven nautical miles – but the guns were right on. Direct hits quickly stopped the train. In minutes another appeared on the same track and that, too, was knocked off.

Crusader was now the UN champion trainbuster. While the gunners were sponging out their smoking barrels and touching up blistered paintwork, the ship raced off to join the fast carriers of Task Force 77. Her fame had gone before her. As she sighted the powerful force – three fast Essex-class carriers, one battleship, a cruiser, and twelve destroyers – the Commander, Rear Admiral R.F. Hickey, USN, welcomed her personally on voice radio. *Crusader*'s uninspiring call sign was "Leadmine," but Admiral Hickey changed it on the spot to "Casey Jones." (The Admiral's call sign was, appropriately, "Jehovah.")

Trainbusting, for want of ships to fight, stayed as the main sport. *Athabaskan* scored two and that made a final total of eight for the RCN. It was a remarkable figure. The combined score by UN ships for the entire war was twenty-eight trains. The Canadians, only three of some eighty destroyers, spent most of their time on the other coast. Their gun armament wasn't nearly as powerful as the USN's. But from their captains down they were masters at using what they had. No ship of whatever size ever matched *Crusader*'s score.

WAR'S END

The fighting ended with an armistice on 27 July 1953. The Chinese and North Koreans were highly unpredictable, and without a full political settlement there'd be no letup. In January, 1954, the Canadian army force was cut but the full complement of three destroyers worked steadily on, patrol after patrol, until the end of the year. Like the navy itself it was first in, last out: *Sioux*, with Commander Gus Rankin, stayed until September, 1955.

Eight of the RCN's eleven destroyers completed twenty-one tours of duty among them – *Cayuga, Athabaskan, Sioux*, and *Crusader* from the Pacific Command and *Haida, Huron, Iroquois*, and *Nootka* from the Atlantic. Over 3,500 officers and men served there at least once. Three were killed and two severely wounded.

The Korean War was hard slogging, often tedious and dull, sometimes charged with danger. Always there was tension. Ships spent 65 per cent of their time under way, with patrols ranging up to fifty days. Most ships' companies were away from home for a year. And this was "peacetime." But morale was extraordinarily high – it was foreign; it was different; there were some breaks for leave in a fascinating country and most ships had a rest period in Hong Kong. Mainly, though, they were doing a job that had to be done, working at it hard, and doing it well. The ships hit the heights of efficiency. From Chinnampo on, the RCN earned a real reputation in the sister navies for resourcefulness, efficiency, and getting things done with spirit and dispatch.

When *Crusader* parted company from Task Force 77 after four days of high-speed screening, Admiral Hickey signalled: "I want you, your officers and your men to know that you leave with the deep and profound admiration of all for your enviable performance during your stay. Your ship operated like a veteran from the beginning. I consider your alertness and efficiency in all your operations an outstanding lesson to sailormen everywhere."

Such accolades are not earned lightly. It could well have applied, other times, other places, to the other ships' companies in Korea. They had done a first-class job, an important one, for the UN, for peace, and for Canada. And they had done a great deal for the navy. Korea brought out in them a standard of excellence, a special and distinctive way of doing the job – their own way. Canadian sailors, in what was now a fast-expanding fleet, had shown themselves again what they could do.

CHAPTER THIRTEEN
THE NEW NAVY

A BANNER YEAR

WHEN VICE ADMIRAL HAROLD GRANT, CHIEF OF NAVAL STAFF, FLEW TO Korea to inspect the destroyers in late 1950, he brought heartening news from Ottawa. The St. Laurent government had raised the navy's ceiling to 13,000 men. A few months later the target was 100 ships and 20,000 men by 1954. It was a tall order. But with the war on and Canada strongly committed to NATO, the climate was right and a good deal was already under way.

There was a popular notion that Europe, in war, could be kept supplied by air, like Berlin, and this had strong promoters. A serious look at the tonnages, however, showed the idea to be ridiculous, and from early NATO strategy sessions it was clear the North Atlantic sea lines of communication must be defended. Stalin's navy already had four times the number of submarines that Germany had at the start of World War Two, and, with German technology and technicians, they were building updates of the Type 21 that was so dangerous in 1945. It could do seventeen knots submerged for a burst, ten knots for eleven hours, dive to 900 feet, and carry twenty torpedoes. In short, it was nearly eight times as hard to detect as the regular U-boat of World War Two and, if caught, five times as hard to kill.

Admiral Grant steered clear of the NATO (i.e., the U.S.) battle fleet. Canada, Grant said, would contribute anti-submarine escort forces. The carrier would be devoted to that role, too, with fighters for air defence. Anti-submarine work, after all, made sense. It was Canada's realm of experience. It called for small ships and many more were needed. The dozen wartime-built destroyers were updated in the early fifties while new escorts were being built. Later, to expand, twenty-one wartime frigates were converted into useful ocean escorts. Mines, with Korea as the reminder, were a cheap and easy threat to Canadian ports. Some wartime Bangors were recommissioned as a temporary minesweeping force; meantime twenty fine little Bay-class minesweepers were laid down starting in 1951, to go into service between 1953 and 1957.

Preliminary design had started in 1948 on a completely new and quite radical escort vessel. Three were approved and in 1950 the first, HMCS *St. Laurent*, was laid down in Montreal. To fight the new enemy submarine they had to be far faster and more powerful than corvettes or frigates. In any war Britain must be counted out for supply, so dependence on the RN went by the board. The navy must rely on North American sources. Unless it was to buy off the USN's shelf, it must design its own ships and work with Canadian industry to build them. That meant an advanced technical and industrial base must be created. The navy's program injected technical advances into industry as never before, not just in building hulls but in a great range of high-tech equipment – electronic, electrical, mechanical. This was a real boost to the economy and made thousands of jobs. As well, the expansion gave a terrific boost to the navy. It was just what Sir Wilfrid Laurier had in mind for Canada in 1910.

The year 1950 was a turning point in aviation, too. The RCAF's campaign against naval air had been blunted with NATO's demands. Indeed, they would have to put some effort themselves into maritime air. And now the spell of RN aircraft broke at last. As a solid reliable plane for ASW the navy bought seventy-five used Grumman Avengers from the USN. They were modified at Fairey Aviation in Dartmouth and that began a long partnership with the aircraft industry.

The "Turkeys," as they were called, were air-sea kindly, rugged, and easy to maintain. Over the next seven years the rising generation of naval aviators learned all-weather ASW in the faithful Turkeys from *Magnificent*'s deck. Pilots at last were getting at least thirty airborne hours a month. They now looked south of the border for attitude as well as aircraft, and safety became respectable.

Rear Admiral George Stephens had laid the technical foundations for an independent navy. By 1956, Rear Admiral J.G. ("Fat Jack") Knowlton, the Chief of Naval Technical Services since 1948, had built a professional and technical staff of some 400. Most, both service and civilian, were brought from the U.K. The Royal Corps of Naval Constructors, a civilian arm of Admiralty, lent Mr. R. Baker, an experienced and innovative naval architect. "Roly Biker," with his broad Cockney, was viewed askance in England as something of a renegade. His ideas were rather too advanced for the notably conservative Royal Corps, but the targets set by Canada's Naval Staff called for his kind of mind and energy. He was made a Commodore and masterminded the design of the St. Laurent-class (to be followed by improved Restigouches and Mackenzies) under Knowlton, who managed the whole shipbuilding, converting, and new equipment program.

For about ten years Canadians were quite concerned about defence. Army and air force loomed far larger than navy in the public view and the share of the public purse. But in ten years, from the early fifties, the navy designed and built forty-one new ships and did major conversions to thirty-three more. Bright young naval architects and engineers got real responsibility for advanced design, development, and production work. As well as sophisticated high-tech industry for Canada, the navy developed an expert officer corps and an in-house capability in warship design and engineering that could take on any future task.

THE CADILLACS

Harking back to the "Rolls-Royce" destroyers of 1933, someone rightly dubbed this new family of war vessels the "Cadillacs." These were ships for the North Atlantic the Canadians knew so well. Excellent seakeeping, long range, good sustained speed, and reliable sonar were essential. Icing up was an old problem, controlled by high freeboard and reduced upper-deck clutter and a reserve of stability that gave the ships a characteristically sharp roll. And they had to be capable of rapid building in quantity. For the first time, a ship was designed from scratch for the Captain to take command in action from the operations room rather than the bridge.

Noise that gave away a ship's position to submarines was controlled by hull and propeller design and machinery mountings. Post-Bikini, the ships had to cope with heavy underwater shock. Contaminated spray and deadly radioactive fallout had to be washed off quickly with spraying systems. No RCN ships or aircraft were fitted for nuclear weapons, but both friends and enemies had them. Either way, ships and men had to survive and keep fighting.

In a new departure, Canadian Vickers in Montreal was the "lead yard." The Naval Central Drawing Office established there guided construction of all new ships and conversions from Halifax to Victoria, with tight naval overseeing and minute attention to detail. The commercial yards did high-quality work.

With the first of the newly built ships RCN standards of shipboard life leaped far ahead of the RN and ran past the Americans. There were comfortable bunks with reading lamps and quality bedding, decent-sized personal lockers, modern electric galleys serving first-rate food in central cafeterias. They had much more refrigeration and freezer space, air-conditioning, greatly improved washrooms and heads, on-board laundry, good supplies of fresh water, and better lighting everywhere. Living at sea can never equal comforts ashore. But wartime sailors who took memories of the little corvettes aboard a Cadillac found themselves in a totally different world. Canada's sailors of the fifties were getting the very best.

The first of the Cadillacs, HMCS *St. Laurent*, went to sea in 1955 under Commander Bob Timbrell, last seen killing U-boats with Chummy Prentice in the Channel in 1944. "Sally the Second" went through all the hoops with the U.S. Navy's Operational Evaluation Command out of Key West. Timbrell and his team quickly found out how to get the most out of their ship. American evaluation showed HMCS *St. Laurent*, the first solely Canadian-designed warship, to be the best of her type ever built.

From the mid-fifties on "Sally" and her sisters symbolized the Canadian navy's unique identity. Twenty of the new family came into service over nine years. The last two of the line came fresh from the shipyards in 1964 with hangars and flight decks. The same year *St. Laurent* came back to sea reconfigured in the now-classic mould of the helicopter destroyer, the Canadian DDH.

NATO'S NAVY

Vice Admiral Rollo Mainguy followed Harold Grant as Chief of Naval Staff in late 1951. The navy wasn't yet transformed but, as Grant said in his farewell signal, it was "close-hauled and beating to windward." A sound basis for a modern navy had been laid on the broad international outlook of Louis St. Laurent and Lester Pearson, the commitment to NATO, and the thrust of the Korean War, plus the industrial nationalism of C.D. Howe, the wartime Minister of Munitions and Supply, then of Reconstruction, and finally of Trade and Commerce.

A sad gap in NATO's and Canada's own strength was the lack of a seagoing Canadian Merchant Marine. Without national policy its wartime strength had virtually disappeared. Canada, though, stood up among its allies, delivered when it spoke, and was heard with due and growing respect.

RN apron strings had often been a lifeline, but over the years they had sometimes caught around the Canadian navy's throat. The strings weren't officially cut, but they were replaced by the bond of mutual professional respect. Canada's navy was on its own now but never alone. As the fifties moved on and it took its expanding place in NATO, it felt its own strong tradition, the thrust of adventure and innovation, of professionalism and pride. Canada's navy was well on its way to running with the very best.

Winston Churchill ran an emotional and eloquent campaign for an RN Admiral to reign over NATO's Atlantic, but he got no support from Canada. The first Supreme Allied Commander Atlantic (Saclant), Admiral Lynde McCormick, USN, hoisted his flag in Norfolk, Virginia, in 1952. The wartime Canadian North Atlantic Command dropped into place as a NATO sub-command. Rear Admiral Roger Bidwell, CBE, Canada's Flag Officer Atlantic Coast, took on the NATO hat, too.

Army and air units were assigned permanently to NATO commanders and stationed in Europe. The naval command structure stayed in place but forces were so mobile and each country had such national needs that ships were committed on paper to NATO command in emergency and for exercises. Admiral McCormick wasted no time gearing up the exercises. Strategy and tactics, communications and command, had to be tested, and a looming NATO exercise was a sharp jab toward excellence.

Fall was the time for the big NATO gatherings. Each winter most east coast ships were off to the Caribbean, west coast ships to California or Hawaii. The kindly weather and the marvellous USN facilities meant top value for training time and dollar. Sunshine and warmth eased painting and maintenance. And there were intriguing runs ashore for young men who did, after all, want to see more of the world than open ocean and downtown Victoria or Citadel Hill. Wives left behind in icy, storm-lashed Halifax never did believe that all hands had in fact been working very hard when they came back in springtime sporting expensive tans.

Uganda (later recommissioned *Quebec*) had circumnavigated South America in early 1946 to announce that post-war Canada was open again for trade. It worked. From time to time there were more such cruises, some to the exotic places of a young sailor's dreams: Japan, Australia, Africa, Malaysia, a host of European countries. Showing the flag in foreign ports saw the ships polished, glittering, impeccable. Ceremonial guards paraded and bands played; dress uniforms, swords, and medals gleamed; bugles and the shrilling Bosun's call greeted foreign officers and bigwigs; cocktails on the quarterdeck under coloured awnings lubricated relations; ships were thrown open to swarms of curious visitors.

To many – especially those on the lower deck who laboured while the officers played well-groomed hosts and were entertained lavishly ashore – these visits were something of a bind. But showing its flag flying over a smartly impressive naval ship has always been a telling way for a country to make its point abroad, whether the point is good will or raw power or goods for sale. Canada's image as a strong NATO and Commonwealth member and a major worldwide trading nation was presented by the navy very well indeed, in ports around the world, and in the summer of 1953, for instance, at a great Review of the Fleet at Spithead, off Portsmouth, when Queen Elizabeth II celebrated her coronation.

That fall it was back to hard business in Exercise Mariner, involving nine NATO countries, 300 ships, 1,000 aircraft, and half a million men at "war" for nineteen days. *Magnificent*, *Quebec*, *Algonquin*, and frigates *Swansea* and *La Hulloise*, as well as three RCAF maritime squadrons of aging Lancasters, took part. The problem posed was control of the North Atlantic and European approaches. Convoys from America must be fought through to supply Europe against "Orange" submarines, surface raiders, and shore-based aircraft – and against a brutal lashing of North Atlantic weather.

One grey squally afternoon the task group, with carriers *Magnificent*, USS *Bennington*, and USS *Wasp*, moved in south of Iceland to strike at airfields in "enemy" hands. *Quebec* was among the surface support. The big formation turned into the wind, flew off the first strike, and resumed course. Forty-two aircraft, including eight of "Maggie's" Avengers, climbed through the glowering clouds toward their targets.

Then, without warning, a dense blanket of fog rolled in, and that meant likely fog in Iceland, too. A fast command decision: planes were recalled; disciplined, precise, the force turned into wind again, straight toward the fog bank, with very little room. Ten planes got aboard – just.

And the fog clamps down. Visibility nil. Thirty-two aircraft stack up overhead. Each carrier controlled approach operator uses radar, talks his aircraft in. On "Maggie's" bridge, with Captain Herbert Rayner, it's quiet, controlled. Below on the fog-swirled flight deck, cleared for emergency, all lights burn. The rescue man in his asbestos suit shifts and checks his firefighting gear. A Turkey's engine down the port side can be heard, coming round, then closer from astern, and closer. The Landing Signal Officer, bats in hand, strains to will away the fog. With radar the pilot still must see the deck and batsman, just that last snatch of visibility, to land on. The plane is heard, throttling back, still closer, coming in, in. Then he guns it, roars up and overhead. No dice. Another tries. Another.

Around drone the planes in the dense grey pall, circuit after circuit, looking for a thinning of the fog. In *Quebec*'s operations room muted radio speakers carry the laconic voices – pilots', controllers', signalmen's – cool and disciplined. The bright spots on the radar scan show the ordered ring of ships.

"Heavy ships move clear" – extra masts are bad news for low-flying planes in fog. Captain Pat Budge on *Quebec*'s bridge works his ship through the murk, past the destroyer screen, out of the formation. "Planes report your fuel states." Shore airfields? Too far now for dwindling fuel. Exercise rules are off and darkness approaches – decision time again. "Aircraft prepare to ditch ahead of the force." A nasty business in the fog, that. "Destroyers station ahead to pick up crews." If they can see them.

An "Orange" submarine, USS *Redfin*, 110 miles away, has been listening and reports: "Ceiling here one hundred feet, visibility two miles." That's enough to ditch safely and maybe get picked up before dark and frigid water do their work. It's just on sunset. Another decision. "Planes with fuel, go for *Redfin*. Remainder ditch." "Roger. Out." "Roger. Out." "Roger. Out." The margins are narrowing to nothing.

Then, from "Maggie's" bridge, the fog is thinning. The flight deck comes to view, the masthead, the other ships. It's a patch of warmer water. But will it last? Controllers call the aircraft back, into the circuit. Lowest in fuel land first. And down they come and drop on deck – any deck – but precisely and with care, because a landing hitch can deal disaster to the friend behind. Every plane gets down, and in mere minutes the fog clamps in. The light fails.

Professionals must face the eternal challenge of the sea. But this was a miraculous stroke and no one had any illusions about it. It made a sailor think.

There were other oceans, other challenges. HMCS *Labrador* opened a new chapter in Canada's Arctic, navigating the fabled Northwest Passage in 1954, but soon she turned civilian with the Department of Transport. Following Lester Pearson's initiative in 1956, which led to the United Nations Emergency Force in Egypt, *Magnificent* offloaded her aircraft to ferry the Canadian contingent. That was a crash operation in Halifax over Christmas. First it was the Queen's Own Rifles. But the Egyptians, violently anti–British, rejected such a name – and uniform. Canada badges wouldn't show up in a rifle sight. Aboard came communications and logistics troops and vehicles. "Maggie" sailed and unloaded at Port Said.

The reward for uncarrier-like operations and many hours of stevedoring was a look at the wreck-littered entrance to the Suez Canal, camel rides at the pyramids, and a memorable rest and recreation stop at Naples. In that steamy seaport the proprietresses of certain places of entertainment sought to redeem a sizable bale of Canadian Tire "money" from the ship's paymaster. It had seemed authentic in the dimmed lights but their bankers declined to accept it in the light of day. Join the navy and see the world indeed.

A NEW GENERATION

Quite a number of first lieutenants and commanding officers of small ships were, by the mid-fifties, graduates of Canada's own naval college. The navy had seized its chance when money was available and opened the Royal Canadian Naval College at HMCS *Royal Roads* in 1942 to train permanent-force cadets. It had been twenty years since the earlier college closed. Now the 100 cadets occupied a fine old stone mansion and some newer outbuildings on a stunningly beautiful estate facing the anchorage off Esquimalt.

Two models for *Royal Roads* were studied: the RN's Britannia Naval College, Dartmouth, and the U.S. Naval Academy at Annapolis. The RN, for untold generations, had sent boys to sea largely from the upper middle class to become officers through a sort of apprenticeship. More modern days continued the class bias and a college was built ashore for schooling a bit beyond secondary level, basic training, and thorough naval indoctrination. Parents paid a fee. Only engineering midshipmen went on to degree level. The executive officers, the big majority, went to sea and more technical training. Intellectual development was up to them. As of yore, "the man-of-war was their university."

The U.S. Naval Academy, by contrast, took high school graduates through stiff competition, gave them four years to a respected science degree, and included naval training and thoroughgoing indoctrination. The RN way produced young, well-trained, hands-on, sea-wise junior officers. Generally, by their first command they were better seamen and navigators, better shiphandlers, and more flexible, innovative tacticians. The results showed at sea. But the American way produced a well-educated officer corps. The results showed in the power of the USN. It was educated admirals versus well-trained juniors.

A war was no time to be starting a university in Canada. In any case, with all the RCN's senior officers cast from the RN mould, the choice was as inevitable as the one made the following year on naval aviation. And it was just as much an albatross. Captain John Grant, brother of Harold, was in command. "Stumpy" Grant was an old Naval College graduate himself, a between-wars schoolmaster. He was a benevolent little martinet who could spot a speck of dust on a cadet's uniform at a hundred yards and ran the place like a senior boys' boarding school in navy blue.

College candidates certainly had to be fit and have good junior matriculation, but the main filter was a half-hour personal interview by a board of senior officers. Their leanings, and possibly the way the word was spread, were clear. Nineteen of the first *Royal Roads* class of fifty came from private schools. There was no thought to Quebec. With an age ceiling and mandatory math and science for entry, graduates of Quebec colleges had small chance of qualifying. Few French Canadians even applied.

From its opening, predictably on Trafalgar Day, things ran very much in the RN mode. Except for the mandatory ice-cold plunge each morning it was little changed from the old college. The norm was two years of education and all-round vigorous naval training on top of junior matriculation. It brewed fine naval esprit and well-trained young officers, though only half stayed in the regular force. Graduates went off to sea as midshipmen for two years with the RN, then did technical courses in the U.K.

In 1947 *Royal Roads* became the RCN/RCAF college. The air force insisted on senior matriculation for entry, and Brooke Claxton was determined to get the three services together at the start. The next year the Royal Military College in Kingston reopened as a four-year degree-granting university for the three services. *Royal Roads* became tri-service, too. The air force, aiming for educated air marshals, had all its cadets go on to RMC for degrees. The navy, however, stayed on course, sending cadets straight to sea after two years, still mostly to RN ships.

Back in the early twenties the shrunken RN had sent a lot of its surplus young officers off to Cambridge to extend their education for a year. The rock-bottom RCN couldn't raise the modest fee of £1 per day for any of Grant's, Reid's, or Mainguy's generations. Who can tell what their attitudes to junior officer training would have been had their minds been thus expanded? It wasn't until 1957 that a study by Commodore Patrick Tisdall went so far as to say "a fundamental knowledge of the sciences and humanities is an essential requirement for command of a modern ship." At that point, finally, the aim was for all officers, executive and supply as well as engineers, to have university degrees. Now, too, all executive and engineering prospects would get both bridge and engine room certificates and all would qualify for command at sea and could become Flag Officers in Command or Chief of the Naval Staff.

In the meantime the Regular Officers Training Plan, which entered officers through the service colleges and universities, wasn't producing enough for the expanding service, especially aviators. To fill the gap HMCS *Venture* started in Esquimalt dockyard in 1954. The Chief of Naval Personnel, Rear Admiral Hugh Pullen, was a traditionalist. *Venture* was a little naval college on the old pattern. To run it Pullen made a sound choice in Captain Robert Welland, DSC and bar. Welland mustered the best of instructor officers and chiefs and petty officers. A lot of adventurous young men who didn't aspire to degrees rose to the challenge. There was a special introductory course run annually in Quebec and a fully French classroom stream in the first year of the two-year course. For the first time ever the navy got good response from French Canada. Over the years *Venture* produced about half the officers for the navy. What they lacked in higher education they made up in know-how and esprit, and a lot reached the top.

Venture, too, was the prime source of naval aviators. Selection and training saw to it that they were smart, quick, innovative, and flexible. From the early fifties, aviators were becoming first lieutenants of destroyers, then commanding ships, then escort squadrons. These were well-rounded naval officers. It was this combination of thoroughgoing sea and air professionalism, for example, that married the helicopter and escort. With the navy's single-minded focus on anti-submarine it was what made the RCN of the sixties the leading ASW outfit among NATO's navies.

AVIATION GROWS UP

Bonaventure replaced *Magnificent* in 1957. She'd been laid down in Belfast in 1946 and in 1952 Canada agreed to buy her for, it was said, some $30 million worth of good Ontario cheese. She came complete with some outstanding post-war RN innovations that were taken up by every navy's carriers: the mirror landing aid that did a far better job than the old "batsman"; the steam-powered catapult that could squirt a heavier aircraft up with much less wind over the deck; and – most important of all – the angled deck. The whole combination brought dramatically better safety and flexibility and far greater peace of mind.

In 1955 the Sea Fury was replaced by the American navy's F2H3 Banshee. They couldn't fly from the unimproved "Maggie" so, waiting for *Bonaventure*, they flew from *Shearwater* air station. The "Banjo" was the only Canadian fighter carrying a guided missile, the heat-seeking Sidewinder. The squadron under Lieutenant Commander Bob Falls regularly beat out the RCAF's CF-100s on intercepts and was rated the top Canadian formation in North American Air Defence Command.

The CS2F Tracker, bravely promoted by Commodore Keighley-Peach, RN, over Britain's Gannet, succeeded the Avenger in 1956. The navy bought 100 built by De Havilland in Toronto under licence from America's Grumman. The "Stoof" was a big, solid, capable ASW aircraft and carried radar, MAD, sonobuoys, and homing torpedoes. It, too, needed the angled deck. The Sikorsky H04S "Horse" helicopters were aboard, too, carrying their dunking sonar.

The navy was nudging hard at *Bonaventure*'s limits. The Americans wouldn't consider operating Banshees from such a small deck. The Tracker was so big that landing a few feet off the centreline a wingtip would hit the island. But Commander Pop Fotheringham was her first Commander (Air), and by now he and his people were seasoned professionals with hard-won experience. They hadn't lost their old spirit of "press on," but it was not "press on regardless." Ship, seamen, aviators, equipment, training came together at last. Now there was work to do to mould them into a top fighting team.

Captain William Landymore took over command of *Bonaventure* in January, 1958. His physical size – they called him "Shadow" at Royal Military College in the thirties – was the only thing small about him. He was a thoroughgoing, energetic, tough-minded professional. Officer to ordinary seaman, sailing with Bill Landymore, or commanding a ship in his task force, you knew exactly where you were.

When Landymore took over, *Bonaventure*'s air operations, like NATO carriers generally, revolved around day flying as they had in the war. One might launch before dawn but preferred to recover before dark. Flying at night was a special exercise. But submarines were in business twenty-four hours a day. Escorts didn't stop pinging at night. The long-range patrol aircraft (LRPA) stayed on the job. So, said Landymore's logic, why not carrier planes?

He told his aviators bluntly that if they couldn't fly around the clock, day in day out, at maximum effort, then *Bonaventure* wasn't worth keeping afloat. He knew people and he'd thrown the gauntlet to the right kind. Besides Pop Fotheringham, the Tracker Squadron CO, Dickie Bird, was very experienced.

The Executive Officer whose job it was to co-ordinate the whole ship's organization was Commander Arthur McPhee. As an aircraft direction specialist he'd been long connected to naval flying.

So hatched "sustained operations" or SUSTOPS. The first target was to keep two Trackers airborne round the clock for five days plus two AS helicopters during daylight hours. (Until the all-weather Sea King they couldn't hover with their sonar ball in the water unless they could see the horizon.) The limiting factor, they found, wasn't mechanical failure or deck crew energy or weather. It was aircrew fatigue. So they boosted the Tracker squadron from twelve to eighteen crews – one and a half per plane. That turned the trick.

Soon "Bonnie's" SUSTOP standard was four Trackers and two helicopters up, plus "Pedro," the faithful rescue and odd-job chopper, when needed. The whole ship's routine was meshed – day, night, any weather, twenty-four hours a day for six, seven, even eight days. Slow undersized carrier and all, give the Canadians an ocean area 200 miles square and they would keep it saturated with airborne anti-submarine forces right around the clock. ASW SUSTOPS became the hallmark of Canada's carrier. The other navies had to run hard to catch up. Innovation, in fact, was becoming the hallmark of the navy itself.

HELICOPTERS AND ESCORTS

When Commander Timbrell and his team were putting *St. Laurent* through her paces in 1955 they chased the world's first true submarine, the nuclear-powered USS *Nautilus*. With a submerged speed of around twenty-six knots and infinite endurance, she was a nearly impossible quarry. She was very noisy, however, and could be easily tracked by passive sonar. *Nautilus* had a conventional submarine hull designed for good seakeeping on the surface. Not so the new USS *Albacore*, which was shaped like a dolphin for top performance submerged. She could "fly" through the water in the range of thirty knots. Such low drag, high speed, and quiet manoeuvrability, given the limitless endurance of nuclear drive, could beat the surface ship.

While *St. Laurent* was at Key West the navy's first anti-submarine helicopter squadron started flying from *Magnificent*. They carried a "dunking" sonar that could be lowered into the water while they hovered. They were invulnerable to torpedoes and far faster than the new submarine. Timbrell's Executive Officer was Lieutenant Commander Pat Ryan, a naval aviator who was quick with a new idea. Ryan had the shipwright shore up the aluminum hatch cover over *St. Laurent*'s anti-submarine mortar well. Naval pilots, always willing to try something new, found it made a tidy landing deck.

The idea of anti-submarine helicopters flying from escorts had come up in World War Two. But now it took its first practical steps ahead. An experimental flight deck was quickly rigged on the stern of *Buckingham*, a wartime frigate. The Americans set about developing a small drone helicopter to carry a weapon and drop it on command from the ship's sonar. The British went for a manned helicopter that could drop a weapon. Only the Canadians had the confidence to go for the whole bundle – the all-weather anti-submarine helicopter with its own sonar, radar, and weapon load, flying from the deck of the small escort vessel, and in North Atlantic weather.

It was a radical combination. The helicopter had to land on a tiny, rolling, pitching, spray-lashed deck day and night. It was a huge, heavy bird and it had to be moved into a hangar for shelter to be maintained. Ingredients for success were the seagoing qualities and configuration of the Cadillacs, a first-rate helicopter, the American Sea King, and Canadian ingenuity, innovation, seamanship, and aviation know-how. After eight years' development Canada's navy on its own brought a whole new dimension in anti-submarine warfare to the navies of the world.

SCIENCE AND SEAMANSHIP

Winston Churchill had called the Battle of the Atlantic "a war of ambuscade and stratagem, a war of groping and drowning, a war of science and seamanship." Science and seamanship got together in Canada's navy in these post-war years. The Naval Research Establishment set up in Halifax in wartime had done some useful practical work, but there wasn't much background in research and development in Canada. Now one main target, the high-speed submarine, focused naval energy and ideas.

The U-boats in the Gulf and off the east coast had escaped detection too easily. Sonar conditions were one main reason – temperature layers, especially bad in Canadian waters, baffled sound beams. The answer, after some practical trials at sea by the ever-innovative Bob Welland, was quite simple – just lower the sonar transducer somehow and tow it along below the layer. The "somehow" was the problem. Welland's first lash-up arrangement in 1947 brought echoes from a submarine booming in at 9,400 yards. It was four times a wartime sailor's fond hope, and a variable depth sonar, or VDS, clearly would be worth a lot of work.

It took time. The heavy, streamlined body containing the sonar transducer must be raised and lowered in rough weather. It had to point in a steady direction and be towed at high speed. A production prototype VDS was at sea in HMCS *Crusader* in 1960. She stuck like a leech to the RN's high-speed submarine *Excalibur* despite all the tricks in the submariner's books. The RN had taken up the VDS, too, but the Canadians' sonar was better. Other navies bought it, and VDS was here to stay.

Displaying the action picture so commanders could make the right decisions fast meant combining radar, electronic, sonar, and radioed inputs from other ships. It was still done by hand and was too slow and imprecise. After the war the USN and RN set huge resources to the problem. The Canadians worked at it, too, and, remarkably, set their sights far above the others. All data, the Canadians said, must be transferred between ships by automatic radio links. Everything would be processed, calculated, and stored using the new digital techniques rather than the old analogue method common for years.

The scientist in the case was communications engineer Stanley Knights, who spotted the crucial connection between digital techniques and radio transmission. The seaman was Commander Dan Hanington. Back in the helter-skelter battle for convoy SC 42, Sub-Lieutenant Hanington in *Kenogami*'s tiny charthouse had tried to shout a cohesive action picture up the voice pipe to his Captain, Cowboy Jackson, on the bridge. Eight months later Hanington did far better in Windyer's *Wetaskiwin* when they teamed with Dyer's *Skeena* to sink *U-588*, because they were better equipped with radar and radio and much better trained. Hanington won the DSC for that one. He knew the problem.

In 1950 a target generated in Toronto was sent by radio to move simultaneously on Stan Knights's scope in the Canadian Naval Electronics Laboratory in Ottawa. It was the world's first radio digital data link, as significant as Alexander Graham Bell's first telephone message. But the USN and RN observers sniffed. "Not practical, too bulky."

Canada pressed doggedly on. In three years "Datar" was working between two ships. Each was loaded with 4,000 vacuum tubes, but Knights collared some very early transistors and slashed the size. The team proposed Datar for *Bonaventure* and the *St. Laurents*. By now, however, money was short, and so was the Canadian attitude. Bureaucrats looked askance at naval developments. If the USN and RN were working on something, then the little RCN shouldn't duplicate it. On the other hand, if the others weren't doing it, there couldn't be a valid need. This was the caution and the underconfidence that so often sold the navy and indeed the country short.

Datar was Canada's unique headstart on all the space-age automatic, satellite-linked communications systems of today. Unhappily, government had no guts for R&D. In 1958 Datar went in the pigeonhole. It was fifteen years before Canadian warships went to sea with a system that could handle things as well as Datar. But the USN had forged ahead on Canadian advances. In 1960 when their first big system went to sea they even acknowledged Mr. Knights as "the father of the naval tactical data systems." Canada's navy wallowed in its own wake.

Another unique project was the hydrofoil. Back in 1943, after the slaughter on the beaches of Dieppe, the Canadian army wanted a high-speed craft to lay smoke in front of an amphibious assault force. The Naval Research Establishment dredged up Alexander Graham Bell's Great War work on hydrofoils in the Bras d'Or Lakes and did some experiments. The project went on the back burner but in the early fifties many naval tacticians, Commodore Jeffry Brock among them, were interested in the "fast, small, and many" concept for screening and fighting the high-speed submarine.

Funds were shy but more experiments and trials produced a proposal from NRE for a 200-ton craft that might tow a VDS. In 1961, stimulated by a sweeping report on the navy's future by Rear Admiral Brock, the hydrofoil project went ahead, and we will pick that tale up later.

Add the helicopter/escort match. Add literally hundreds of other projects – corrosion protection, replenishing at sea, the first wide-band radar direction finder akin to HF/DF, new sonars, and on and on – and Canada's navy racked up an amazing record. From canvas and cordage to command and control, navies have always had to be on the cutting edge of technology. The endless, varied, harsh environment of the sea; the self-sufficiency needed by every unit; the need to fight alone as well as in a mighty concert of sea-based strength – all these call on the best, on innovation, imagination, and a sense of adventure pointing to new horizons. This is the long-standing tradition of the sea.

THE NAVAL RESERVE

After the war the Reserve was looked on as the base for mobilization in the event of a future war. The Royal Canadian Navy (Reserve) had divisions in twenty-three cities and authorized strength of 18,000, including 3,000 in air squadrons. The "wavy" stripes were dropped at last. But when the Russians built their Bomb the spectre of nuclear war meant you had to fight with what you had. So the Reserve shrank.

The lessons of Walter Hose hadn't been forgotten, however, and a lot of effort went into training. Reserve Wrens came back in 1951. The Flag Officer Naval Divisions hoisted his flag in Hamilton in 1953 and started the Great Lakes Training Centre for new entry and sea training. Five naval air squadrons had their own aircraft. They flew operational types in the summer and a lot of pilots qualified in deck landing. Reserve strength at the end of the fifties was 4,600.

Each division had a small regular force staff and supported the winter training for the University Naval Training Divisions. UNTD cadets – the "Untidies" as they called themselves – went through regular cadet training in the summers at the naval schools and at sea. They became the prime source of well-trained Reserve officers and some joined the regular force. Too, they were a well-informed link between the navy and the civilian world.

MARITIME COMMAND

The RCAF had kept maritime air low in its priorities. For over twelve years only old wartime Lancaster bombers modified for the ASW role were used. In

1958 they got the first of thirty-three Argus planes, an outstanding Canadian-built long-range ASW aircraft. The next year Maritime Headquarters Atlantic was formed under the Flag Officer Atlantic Coast, Rear Admiral Hugh Pullen. The Air Officer Commanding RCAF Maritime Command became his deputy. There was a similar arrangement out west under the Flag Officer Pacific Coast. All maritime sea and air operations were now firmly under navy control.

In the Joint Maritime Warfare School in Halifax, in exercises, in the operations rooms, and at the sharp end out at sea, sailors and aviators in light and dark blue worked as one to keep a controlling hand on the common enemy, the Soviet submarine. Saclant had put up a standing prize of a case of Jack Daniels Kentucky Sour Mash Bourbon Whiskey for the unit, air or sea, that forced a Soviet submarine to the surface. It had been won more than once. There were plenty of submarine contacts by the sound surveillance system called SOSUS, which had listening arrays sitting on the bottom off Nova Scotia and Newfoundland. Wrens had come back into the regular Navy in 1956 under wartime senior officer Commander Isobel Macneill, and among their duties was operating SOSUS at the Shelburne, Nova Scotia, station. Patrol aircraft would follow up contacts, and ships might then be sent. Submarines were photographed alongside Soviet fish-factory ships on the Grand Banks, and ships and aircraft patrolled the nooks and crannies of Newfoundland and Labrador and ranged the reaches of the North Atlantic.

FIFTY YEARS A NAVY

In 1960 the navy was fifty years old. In the regular force were 20,000 men and women, fully half of them at sea, fifty-five fighting ships and fifty aircraft, and a swarm of auxiliaries and tenders. New ships were on the building ways and new anti-submarine helicopters on order. There were close working ties with the RN and USN. The White Ensign still flew and uniforms were nearly identical, but the umbilical cord to mother RN had gone.

The late fifties had brought recession, so there were financial constraints and, consequently, fewer people than needed and too few ships to honour fully NATO commitments. Half the new minesweepers had been sold to NATO partners. The chronic reluctance of Canadians to spend money on defence in peacetime meant that pay lagged behind that of civilian counterparts. But the navy had hit its stride.

"Hard-over Harry," Vice Admiral H.G. DeWolf, the Chief of Naval Staff since 1956, took the salute at the fiftieth anniversary sail and fly-past in Halifax, gleefully arranged by that arch-patron of pageantry, Rear Admiral Hugh Pullen. DeWolf, the brilliant fighting Captain of war-famed *Haida*, had reached the pinnacle of his distinguished career of forty-two years. He had joined the old college from his Halifax home in 1918, so he had seen the navy in a burst of Great War action; he had experienced its bare survival for twenty years and its incredible growth in wartime; he had witnessed the post-war lapse, then helped to bring it back to what it had become.

His navy now totalled a carrier, fourteen spanking new St. Laurent and Restigouche-class destroyer escorts, nine destroyers – his gallant *Haida* still among them – twenty-one ocean escort frigates, and ten minesweepers. It had an envied record of designing and building its own ships and equipment. It had boosted the nation's growth in sophisticated shipbuilding and leading-edge electrical and electronic technology, and it created skilled employment for thousands of Canadians. It had added enormously to knowledge of the Arctic. Its reputation in ASW was second to none in NATO. Its people were as fine as one would find in any navy, anywhere.

Certainly DeWolf would have preferred a bigger fleet. It fell short of the country's needs and obligations. But Canada was stepping into the sixties with a first-class navy and there were new ships on the ways. And numbers alone are not the measure of a navy's strength – a real esprit shone on that fiftieth anniversary from the gleaming ships and faultless uniforms and the tight formations flying overhead.

That year Harry DeWolf turned over as Chief of Naval Staff to Vice Admiral Herbert Rayner, DSC and bar. Twenty years before he had turned over command of *St. Laurent* to Rayner during the Western Approaches battle, and the two had fought together in the Channel in 1944. Now their new navy was on a steady course, well-found and set to serve the country well.

CHAPTER FOURTEEN
THE NORTHERN GATE

MARTIN FROBISHER, THAT LUSTY ELIZABETHAN SEA-DOG, CLAIMED THE discovery of the Northwest Passage to be "the only thing in the world left undone whereby a notable mind might be made famous and fortunate." Many nineteenth-century Royal Navy explorers who groped through the awesome, ice-bound channels in their wooden ships, without finding the Passage, have been recorded in heroic terms. John Franklin is best remembered, though less for achievement than because he and all his people perished. But for the first half of the twentieth century, with Arctic geography roughly sketched, Canada's navy, like the country itself, paid slight heed to the frozen hinterland lying at its northern gate.

In World War Two, with Canada's consent, the U.S. built Arctic weather stations and a chain of airfields called the Northwest Staging Route to ferry aircraft to the Russians. At war's end those great circle routes for intercontinental aircraft showed as straight lines on the kind of map most people hadn't heeded much before – the north polar projection. For the first time the world looked at itself from the top and saw the Arctic as the crossroads of the modern world.

In a very short time it was the projected path for the rockets and the bombs. Where Canadians sat, the border between the great power blocs wasn't between East and West. It was between North and North, and Canada, a sprawling buffer for the United States, faced Russia across the Arctic Ocean. Suddenly and emphatically, the Arctic became the strategic cockpit of the world.

Vice Admiral G.C. Jones, the CNS, was slow off the mark. The navy took no hand in starting the Canada/U.S. Joint Experimental Station for cold weather work at Churchill, Manitoba. It didn't join the USN's big Arctic exercise, "Nanook," in 1946. Admiral Reid the next year advised against getting into Arctic operations. Naval ships weren't designed to run with safety in ice-infested waters. Reid didn't even send token representation to join the USN in building more Arctic weather stations in 1947.

Mackenzie King was looking north if the admirals weren't. He was against keeping *Warrior* but agreed to one carrier *if* it could be used up there. *Magnificent*, according to the RN, was "arcticized," i.e., she had a half-decent heating system and cold-weather engineering for upper-deck machinery. She certainly couldn't operate in arctic ice – no carrier could. In any event, she replaced *Warrior* in 1948.

The Prime Minister had made a clear point. The North was important, and the navy should pay heed. Design studies started late in 1947 for an arctic patrol vessel. Harold Grant, by this time the Chief of Naval Staff, had the wit to send *Magnificent* and two destroyers into Hudson Bay the following year. Then *Swansea* visited Frobisher Bay and the little naval auxiliary *Cedarwood* sailed with a Canada-U.S. scientific expedition from Esquimalt through Bering Strait into the Chukchi Sea. These were gestures. Until 1954, apart from the thin line of the RCMP patrols to Inuit settlements, Canada's Arctic waters were the sole domain of the USN.

Proper presence in the North called for the navy and it must have the right kind of vessel. HMCS *Labrador* was approved early in 1949 and was the first new navy ship to be laid down since World War Two. The U.S. Navy was the technical source. The basic design was their Wind-class icebreaker. *Labrador*'s Captain-designate, Captain Owen Robertson, spent two years with the U.S. Navy and Coast Guard before his ship commissioned, learning the Arctic business.

"Long Robbie" – he was enormously tall – was a fine practical seaman. Among many wartime exploits, he got a blazing American ship, SS *Volunteer*, which was loaded with ammunition, safely clear of Halifax harbour. It was a nerve-stretching operation alive with memories of the devastating blast of 1917. That won him the George Medal. He was in charge again after a huge explosion at the Naval Magazine on Bedford Basin in July, 1945. The fire burned for four days as Halifax and the navy held their collective breath until Robertson and his firefighters won.

Robertson was used to the unusual and the Arctic was an exciting prospect. It was, is, and always will be sombre, awesomely beautiful, and cruel. A limitless challenge and overpoweringly vast. From Cape Chidley at the northern tip of Labrador to the Alaskan border the coast sprawls across 70 degrees of longitude – one-fifth of all the world at latitude 70° North; in a straight line that's about 2,000 miles. The Arctic archipelago is the largest group of islands in the world. The coastal group – Baffin, Somerset, Prince of Wales, King William, Victoria, Banks, and lesser ones – is divided from the northern Queen Elizabeth Islands by Lancaster Sound, Barrow Strait, Viscount Melville Sound, and M'Clure Strait. This is called the Parry Channel and it is the axis of the Northwest Passage.

For over half the year the sea is covered with ice averaging nearly two metres thick. Where it has ridged and rafted, it's far thicker. In the brief and brilliant summer the straits and channels winding through the islands are open, more or less, with zero to nine-tenths ice cover depending on the area and conditions of the year.

Most of Baffin Bay is wide open in summer, though there are thousands of icebergs – giant, glittering, many-coloured menaces for the unwary. Open water extends westward through the Parry Channel as far as Barrow Strait in a bad year, and to M'Clure Strait (between Melville and Banks islands) when conditions are good. In rare years there is clear passage north of Banks Island right to the Beaufort Sea. The shallow mainland coast opens pretty well each summer from Simpson Strait, past the mouths of the Coppermine and Mackenzie rivers, right through to Bering Strait. Brilliant summer sun dips below the horizon for an eerie twilight. Gales and blinding snowstorms strike from nowhere. Navigation marks are few. Soundings, even today, are sparse. It is a place that still demands the best of a "notable mind."

HMCS *LABRADOR*

Robertson went north with the USN and Coast Guard and fed experience back to the drawing board. Thus *Labrador* got a hangar and enlarged flight deck for three helicopters. There were big improvements over USN communications and radar. In line with the new navy, the living and recreation quarters were quite superior.

Icebreakers are quite round bottomed to work in ice. They can't have the fixed bilge keels that steady a conventional ship, so they have an extraordinary roll in the open sea. *Labrador* got retractable stabilizing fins, which helped. Icebreakers are deep-drafted and have big screws tucked well below the reach of tumbling surface ice. The common action is to drive the ship forward so the bow mounts the ice and the weight of the ship breaks it downwards. One technique is to roll the ship by pumping water from side to side between heeling tanks. *Labrador* could pump at the remarkable rate of 40,000 gallons per minute. Similar tanks and pumps were fitted for trimming fore and aft. Her six diesel electric engines delivered 10,000 shaft horsepower. For her 6,900 tons displacement, she was well up to the job.

Labrador, though, was not to serve simply as an icebreaker, a ship to get other vessels through. Ice-breaking for her was a means, not an end. She was to patrol northern waters, building knowledge and experience for future operations. Along the way she would support Arctic bases, do hydrographic and scientific surveys, provide rescue and limited salvage service. She would break ice as she needed on the way.

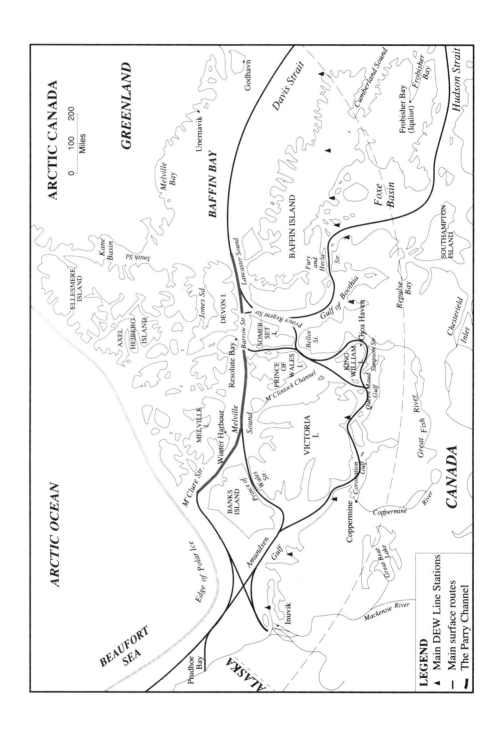

The new ship commissioned in Sorel, Quebec, on 8 July 1954 and had just two weeks to get to Halifax, get organized, and sail for the summer season in the North. In that briefest time her new ship's company learned to run a new, completely strange ship, tested, tried, calibrated all her complex equipment, stored and provisioned for three months, embarked strange cargo, such as eighty tons of coal for the RCMP at Alexandra Fiord, and flew on her three helicopters.

OPENING THE ARCTIC

Often in our own time, just as in Frobisher's, the Far North is styled as our last great adventure. Few of *Labrador*'s company had been anywhere near it before. All entered the mysterious realm in the tracks of some of the greatest mariners and most intrepid explorers of human history. Martin Frobisher himself sailed in 1576 on the first expedition organized specifically to find the Northwest Passage, more than ten years before he fought the Spanish Armada with Drake and Hawkins and that brave company of old free-booting friends. The driving force to the Passage then was commerce, the riches of the East the prize.

Right of discovery, in the manner of the time, marked the Arctic islands as British from the sixteenth century. Whalers from England, Scotland, Germany, and Holland followed the explorers. But a rich whaling ground was a well-kept secret. They were fine seamen but few were literate, and no records were kept; hence, no new territorial claims were made.

With Napoleon beaten in 1815, a great navy lay idle with thousands of seasoned professionals eager to make their mark. Britain turned to the north in a burst of Arctic exploration that caught the imagination of the Victorian age. A Northwest Passage was eventually confirmed by Captain Robert M'Clure while searching for the long-lost John Franklin. M'Clure approached from the west via Bering Strait in 1854 and was blocked by ice before he reached the point achieved from the east by Lieutenant William Parry in 1819. Parry, sailing into Lancaster Sound, had seen open water ahead, seized his chance, and got past longitude 110° West to win a prize from Britain's Parliament of £5,000. M'Clure forged the final link by sledges, manhauled across the intervening ice. There was indeed a passage across the top of North America that might be navigated in a single season when ice conditions were right. But it was not for ships of Queen Victoria's day.

Britain lost interest in the Arctic. The Northwest Passage and the islands, after all the lives and treasure spent, had no commercial value. In 1880 she turned over the last of her North American possessions, except Newfoundland, to the young Dominion. Giving the Arctic islands to Canada, so the thinking went, should at least keep them from the Yankees.

Americans were increasingly busy in the Arctic. There had been some Franklin searchers and then, around the turn of the century, polar attempts by

Robert Peary and Dr. Frederick Cook from the rim of Ellesmere Island. Their feats, and some questionable claims, roused raging controversy and great international interest, but Canada's national interest in the North burned low.

Between 1898 and 1902, Norwegian Otto Sverdrup travelled Ellesmere Island and discovered islands off its western coast, hence those distinctively Scandinavian names. Long negotiations led in 1931 to Canada buying out Norway's claim to Sverdrup's discoveries. The other great Norwegian contribution was Roald Amundsen's. He set off in 1903 to locate the Magnetic Pole and navigate the Northwest Passage along the Canadian coastal route. He took his forty-seven-ton herring fisher *Gjoa* into Lancaster Sound and south through Peel Sound and spent two winters in Gjoa Haven on southeast King William Island, a third in the western Arctic. *Gjoa*'s engine plugged faithfully along and Amundsen finished his work in 1906. The Northwest Passage, with a very small party in a very small vessel, had at last been won.

SUGGESTIONS OF SOVEREIGNTY

American whalers had become more and more active and by 1900 the feeling grew in Canada that the U.S. might try to take the islands over. A geological survey and flag-planting expedition went off in 1903 and the North West Mounted Police began collecting customs and regulating liquor and the law. American action, or fear of it, is a not unusual force in Canada's history. It finally triggered some interest in the basic business of sovereignty in the Arctic islands.

Meantime, L.P. Brodeur, the Minister of Marine and Fisheries who played such a key part in starting the navy, was the driving force in upholding northern sovereignty. In the early years of the century he made sure a Canadian presence was maintained, slight though it might be, with regular expeditions and patrols. Captain Joseph-Elzear Bernier commanded CGS *Arctic* on northern voyages between 1904 and 1911. She was small: 762 tons with a fifty-horsepower steam engine. Sealers had been working the Newfoundland pack for generations so her design was right. The main aim was to confirm sovereignty. Bernier was an experienced and capable mariner. He brought back a wealth of information and did a lot of valuable surveying in the islands. But he was more intrepid than imaginative.

In 1908 *Arctic* lay in M'Clure Strait, beyond Parry's farthest point of 1819, and ice-free water stretched ahead as far as Bernier could see. The way looked clear, indeed, to skirt the north shore of Banks Island, where no ship had gone before. If so, Bernier might open a new Northwest Passage in a single season. He knew that Amundsen's route along the mainland coast was too shallow for merchant ships of size. The way that lay ahead could be a commercial route and he believed his *Arctic* could have made it. But as he "had no instructions to proceed through the Northwest Passage" he turned back to Winter Harbour to lay up for the season. His chance was gone. On his next voyage he had instructions to press on if conditions allowed. They did not. He had missed his moment and it never reoccurred.

But Bernier was a prodigious achiever. He planted innumerable cairns and survey marks. He surveyed by sea and by dog-sled and built a rich knowledge of Arctic navigation. He planted a plaque on Melville Island, on Dominion Day, 1909, asserting Canadian sovereignty over "the whole of the Arctic Archipelago lying north of America from Longitude 60 West to Longitude 141 West." Bernier followed the old tradition of naming corners of the Arctic for benefactors. Baffin had so named Lancaster Sound; James Ross named Boothia Peninsula after his backer, who distilled the well-known Booth's gin. Conspicuous spots were running low but Bernier named Brodeur Peninsula at the northwest corner of Baffin Island and remembered the Minister's birthplace by naming an island Beloeil.

The next notable Arctic prober was Vilhjalmur Stefansson. He travelled the coast from Point Barrow, Alaska, to Victoria Island, 1908-12, and then led the Canadian Arctic Expedition of 1913-18. Stefansson lived off the land, travelling vast distances over the ice through the western islands and out on the Beaufort Sea. He supported men and dogs by hunting, and he made the last of the world's land discoveries on the far fringes of the western Arctic and Queen Elizabeth Islands.

Stefansson wrote of the Arctic as a region to be lived in, used, and developed. His was the vision of a "Polar Mediterranean," a world crossroads. If exploited and controlled, he said, it would make Canada a great power. Stefansson was erratic and controversial, and, like most prophets, he was reviled by many in his time.

Captain Bernier took *Arctic* north again after the Great War, then other mariners with other vessels continued the yearly patrols until 1940. There was little thought about the land or the hardy, resourceful native people who lived on it. The RCMP patrolled the islands and channels each year with small vessel and dogs. Their famous little schooner *St. Roch*, commanded by Staff-Sergeant Henry Larsen, was the first ship to sail the Northwest Passage from west to east, in the years 1940-42. She wintered twice en route. Then, in 1944 she did the full passage for the first time ever in a single year, from east to west through Parry Channel and Prince of Wales Strait.

LABRADOR IN THE ARCTIC

In 1954 Canada's navy was at last properly in the Arctic. At the end of July *Labrador* steamed up Lancaster Sound and anchored off Resolute Bay, Cornwallis Island. An airstrip and a weather and scientific station had been there since 1947. The ship's company did the first survey, set up beacons, and so opened Resolute to resupply by heavy ships. *Labrador*'s draft of thirty feet made her the deepest ship ever in great areas of these sketchily surveyed waters. Captain Owen Robertson needed a full combination of ancient seafaring sense and modern technical skill. He, his Executive Officer, Commander Mac Leeming, and his Navigator, Lieutenant Tom Irvine, had those in full.

In her first season, supply tasks took *Labrador* well north in Kane Basin. On that stretch she had a howling, yowling deck cargo of seventeen dogs belonging to RCMP Special Constable Ariak. The ship delivered him, his family, and his dogs along with the cargo of coal to Alexandra Fiord. She rescued a Boston dragger called *Monte Carlo* from a losing gamble with the ice. Then she headed west through Parry Channel and joined the USN's Beaufort Sea expedition – she surveyed and collected hydrographic, oceanographic, and scientific data through Prince of Wales Strait, Amundsen Gulf, and the Beaufort Sea.

Finally, she passed south through Bering Strait to the Pacific during the last week of September. HMCS *Labrador* thus was the first warship and first large ship of any description to complete the Northwest Passage. Home to Halifax via Esquimalt and the Panama Canal made Robertson's *Labrador* second only to Larsen's little *St. Roch* to circumnavigate North America. More than this, she had shown herself the finest Arctic vessel in the Western world. Manned by an outstanding ship's company, she was ready for any challenge the North could provide.

THE DEW LINE

The Soviets had the atomic bomb and a growing strategic bomber force by 1949. Four years later they exploded their first thermonuclear device. With the spectre of Armageddon over Arctic seas, Canada and the U.S. agreed to build the Distant Early Warning line along the Arctic coast and islands. Work started in 1955. The gigantic sealift task fell to the U.S. Navy's Military Sea Transport Service. *Labrador*, with a year of hard experience, was ready. She was turned over to USN operational control and flew the only Canadian flag in a huge flotilla. But her lone representation of Canada in the northern seas was no mere token.

Captain Robertson was given command of the Eastern Arctic Task Group with twenty-three ships. For staff he had his own ship's officers, one additional USN officer, and a U.S. Army colonel in charge of 3,000 soldiers. Their challenge was to land enormous loads of construction equipment and materials by landing craft over Arctic beaches. Often these had first to be charted and cleared. Robertson's opposite number in the western Arctic, a USN rear admiral, had some seventy ships and a staff of thirty.

The giant DEW line construction job employed 25,000 people, and it was done with amazing speed. By 1957 twenty-two radar stations, mostly on

CGS *Arctic* in the ice of Baffin Bay, 15 August 1906. Under command of Captain J.-E. Bernier the little vessel, less than 800 tons with a 50-horsepower steam engine, surveyed and placed navigation marks over thousands of miles of Arctic coastline. In 1909 *Arctic*'s Bernier planted Canada's formal claim to all the Arctic archipelago. (*National Archives of Canada*)

HMCS *Labrador*, the navy's first and only Arctic patrol vessel, is dwarfed by an iceberg near the entrance to Lancaster Sound. Beside the helicopter hangar is "Pogo," the rugged little launch that helped *Labrador* accomplish so much survey and hydrographic work during her four brief Arctic seasons in naval hands. (*National Archives of Canada*)

Vice Admiral E.B. "Whitey" Taylor, USN (Commander Anti-submarine Forces Atlantic), is flanked by Air Commodore W. Clements (Commander Maritime Air Command) and Rear Admiral Kenneth Dyer (Commander Canadian Maritime Atlantic) at a briefing at Greenwood Air Station by Group Captain Ralph Gordon (commanding the station) in October, 1961. A year later such close personal liaison paid off and these were the key people in the smooth and effective co-operation between American and Canadian forces in the Cuban missile crisis. (*Department of National Defence*)

HMCS *Mackenzie* arrives in Halifax from the builders, Canadian Vickers Limited, Montreal, in October, 1962. The Mackenzies, like the Restigouches, have the British 3-inch 70-calibre rapid-fire twin gunmounting forward. It was highly complex and only the RCN fitted it in small ships. Exceptional standards of skilled maintenance – by this time common throughout the navy – kept it working. (*Department of National Defence*)

Hoisting the Canadian Ensign, hauling down the White, 15 February 1965. *Bonaventure*'s ship's company parades on the flight deck in San Juan, Puerto Rico, to say a nostalgic good-bye to the White Ensign, under which the navy had served since 1910, and to honour its replacement with the new Canadian flag. (*Department of National Defence*)

A Sea King ready to land on *Assiniboine* in 1964. Starting with sea trials in 1956 the RCN achieved what no other navy would try – flying a full-sized anti-submarine helicopter from a small ship in all weathers. The original St. Laurents lost some armament and got a split funnel to squeeze in the hangar. The square on the flight deck is the "beartrap," which clamps around the helo's probe and holds it firmly on the rolling deck. At the stern is the handling equipment for the Canadian-designed Variable Depth Sonar. (*National Archives of Canada*)

HMCS *Okanagan*, one of three British-built "O" class diesel-electric submarines that commissioned 1965 to 1968. The key anti-submarine role of submarines was re-demonstrated in the Cuban crisis of 1962. These exceptionally quiet boats were outstanding in that role but fell increasingly behind the improvements and quiet running of nuclear-powered submarines. (*Department of National Defence*)

Soviet Hotel-class nuclear-powered submarine, photographed by a Maritime Command Argus, lies disabled in heavy weather 600 miles northeast of Newfoundland in 1973. She spurned Canadian and American offers of help and was eventually towed home by this Soviet tug. She carries three nuclear-tipped ballistic missiles in her sail. (*Department of National Defence*)

HMCS *Bras d'Or*, the world's first ultra-high-speed open-ocean warcraft, "flies" at 63 knots off Halifax in 1970. The 200-ton ship was more comfortable at 40 knots in ten-foot seas than a destroyer was at eighteen. Ever-decreasing navy budgets and government reluctance to finance research and development sank *Bras d'Or* at the time of certain success. (*Department of National Defence*)

Preserver, commissioned in 1970, the last of three operational support ships, fuels *Assiniboine* (to starboard) and *Margaree* in the Caribbean in 1971. The OSS can provide everything a ship needs to stay indefinitely at sea in fighting trim – ship and aviation fuel, ammunition, provisions, essential spare parts, extra helicopters. (*Department of National Defence*)

Iroquois, the first of the four new Tribals, fires a Sea Sparrow anti-aircraft missile off Puerto Rico in 1976. She was the first all gas-turbine propelled ship in the NATO navies and the first frigate to fly two all-weather helicopters. She has an Italian rapid-fire 5-inch gun forward, American Sea Sparrow anti-aircraft missiles with Dutch radar control and Canadian handling system, Dutch warning radar, Canadian beartrap and helicopter handling system, and Canadian variable depth and hull-mounted sonars. (*Department of National Defence*)

Iroquois rides high on the new "synchrolift" marine railway in Halifax dockyard, December, 1986. Dwarfed by her near 4,000 tons is thirty-four-year-old *Skeena*. A big modern ship repair and maintenance complex and an up-to-date operations and administration building were added to this dockyard in the eighties. Such facilities, though not obvious when counting ships at sea, are vital assets in national and alliance terms – as their near-total lack at the start of two world wars attests. (*Department of National Defence*)

Marching off the old Queen's Colour, 1979. This Colour was presented to the RCN by her Majesty in 1959 (during her visit to open the St. Lawrence Seaway) to replace the King's Colour presented by her father in 1939. She presented her new Colour, suitable to the change of ensign, in 1979 to a naval parade in Canadian Forces green. The Guard for the old Colour was dressed in old navy uniform, though the petty officer second class on the right is wearing a moustache. Before unification, sailors wore full beards or nothing. (*Maritime Command Museum*)

The Standing Naval Force Atlantic (Stanavforlant) in close "photo-op" formation off Gibraltar. *Iroquois* is third from the left. (*Department of National Defence*)

Kootenay rides herd on a Soviet Kara-class cruiser 100 miles off Vancouver in 1982. The Soviet navy sent this powerful ship plus one Kashin-class and an oiler to monitor North American surveillance systems. *Kootenay*'s anti-submarine outfit is visible aft: the box-like Asroc rocket–launched anti-submarine torpedo mounting; the two wells for her six-barrelled anti-submarine mortar Mark 10; and her VDS right at the stern. (*Department of National Defence*)

Women went to sea for trial in the diving tender *Cormorant* in 1980. In 1989 they were accepted in seagoing billets in all ships but submarines. (*Department of National Defence*)

Canadian soil, stretched their web from western Alaska to Baffin Island. The U.S. paid the bills and employed Canadian companies and labour; Canada kept ownership of the Canadian sites.

Labrador, by then commanded by Captain T.C. Pullen, worked the eastern DEW line again in 1956. The pace was off a little but ninety-five ships still landed 250,000 tons of dry cargo and three million barrels of fuel. Pullen, First Lieutenant of *Ottawa* when she was sunk, had a wealth of experience, a wide-ranging intellect, and the right balance of sound judgement, initiative, and drive. He came of a naval line: his older brother was a rear admiral; their forebears had explored these very waters, as attested on the charts. Pullen's executive officer was Tony Law, who had commanded motor torpedo boats through many gunfights in the Channel. Quick of mind and soft-spoken, Law led with a sure and subtle hand. Here he followed his work as a war artist by recording remarkable images of the Arctic.

Pullen observed in a report: "The Americans have operated thin-skinned ships in all areas of the Arctic, thus gaining much knowledge. They have done more pioneering, surveying, charting, oceanography, and exploring in Canada's northern waters than in all history." Canada was back in the starting blocks, and *Labrador* and her company had much to learn, but they did learn and they did contribute in important ways.

Besides their sealift duties, *Labrador*'s people made major revisions to ten charts and produced twelve completely new ones, opening innumerable harbours and channels to deep-draft ships. In her last two seasons under Pullen she navigated and charted Bellot Strait for the first time, discovered a deep channel into Frobisher Bay, and surveyed and erected beacons around Foxe Basin. That made a huge area newly safe for navigation. Oceanographic observations were taken by the thousands. Meteorological data piled up.

The exploits of earlier mariners cast long shadows in the Arctic sun. Reading of their trials and tragedies and achievements brought more than passing wonder to the ship's company, travelling as they did in such relative luxury. Specially memorable to Tom Pullen was anchoring off Beechey Island in Erebus Bay precisely where HMS *North Star* anchored 104 years before. His great uncle, Commander W.J.S. Pullen, RN, had been in command, and the Master was another great uncle, an earlier T.C. Pullen. *North Star*, on the Franklin search of 1852-54, spent two years trapped in ice that *Labrador* could have shrugged off with a few turns of her screws. She was a far cry, too, from Bernier's little *Arctic*. In his 1911 report Bernier wrote, "The wind diminished, the ice slackened, the Engineer got up steam . . . and an attempt was made to force the *Arctic* through the ice with the aid of boathooks." Boathooks! Things had advanced a fair bit in forty odd years.

The fund of data compiled by *Labrador* added enormously to the safety of surface navigation. It prepared also for the onset of submarine passages beneath the ice. A new major piece was about to come into play on the strategic chessboard of the world.

UNDER NORTHERN WATERS

World War Two U-boats operated in the ice-infested Kara Sea off northern Russia. In 1946 USS *Atule*, with developing instruments, crept half a nautical mile under the ice in Kane Basin. The next year USS *Boarfish* ran thirty miles beneath the pack in the Chukchi Sea. In 1952 *Redfish* spent nine hours below the great revolving mass of ice west of Banks Island called the Beaufort Gyre.

Advances came with new sonars to detect icebergs and keels projecting downward from the pack; the inertial navigation system, a gyroscopic device, kept a very accurate position underwater, though it had to be aligned every few days with a peek at the stars through the periscope. But the major leap came with nuclear propulsion. USS *Nautilus* came very close to the Pole in 1957, then the next year crossed the top of the world from Pacific to Atlantic beneath the ice the whole way.

A submarine that doesn't have to surface can cruise indefinitely under the Arctic ice and thread through several of the channels in the Canadian archipelago. USS *Seadragon*, under Commander G.P. Steele, made the first submerged transit of the Northwest Passage via Parry Channel and M'Clure Strait in 1960. He had Commodore Owen Robertson aboard. Once past the historic point the submarine turned north and popped up in a polynya a mile from the Pole. It was almost old hat, but still it was something to celebrate, so on a warm, sunny 27th of August the crew had a rousing game of baseball on the ice.

In the cheerful horseplay, though, Robertson had a sense of deep chagrin. Canada's navy was out of the Arctic. HMCS *Labrador*, two years back, in 1958, had been turned over to the Department of Transport.

PULLING OUT

Even if surface warships were strengthened for ice, movement was too limited to do much against enemy lodgements or submarines. A government directive put top priority on fighting ships, and there was no denying that *Labrador* lacked a direct military function. NATO commitments were honoured in those times and the *Labrador* crew could man another ocean escort. Cabinet ordered spending cuts for 1958-59 and didn't see the long-term importance of keeping the navy in the Arctic. Transport would run her more cheaply.

It is fair to say that *Labrador*, in her four short seasons in the navy, contributed more to knowledge of the Canadian Arctic than any single ship had in this century. Naval officers are reared to lead, to take the initiative. They learn to handle complex operation orders and act on them in endlessly varied situations. They're taught to grasp the overall aim of their commander, interpret it according to the situation at hand, and get on with what has to be done. They'll take responsibility for action on the spot and don't need to ask for further orders.

Transport's officers were very capable seamen and icebreaker captains. There's a great difference, however, in being brought up in the merchant service, where ships are far less versatile and the stress is on safe passage from A to B. Joseph Bernier turned back from a clear passage to the Beaufort Sea because he had no orders; William Parry had seized his moment and driven on. Merchant seamen are skilled in their own jobs and self-sufficient like all who follow the sea. But a merchant, Transport, or Coast Guard ship's company carries nothing like the range of technical skills of a naval ship.

In four brief seasons under the outstanding leadership of Captains Robertson and Pullen, *Labrador* and her company delivered brilliantly on all counts. Had government come up with enough to keep her in the navy she certainly could have brought a lot to science, hydrography, and oceanography. As well, she would have been invaluable in training and in shaping concepts for operations in an area of looming importance in the world. In addition, there would have been an ongoing exchange with the USN. Navies talk to navies when there's valuable information to trade and recognized experts do the trading. Canada might then have faced far earlier the meaning of the new submarines and found ways and means to exert control and uphold sovereignty in Canadian waters. She might have some bargaining chips in hand rather than be left to lean helplessly on her southern friend and neighbour to make the running in the North.

In 1969, when Arctic oil and minerals boomed in world importance, Exxon Corporation sent the supertanker *Manhattan* through the Northwest Passage. The Canadian Coast Guard icebreaker *John A. Macdonald* helped her through. The icemaster on *Manhattan*'s bridge was Captain Tom Pullen. He was retired from the navy and in a second career as the leading expert on northern marine operations. That voyage turns another chapter in the opening of the seas beyond the northern gate.

CHAPTER FIFTEEN
THE BRINK
OF WAR

PRESIDENT KENNEDY SPOKE ON TELEVISION AND RADIO AT 6 P.M. ON Monday, 22 October 1962. What he had to say electrified the world. The Soviet Union had medium-range nuclear ballistic missiles positioned in Cuba that could vapourize Washington, Panama, or Mexico City. Sites were being built as he spoke for intermediate-range missiles that would reach 2,200 miles – to any city in the eastern two-thirds of North America. And he said: "... to halt this offensive build-up a strict quarantine on all offensive military equipment under shipment to Cuba is being initiated. All ships of any kind bound for Cuba, from whatever nation or port, will, if found to contain cargoes of offensive weapons, be turned back."

"Quarantine" – to go into effect at 10 a.m. on 24 October – was another word for blockade. Ships were heading for confrontation on the high seas. America's Strategic Air Command was airborne on full alert with nuclear weapons in the bomb bays. So, certainly, was its Soviet counterpart. Six U.S. nuclear submarines somewhere under the trackless sea had their Polaris ballistic missiles programmed for cities in the Soviet Union.

Around the world people hung on Kennedy's words and their world hung by a thread. The awful fear that had lurked deep in their minds for ten long years burst to the surface. Suddenly, the world they knew could be snuffed out in a suicidal nuclear exchange. The United States and the Soviet Union were on a collision course to war.

THE READINESS BUSINESS

Soviet missiles and arms – the dramatically visible ones – were stunningly new in the Western Hemisphere. Their submarines, though, had been probing and pushing in the northwest Atlantic for years and that was very much the daily business of Rear Admiral Kenneth Dyer, Flag Officer Atlantic Coast. In the NATO structure, Dyer was Commander Canadian Maritime Atlantic under the Supreme Commander Atlantic, Admiral Robert Dennison, USN. In his headquarters in Norfolk, Dennison was also the U.S. Commander-in-Chief Atlantic. One of his key officers was Vice Admiral E.B. "Whitey" Taylor, who commanded anti-submarine forces in the Atlantic.

Day in and day out, besides the NATO connection, the two navies worked hand in glove under the Canada-U.S. defence agreements that had been in place for years. Ships exercised together regularly and so did staffs. Dyer and Taylor between them kept tabs on Soviet submarines. The SOSUS monitoring stations at Shelburne, run by RCN Wrens, and the USN station at Argentia were part of the Atlantic underwater surveillance net. They could detect snorkelling or surfaced submarines at very long ranges and identify them with varying success.

In 1962 the Soviet surface fleet was growing fast but still was no match for the U.S. Navy. In submarines, though, they were formidable; in 1960 they had about 500 of all types. The first post-war home construction, the Whiskeys and Zulus, were high-performance diesel-electrics modelled on the German Type 21s that could do fourteen-sixteen knots submerged. From the mid-fifties their ocean-going attack fleet stayed around 220 boats, adding new improved classes like the Romeos and Foxtrots and tucking the old into reserve. Their torpedoes could carry nuclear heads, expensive against merchant ships but very dangerous for fleet units.

The Soviets had moved much faster than the West in anti-ship guided missiles. Cruisers and destroyers bristled with them and some Whiskey submarines could fire missiles from the surface by the late fifties. Soon ranges went to 250 miles with targeting data by an aircraft at long range. For propulsion, some Zulus tried the Walther high-test peroxide method, but there were safety problems. Nuclear propulsion was a much better bet, and some November-class torpedo-armed nuclear-powered attack boats went to sea in 1958. The nuclear-driven Echo II attack boats clattered along at a noisy twenty-five knots by 1961 and carried eight surface-to-surface missiles. Their targets were the carrier forces.

The Soviets were well behind the Americans' underwater-launched long-range Polaris strategic nuclear missile, but already some Zulus had been armed with surface-launched ballistic missiles – range 300 miles – with megaton heads. Golf-class diesel-electrics and Hotel nuclears with the same ballistic missiles were in service by 1962. They weren't Polaris, but sitting off the eastern seaboard they were nightmare weapons that could strike New York, Boston, Washington, Norfolk, Halifax with a fraction of the flight time of bombers over the Pole, or even missiles from Cuba.

The idea in the navy's day-to-day Cold War was to keep the opposition under pressure, define and analyse his operations, and work out ways to handle them. Taylor had a standing carrier group called Task Group Alfa that developed anti-submarine tactics. The Joint Maritime Warfare School in Halifax kept right on top of tactics and techniques and worked out new ones. The navies exchanged intelligence, and direct phone lines joined Halifax and Norfolk.

If Shelburne got a submarine contact, for instance, out would go an Argus from Greenwood. It might get a radar contact on a conning tower or snorkel, or it could sow a wide field of special sonobuoys to pick up the submarine's engines. Then it would sow more sonobuoys and narrow down the contact. Ships might go to the scene. Between ships and aircraft they'd hold and track. Ships had their sonars, much improved. The aircraft would use MAD, improved on wartime's "magnetic anomaly detector," to keep tabs. In a real war, the plane would have dropped a homing torpedo, developed from wartime's "Fido," using MAD. In the USN, if nuclear war was on, the plane could drop a nuclear depth charge. A peacetime hold-down used no weapons, but it was still the old wartime "hunt to exhaustion." They'd hold contact if they could until the target had to come up and breathe. In any event, it was a lot better for practice than a friendly "Mechanical Mouse." Besides, they could claim Saclant's case of Jack Daniels whiskey for their trouble if they won.

Regular patrols flew from Canadian and American bases. When submarine activity was high, ships stayed out on station. Every Soviet ship, from trawler to supertanker to submarine, was part of their total navy. Their fishing fleets on the Grand Banks and George's Bank off Cape Cod had to be watched with care. Tucked among legitimate fishermen, some Soviet trawlers were fitted for "Elint" – electronic intelligence gathering – and they could be communications links with submarines and could tamper with the transatlantic cables, still vital links with Europe. Soviet factory ships were sources of supplies and fuel. Surface ships with similar diesel engines could mask a transiting submarine's sound signature. They had to be monitored; the pressure must be kept on.

Dyer had thirty-nine warships in his command. Ten were in regular refit, docking, maintenance, or repair. That made twenty-nine available for operations in October, 1962. Of those, *Bonaventure* and five destroyer escorts were in U.K. waters. Two or, better, three Restigouches with their improved sonar, anti-submarine mortar, and homing torpedoes could handle a Soviet conventional diesel-electric. Give them helicopters and, give or take the thousand and one imponderables of ASW, they could probably kill a nuclear-powered boat. But this enemy could pack a nuclear punch in torpedoes or missiles against the Canadian ships' high-explosive mortar bombs. Besides, no Canadian ship had a weapon that would shoot down a guided missile. If it came to a shooting war, Canadian destroyer captains had some food for thought.

If Soviet activity in the northwest Atlantic increased at any time, it was up to Dyer to react. In early October submarine activity *was* increasing – at exactly the same time the situation was coming to the boil in Cuba. On 11 October Dyer boosted his air surveillance with more and longer Argus patrols.

READINESS IN ACTION

On 17 October the extra vigilance paid off. An Argus from Greenwood got a solid submarine contact 225 miles southeast of Nova Scotia called Bravo 27. On the same day a U.S. Navy aircraft far to the east spotted the Soviet navy oiler *Terek*. She was fitted for refuelling submarines and this was not her usual beat. The next day a U.S. military tanker sighted a submarine in the Caribbean 130 miles off Venezuela. More patrols and photo recce flights took off from Canadian and U.S. airbases. Special targets were the fishing fleets. The known Elint trawler *Shkval* was spotted and shadowed.

On the 21st *Terek* was seen again, northwest of the Azores and heading toward the Caribbean at fifteen knots. Then an aircraft caught her fuelling a Zulu over her stern. The photos showed the submarine's fouled hull. She had been on patrol with a lot of submerged time for quite a while. Her sound signature matched with an earlier track off the eastern seaboard. Now she was topping up in the Atlantic, which the Soviets didn't normally do, so it appeared she was going back on station rather than rotating home. The ballistic missile boats were out and they were forcing the pace. How many were on station?

On 22 October, with SAC bombers on airborne alert and blockade orders out to his Atlantic fleet, President Kennedy made his speech and all the U.S. forces went to Defence Condition 3. The submarines on Dyer's plot could oppose the U.S. blockade and could threaten any U.S. strike and assault forces around Cuba. Or they could just lie quietly disposed for action against fleet units and shipping if and when war began. And should that happen, some of them were part of the Soviet nuclear strike force.

Whatever way Dyer looked at it, North America was under direct immediate threat. That included Canada. All the long-standing arrangements and government-to-government agreements said if one partner boosted its defence condition, the other followed. Ottawa, of course, was fully posted. The operations room in Ottawa, under Rear Admiral Jeffry Brock, Vice Chief of Naval Staff, showed the essential picture. The Chief of Naval Staff, Vice Admiral Rayner, was in close touch with the Minister, Douglas Harkness.

Dyer now expected the message from Ottawa at any moment. It would be the Alert State of Military Vigilance, the Canadian equivalent to Defcon 3.

Then all aircraft would take off with war loads, live torpedoes. Ships would get out on special stations under war conditions. Alternate operational head-quarters and communications would be manned. Maintenance ships, shore-based aircraft, and logistic support would be dispersed. War, nuclear war if it came, would flash in an instant. It was terribly, overwhelmingly close.

The clock ticked, but nothing came. Dyer phoned the Chief of Naval Staff, but Rayner's hands were tied. He couldn't do what everything in his cool, precise, professional mind was telling him. He couldn't signal the alert with-out permission from his political masters. In this most perilous crisis that had ever faced the world, the Prime Minister of Canada, the man who must take the vital decision, would not make up his mind.

POLITICAL PARALYSIS

A few hours before Kennedy's speech, presidential envoy Livingston Mer-chant flew into Ottawa with photos of the missile bases. He briefed Prime Minister John Diefenbaker, his Secretary of State for External Affairs, Howard Green, and the Minister of National Defence on what the President was about to say. Douglas Harkness recorded the Prime Minister telling Merchant that "in the event of a missile attack on the United States from Cuba, Canada would live up to its responsibilities under the NATO and NORAD agreements." Waiting for the first strike would render the decision futile but, as the spectre of nuclear annihilation hung overhead, Diefenbaker refused to make that key decision to put Canada's armed forces on alert.

Within minutes of Kennedy's broadcast, the chairman of the Chiefs of Staff, Air Chief Marshal Frank Miller, told Harkness that all U.S. forces were on Defcon 3. He asked for authority to order the Canadian forces – especially the NORAD component of the RCAF – to the same level. The air forces, unlike the navies, were under a single command for continental air defence and having the Canadian part of it at lower readiness was impossible. Harkness had to ask the Prime Minister, and Diefenbaker wouldn't decide without the cabinet. But because the House was sitting, he refused point-blank to call a meeting until morning. Morning! Harkness, a wartime fighting soldier with a level head and orderly mind, could scarcely believe it. All he could do was tell Miller to go to maximum preparedness short of an alert.

On the morning of the 23rd, Soviet ships were seen heading for the blockade line. At the cabinet meeting Diefenbaker and Green were against an alert. The Prime Minister said it would unduly alarm the people. He and Harkness had hot words. Harkness believed he refused "because of a patho-logical hatred of taking a hard decision." There was another factor. Diefenba-ker mistrusted President Kennedy. Underlining that, he and Howard Green had backed a UN move for an inspection in Cuba to confirm the missiles were actually there.

The Minister met the chiefs again. They trusted Harkness and he trusted them. They were equally appalled. There was no alert but the Minister said to go ahead with all necessary measures "in as quiet and unobtrusive a way as possible." They spoke to their senior commanders by phone. Harkness kept the Prime Minister posted on the escalating events. At last he got him to call a cabinet meeting for the 24th – they met but weren't unanimous, and again the Prime Minister refused to decide himself.

Then Air Chief Marshal Miller reported that SAC and some U.S. naval forces were at Defcon 2: "Immediate enemy attack expected." With this the Prime Minister agreed to an alert for the Canadian component of NORAD forces only. There was no mention of the navy.

In the House of Commons that day, S.P. Ryan, MP, questioned the Minister of Defence. Was Canada assisting in any way in the "policing" of the Atlantic to prevent entry of weapons into Cuba? Were we assisting in "some ancillary fashion?" Harkness answered "no" on both counts. In fact, the mutual defence operations already taking place at sea were of very real "ancillary" help to the United States. Dyer had set his command in motion as for Alert. If the Minister did know any of the details, he hardly could have answered otherwise.

The following afternoon, 25 October, the Prime Minister said in the House of Commons: " . . . all Canadian military forces have taken necessary precautionary measures to improve their readiness to meet any serious developments. The Canadian component of the NORAD forces have been placed on the same level of readiness as the American forces under NORAD operational control." Long leave and movement of forces dependants overseas was suspended, he said, and "the government approved the measures that the forces would have to take in the event that the present crisis leads to a more serious situation."

All very consoling to the populace . . . But if one kept half an ear to the radio or half an eye to TV, one knew the palpable fear that gripped the world. Diefenbaker's "more serious situation" could only be war itself. The world was on the brink, and officially only the NORAD component of Canada's armed forces was on alert. It had taken two days for the Canadian government to get its trousers up to its knees. But the navy's Atlantic command was moving briskly and effectively.

NAVAL ACTION

The Naval Board had met twice on 24 October. It sedately initiated the "Discreet Level of Military Vigilance" for Headquarters only. This simply meant running through the check-off list of plans, communications, and security arrangements and setting up interdepartmental liaisons and other administrative matters. Although long leave had been suspended, to avoid public alarm those on leave weren't recalled. *Bonaventure* and her destroyers were ordered back from Portsmouth, but "at economical speed." At no time did the navy or the maritime air component of the RCAF go officially to any higher degree of vigilance than "Discreet."

Rayner could say nothing more to Dyer than "do what you have to do." But he knew his man. Quite apart from honouring commitments to an ally, what sea commander since Pearl Harbor would let his ships be caught in harbour with war in the wind? Best, too, if Rayner didn't know in any detail what Dyer was about; he might be asked and he was a man of utmost probity. So the quick and simple solution was "exercise." Dyer could run what exercises he liked without bothering Headquarters at all.

A Canada-U.S. convoy exercise was due in late October. The USN had understandably pulled out but Dyer put ships and planes to work on substitute "national exercises." That is what the press, quite deliberately, was told. But the forces were disposed to meet a threat that was chillingly real. The emergency plans for dispersal had been exercised two weeks before. They were repeated, in earnest. *Cornwallis*, the training base in the Annapolis Valley, became the alternate headquarters. Admiral Dyer stayed in Halifax because if he had cleared out it would have been hard for Rayner to explain. Sydney and Shelburne became alternate naval ports. Short-handed ships were brought up to scratch by pulling people from shore courses. Greenwood air base dispersed some aircraft to Saint John. Ships in maintenance, trials, and work-ups were pushed forward. Fuel, ammunition, stores, and dockyard services were available around the clock.

THE SUBAIR BARRIER

Operations plans under Defcon 3 called for a "Subair Barrier" across the Greenland-Iceland-U.K. gaps. Intelligence on Soviet submarines moving down was vital; but with such heavy U.S. involvement to the south, Halifax and Norfolk jointly decided to pull the barrier closer to home. On the 24th, while Diefenbaker dithered, the Argentia Subair Barrier went into force. It stretched from Cape Race, Newfoundland, some 600 miles southeast to a point about 300 miles from the Azores and was 100 miles deep. Across this great arc were disposed ten USN submarines and the two RN submarines based in Halifax under Canadian operational control – HMS *Alderney* and *Astute*. Seventeen USN Neptunes were sent to fly out of Argentia. The twenty-four operational Argus aircraft from Greenwood, which had been hard at it for two weeks, were divided between surveillance and barrier patrol. Eight more joined from the training squadron at Summerside.

The Soviets' rather noisy diesel-electric boats were vulnerable to detection while snorkelling or running on the surface toward their stations. Some were picked up first by the SOSUS net in the Greenland-Iceland-U.K. gaps. The

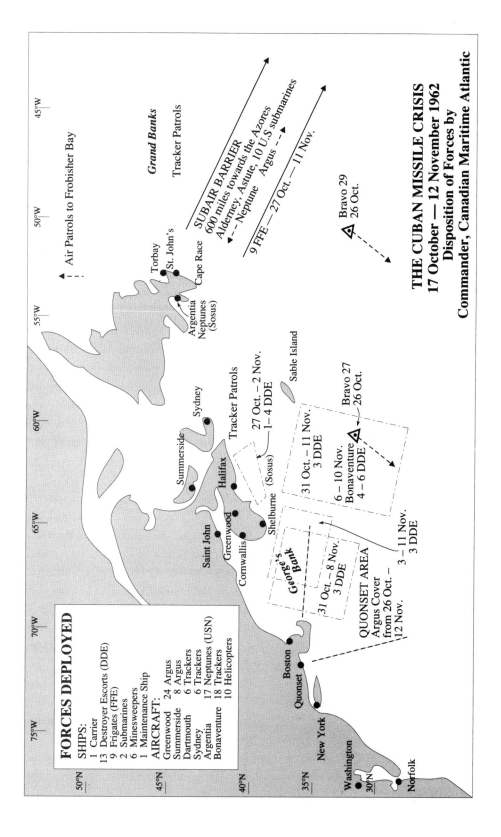

FORCES DEPLOYED

SHIPS:
1 Carrier
13 Destroyer Escorts (DDE)
9 Frigates (FFE)
2 Submarines
6 Minesweepers
1 Maintenance Ship

AIRCRAFT:
Greenwood 24 Argus
Summerside 8 Argus
Dartmouth 6 Trackers
Sydney 6 Trackers
Argentia 17 Neptunes (USN)
Bonaventure 18 Trackers
10 Helicopters

THE CUBAN MISSILE CRISIS
17 October — 12 November 1962
Disposition of Forces by
Commander, Canadian Maritime Atlantic

object of the barrier was to track them as they moved south, feeding information into the plots ashore and afloat, so they could be picked up by hunter-killer forces stationed behind the barrier.

Barrier submarines, running slow and silent, were the on-line listening posts. The long-range patrol aircraft laid lines of sonobuoys, monitored them on each successive sweep, and replaced them when they reached the end of their limited life. They listened on their radar search receivers and searched in short bursts of active radar for snorkelling or surfaced boats. They checked out surface ships, too, that could be making for Cuba.

The Maritime Command Arguses were key players from the start. They had a much longer radius than the U.S. Navy's Neptunes. They could cover the far southeast end of the barrier – 1,000 nautical miles from Greenwood – with plenty in hand for patrolling and developing contacts. Three of them were constantly on station – six hours out, eight on station, and six back – twenty hours per flight. Dyer used every available aircraft and burned aircraft hours at the full wartime rate.

And they carried full war loads – 8,000 pounds in depth bombs and MK 43 acoustic homing torpedoes. The torpedo batteries were charged and ready for instant use. That was irreversible and expensive, only carried out before a practice drop, or in war. They sowed hundreds of sonobuoys, and stocks ran low. A phone call to Whitey Taylor and the USN flew in an extra 500 – no charge. Canadian ships and aircraft didn't have nuclear anti-submarine weapons but the U.S. Navy did. If they were used the tactics were common doctrine.

CRISIS RISING

By the 24th the Commander-in-Chief of the Atlantic fleet assessed at least three Soviet submarines in the North Atlantic that "could reach the quarantine line in a few days and could be a substantial threat to that force . . . and . . . could be a deliberate counteraction by the Soviets against quarantine forces." He ordered Task Group Alfa – ASW carrier *Randolph* and a destroyer squadron – south to protect the strike carrier *Independence*. On the blockade front on 25 October, twelve of twenty-five Soviet ships heading for Cuba turned back. The next day a Soviet-chartered freighter was stopped by a USN destroyer, searched, and allowed to proceed.

Now an Argus detected another submarine 450 miles south-southeast of Cape Race. This was Bravo 28. It popped up again later and was tracked heading south. The same day off Cuba the strike carrier *Enterprise* heard a Soviet submarine's radar. It could be snapping a range for firing torpedoes. Her destroyer screen made sonar contact, then lost it. The strike force drew smartly back into shoal water south of Jamaica to make things tougher for the subs.

Admiral Taylor had more on his plate than he could handle. Thus, beginning on 25 October Restigouche-class ships of the 5th Canadian Escort Squadron covered the George's Bank, off Cape Cod. This was a critical and difficult area. Missile-firing Zulu submarines in range of Boston and New York could sit on the bottom and take advantage of the difficult sonar conditions, the heavy surface traffic, and their own support vessels among the fishing fleet. The area needed air cover as well as ships, but Taylor badly needed the Neptunes from Quonset Point Naval Air Station down south. On the 26th Dyer took their patrol area over, too, and assigned Argus cover.

The maintenance ship *Cape Scott* moved to Shelburne, which became the 5th Escort Squadron's dispersal base for support and fuel. Captain Patrick Nixon, DSC, the squadron commander, who had three U-boats to his credit from 1944, stayed at sea. When the ship he was riding had to go in to top up he and his staff swung to the next by jackstay. They ranged from George's Bank to Sable Island in some filthy weather, checking shipping, chasing electronic intercepts, searching for submarines, ready to move to contact areas. Nixon had six Restigouches available. *Mackenzie*, the latest addition to the fleet, commissioned in Montreal three weeks before by Commander Tony German, raced through equipment trials and work-up to get ready.

Trackers from *Shearwater* swept the inshore areas and fishing banks. A detachment swiftly deployed to Sydney, while Torbay, Newfoundland, became an advanced airbase. The two available older destroyers of the 3rd Squadron patrolled offshore Nova Scotia with one of the 5th. Nine of the high-endurance Prestonian-class frigates of the 7th and 9th Escort Squadrons backed the Subair Barrier.

Dyer was "in hourly touch with Whitey Taylor in Norfolk. Mark you, he didn't know much that was going on [off Cuba] because Kennedy kept butting in, speaking directly to the forces himself." In the U.S. the time-honoured chain of command was cut. With such astronomic stakes, the split-second pace of events, and the awesome responsibility on the President, the urge to take direct charge was overwhelming. Modern communications gave him the means. He and his staff talked to destroyer captains on the blockade line directly from the White House basement. Short-circuiting command meant that key people like Taylor were often in the dark. It caused friction and confusion and a highly charged collision between the Secretary of Defence and the Chief of Naval Operations right in the Pentagon's Flag Plot.

Commodore J.C. O'Brien, the Canadian naval attaché in Washington, knew that heavy American commitments in the Mediterranean and Pacific meant Canada "had more ready forces in the ASW business in the Atlantic than the Yanks did." All Washington knew the Canadians had dragged their feet on NORAD and still hadn't put their navy on alert. Knowing Ken Dyer, O'Brien knew he'd be doing all he could to help, but as nothing was official he was in the dark. He got into CNO's Flag Plot. Sure enough, their dispositions showed no Canadian identity. O'Brien saw it was vital that the top of the USN knew exactly what Canada was really doing. He asked Headquarters in Ottawa for a message spelling it out to the Chief of Naval Operations. Vice Admiral Rayner sent a personal communication but it was disappointingly unspecific.

In the vacuum left by no higher direction, the right things were being done. Dyer's Chief of Staff, Commodore James Pratt, flew to Norfolk for Admiral Dennison's morning briefings as they were piped simultaneously to Washington. He was back in Halifax to brief his own Admiral at noon. Dyer kept Rayner in the picture by telephone and with copies of operational summaries. He had Rayner's word on the telephone that he'd back him if lightning struck from aloft. That was enough. They knew each other from a long time back; also, Rayner knew Harkness would never let them down. And Harkness knew Diefenbaker. The key was not to raise the matter of the navy with the Prime Minister at all or he'd likely give a petulant "no."

Tension mounted. Work on the Cuban missile sites went on. On the 27th another Soviet ship closed the blockade line. A U-2 reconnaisance plane was shot down over Cuba; another strayed into Soviet airspace. Halifax harbour was all but empty. The nuclear-war tote board coldly called it a second-strike target. But Boston certainly was first strike, and fallout from Boston would blanket Nova Scotia in a day. Halifax looked to its civil defence. Navy men went off to sea with the nightmare of their families snuffed out in the onslaught while they lived on fighting – for a time.

Then, on 28 October, Soviet Premier Nikita Khrushchev seemed to back down. He agreed to withdraw the missiles from Cuba if the U.S. pledged not to invade. The world breathed – except for those who knew. Words from Chairman Khrushchev were one thing, deeds another. He faced a humiliating defeat. Could he keep control of his own country or forces? How would the Soviets react? The U.S. suspended the blockade but kept all ships on station to watch and wait at full alert.

Under the sea there was no letup. That same day Task Group Alfa caught a Soviet Foxtrot submarine on the surface. A defect stopped her from submerging. She was kept under tight surveillance and finally taken in tow by a Soviet tug. On 30 October, Rayner noted to Naval Board that "while there had been a temporary relaxation in political tension over Cuba, there was, as yet, no indication of improvement in the general military situation."

On the 31st another Foxtrot was forced to the surface by the USN after thirty-five hours of sonar contact; on 1 November Admiral Taylor summarized for Dyer: on their plots were seven positive submarines, one probable, five possibles, and at least one replenishment ship. There had never been such activity before. Taylor asked for increased surveillance. He expected to keep it up indefinitely with U.S. forces at near-wartime levels.

There was no letup by Dyer's forces either. The Arguses did the lion's share of the 120 air hours per day on the Subair Barrier, and they did area surveillance and additional patrols up Davis Strait to Frobisher Bay. The elint trawler *Shkval* and another suspect, *Atlantika*, were shadowed continuously by Canadian ships and aircraft. Ships rotated to the alternate harbours from their patrol areas for fuel and provisions and headed straight back on station. The barrier submarines stayed silently on watch.

Bonaventure got into Halifax on 2 November. Her consorts, five older destroyers of the 1st Escort Squadron, topped up and sailed to bolster the patrols. The carrier fuelled, stored, ammunitioned, loaded more aircraft, and sailed for a point northeast of Bermuda, at about the latitude of Philadelphia. With five ships of the 5th Squadron, she was immediately behind the Subair Barrier astride the most direct route for submarines making for the Caribbean. Like George's Bank and Quonset, this let another U.S. task group move further south and so strengthened the American hand near Cuba.

Commodore Robert Welland flew his broad pennant in *Bonaventure*. He'd taken over from Bill Landymore as Senior Canadian Officer Afloat while the ship was in Portsmouth. Captain Fred Frewer was in command and Commander (Air) was Bob Falls, one of the first fighter pilots to land on *Warrior* in 1946. It was an experienced, well-honed team that ran five days of sustained operations. Eighteen Trackers and nine helicopters flew constantly, the Trackers around the clock. The navy's first replenishment ship, *Provider*, wasn't due in service for a year, and the USN's were too busy, so "Bonnie" had to keep her own consorts fuelled and count her days on station.

Before she ran out of fuel herself, on 12 November, the crisis was over and the whole naval operation wound down. The Subair Barrier was folded. Ships returned to harbour and dropped back to peacetime routine. Sailors and airmen caught up on precious time with the families they thought they might never see again. None would forget that war *could* happen. None would forget that the job they'd done 2,000 miles from the blockade line was part and parcel of the total readiness that had stopped aggression in its tracks; or that their Admiral, Ken Dyer, was a courageous leader who had done what had to be done when Canada's political leadership had so shockingly failed the test.

RETROSPECT

There were twenty-nine established submarine contacts in the western Atlantic during the crisis. Some were lost, then picked up again and identified by their sound signatures. Some were followed for many hours and some for days by permutations of the shore, ship, and airborne detection and classification systems. There was the ever-improving SOSUS; sonobuoys picked up underwater sound and relayed it to aircraft, who sorted it out in systems with names like Jezebel, Lofar, Codar, and Julie; sonar, radar, radar search receivers, HF/DF probed and searched; the well-peeled human eyeball was as essential as it ever was. Six submarines were actually sighted near the Cuban operations.

A tally was made by the RCN's ASW operational research team of "exposure contacts" of Soviet submarines in the western Atlantic. It included contacts obtained by the various ship, submarine, and airborne detection methods, but not SOSUS. In 1958 there were four contacts; 1959 had nineteen; 1960, twenty-one; 1961, twenty-two; 1962 (23 October to 15 November only), 136. As their side got busier, ours got better.

There is no question that Canada's navy played an effective role. Admiral Dyer deployed twenty-two specialized anti-submarine ships, two submarines, *Bonaventure* with her twenty-eight aircraft, twelve more Trackers flying from shore, thirty-two Arguses out of Greenwood and Summerside. That made twenty-five ships and over seventy Canadian aircraft out on ASW plus the maintenance ship, tenders and auxiliaries, and six minesweepers getting about their important business in harbour approaches. The whole force was manned by highly trained professionals. Ken Dyer recollected in 1986, "We had a neat little force there." A neat little force indeed.

War did not happen. But to those who were directly involved on, over, and under the sea and in headquarters ashore, it could have burst into searing fury at any time. The crisis was played with all the stops pulled out. Taylor issued no orders to Dyer. Nor did Rayner. For different reasons, neither could. But for the same reason they didn't need to. That "band of brothers," Nelson's basic way of running things at sea, by mutual understanding and a firm grasp of the basic aim, was alive and well in North America in 1962. The navy, with Maritime Air Command, honoured Canada's duty to stand by her North American ally, without one scrap of paper, memo, minute, or message, or one public announcement to give it direction or approval.

BRAVO ZULU

The Organization of American States – Canada only became a member in 1990 – had unanimously backed the U.S. stand over Cuba. Two Argentine and two Venezuelan destroyers got to Trinidad by 8 November. With a USN destroyer they formed Task Force 137 and sailed on 12 November, the day the crisis passed, "in special formation for aerial photos" to patrol the Antilles Passages for eight days. The Dominican navy sent two escorts to San Juan, where they were found unfit for sea.

Americans are ever generous with their thanks. At ceremonies in San Juan and Trinidad, each officer and man got an American Certificate of Participation, Dominicans included. The patrol ships got commemorative brass plates.

Admiral Dennison's account said, "The contribution of the Latin American navies was noted in the world press. . . . CNO hailed the Latin American participation as an historic milestone in hemisphere relations and personally thanked his counterparts."

Dennison's *Historical Account of the Cuban Crisis* had no summary of Canadian forces or operations and only four passing mentions of Canadian units. Latin American involvement got five pages. Those few who really knew what had been done by the Canadians also knew very well it lacked political authority. Like Whitey Taylor, they thanked their Canadian counterparts most sincerely – but in classified messages and personal calls alone – a public backslap from the U.S. Navy and the heads of their good friends could roll.

Certificates and brass plates for doing one's duty were not avidly sought by Canadian sailors. But the simple naval flag signal BZ – Bravo Zulu, Well Done – from the highest masthead always was, is, and will be a treasured accolade. What they had done was just an exercise called "Cubex." No one, other than individual commanding officers, said to their men, "Well done."

Canadians, as reflected in the press, were as appalled at Diefenbaker's indecision on NORAD as they were horrified by the spectre of nuclear onslaught across the Pole. All thought was to the air. No newspaper or commentator, then or later, even speculated on the navy's actions in the crisis. No question, other than Mr. Ryan's, was raised in the House of Commons, even to pry into excess expenditures. A year later Admiral Rayner said simply to the House Special Committee on Defence that the Cuban crisis "proved to be a most realistic test" and the navy was brought, "as quickly as possible, to a high state of operational readiness." Still no one asked, "How high?"

In the democratic tradition, military action stems from government policy alone. By that token, perhaps one Minister of the crown and two Canadian admirals were wrong. But they acted in line with defence agreements in place since 1940. What the navy and maritime air did should have stirred the hearts of their countrymen in a time of national shame. It should have brought the unbridled praise of the highest in the land. Had it been generally known in the U.S. it would surely have cleared the sour American memory of Diefenbaker and of a Canada dragging her feet when the chips were down. It would have left a grateful memory of sharing the defence of the continent when it counted. Too, it would have shown Canadians right across the land, like nothing else, just what a navy was.

But no one spoke. The Minister couldn't without saying he'd defied the Prime Minister. The admirals couldn't without hurting the Minister who had run interference at risk of his political life. The Soviet navy knew, of course, but had no reason to speak. The service, as always, stayed silent.

And the rest of the country didn't know enough to ask.

CHAPTER SIXTEEN
FLYING HIGH

"BONNIE"

BONAVENTURE'S OCEAN AREA IN THE CUBAN CRISIS GOT CLOSE ATTEN-tion around-the-clock for five days and she could have kept it up a good deal longer. Sustained operations were well-oiled routine. Captain Fred Frewer had taken over command from his classmate, John C. "Scruffy" O'Brien, in mid-1961. Frewer, with five wartime years on the convoy lanes and a couple of destroyer commands of his own, had been Executive Officer in *Magnificent* five years back.

"Bonnie" was really too small, too slow, and too crowded. Designed for the RN in the early forties, she was built for hammocks and RN-style messing. The conversion to bunks and dining halls was less than ideal, and living spaces were tight with small lockers and little room for relaxing – even chief petty officers were stacked four high. With time, the ship bulged with new equipment and men to run it. She was cold in winter and brewed up like an oven in the tropics. She wasn't nearly as livable as the Cadillacs but there was strong, experienced leadership and a spirit that bespoke pride from top to bottom in doing a tough job well. "Bonnie" was a happy and efficient ship.

The spring of 1961 was quite typical. In March she searched the Emerald Bank for fishing vessels in distress in a severe storm. Three of them, out of Lockeport, Nova Scotia, were lost with all hands. The ship's company made a big contribution to the Lockeport Relief Fund for the sixty children who had lost their fathers. The same month they sent a fat cheque to the Salvation Army, the Red Cross got 457 pints of "Bonnie" blood, and a special fund was raised to help a petty officer from *Iroquois* who lost five children and was badly burned trying to get them clear of his blazing house. *Bonaventure*'s men were ever-generous and warm-hearted.

Her calling card in foreign ports was the children's party. The invitation always went in advance, especially for disadvantaged kids. In Portsmouth, Trinidad, Stockholm, Hamburg, Belfast, Rotterdam, Toulon, wherever the ship was alongside to draw breath between exercises, out came the clown and pirate costumes, the miniature merry-go-rounds and the mock-up airplane rides and the train hauled by the flight deck tractor. Enthralled youngsters swarmed over the ship and the airplanes, ran races on the flight deck, gorged themselves on gallons of ice cream and soft drinks, mountains of hamburgers. Sailors who saw too little of their own children enjoyed the parties as much as their young guests.

At 20,000 tons with twenty-two knots, *Bonaventure* fell far short of U.S. Navy standards. The Americans held that their wartime Essex class at 40,000 tons was the bottom limit for any carrier. It was distinctly in American interests to see Canada's navy properly equipped, and after Cuba they offered fully updated Essex-class carriers with the latest equipment for the knock-down price of $4 million apiece. The offer stayed on the table for a year. *Bonaventure* was due for a mid-life refit in 1966 that would cost twice that. But the big carrier would mean more aircraft and more men, and the fiscal lid was on. Naval Staff put on no campaign to buy. As it turned out, *Bonaventure*'s refit ran to $17 million – the price of four ready-fitted Essex-class carriers with change.

The government's money belt stayed tight but gains came with energy and initiative. Jezebel, for example, was a new submarine detection and identification system developed by the U.S. and Canada that used a special sonobuoy to pick up low-frequency underwater sound and send it to the parent aircraft for analysis. The airborne equipment was for large shore-based aircraft only, but squadron electronics officer Lieutenant Gary Crosswell fixed that by putting together receiver-transmitters from Heathkit parts and fitting them in the Trackers to relay Jezebel data to *Bonaventure*.

Under Commodore Welland's direction in a Can/Brit exercise in 1963, Lieutenant Commander Ben Oxholm and his Trackers used the lash-up Jezebel with dramatic success, getting excellent probability areas on RN "enemy" submarines in a mysterious way quite unknown to the RN. For Bob Welland it was a nice switch. From being miles behind the British with equipment in the war, he couldn't even tell them what he had because the U.S. hadn't cleared it for anyone else.

Keeping up the standard kept *Bonaventure* very busy. In an average year she took 2,500 deck landings and steamed 42,000 nautical miles – nearly twice around the world. That took about 180 days at sea and she was away from her home port a good deal longer than that. Weather was always a factor. The Canadians earned the reputation for being steadily on task when bigger carriers hunkered down. Winter training might take place off sunny Puerto

Rico but business-like NATO exercises were on the harsh ocean long familiar to Canadian sailors.

LOOKING AHEAD

In 1961 the Ad Hoc Committee Report on Naval Objectives (Rear Admiral Jeffry Brock, chairman – it was called the Brock Report) made a series of far-reaching and imaginative proposals for the future shape of the navy. Rather ahead of conventional thought, Brock said the navy must handle not just general nuclear war but the whole range through conventional conflict to brushfire wars and police action. The navy, therefore, should broaden its capability from the narrow focus on ASW.

A series of general purpose frigates should follow the Cadillacs. In conceptual design, they would each carry a helicopter and be able to support forces ashore. They would have good anti-submarine capability but be much stronger in air defence than the predictably vulnerable state of even the most modern Canadian ships. Next, all the new destroyer escorts should be converted to carry anti-submarine helicopters. There should be more operational support ships to multiply the effectiveness of fighting ships by extending their time on station. Six American diesel-electric anti-submarine boats should be built in Canada with six nuclear-powered possibly to follow. It might have been remembered that Canadian Vickers in Montreal had successfully built American H-boats during the Great War. As a future vehicle the hydrofoil should be pursued.

The report, as a blueprint for the future, was very favourably received by government in 1961, and the Cuban crisis proved the points on submarines and support ships. What the country would pay for remained to be seen.

SUBMARINES

Only in the late 1950s did the navy conclude it must have its own submarines for more than anti-submarine training. Post-war training needs had been inadequately met by borrowing from the RN and USN. Then, from 1954, three boats of the RN's 6th Submarine Squadron were stationed permanently in Halifax, under Canadian operational control. In return the RCN paid operating and maintenance and kept about 180 volunteers for submarine service in Britain, training and serving in RN boats. West coast ASW training depended on borrowing from the USN at their convenience until an old American boat on permanent loan was commissioned with a Canadian crew as HMCS *Grilse* in 1961.

It was clear, however, that the most potent addition to Canada's anti-submarine armoury would be submarines. Best in the long run would be submarines with nuclear power. Commander R. St. G. Stephens (an engineering officer, son of the notable wartime Engineer-in-Chief) was the first

Canadian involved in nuclear propulsion in the U.K., where the RN was developing its first boat using American power-plant technology. By 1960 Stephens was involved in a series of technical studies with Captain S.M. Davis, which concluded American-designed nuclear boats could be built in Canada. The cost, about $65 million each, was twice the price of a new Cadillac. By 1960 a Canadian submarine service was approved. The question of which boat wasn't decided, though Admiral DeWolf certainly favoured six conventionals for the price of one with nuclear power.

In 1963, in spite of the Cuban crisis the year before, the Brock Report's proposal for six American conventional boats proved too rich. Government approved three boats only, and for the lowest price they would be RN Oberon-class and built in Britain. The Oberons were very quiet, capable, diesel-electric anti-submarine boats, and there were plenty of well-trained submariners by now, thoroughly versed in British equipment.

UP AND ON

Provider, the first Canadian operational support ship, had commissioned in 1963. She carried fuel for ships and aircraft, ammunition, stores and provisions, and had a flight deck and hangar to carry three Sea Kings. Previously the navy had to borrow such ships from the USN or RN. In 1964, new Sea King helicopters, built in Montreal to RCN specifications, flew aboard *Bonaventure*. All-weather, all-up machines, with sonar, radar, and homing torpedoes, they gave a huge boost to ASW, and within two years Sea Kings began to fly from nine converted destroyer escorts.

Operating big helicopters from small ships was a new dimension. Shoehorning all the new hardware into the St. Laurents and Annapolises was a ship-construction naval-engineering aviation marvel. Flying that Sea King on and off the tiny, gyrating flight deck day and night in all weather was feasible only with the Canadian-designed "beartrap" deck handling equipment. New techniques, new tactics had to be developed. Operational limits had to be tried and extended. Deck handling and maintenance had to be managed in far wetter, saltier, tighter, and tougher conditions than anyone's navy had ever tried before.

Eight general purpose frigates were approved by cabinet in 1964 to replace the last of the wartime destroyers. HMCS *Ojibwa*, the first of the new submarines, was due to commission in 1965. Thus, coming on stream in 1964 was an evolving navy, leaps ahead even of Dyer's "neat little force." Hearts were high.

ILL WIND

In early 1964 the new Minister of National Defence, Paul Hellyer, spent a couple of days' familiarization in *Bonaventure* off Bermuda. With him was

Vice Admiral Herbert Rayner, Chief of Naval Staff. Captain Robert Timbrell was in command of the ship.

This was the Minister's first and only trip to see the navy at work and he was among as fine a group of sea and air anti-submarine experts as he'd find anywhere, and an exuberant lot of naval aviators. Gently reminded of his brief, landbound RCAF service during the war, Hellyer was kitted out and coaxed into a Tracker co-pilot's seat for a catapult launch. The pilot, he was assured, would be the most experienced in the navy. When the pilot appeared, white of hair, patch over one eye, he tottered across the flight deck with a cane and poked blearily at the aircraft's innards. The deck crew lifted him, quavering inanities, reverently to his seat. If naval aviators have a failing it is perhaps in thinking everyone has their slapstick sense of humour. In fact, they were dealing with a man who had no sense of humour at all. History cannot confirm that Hellyer harboured special ill-will toward naval aviation as a result, but within five years it was all but destroyed.

A JOB TO BE DONE

There was always a job to be done at sea. In the winter of 1964 *Bonaventure* carried Canada's contingent for the UN peacekeeping force to Cyprus, as *Magnificent* had done to Suez in 1957. Not to be caught with his ASW trousers down, Captain Timbrell squeezed twelve Trackers in with the fifty-four army vehicles and 400 tons of stores. After he offloaded in Famagusta and paid a call on Archbishop Makarios, he got on with a carrier's regular business.

The Soviet submarine and surface fleets were growing and getting more aggressive. In the Baltic, to and from a flag-showing visit to Stockholm, *Bonaventure* was shadowed by a Riga-class destroyer; she was buzzed by Blinder aircraft and East German MTBs. Everyone's game, of course, was to startle an intruder into transmitting on gadgets he wanted to monitor. Back outside the Skagerrak the Trackers spotted a Foxtrot submarine. Progressively, more "uninvited guests" turned up among the submarine contacts scored on exercises.

Around the world, while *Bonaventure* was in Cyprus, three west coast ships were in a major Commonwealth exercise in the Indian Ocean. Indonesia's President Sukarno had been rattling his sabre at Malaysia from across the Malacca Strait, and this live show of solid Commonwealth naval strength carried a powerful message. Tun Razak, deputy prime minister of the burgeoning Malaysian federation, told the Canadian captains just how much their country's tangible presence meant to his country.

Mackenzie, *Fraser*, and *St. Laurent* worked with carriers, frigates, cruisers, and submarines from Australia, New Zealand, India, Pakistan, and Britain. To this professional band of brothers, all rooted in the same naval tradition, the most intriguing ship of all was *St. Laurent*, with her new flight deck, hangar, and beartrap. She'd been converted in Esquimalt and was heading the long way around to Halifax to start helicopter operations. *Mackenzie* and *Fraser*, returning to Esquimalt via Hong King and Japan, effectively boosted Canada's trade and relations along the Pacific rim.

The tight little navy of 20,000 men and women stood on its own merits in 1964, running at full stride and with the very best, and it capably represented its country's interests on the international stage. But while all this was going on across the oceans, Paul Hellyer tabled his 1964 White Paper on Defence in the House of Commons. As *Mackenzie* and *Fraser* made their way back to Esquimalt and *St. Laurent* went west to Halifax, the word came through. No one really understood what was going to happen. But the fact was that the navy, flying at its highest ever in peacetime, was about to endure the unhappiest upheaval in its history.

CHAPTER SEVENTEEN
INTEGRATION AND UNIFICATION

FACED WITH RISING COSTS OF ARMS AND COMPETING SOCIAL PRIORITIES, Lester Pearson's Liberal government tabled a White Paper on Defence in March, 1964. Tucked blandly away on page twenty-three was this:

> Following the most careful and thoughtful consideration the Government has decided there is only one adequate solution. It is the integration of the Armed Forces of Canada under a single Chief of Defence Staff and a single Defence Staff. This will be the first step towards a single unified Defence Force for Canada. . . . Sufficient savings should accrue from unification to permit a goal of 25 percent of the budget to be devoted to capital equipment being realized in the years ahead.

That short statement led to the most revolutionary change in the armed forces of any developed country in this century, effectively abolishing the navy, army, and air force and forming a single new service. It was a unique process, especially in a country that has always moved cautiously in reforming its institutions. And in that process, the navy was the most embattled and the most deeply wounded of the three.

At Headquarters, while the navy steamed hard, it had trouble keeping up. Its equipment needs were always more complex and more costly than those of the other two services. That was the nature of navies. But it was the smallest of the three and it kept a higher proportion of its officers at sea and in operational posts – which, by and large, is where they wanted to be.

Technical officers found Headquarters a challenge for their particular profession but most executive officers looked to seatime for professional development and promotion. To many, their stint in Ottawa was a penance to be avoided. The RCAF was lushly complemented. Air force pilots finished operational flying with many years left for staff training and duties. A peacetime army always has a surfeit of well-trained staff officers.

The army and air force were also big enough to have their own staff colleges. Some naval officers attended them, and a few went to the United States. But the main staff training mecca for RCN officers was the Royal Naval Staff College, Greenwich, England. It offered good higher naval education and produced capable operations officers for fighting a war. What was badly needed was skill in the machinations of Canadian politics and public administration to win the peace. The small Naval Staff had to deal with the convolutions of over 200 interservice committees, and in the Headquarters battle for dollars the navy was invariably outranked and outnumbered, and quite often outwitted.

CUTTING COSTS

The momentum of the vigorous naval programs of the fifties wasn't reinforced in succeeding budgets. Cutbacks began with recession beginning in 1957. Manpower shortages led to high sea/shore ratios. Equipment costs spiralled as hardware got more complex and inflation took hold. Keeping the lid on budgets meant spending on equipment dropped. In 1954 over forty-two cents of every defence dollar had gone to buy equipment. By 1963 it was fourteen cents and falling. The navy, as always, was the most capital-intensive of the three, spending over 25 per cent of its portion on equipment.

Then John Diefenbaker's government fell on the issue of nuclear weapons in February, 1963. In the April election campaign Lester Pearson promised a Liberal government would honour Canada's nuclear commitments to her allies, then negotiate a non-nuclear role. He also made a not unexpected promise of a searching review of defence policy. Pearson squeaked in with a minority. His Minister of National Defence, Paul Hellyer, approached his task with energy, single-minded purpose, and considerable ability – with knife in hand.

Cutting the administrative fat, streamlining the department, eliminating waste and overlap and thus releasing money for equipment had been sound objectives pursued with mixed success for years. The first post-war Minister, Brooke Claxton, reform-minded as he was, had pushed the reluctant services into tri-service colleges, common pay scales, equivalent rank structure and legal services, and a standard code of discipline. Then he established a Chiefs of Staff Committee with a permanent chairman, though each Chief still had direct access to the Minister to represent his service's views.

The army had provided dental care to all of the services for years. Later, the medical, postal, and chaplain services were amalgamated. There was one school for musicians and for basic flying training. In Headquarters the personnel functions of the three services were put in one building, operations in another, supply and technical services in a third. A veritable jungle of interservice committees developed. The organization creaked.

AIMS AND AMMUNITION

In 1963 a royal commission on government organization chaired by J. Grant Glassco said DND suffered administrative confusion, with triplication of effort in some fields. The maze of interservice committees, Glassco said, tended to obfuscate and procrastinate, not expedite. It seemed to a lot of officers that the Glassco Commission was right on many counts. On the face of it a great deal of money could be freed up for operational use by amalgamating budgeting, supply, accounting, civil construction, and general administration. Smaller overheads in Ottawa meant more ships and aircraft out at sea. A good housecleaning could certainly have done a power of good, but no particular initiative had come from the Chiefs of Staff. To Paul Hellyer, the Glassco Report was ready ammunition.

The Department of National Defence was, in fact, a graveyard for politicians – too little patronage to purvey; too much spent with no apparent social benefit; endless questions of cost overruns. It was seen as the money-eating ogre that Canadians wished would go away. Also, it was very hard to control. In other departments one professional deputy minister reported to his elected minister; in Defence six powerful people could knock on the Minister's door – the chairman, the three service heads, the chairman of the Defence Research Board, and the deputy minister. Inevitably, there was conflicting advice. It was an enormously demanding ministry with a minimum return to its political head.

Hellyer saw that the chance of personal political capital in this wilderness lay in some startling innovation, getting a name for dynamism. He had publicly run down the navy before the election, saying in effect that it couldn't find modern submarines and its principal role should be supporting a mobile force for brushfire wars and peacekeeping. Early in his reign as Minister he made the classic move of taking control of public communications. Wing Commander William Lee, the RCAF Director of Public Relations (Air), moved into Hellyer's office. Lee's exceptionally effective RCAF directorate, the army's Directorate of Public Relations, and the tiny Directorate of Naval Information were cut down, amalgamated, and made responsible to the deputy minister rather than to the service heads, and thus up the line to the Minister (via Lee).

Hellyer thus harnessed a big professional team to promote his singular views. At the same time he had pulled the teeth of the Chiefs of Staff in case they were of a mind to work up public support through the press.

Lee, a skilled hand with the media, was also a long-term advocate of unifying the forces, an idea that was raising debate in Britain and elsewhere.

Whatever the source, toward the end of 1963 Hellyer grasped the idea of a single service under a single Chief. Unification would be achieved via the intermediate step of integrating Headquarters and the commands on functional lines.

The White Paper was Hellyer's own. Historian Daniel P. Burke recorded that the draft was "written in longhand by Hellyer in eighteen days in late November and early December 1963 with scant input from his personal staff and none from the officers and civilian officials who had traditionally performed this function." He then got Prime Minister Pearson's own approval during the Christmas recess without a word to the Chiefs of Staff or his cabinet colleagues.

His mid-January visit to the fleet at sea off Bermuda was his first and only exposure to the navy on the job, but he had already made up his mind. In his view the highly trained career professionals he saw at work could be made interchangeable with equally specialized people from the other services by reorganizing things his way. In Halifax he was briefed by the Flag Officer Atlantic Coast, Rear Admiral Jeffry Brock. Two such determined, egocentric men were bound to tangle. Within six months they met head on.

Hellyer discussed his White Paper with the Chiefs of Staff in early February before he took it formally to cabinet. All of them supported the principle of integration (though they didn't know the details). Unanimously, they opposed unification into one service. The Chief of Naval Staff, Vice Admiral Rayner, was the most vigorous in his objections. He urged the Minister, without success, to strike all reference to unification.

Rayner was a thoroughly professional sea officer with a fine record of command. He was held in respectful regard by those who served under him for his quiet competence and deep concern for his people. He was a man of strong religious conviction and utmost probity. Such a professional gentleman could not believe that something so fundamental as dismantling and restructuring the armed services of Canada could become government policy without the concurrence of the Chiefs. But he was not dealing with someone like himself, and Hellyer had set his course already. His tacit stance was that the Chiefs could do his bidding or resign.

Other than this key issue, the White Paper had no great content. It shuffled the priorities for defence. Peacekeeping was placed at the top in deference to Mike Pearson's international outlook; there was stress on mobility to help deal with "brushfire wars"; Canada would stay in NATO (Pearson, of course, had had a major hand in its beginnings) and would keep its place in NORAD; the navy would continue its ASW role; Bomarc anti-aircraft missiles, fighter and strike aircraft, and Honest John missiles in Europe would keep their nuclear tips. Procurement would concentrate on: re-equipping the army as a mobile force; air and sealift for its deployment; new tactical aircraft; and maintaining "a relatively constant improvement in Maritime anti-submarine capability." There was not much encouragement for the navy in that. The new construction program had been on hold since the change of government.

Making the case for reorganization, integration, and ultimately unification, Hellyer drew heavily on the Glassco Report, but cabinet wasn't particularly interested in the details. Hellyer could do what he wanted so long as he saved money. With Walter Gordon, the Finance Minister, he agreed to a budget of $1.5 billion per year with 2 per cent for inflation. As inflation was already running at 3.5 per cent, that meant a steady decrease in funding, and when it climbed the Defence allocation declined even further. Succeeding cabinets were quite happy to perpetuate the trend.

INTEGRATION

Hellyer's first step, integration, came quickly. In July, 1964, Parliament abolished the chairman and three Chiefs of Staff and replaced them with one Chief of Defence Staff. The first was Air Chief Marshal Frank Miller. On 1 August Vice Admiral Rayner, the last Chief of Naval Staff, was prematurely retired. Rayner unquestionably fought to his limits as he saw them for the ultimate preservation of the navy. He worked strictly inside the department and within all the rules of propriety, and he made no public statements until he voiced his measured opposition to the House Standing Committee on Defence in 1967. But that was too late.

With Rayner's retirement the Royal Canadian Navy had no head. The senior sailor was the highly regarded Vice Admiral Kenneth Dyer, Chief of Personnel in the integrated Headquarters, but he could speak officially only for the "personnel function," not for the navy. In the integrated NDHQ the small naval component was all but submerged. "Integration" was going to be difficult enough to manage, but it wouldn't reach beyond the command level and hit the sharp end – the people out at sea. No one knew, though, what might lurk beneath the surface of "unification."

Dyer and the rest of Headquarters tried valiantly to reorganize along with HQ personnel cuts of 30 per cent. Expertise and direction crumbled. The Naval Air Staff, for example, was slashed and found itself reporting to an RCAF Wing Commander who answered to a Group Captain, neither with any carrier experience. The naval Commander developing requirements for gun and missile systems for the general purpose frigates became responsible to a Brigadier – a fine field soldier who readily confessed no knowledge of the subject. He could only rubber-stamp policy proposals en route to the desk of a Major General who was no better informed. Expertise, experience, mature, informed professional judgement, leadership – all gave way to cure-all concepts of management. If the "organigrams" defined things neatly, then things must work.

Two navy coast commands, four army geographic commands, and five air force functional commands were put in the pot. Out came seven functional commands: Maritime (the navy, with Maritime Air, headquartered in Halifax with the deputy commander in Esquimalt); Mobile (combining army and tactical air headquartered at St. Hubert); Air Defence (at North Bay); Air Transport; Training (in Winnipeg); Communications; and Materiel (in Ottawa).

On publication of the White Paper in March, Rear Admiral Jeffry Brock had made his disagreement quite plain. Integration, he said, meant that no navy senior officer would now have access to the Minister, and ultimately the Prime Minister, on important naval matters. This was precisely what Walter Hose said when he dug in and saved the navy in 1922.

Brock spoke forcefully to the Parliamentary Standing Committee on Defence in Halifax in late July. Hellyer called him to Ottawa in August and summarily fired him, then told the House he'd retired him for economy. Back in Halifax, the ships and dockyard people gave their Admiral a rousing send-off. When his final retirement date passed he was busy in Ottawa advising the opposition fighting unification in the House. His successor in the Atlantic Command was Rear Admiral William Landymore.

Landymore, as Maritime Commander Atlantic and Commander of the NATO Atlantic Sub-Area, had to keep ships and aircraft effective. But the new Maritime Command was losing control over the dockyards, repair facilities, and logistic support of the fleet to the integrated Materiel Command in Ottawa. He was also losing the fleet schools on the coasts to Training Command headquartered in Winnipeg. As was so clear in the war, shore support and training were essential parts of fighting effectiveness at sea and had to be in the Admiral's hands. In the meantime, Bill Lee built his Minister's image as the man-in-charge and service people got the latest information not through the chain of command but via the press.

In November at a senior officers' briefing the Minister announced that unification was on the way. He didn't define what it meant, but it was coming – regardless. Landymore told Hellyer he couldn't accept any plan that meant demolishing the navy. In his professional opinion, economy and proper command and control could be achieved by integration alone. Unification was unnecessary and highly unpalatable to the vast majority, he said – and Landymore knew his people. He simply couldn't believe that it would, in the final analysis, come to pass.

In December the five-year equipment program was announced. The eight general purpose frigates were dropped. The navy would get four larger helicopter-carrying destroyers (the new Tribal DDHs), two more operational support ships, conversion of seven Restigouches to carry anti-submarine rocket torpedoes rather than helicopters, twelve more Sea Kings, and updated

ASW equipment for the Trackers, Arguses, and Neptunes. Also, *Bonaventure* was to get a mid-life refit. At the same time there'd be deep cuts in personnel. Through 1965 many elected to go. Where retirement served economy they left with a separation allowance, early pro-rata pension, and a handshake. Many more had their services simply terminated.

MATTERS OF MORALE

In the spring of 1965 the Minister suddenly announced to a senior officers' conference – still without defining what unification meant – that there would be a single walking-out uniform and the same rank names in all services by Canada's Centennial on 1 July 1967. Dyer, the Chief of Personnel, had no prior notice or consultation. The first word the services had was in the newspapers.

Bill Landymore, head of Maritime Command and thus of the operational navy, was a tough-minded, tireless professional and a first-rate leader, but in a single year, morale had plummeted from the heights to a slough of uncertainty, frustration, and fear. Too many trained, experienced senior people were leaving. Recruiting was falling short by 40 per cent. The navy was a tough enough life as it was. Who wanted to face such uncertainty? All of this stemmed from Hellyer's personal decisions. But numbers and morale were very much the Admiral's problems. He was the one who had to keep the fleet effective.

Landymore's was by far the biggest operational command in all the services. He was by custom a frequent visitor to the ships and spoke to men of all ranks and he was gravely disturbed by their concerns. In late June he wrote to the CDS, saying that "the choice seems either to live with a service which will have no heart in its work for years to come, or pursue integration with all its benefits leaving the matter of identity totally intact. I most strongly urge the second alternative. It is requested the Defence Council be made aware of the foregoing observations." He received no reply to his letter.

To shore things up Landymore spoke that summer to closed meetings of lieutenant commanders and above. He told them that forming a single service would take an Act of Parliament and he was sure good sense in the House would prevail. He personally saw no merit in taking away the navy's identity, but he would represent their viewpoint, whatever it was. After discussion he asked them to indicate their agreement or disagreement on five points; first, he would represent their views; second, they could speak openly about their own views in and out of the service until the law was changed by Parliament; third, they would not consider loss of identity inevitable and become apathetic; fourth, they would not ask to be retired because they couldn't accept the theory of unification (he pledged that if their viewpoints were ignored he alone would take appropriate action in protest); fifth, for the information of others the meeting had discussed morale. Of 367 officers at the meetings, three didn't fully agree. Landymore reported what he'd done and the views of his officers to the Chief of Personnel.

TWISTING THE TRUTH

Hellyer heard about the meetings and considered disciplining the Admiral for brooking critical discussion of government policy – Landymore had put himself legally on thin ice – or simply firing him as he had Brock. But two top operational commanders in a year? And Landymore had been made integrated Maritime Commander by the Minister himself. Besides, there weren't enough admirals around to convene a court martial.

For months the commands were entirely in the dark about unification. There was no definition, no study of what the consequences might be. In February, 1966, Landymore sent his own appreciation to Ottawa, saying again, "integrate, don't unify." On 14 April a *Globe and Mail* article quoted a Defence Department spokesman "that naval officers still retain to some extent an above decks, below decks mentality . . . . Sailors don't just scrub decks and set sail now, they're skilled men and the old attitude of officers just doesn't fit. We're trying to change that." It was a gratuitous, unfounded attack, attempting to deflect blame for sagging recruiting and re-engagement away from the spectre of unification. The spokesman was "Leaky" Lee, as he'd been dubbed by now. Landymore officially requested a denial or a public apology and got nowhere. The Minister's men could fire at the navy at will. There was no way to fight back.

Then, in June, Landymore was called to Ottawa to give evidence on Naval Estimates to the House Standing Committee. Before the meeting he submitted his report to the Minister and two fundamental points were cut out by Lee. The Admiral had shown statistically how numbers had run down since early 1964 to a shortage of 3,500 men and how slumping re-engagement of the vital chiefs and petty officers was cutting into the hard core of the fleet. This seriously affected his ability to meet operational commitments. The second point was a warning about the aging fleet. Building only four new ships instead of the eight frigates previously approved meant he wouldn't be able to do the job the government required.

Landymore, believing he had no choice but to obey his Minister, choked down his disgust and delivered the report as changed. Hellyer had effectively stopped expert evidence key to the defence of Canada from being heard by Parliament. Questioned by the committee, Landymore said that morale was bad; there was a great deal of unrest; the navy as a whole was against unification; identity was vital for servicemen and the uniform a most important part of it.

The Minister sent for Landymore in late July. He would make not a single concession on naval identity even though he had recently agreed that Highland regiments could keep their kilts. Army regiments and corps could still be "Royal" but not the Royal Canadian Navy. Landymore repeated he could not support any move that destroyed naval identity. Hellyer asked for his resignation. The Admiral chose to be fired. Outside the Minister's office he ran into Rear Admiral M.G. Stirling, who had come from his west coast command quite independently to tell the Minister he couldn't support unification and would resign. Hellyer accepted on the spot. Admirals Dyer and Welland were retiring prematurely, too.

The only thing Landymore could do now was see the Prime Minister, and the only way he could get to him was through David Groos, Liberal MP for Esquimalt, retired Commander, RCN, and chairman of the Parliamentary Committee on Defence. Groos agreed to arrange the meeting only if Landymore wouldn't raise the matter of the altered testimony. Landymore had to agree. He told Pearson of his firing and of the early retirements of three other admirals. Pearson said he agreed with the integration policy. He didn't know what Hellyer intended about unification but he reaffirmed what he himself had said on a visit to *Saskatchewan*'s ship's company: the government wouldn't interfere with naval traditions.

DECAPITATION

In a few weeks retirements were announced: Air Chief Marshal Miller (CDS), Vice Admiral Dyer (Chief of Personnel), Lieutenant-General R.W. Moncel (the Vice Chief), Lieutenant-General Frank Fleury (Comptroller General), and Rear Admiral Welland (Deputy Chief of Operations). Miller was the only one who had reached retirement age. All left by choice or under stress, quite unable to deflect the course of events. Dyer, for one, still didn't know what Hellyer intended by unification and had told the Minister he couldn't go on. The new CDS was General Jean-Victor Allard, an ebullient field soldier who enthusiastically endorsed the new direction, whatever it might be.

In July, 1966, only two of the top thirteen officers in the Canadian forces had held their appointments for more than a month. In two years the six senior admirals – Rayner, Brock, Dyer, Landymore, Stirling, and Welland – had gone before their time. The press coined the phrase "Admirals' revolt." But there was no collusion: each acted quite independently; each was equally convinced that elimination of the navy in favour of a single service was dead wrong; each tried to deflect a rigidly determined man from his arbitrary, single-minded course; each suffered early retirement. Only Brock, then Landymore after he was fired, spoke out publicly. Revolt it never was.

Back in Halifax, Landymore read the message stripping him of his command. When the Minister released his story the Admiral gave his own to the press. Hellyer countered that if the government backed down they would have to get a new Minister, and Landymore went down with guns blazing.

To the navy, Bill Landymore was a hero. With his wife he was given a send-off from the Halifax dockyard such as never seen before. Ships' sides and roadways were lined with cheering sailors and civilian employees. Every ship in harbour flew signal flags spelling Landymore's name; above them flew flags BZ: Bravo Zulu: "Well done, Landymore." There was nothing else to say.

UNIFICATION

Hellyer sent for Commodore O'Brien, Senior Canadian Officer Afloat, and offered promotion and the Atlantic Command. O'Brien got assurance from the Minister, General Allard, and Defence Council that the shipbuilding and aircraft programs would go ahead, that there would be no further reduction in the size of the fleet. Specifically, it would be maintained at the level of the modernized *Bonaventure*, twenty-four destroyers (including the new Tribals), sixty-eight Trackers, thirty-two Arguses, sixteen Neptunes, and all the new Sea Kings and the support ships. Further, the Maritime Commander would report directly to the CDS. There was no agreement on uniform or ranks. O'Brien took the job. Within three years a good portion of those undertakings, and the Prime Minister's personal pledge, went down the drain.

In September, Hellyer visited Halifax for the first time in over three years. Answering a question from the floor on the subject of uniform at an all-officers meeting, he commented that the navy seemed to think their uniform was ordained by God. The response was a full-throated roar of outrage. Admiral O'Brien had to jump in and order silence. This outburst by a group of career officers at their Minister was absolutely without precedent. The question had been asked, respectfully but pointedly, by Lieutenant Commander Nigel Brodeur, whose father and grandfather had played such leading parts in the history of the RCN. Feelings in the navy ran very deep. Hellyer had learned nothing. In spring, 1964, a CPO asked him publicly why, if unification was the answer, Canada should be the first in NATO to try. His reply: our allies were worried that while reorganizing they'd lose operational effectiveness – but with us, *it doesn't matter*.

He only hardened. He bore on implacably, against advice from his staff and colleagues to ease off. He was on his own flight toward the party leadership and he had to win, and win hands down. The next step was the Unification Bill. In the debate the Minister was assailed for tampering with Landymore's testimony. When the bill went to committee it was a marathon. In 1944, Chairman David Groos had commanded *Restigouche* in the hurly-burly battles off Brest. He had also been in command of *Crescent* in Nanking in 1949. Now, the unification battle sent him to hospital with a heart attack before the committee hearings were over.

Landymore systematically documented the Minister's alterations to his earlier testimony. He called for setting unification aside or, if it was inevitable, at least scrapping the common uniform and army ranks and allowing those who disagreed to have an honourable release without losing their pensions.

When Hellyer was pressed for his reasons for firing Landymore, he said it was for "eighteen months of consistent disloyalty to the people he was paid to serve." It was a shocking charge. He added that the Admiral, since November, 1964, had been working against government policy by holding anti-unification meetings with officers. Landymore again documented his actions. Hellyer grudgingly conceded. Without condoning the Admiral's actions, he accepted his statement "that there was no disloyalty to his service or his country." Other than serving officers, the great majority of witnesses – Generals Moncel, Fleury, Simonds, Foulkes, Air Marshals Miller, Curtis, Hendricks, and Annis, Admirals Rayner, Landymore, and Brock – called unification seriously in question. But the Liberal-dominated committee passed the bill back to the House substantially unchanged.

The Prime Minister throughout had exercised neither leadership nor constraint. Now his enthusiasm waned with the controversy. It took two threats of resignation from Hellyer to keep it on the order paper. Finally, the Liberals invoked closure on third reading to ram it through. That happened on 25 April before the House recessed for the gala opening of Expo '67. That summer Canadians were treated to a splendid travelling tattoo put on by the three traditional services, still in their own uniforms. In return Canada's Centennial gift to her armed forces was destruction of their time-honoured institutions and a new, undefined service that few wanted or even understood.

The last legality came on 1 February 1968, when amendments to the National Defence Act ended the life of the Royal Canadian Navy, the army, and the RCAF and rolled them into the Canadian Armed Forces. The common green uniform displaced navy blue, light blue, and khaki in 1970.

For his own political ambitions Paul Hellyer decided on a massive, entirely theoretical restructuring of the armed services that he and close personal advisers conceived. He never defined it, never examined it, never listened to the counsel of his legally appointed professional advisers. He flouted Parliament. He rammed unification through and left others to figure it out, and experimented recklessly with the careers of 120,000 people, reducing the defence establishment to impotence for a long time. In the process, the navy suffered a deep and lasting wound.

Certainly, it was the service most strongly opposed to unification. The navy goes to sea. It is a very distinctive, uncomfortable, and demanding way of life, and it's not for everyone. A navy cook is not only a cook and a baker; he's also a sailor who tends to ship's duties. He goes into action as part of his ship's fighting team. He must deal with fires and flooding, handle ammunition, save lives. A naval officer follows the ancient and demanding profession of navigating the sea as well as that of arms. Everyone who goes to sea in the navy has to be a "Jack of *all* sea trades and a master of *one*." The navy, so different as a profession and a way of life, had the most to lose.

EVISCERATION

The opposition had made hay in the House of Commons and scored heavily on Hellyer. But by then his purpose was beyond recall, hardened no doubt by Brock and Landymore, abetted by a skilfully handled press. The services drew small support from Canadians overall. In the public's eye the navy dragged its feet: the admirals revolted because they and their navy were too set in ancient ways. They drew the barbs of cartoonists, not the rationale of thoughtful editorials. The public focused throughout on the obvious symbols like uniform and rank and found them picayune. Deeper issues, such as operational effectiveness and the real meaning of morale, were simply not understood. Brass-bashing was always a popular sport. The country watched, with derision if anything, but not with any concerted outrage as three Canadian institutions disappeared. And certainly there was no wide feeling that in military affairs one politician could possibly be wrong and every one of his senior professional advisers right. Paul Hellyer, and Bill Lee, had called the shots right. To a point.

He moved from Defence to Transport, taking Lee along, and they continued pursuit of the real aim, the Liberal leadership. But from the time of Landymore's stand it began to come through that Hellyer had taken his iron-willed image too far. Before the Liberal leadership convention *Maclean's* magazine noted his "reputation for arrogance . . . like a teacher who says 'you speak out of turn boy and out you go.'" On the convention floor in March, 1968, he ran to form. After the third ballot he rejected all advice, including Lee's. He refused to release his delegates to try and stop Pierre Trudeau and became his own cheerleader, shouting "Go, Paul, go!" Trudeau won on the fourth ballot.

Watching Paul Hellyer sink himself gave sour satisfaction to many. But the havoc he had wrought for his own ambition was only the softening up. The services were gutted of experienced leadership, and too many more took their energies and ambitions elsewhere. Integration on its own could have achieved such benefits as did accrue. Certainly some did, though the promised 25 per cent for new equipment never materialized. Scaled up to the other services, sailors got better housing, social services, and benefits. They got sea-pay, personal flights on service aircraft, and the Canex retailing outlets. But numbers shrank – the navy to half its former size – and equipment aged without replacement. Far from Hellyer's prediction, no other country followed suit.

The Canadian Forces became the best-paid, best-fed, and, as time went on, the worst-equipped armed forces in the Western world.

The next fifteen years under Prime Minister Pierre Trudeau would see steady erosion of the nation's defence. The navy, which Paul Hellyer had savaged, dwindled over the ensuing years to a shadow of its lusty self.

CHAPTER EIGHTEEN

CLIPPED WINGS

WHILE ADMIRAL LANDYMORE WAS FIGHTING TO KEEP THE NAVY ALIVE and sorting out integration in the new Maritime Command, the Cold War kept up its persistent demands. The threat, indeed, increased. In 1964 *Jane's Fighting Ships* reported baldly that "The Soviet Navy has the most powerful submarine fleet the world has ever known." Each year their attack fleet improved and more of them had nuclear power. Then within three years they added twenty-five nuclear-driven Yankee-class "boomers" carrying nuclear-tipped strategic missiles that could be fired submerged. In that department they were fast catching the USN and posed a major direct threat to North America.

In the fall of 1966 *Bonaventure* went to her major mid-life refit at Lauzon, Quebec. Costs climbed sharply as the refit ran its course. The ship was out of action for eighteen months and the squadrons meantime flew as guests in American carriers to keep in shape. Flying back aboard "Bonnie" again in October, 1967, they found her flight deck awfully small.

Captain Bob Falls was now in command and another ex-fighter pilot, Commander Allan "Smokey" Bice, was XO. For that winter's training around Puerto Rico the carrier took the two new Canadian submarines, *Onondaga* and *Ojibwa*, and *Provider* for underway replenishment and support. There were fewer escorts now. War-built destroyers and frigates were disappearing without replacement.

The aviators always played the game to the hilt and, as always, there was risk. In "Maple Spring 69" in the Caribbean a catapult strop broke on takeoff. The Tracker couldn't get airborne, flopped over the bow, and was literally run over by the carrier. Somehow the crew got clear and they actually bounced along the bottom of the ship. Two of them passed right through the turning screws and popped up in the wake.

Sub-Lieutenant Réal Dubois, flying Pedro, the rescue helicopter, was over in seconds to pluck Lieutenant Jack Flannagan from a crimson pool of his own blood, his leg sheared off by the screw. These were shark waters but Leading Seaman Cameron jumped straight in. With the hoist operator he got Flannagan aboard and they put pressure on the spurting leg. Moments meant life and Dubois got him straight to the flight deck, then picked up co-pilot Chuck MacIntyre and Leading Seamen Bill Smith and Bob Winger. Flannagan was back flying Trackers in a year with an artificial leg; then he flew Sea Kings in destroyers. MacIntyre and Dubois were soon outside as Air Canada pilots.

Professionalism doesn't stop accidents entirely. In the first ten growing years of Canadian naval aviation there were sixty-two deaths; in the last twelve years, from 1957 to 1969, there were thirty-five. In that second period the numbers of airborne hours and deck landings in round-the-clock all-weather operational flying had far more than doubled.

TRUDEAU TURNS AWAY

The Soviets' iron hold on Eastern Europe was dramatically confirmed when their tanks rolled into Czechoslovakia in 1968 to crush the move toward liberalism called "the Prague spring." The following spring Prime Minister Pierre Trudeau made a major change in Canadian defence policy. Suddenly, top priority was protecting national sovereignty. Canada's support for NATO was cut by almost half. The aim in Paul Hellyer's 1964 White Paper "to maintain a relatively constant improvement in Maritime anti-submarine capability" went down the drain. In September, National Defence Headquarters announced that *Bonaventure*, rejuvenated though she was, would be retired. With budget constraints and social-political priorities, she was deemed too costly to keep afloat.

During "Bonnie's" last crack at the exercise circuit the message came to disband the Tracker squadron, VS 880. There was rage, disgust, sadness for the end of a tight, top service and questions about their own future. But they swept all that to the backs of their minds. For the last time they flew in the rough stuff, logged more hours than anyone else's aircraft, and pressed on "killing" submarines when the others had stopped flying. At one stage they spotted fifteen Soviet submarines escorted by three Kresta-class destroyers. One of the Krestas glued herself dangerously close to "Bonnie" and gave Captain James Cutts, who was a cool and expert shiphandler, some bad moments. The year before Bob Falls had had to go full astern to avoid a Kotlin that got too close. Such events were getting common. But as the Soviets waxed bigger and tougher and flexed their muscles at sea, Canada was pulling in her horns.

THE END OF NAVAL AVIATION

Earlier the Auditor General had noted that the cost of *Bonaventure*'s refit had doubled over the estimate. Estimating for a refit is imprecise at best. New defects always come to light when plating, piping, hull fittings, and machinery are opened up for inspection and repair. An allowance is always made, but *Bonaventure* was wartime construction, more than twenty-three years old, and had never had a full overhaul.

Questions were hurled about the House. The press focused on titillating refit trivia like luxury items in officers' cabins and the cost of moving furniture. Parliamentary committees puffed around the ship and huffed as they never did on the real defence issue of the day, namely Canada's retreat from her long-time alliances. *Bonaventure* became a synonym for mismanagement, which caught the public's imagination as the ship and her sailors, her aircraft, and those who flew them never did when they were at sea serving their country's needs. The fault was not in overspending but in underguesstimating. The damage was in failing to justify the higher costs logically and publicly. The implication was ineptness by the same kind of barnacle-bound admirals who had fought unification. The navy got no media or political defence, and the cartoonists had a field day. Ridicule always wins.

Only one wartime destroyer and one converted frigate remained. The three new submarines were running on the east coast. *Protecteur* and *Preserver*, the new operational support ships, were due in 1970. The four Tribal DDHs were under construction for 1972-73. There were seventy-one updated Trackers and forty Sea Kings in service. The limited equipping plan to which Hellyer had agreed in 1966 was coming along. But now the numbers in the unified Canadian Forces were being cut again and something had to go.

Naval aviation en bloc – carrier and aircraft and people and shore support – was a juicy chunk of the budget. Carrier sailors could man the new ships. All the *Bonaventure* flack blurred the basic issue: Trudeau's drastic cutback on Canada's commitments to her allies. Politically, it was easy to retire *Bonaventure*, and that put an end to Canadian naval aviation. The operational core of Canada's seagoing contribution to NATO and continental defence was gone.

Twenty-three years of struggle built an esprit and capability in naval aviation that was second to none. Pop Fotheringham was one who could say with calm certainty and justifiable pride that "it all combined to produce the finest and most professional group of aviators in any man's navy, anywhere." Fotheringham had flown from RN and USN carriers *Warrior* and *Magnificent* and had made the first deck landing on *Bonaventure*. On 12 December 1969 he made the last.

THE LAST FLY-PAST

As *Bonaventure* came back to Halifax from her last operation all aircraft flew off to Shearwater except four Trackers, one Sea King, and the rescue helicopter. They were to launch in a farewell to the city as "Bonnie" steamed up-harbour. Then they would join the final all-up fly-past with the Maritime Commander, Vice Admiral O'Brien, taking the salute.

But the wind was wrong and at the crucial time the catapult broke down. That meant the last Trackers would have to go ashore by lighter. But going out with a whimper was simply not for VS 880, for *Bonaventure*, or for the navy. Captain Jim Cutts and Squadron Commander Dave Tate conferred. Cutts took the ship past the dockyard into Bedford Basin. Then he rang up engine revolutions and raced the bulky lady around the basin like a destroyer, helm hard over, nearly nicking the shoal buoys. He gave Tate and his boys seventeen knots of wind along the deck. The final four roared the full length of it to take off. Then they gave their favourite bird-farm one final beat-up and joined the last fly-past.

Another kick at the old "cracking show"? School-boy games? Bravado? No. These were seasoned professionals. They knew exactly what they were doing. They were flying top-class airplanes maintained and handled by the best of naval airmen. They had never lost the old press-on spirit from the early days, and they had always pushed the limits. But they did not press on *regardless*.

Lesser aviators, run-of-the-mill sailors, politicians who airily toss away hard-won traditions, the land-bound who have never known planes and people and ships at sea would hardly understand. But the ghosts of Bedford Basin – the seamen of those convoys of a thousand sail and a hundred steamships that had gathered there in wars over 200 years – they would off-caps and cheer. So would Walter Hose, Leonard Murray, Chummy Prentice, John Stubbs, Alan Easton, Hammy Gray, Harry DeWolf, the thousands who toughed it out in the little ships in the great Battle of the Atlantic. They would have done the same thing themselves.

CHAPTER NINETEEN
CHANGE ON CHANGE

UNHAPPY TIME

WHEN THE NATIONAL DEFENCE ACT WAS AMENDED ON 1 FEBRUARY 1968 to end the legal life of the Royal Canadian Navy, four years of controversy and a lot of bitterness had already left their mark. The pride the navy had built in itself, by itself, had been hard hit. This unhappy, unsettled time led right into an era of more cuts. To the navy, the country didn't seem to care about the dwindling fleet or alliance commitments. At the same time, people had to swallow change upon change upon change.

When Admiral O'Brien took over as Maritime Commander from Admiral Landymore in 1966, he was the right man to steer the service through another sickly season. He had an agile, inventive mind, a strong, buoyant personality, and a reputation as a sea commander who knew his business. Ships still must go to sea; planes must fly; the job had to be done with what there was at hand. Headquartered in Halifax, he ran the west coast, too, through his deputy in Esquimalt. Operations scaled down as the wartime escorts and *Bonaventure* disappeared, but there was one major gain; all Maritime Air was now part and parcel of Maritime Command.

In Ottawa the tri-service committee thickets were slashed. Economies, pretty well completed by the end of the integration stage in 1967, had badly thinned out expertise. The senior naval officer at Headquarters, Vice Admiral Ralph Hennessy, was the Comptroller for the Forces but not the navy head because theoretically there was no navy. De facto, the boss was O'Brien, who was soon a Vice Admiral, too. Headquarters, he found, was pretty much of a shambles until 1970, but Rear Admiral Terry Burchell, who had headed Naval Technical Services, was the key man there. The navy had the only core of highly trained technical officers and systems engineers who had run sophisticated programs. Whatever the organization charts said, Burchell and company got the most they could for O'Brien from the shrinking pot.

Putting the naval dockyards and ship repair units under Materiel Command in Ottawa had been one of the unwise and unworkable moves. Dockyard support and ship repair were essential parts of front-line fighting readiness, as so clearly seen in war. O'Brien ran a determined fight and finally got them back.

Initial training, education, and interchangeable trades training could certainly be run by a separate command. But the ships needed the fleet schools in Halifax and Esquimalt for technical and team training to keep themselves efficient. School staffs had to stay in touch with ships to keep their training right to the point. Finally, the instructors themselves were part of the sea/shore ratio. Training was as important to fighting efficiency as dockyard support and it belonged to the operational commander without a fifth wheel in Winnipeg. After another long fight the fleet schools came back under Maritime Command in 1971.

THE HIGH-SPEED HYDROFOIL

One bright spark in the gloomy turn of the seventies was the navy's open-ocean hydrofoil, HMCS *Bras d'Or*. She was Canadian to the core. Lieutenant Barry German watched Alexander Graham Bell's hydrofoil skimming Cape Breton's Bras d'Or lakes back in 1917 and reported ''she went like smoke'' at an incredible sixty knots. After the war the navy helped Bell with high-speed towing behind the destroyer *Patrician*, but there wasn't a cent in the navy's budget for development. Then in 1943 the Canadian army asked for a high-speed smoke-laying craft to cloak amphibious landings and reduce slaughter on the beaches as had happened at Dieppe. The Naval Research Establishment in Halifax recalled Bell's invention and worked on a hydrofoil solution with a V-shaped ''surface-piercing'' foil. It went on the back burner in 1945.

In the early fifties, trying to find ways to beat the high-performance submarine with limited sonar, tacticians split on big sophisticated escorts versus small, cheap, and many. NRE scientists had meanwhile plugged quietly away at their hydrofoil design with test craft. By 1959 they had enough confidence to propose a 200-ton open-ocean hydrofoil as a practical proposition for anti-submarine work.

By this time the dazzling speed of the nuclear submarine was shouting for novel solutions. Britain was working hard on hovercraft. The USN had a hydrofoil using different submerged-foil techniques. NATO urged Canada to press on with her surface-piercing project. Naval Board, stimulated by the Brock Report of 1961, approved development work. Light aluminum structure looked the best bet and in 1963 a design contract went to De Havilland Aircraft of Canada.

Shipbuilding was a pretty conventional industry and De Havilland brought a lot to it that was completely new. The prototype fast hydrofoil escort was built at Marine Industries Ltd. in Sorel and was the first warship ever constructed upside down. It might offend the seaman's eye but it made for better welding. Marine Industries was tops in aluminum welding through building the St. Laurents. This was Canada's first marine powering by an aircraft type gas-turbine engine and the experience fed forward into the Tribal class. Technical mastermind was marine/air engineer Captain Dudley Allan.

An accidental fire in the yard unfortunately set completion back about a year. But NRE scientist Michael Eames – the man who made the variable depth sonar run – had done his hydronamic work brilliantly. Add innovative design and imaginative engineering and the project paid off. By the summer of 1969 HMCS *Bras d'Or* was gloriously riding high on her foils off Halifax with a naval crew under Commander Constantine Cotaras.

But *Bras d'Or* was on borrowed time. The delay and cost of the fire told, and the deep cuts in the Defence budget had the Forces on the ropes. Exotic activities, however promising, were the first to draw the jaundiced eye and the budget-cutter's knife. The opposition sniped at such a high-profile project; the government side of the House, backing off defence, questioned navy management.

In the next year, though, *Bras d'Or* met all the Naval Staff targets. Running hull-borne on her slow-speed diesel she handled twelve-foot waves as ably as a destroyer. The foils deep under water made her steadier than a destroyer. With her powerful gas turbine turning two propellers the foils lifted the hull and she "flew" actually clear of the water – at sixty-three knots in four-foot waves. In big ten-foot waves she cruised at a remarkably stable, steady forty-five.

In 1970, with green uniforms and army ranks, *Bras d'Or*'s new CO was Lieutenant Colonel Gordon Edwards. He had joined as an ordinary seaman in 1948 and served in Korea in *Athabaskan*. Commander Bob Welland was ever alive to the potential of his men and Edwards was picked from the lower deck for air officer training. He flew fighters – Sea Vixens, Sea Furies, and Banshees – from British, Canadian, and American carriers, was Operations Officer in a destroyer, XO of a frigate, and capped that with three years in command of *Assiniboine*. He brought to *Bras d'Or* a fighter pilot's dash, a seaman's steady eye, personal flamboyance, and a sense of fun and adventure that swept things along, difficulties be damned.

In heavy weather *Bras d'Or* literally ran rings around the destroyer *Saguenay*. She was more comfortable at forty knots in ten-foot seas, so *Saguenay*'s captain observed, than his own ship was at eighteen. Edwards proved out fuelling and storing under way with support ship *Preserver* en route to Bermuda. Flying in the winding channel at fifty knots past the coral heads and dropping down like a great sea bird off the Princess Hotel was the kind of flourish Edwards loved – and had the skill to carry off.

He took her over to Norfolk and blazed past a startled USN destroyer squadron in historic Hampton Roads at forty knots, then eased alongside for a couple of days of show and tell. There were many problems to solve, certainly. But her breathtaking performance proved out what Alexander Graham Bell started on Cape Breton over fifty years before. Canada had the only proven, ultra-high-speed, open-ocean warcraft in the world.

She needed some engineering modifications and her suit of fighting equipment, already developed, had to be fitted. Then she was to do full ASW trials. The idea was to cruise quietly, hull-borne, sweeping with her VDS and electronic warfare detectors. On getting contact she could move at "jump speed," working with another unit to contain even the fastest submarine and attack with homing torpedoes. Analysis showed two hydrofoil escorts about equal to one frigate. At $28 million per copy she cost less than half a Tribal, and she carried one-eighth of a Tribal's crew. With guided missiles she would make a potent surface striker. She could carry an automatic gun for policing, cover big surveillance areas fast, and safely handle the worst of North Atlantic weather. Science and seamanship had combined to create quite an addition to the naval armoury.

But in late 1971 Defence Minister Donald Macdonald stopped the work after $52 million had been spent, including the fighting system at about $10 million (and the fire, which added $6.5 million). It was a bargain, especially as it had also paid for pulling Canadian shipbuilding right into the computer age, brought in sophisticated quality assurance, developed the marine use of exotic steels and aluminum structures, and introduced gas-turbine marine propulsion.

Another $6 million would have fitted the fighting equipment, done an operational evaluation, and wrapped the whole thing up. There was potential for offshore sales if not for Canada herself. Unfortunately, there were no marks for fuelling the economy, and Macdonald's 1971 White Paper sheered away from ASW. Maritime Command had far too little money for running its conventional fleet alone. The budget was frozen, and the Tribals were nudging up in cost. Faced with the choice, operational commanders preferred the devil they knew.

Canada has shown great talent for R&D but small courage. There is a certain parallel with the Avro Arrow fighter, ditched by John Diefenbaker in 1959 after costing over $400 million. *Bras d'Or*, at one-tenth the cost, was just as far ahead of her field in her time. But unlike the Arrow, there was no clouded question-mark on her design and her engineering problems were defined and clearly fixable.

Bras d'Or was gutted. Government refused to put good money after good, and she ended her days standing sadly on her foils like a stranded water spider at the Bernier Marine Museum at l'Islet-sur-Mer, Quebec. Alexander Graham Bell would surely have applauded the naval vision and advanced technology that she represented just as warmly as he would have condemned the lack of guts to go the distance. Tactically and technically, Canada's navy could run with the very best, but it had to give up the risks and rewards of innovative ventures. In the shrivelled seventies, survival was the order of the day.

DOWN THE DRAIN

Meanwhile, replacements for the Arguses, as well as new fighters and tanks, had gone down the drain with Defence Minister Cadieux's 1969 budget, frozen at $1.8 billion for three years. The four Tribals continued to completion but nothing came after that. Capital spending slumped. By 1973 it was at an all-time low of 9 per cent of the total Defence budget. The Commons Defence Committee heard evidence that France spent 40 per cent on capital programs, West Germany 30 per cent, most NATO countries 24 to 30 per cent. Canada's lolled around 10 per cent for fourteen years. Pay shot up and personnel costs ate up two-thirds of budget – almost double that of any other Western nation. Pay and maintenance together took up 89 per cent. The United States was worried when pay and maintenance combined at 46 per cent.

Western nations were still trimming defence, but Canada had long since dropped below what all the rest took as prudent limits. Yet the country wasn't poor. Gross Domestic Product, increasing steadily, more than doubled in constant dollars between 1963 and 1985. Of sixteen NATO nations Canada ranked a steady fourteenth in defence spending as a percentage of GDP. Below her stood Luxembourg and then Iceland, which kept no armed forces at all. The navy lay becalmed at 9,500 all ranks, the lowest since the doldrums of the late forties.

RESERVES

The Naval Reserve had stood at an authorized 4,600 all ranks in the early sixties under its own command in Hamilton. In 1964 it was chopped below 3,000. The idea was that a big war would be nuclear, with no time to mobilize. The concept of conventional war accepted in 1961 was conveniently forgotten. It would only be the "brushfire" type in the Third World, gun-boat stuff to be handled by a small force of professionals. Direction of all Reserves was unified in Ottawa, which virtually orphaned the Naval Reserve from the active force. O'Brien launched another campaign and in 1969 the whole Naval Reserve came to Maritime Command, with its own Headquarters in Halifax, but it stayed as small.

In the meantime, the University Naval Training Division died. After twenty-five years of producing well-trained junior officers for the Reserve (and many for the permanent force) it was rolled into the unified Reserve Officer University Training Plan in 1968. People missed identification with the service of their choice, and Naval Reserve divisions, cut as they were, ran short of qualified officers. A strong naval link across the country dissolved.

In the late sixties NATO accepted the doctrine of "graduated response": as in the Brock Report, war without immediate nuclear devastation was on the cards; much stronger conventional forces were needed and Reserves would have reinforcing roles. The ceiling nudged up to 3,600. Whatever system might be used to get shipping across the oceans, it had to be pulled under control, organized, and kept moving right from day one. Maritime Command needed a trained and ready organization and naval control of shipping (NCS) became the main role for the Reserves.

FAREWELL TO RUM

One hoary inheritance from the RN was the navy's tot, the daily free issue in ships of 2½ ounces of overproof rum. For junior hands it was diluted in two parts of water. From the fifties the sailor could supply his own mix – watered or with Coke and ice cubes, it was still a rousing belt – or he could draw two cans of cold beer or take a little money instead.

It was a merry old institution. The Coxswain and the supply petty officer and the witnessing officer officiated every noon at the brass-bound rum tub suitably emblazoned "The Queen God Bless Her," pouring each man his measure to be drunk on the spot. Cheering though it was, rum was rife with problems. Men hid and hoarded it, bartered and binged on it. It was a time-consumer and an administrative headache, at the root of countless breaches of discipline. And certainly it slid many good men down the alcoholic's slippery slope.

Officers had protected the rum issue as much to preserve their privilege of duty-free liquor in the wardroom as for the men's enjoyment. But such a one-element privilege could never survive unification. The alternative: authorize bars on board. Now, like his officers, the sailor could buy an alcoholic drink at regulated hours and have it in the cafeteria or the comfort of his mess. It enhanced the ship as his home. It was the sensible answer for civilized people, and it wasn't abused.

UNIFORMS

The big symbolic change – green uniform for all – appeared in ships in 1970. Now all hands wore the same uniform, distinguished only by rank stripes and, for officers, gold leaf on the cap. Apart from looking like soldiers, the distinction was gone between the navy's working hands, who had worn the traditional seaman's rig, and the petty officers first class and the chiefs, who ran the show. The new uniform was certainly Canadian, which was appropriate. Overall, though, it was simply no match, in both navy and civilian eyes, for crisp blue and white and gold, bell-bottoms, and the universal nautical cut that marked a man a sailor – and proud of it – anywhere in the world.

Generally indigestible though the new uniform was, it hardly matched the heartburn that came with foisting soldiers' ranks on sailors. An admiral became a general, a leading seaman a corporal. It rubbed more salt in the wound to lose the honoured, battle-tried title "Royal Canadian Navy" while mere units of the "land element" – Royal Canadian Artillery, the Royal 22nd, the Royal Canadian Regiment, *et al.* – kept their "Royal" as well as their traditional ceremonial uniforms. In any event, a more sensitive Minister, Maurice Lamontaigne, restored a modicum of naval self-respect by giving back the old ranks in 1971 and uniform gradually subsided as an issue.

NAVAL AIR

After losing *Bonaventure* in 1970, the aviators themselves made a determined drive to keep the Tracker squadron for coastal patrols from shore, and there were the shipboard helicopters to fly. Still, a lot of naval aviators left the service. Others found their way to the Argus squadrons or moved to Air Defence or Mobile Command. Naval air and ground crews, in fact, formed the core – particularly in the helicopter units – of Mobile's growing Tactical Air Group, and as time went on ex-naval air people filled most of their senior positions.

Then, in 1975, a new Air Command gathered all aviation under its wing and supplied its "customers," Maritime and Mobile, with aviation as required. The helicopter sea detachment was the toughest challenge in Canadian forces aviation. Flying off that gyrating little deck, skimming the wave-tops in all kinds of weather, and living a seaman's life in a stomach-churning ship were challenge and adventure. But it was less than appealing for those not bred to salt water. Only a year later there was a shortage of pilots and maintenance men for the ships and Headquarters broke a pre-unification pledge, pressing ex-RCAF people to go to sea.

The naval officer aviators and their seaman-trained air and deck crews, who had played such a strong role in getting the Canadian navy to its prime place, would be no more.

THE HARD SEA TRADES

When unification got down to detail there was little in common between most naval seagoing trades and those of land and air. A ship must operate completely on her own and sailors have to maintain unique complex equipment as well as operate it. The "hard sea trades," as they were called, made up around 85 per cent of a ship's company. The rest were the interchangeable ones – medical, finance and administration, stores, victualling and catering trades. Sea drafts for interchangeable tradesmen from the other commands were volunteer at first, but with shortages some had to be pressed. All had to learn about ships, and it was costly in people, effort, and time.

The four new Tribals at sea from 1973 brought in a whole new age. Gas turbines drove them, solid-state electronics were in, and pretty well everything was run by state-of-the-art digital computers. All this required a special service centre ashore with a complete Tribal-class computer system to develop software, test and repair components from ships, and train the programming officers and computer technicians. It was better to take an experienced sea officer and teach him programming than try to teach naval tactics to a programmer, and the training was first rate. The techs' intense three-year course was unmatched anywhere in Canada.

Yet, no new ships were in sight so the old "steamers" would be in service indefinitely. That meant new men still had to train as well in antiquated but complex systems built before they were born. Vacuum-tube technology lived on in Canada's navy, and the only source of tubes was behind the Iron Curtain.

WOMEN IN THE NAVY

With unification most Wrens lost their naval connection. Treatment of men and women certainly hadn't been equal. Until the late sixties, women had to leave the service on marriage, and not until the seventies could they stay if they got pregnant. A lot of marriages were in-service. "Career managers" who dealt with people's destinies from Ottawa did their best to keep couples at least in the same geographical area. In 1980 women at last got into the military colleges.

Going to sea appealed to the adventurous and women began training with the Naval Reserves in coastal craft in the seventies. Combat duty for regular-force women was hotly debated, and from 1980 the diving support ship *Cormorant* included a dozen females for trial. Most enjoyed it as a one-time adventure. Not one volunteered for a second draft.

In 1987 operational support ships and non-combatant vessels were opened to women. Privacy in crowded ships and strength and endurance for heavy duties and emergencies were studied. Should women, for example, be trained in the hard sea trades? Certainly they could acquire the skills, but it was more expensive because far fewer women than men re-engaged and a very small number went the full career. Female hull technicians – the modern equivalent of the ancient trade of shipwright – were in training in 1988. Should they share the sea/shore ratio? In 1989, ready or not, all ships but submarines were opened up to women under Canada's Charter of Rights and Freedoms.

"CIVILIANIZING" THE FORCES

In 1972 National Defence Headquarters was "civilianized." In the democratic tradition, of course, elected politicians control the military. That could be nerve-wracking, as it was during the Cuban missile crisis; it could be baffling, enraging, and destructive, as it was during unification. Political control was routinely frustrating for senior officers, reared in a precise profession, who had to deal with a succession of partially informed masters as the political winds shifted through the ten years it took to bring a new shipbuilding program to fruition. But it was democracy and it was right.

Politicians and the military are uneasy bedfellows at best. The sixties bred deep suspicion and Prime Minister Trudeau's anti-military attitude didn't help. Delays and cost overruns in major projects were easy to blame on senior officers' mismanagement. The navy wasn't alone, but *Bonaventure*'s refit stood out. So did the money spent (it was too easy to say "wasted") on the hydrofoil project. Then there were cost overruns on the four new Tribals.

Bras d'Or and the Tribals were the most advanced surface vessel design and engineering projects in the Western world. But in Canada, rather than praise for remarkable achievement, they drew unfocused criticism for high cost. The political reaction was to increase civilian control. In 1972 a huge reorganization melded the Canadian Forces Headquarters with the civilian Department of National Defence. The deputy minister was put on the same level as the Chief of Defence Staff. Large sections, even the strictly military ones, came under assistant deputy ministers, either serving officers or civil servants. This was not the traditional overall civilian control but actual direction by civil servants of many aspects of naval and military affairs.

Admiral Landymore's basic point that decisions about sailors and the sea must be made by sea-experienced officers was buried even deeper. In addition, the civil service had changed. A professional bureaucrat no longer spent a productive, continuous career in one department climbing increasingly familiar ropes. The smart ones hopped from one department to another, bent on fast promotion. Expertise was dissipated. All departments cost more and produced less.

Servicemen of skill, dedication, and experience were leaving disenchanted. Pay, it was thought, might do the trick. In 1972, the Forces went on par with the public service and got an immediate 12 per cent boost. But here were the seeds of silliness. Big public service pay hikes through the seventies sucked at the federal budget; that meant less for defence. But Forces pay, now out of the Forces' control, kept pace. That meant even less for equipment.

As well, in the civilizing, Forces ranks were equated with civil servants; for bureaucratic balance, shoals of service people were promoted quite unneeded. By the mid-1970s there were 106 admirals and generals, and, overall, one officer for every 4.5 in the ranks – the most by far in any developed country in the world.

Civilians blossomed at the working level, too. By 1978, with uniformed personnel down to 78,000, the civilian employees of DND had climbed to 37,000. Immovable civil servants proliferated. Sailors perforce spent even more time at sea.

BILINGUALISM

The Official Languages Act of 1969 meant historic change in Canada that had to be reflected in the Forces. It was an obvious place to start: units were spread across the land; a highly developed training and education system was in place; people in the forces did what they were told and there were no unions to argue the toss.

A country's armed forces should be a unifier, but in Canada the historic reluctance of most Québécois to rally to what they generally viewed as foreign wars was stuck in the country's psyche. The beginnings of a navy had been bitterly fought by Henri Bourassa in 1911 and Laurier lost power. The conscription issue of two wars had been wrenchingly divisive. A number of French-Canadian army units had outstanding battle records, and the only permanent French regiment, the Royal 22nd, the famous Van Doos, had as gallant a history as any unit anywhere. But the language of the army majority was English, and in the navy and air force, one worked in English across the board. English was also the communications language of NATO.

French Canadians who had joined the navy – a few in peace, many in war – toughed out the language barrier on their own. From the fifties, the French new entry got systematic help with English. So did the cadet at *Venture* and College Militaire St. Jean. After that, though, it was sink or swim in the English sea. When they formed families they had to live in an English milieu, so the young French Canadian needed more than the average flexibility and determination to stick with it and succeed.

The aim, for a national institution, was fundamental and right. Working toward it brought all the stress of any kind of affirmative action. In the sixties 27 per cent of new recruits were French but the dropout rate was very high. The first move was for more French-language units like the Van Doos. The destroyer escort *Ottawa*, based in Halifax, became the first navy FLU in 1969.

The cherished criterion of merit for promotion was bent to fill some billets according to mother tongue. In 1970, 28 per cent of all ranks was earmarked Francophone. Some Anglophones were certainly hurt in the process, and some Francophones found their well-merited promotion treated with scorn.

And for every genuine case of unmerited promotion, imagined grievances were legion. Then came objectives for bilingualism. All Francophones in the navy were bilingual but few Anglophones spoke French. In six years, came the edict, 40 per cent of commanders and above and 35 per cent below were to reach "bilingual level four." By 1980 it was to be 60 per cent and 55 per cent. Tremors ran through the Anglo ranks and they queued up for language courses.

To the open-minded this was an opportunity their schooling hadn't given them. As well as being vital to a top-level career in a two-language country, it offered a valuable new cultural dimension. To others it was an imposition to be endured. For those who just couldn't grasp a second language, career prospects narrowed.

The goal was right but the taste was sour. The expense was legitimate because of the nature of the country, yet it was hard to swallow when there was no money for fighting equipment. The government, which had made such drastic cuts, gave no manpower margin to fulfil the language guidelines. Hence, there was less time for the technical training that people needed to get ahead and to cope with the spiralling maintenance problems of an aging fleet. It all hit the Maritime Commander and Canada's defence where it hurt – in readiness at sea.

Eventually, language training got built into the system and two workable languages became part of a vigorous officer's or senior sailor's kit. Certainly the navy was a long step ahead of L.P. Brodeur's frustrated attempt of 1910 to allow French applicants to write their cadetship exams in their mother tongue. And a Canadian navy could not help being the better for that.

TRAINING OFFICERS

In the early sixties all junior officers went to sea after service college, university, or *Venture* to qualify both on the bridge and in the engine room. Their obligation after full free university education was only five years' service. The shrinking navy was hardly an enticing place for an ambitious young man, and far too few stayed on. Naval officers split again into two career streams, the upper deck, called Maritime Surface and Subsurface or MARS, and the Maritime Engineer or MARE. There was no bar to engineering officers commanding ships if they qualified and reaching top operational command.

Back in 1968, while Training Command was all-powerful, HMCS *Venture* was closed and all Canadian Forces officers entered together. Their initial training was a good filter and a start on leadership, but the unified training after that was inadequate for junior naval officers and *Venture* reopened in 1976. It was named the Naval Officer Training Centre and belonged to Maritime Command. All junior naval officers from colleges and universities went through it. There weren't enough from these sources, so *Venture* ran one-year courses for high school graduates with plenty of hands-on sea training. Over half the naval officers of the early eighties came from this program. If they didn't have degrees – and many picked them up later – they could still run with the very best at sea.

In the dirt-poor times of the seventies and eighties the Maritime Commander invested all he could in officer training. He put four part-manned Mackenzie class, six of the old Bay-class minesweepers, and a flotilla of yard craft into the West Coast Training Squadron. The Squadron Commander ran the whole Naval Officer Training Centre, *Venture*, ships and all. Out came a stream of first-class junior sea officers with skill in practical seamanship and navigation, a grasp of practical engineering, and good all-round naval knowledge. About half had degrees, and close to a third of the university graduates went on to higher degrees. The staff colleges linked the services at the higher level, Headquarters staffs were better armed for the bureaucratic battle, and when the dust had settled great steps had been made in professional development. The system that evolved worked for the country and produced a well-educated and thoroughly trained officer corps.

And nothing disturbed or changed the irreplaceable part of the naval officer's endless training that is passed from senior to junior, from old hand to seasick neophyte, from Captain to his watchkeeping officers and down the line. Year after year, generation upon generation, by example, by coaching, by being given the job to do, by quiet conversations in the long watches of the night, the most essential training of all continued as it always had. Change there might be, but through long frustrating times the heart of the basic navy stayed the same.

BACK TO NAVY BLUE

Joe Clark's Progressive Conservative government, which won the election of 1979, set up a task force on un-unifying unification. Its chairman was George Fyfe, who had survived sinking as a DEMS gunner in merchant ships, retired from the navy as an Ordnance Commander, and became a senior civil servant. People in the service were cautious with their evidence. With all the traumas over the previous fifteen years they had worked things out reasonably well. The three services weren't really unified, just Headquarters was. They didn't want to open wounds. What they needed was money to rebuild. When Trudeau's Liberals came back in February, 1980, Fyfe's unfinished work went into the wastebasket.

Then, in the campaign of 1984, Brian Mulroney's Progressive Conservatives promised a few thousand more people and restoration of separate service uniforms and traditions. Once in power the Tories boosted manpower modestly and the Defence Minister, Nova Scotian Robert Coates, announced new uniforms for 1985, the navy's seventy-fifth anniversary.

Canadian navy blue, when it came to it, was actually black. The old eight-button jackets for officers, six-button for chiefs and petty officers, and square rig for junior ranks were no more. All hands from admiral to ordinary seaman got the same six-button fore-and-aft jacket made of the same issue cloth. The distinctions were in rank stripes and the gold leaf and badges on the caps. The air force had their light blue, the army kept the green, and the interchangeable administrative trades could choose the uniform they preferred. Penny-pinchers and curmudgeons be damned, for the navy it was a breath of fresh sea air. The fact is that, except for uniforms, unification according to Paul Hellyer never came about. Sea, land, and air remained distinct, as they always would.

Out of all these years of wracking change came a well-integrated Head-quarters. It was heavily bureaucratic, huge for the size of the fighting end, and it moved with glacial caution. But logical planning and procurement meant each service's priorities got a fair share of the meagre pot. Shared services and facilities were working economically and well. What were badly needed, however, were new ships, aircraft, and equipment to fill the ever-widening gap – and many more people to man them. The part of the Tory promise about restoring traditions wasn't required. Navy traditions, the ones that counted, never died.

CHAPTER TWENTY
TROUBLED TIMES

DEFENCE IN THE SEVENTIES

IN THE LATE SIXTIES BRITAIN, FRANCE, AND THE U.S. SEETHED WITH INTER-nal strife. In Canada there were mailbox bombings, riots and looting in Montreal during a police strike of 1969. In 1970 came the FLQ "state of apprehended insurrection" in Quebec and Prime Minister Trudeau invoked the War Measures Act and called in the troops. Internal security became, in his view, a serious concern.

Defence Minister Donald Macdonald's 1971 White Paper *Defence in the 70's*, spelled out the course the Prime Minister had set when he halved the NATO forces in Europe. Top priority now was protection of sovereignty. Defence of North America came next, then NATO, with peacekeeping at the bottom. The White Paper assumed continued mutual deterrence between the superpowers, growing détente, arms control, and negotiated reduction in nuclear and conventional forces. It noted the growing global range of Soviet naval power and the great increase in missile-firing submarines. The only direct threat to Canada was seen as a nuclear attack on North America. Astonishingly, though, there would be less emphasis on anti-submarine, which meant the U.S. must carry an even bigger share of North American defence.

This inward-turning view came right in the face of a strong NATO appeal for more and better anti-submarine forces and replacement of over-age ships. Failure to cover Canadian ocean areas on both coasts was a tacit invitation to the U.S. Navy to take over – a fundamental aspect of sovereignty that the White Paper had not chosen to address. On the other hand, Maritime Com-mand's coastal surveillance task grew as inexorably as its resources shrank.

In 1970 the traditional three-mile territorial limit was extended to twelve and the Arctic Waters Pollution Act set a hundred-mile control zone around the Arctic islands. In 1974 Canada joined the International Commission for Control of the Northwest Atlantic Fishery to combat flagrant overfishing. By then the Maritime Commander, Rear Admiral Robert Timbrell, had twenty-four ships on paper, but with their advancing age and too few people he could only sail twelve. Then, in 1977, Canada pushed her offshore fishing and economic zone to 200 miles, thus charging Marcom with active surveillance of 5.8 million square miles. Far from more ships, planes, and people for a vastly bigger job, Vice Admiral Douglas Boyle, the Maritime Commander who relieved Timbrell, had a fraction of the forces his predecessors had ten and twenty years before.

Since the fifties every Flag Officer had worried about the huge East bloc fishing fleets. Among them were snoopers – electronic and oceanographic intelligence gatherers. They could cover and even supply Soviet submarines at sea. Rear Admiral Hugh Pullen sent single destroyers and aircraft on random patrols starting in the late fifties, when submarines were spotted alongside factory ships on the Grand Banks. Fishing vessels masked submarine movements, visually, electronically, acoustically. They hauled enormous catches, too, and fished where they chose.

Soviet vessels visited Halifax and St. John's freely for supplies and repairs. Some were well kitted out with monitoring gear. Navy techs couldn't tune their radar or sonar sets with them about. As computers and radio data links multiplied, so did the dangers of electronic intelligence gathering. Commercial telephone microwave services linked the logistics computers in Halifax, Ottawa, and Borden. Information plucked from the air could draw a tidy picture of operational readiness.

There was no curb on the Soviet movements and the problem grew and grew. In 1977, Admiral Boyle noted there were 300 to 400 vessels in his east coast area of surveillance on any day – 20 to 50 per cent were Soviet. Policing by unarmed government vessels has limited effect without naval muscle on call to back it up, but it was ridiculously expensive for a frigate to carry a couple of fishery inspectors around the Banks; or, as happened in 1976, for the 4,200-ton *Iroquois* to chase three Cuban vessels spotted fishing illegally from the air. Fisheries did pay for the fuel, which helped keep the parched fleet going.

Admiral Sergei Gorshkov, the builder of the modern Soviet Navy, said in 1976 that "maritime transportation, fishing, and scientific research on the sea are part of the Soviet Union's naval might." Gorshkov understood history well and was forging a massively potent total maritime weapon. Vastly beyond the needs of defending the homeland, it aimed plainly at projecting Soviet power worldwide. East bloc merchant services, at highly subsidized rates, were carrying more and more of the world's cargoes while free world shipping rusted. Gorshkov's fighting fleet grew steadily in size and effectiveness. It challenged U.S. and allied strength in the Mediterranean first, then reached progressively around the world. The Soviets were getting into aircraft carriers when smaller NATO navies were dropping theirs. They were steadily adding more strategic missile submarines and more nuclear-propelled boats to their largely conventional attack fleet.

Their nuclear attack submarines were now slipping through the Canadian Arctic islands into Baffin Bay and straight down to the hinge of the North Atlantic trade route off Newfoundland. Thus they sidestepped the surveillance in depth strung across the Greenland-Iceland-U.K. gaps. Against Arctic intrusions Boyle could deploy two Argus patrols per month. He had no way of knowing what passed beneath the ice.

Boyle had inherited the Maritime Command from a disillusioned Timbrell. Ferret-like, he pursued economy in every conceivable cranny. He cancelled gunnery practices, opted out of NATO exercises and fleet training, restricted use of staff cars and trucks, reduced speed of ships and aircraft. He even descended to the minutiae of ordering all letters typed on both sides of the paper and half the light bulbs removed from shore-side offices – his own included. A smile rarely softened his tight-pressed lips or eased the intensity in his eyes. He drove himself even harder than his people, with nothing to offer but more of the same.

A HANDFUL OF SHIPS

Here and there a light did shine. Canadian sailors could be as proud of their four new Tribals as the previous generation had been of their Cadillacs. These were fine ships, the centre of attraction and open admiration wherever NATO (and Soviet snoopers) gathered. It was a real boost to be running state-of-the-art equipment. By 1977 they and their helicopters were proven in all sea conditions. They were "first among the finest ships in NATO" and remarkably trouble-free. The best equipment is only as good as those who run it and their crews led the pack with their helicopter/frigate combination. They ran with real flair, innovation, and operational savvy.

The new support ships *Preserver* and *Protecteur* were also top of their class. Replenishment at sea or RAS had been a spirited game at the receiving end since those record-shattering runs in Korea. *Provider*, though, was the first Canadian entry in the supplying field. She went to sea in 1963 with that fine experienced seaman, Captain Tom Pullen, in command. Home-grown innovations led the way to *Preserver* and *Protecteur* being the best naval supermarkets afloat.

The "O" boats ran their quiet operations smoothly and efficiently, but the underwater business in the real world was leaving them way behind. The old steamers, with their single helicopter and a core of long-term navy hands, were good, too, at the anti-submarine game. But they lagged progressively in communications and data links and suffered chronically from age.

Boyle had no option but to continue squeezing. Training for fighting gave way. He cut operations by a third in 1974. The annual spring exercise off Puerto Rico was cancelled for the first time in most sailors' memories to save fuel – for sovereignty patrols. Northern surveillance flights were cut out for three months until outcries in the House forced their resumption in January, 1975 – at one per month. MPs were easily satisfied.

That same month Defence Minister James Richardson announced more cuts with the statement that they would "not impair to a significant degree our ability to continue to ensure the maintenance of our sovereignty in the North or any region in Canada."

THREE SERVICES AGAIN

To meet Richardson's cuts Boyle was told to lop off 590 positions. New aircraft had top priority over ship replacements. That had been the recommendation of Boyle's predecessor, Rear Admiral Robert Timbrell. The Argus was very long in the tooth and running out of spares and several of the original thirty-six had been stripped to support the rest. So Boyle shut down one Argus squadron, cut the 590 positions out of administrative overhead, and kept all twenty-six aircraft flying.

That stirred a hornet's nest. It crystallized the old air force resistance to the navy having Maritime Air. Pressure came on Richardson from the retired network and as a result Air Command was formed. The navy lost direct control of all its aviation but thus came the tacit return to three services. A nice paradox. Maritime Command also had to shut down the forward facilities at St. John's and Frobisher Bay, a blow to operational flexibility in peace or war. To meet the payroll Boyle drained his fuel account, and ships got ninety days rather than 120 days at sea each year.

BOILING OVER

In the spring of 1975 Admiral Boyle briefed a caucus meeting of Tory MPs in Halifax and his frustrations overtook him. His resources, he said, were inadequate and "if we can't put up then we should shut up and surrender our sovereignty to the Americans." Soviet activities in Canadian waters were increasing at an alarming rate, while he had to keep ships alongside for lack of fuel. The government, he said, was "falling down on defence commitments to allies."

Reporters, as well as opposition MPs, were at the question/answer session, and Boyle's words were widely reported. He was quickly on the mat in front of the CDS, but MPs praised his briefing in the House. Defence Minister Richardson actually commended the Admiral's "excellent statement . . . the kind of factual information that should be more widely known by the Canadian public." Boyle was, after all, the senior adviser to government on naval operations, charged with the responsibility of meeting its commitments at sea. Public criticism of major government policy, on the other hand, is unacceptable in a serving officer. But Richardson certainly didn't want another Landymore or Brock. As he shrewdly guessed, the public took little more than passing note. No one rallied. There was no outcry, no action. Canadians didn't want to know about their navy.

By 1977 Boyle had stretched the time between refits from twenty to forty-eight months to save money. For aging ships this was pushing the limits of safety. Helicopter crews were so short that flying operations were curtailed again. For Springex '77 the professional ranks were fleshed out with 250 Reservists and Sea Cadets – teen-aged, one-night-a-week cadets – so that one more ship could get away from the wall.

Even in this wretched state Maritime was the biggest Command in the Forces. Marcom's responsibility was awesome: he had direct responsibility for maritime sovereignty on three coasts; he co-operated, with what little he had, with U.S. forces in defence of North America; he was NATO Commander of the Canadian Atlantic sub-area; he was Canada's Eastern Regional Commander responsible for aid to civil power, pollution control, and support of other government departments; he was head of the Naval Reserve in nineteen divisions across the land. Topping it off, he was responsible for the Canadian Rangers, a scattering of native people in the Far North who provided reconnaissance as they got about their travels on the tundra and the icepack. In fact, the Rangers were the only "system" in Maritime Command that by some bizarre chance – perhaps while seal hunting through the ice – might actually detect a submarine passing through Canadian Arctic seas.

Boyle spoke again and again at public meetings and service club luncheons. His message was the growing Soviet threat and the shrinking Canadian capability. He told everyone who would listen that the St. Laurents would be thirty years old in the eighties. Without immediate replacement, Canada would fall ever further from its dishonoured NATO commitment. When he said bluntly and publicly that the Soviet build-up was leading to open conflict in the eighties, he overstepped the bounds – and the incoming and first naval CDS, Admiral Robert Falls, had to muzzle him. Boyle declined to take a desk in Ottawa to do an economic impact study and resigned eighteen months before retirement.

A few months later, retired Admiral Timbrell went on the record with an assessment close to Boyle's. Meeting commitments, he said, called for thirty-six destroyers, a dozen minesweepers, ten submarines capable of under-ice operation, four supply ships, and thirty-six LRPAs. That meant 22,000 sailors and 6,000 airmen all told. But Admiral Falls said six patrol frigates were being considered – that was the government line, and that was that.

Vice Admiral Andrew Collier, who won his DSC navigating Jeffry Brock's squadron up to Chinnampo in the Korean War, was Boyle's successor as Maritime Commander. This first *Royal Roads* graduate to reach Flag rank took over a starved, storm-savaged navy. There was little but the spirit of the few to keep it afloat, little an Admiral or anyone could do – other than resign – but lash himself to the wheel and ride it out.

BAND OF BROTHERS

There was one strong leading-light in this gloomy passage. In 1968 NATO's Supreme Commander Atlantic had pulled a half-dozen destroyer-sized ships of the different nations into a combined squadron called the Standing Naval Force Atlantic (Stanavforlant). The Commodore came from each country in rotation for a year.

The squadron worked on operational efficiency and tactics, especially in ASW. It showed NATO solidarity to the world and gave Saclant a force of his own for surveillance and for monitoring Soviet exercises. It was a ready squadron for emergency; it could go straight to the vital northern flank off Norway in time of tension, for example. Finally, it was a worked-up nucleus. Around it a bigger NATO force could quickly form.

The Canadians' helicopter operations quickly became a centrepiece and an example. So, in spite of the limits of the old Cadillacs, did their capable round-the-clock, ever-ready shiphandling and seamanship. Canadian operational support ships often were along, and they were the best in the game.

Canadian Commodores Douglas Boyle, Dan Mainguy, and Gordon Edwards had notable stints in command of the Standing Naval Force. For example, Edwards had twenty-seven NATO ships in rotation in 1978-79, averaging seven at a time. *Iroquois, Huron*, and *Algonquin* took turns as flagship as the Tribals were by far the best fitted for the job. *U-10* and *U-14* – fine small submarines of the reborn Federal German Navy – joined for exercises, and a new generation matched wits with U-boats. This time it was the Canadians on the North Atlantic who had the best ships and equipment and the best-trained crews, but there were far too few of them to have much impact on the allies' cause.

Come wind or weather and around the clock, there was one helicopter out on task from a single spray-lashed Tribal's deck; and the second was most likely at short notice, set to go. Ship for ship, man for man, they held the lead. Stanavforlant, for twenty years, had a great deal to do with keeping the tiny navy tails-up in troubled times.

CHAPTER TWENTY-ONE
THE EIGHTIES
AND ONWARD

MAKE DO AND MEND

THERE WAS A CHANGE IN THE WIND IN THE EIGHTIES AS A DISILLUSIONED Europe turned from détente. The Soviets had invaded Afghanistan in 1979. In the Canadian election campaign that year both Liberals and PCs promised 4,700 more people for the Forces and 20 per cent of the defence budget for capital spending. In Europe a huge modern Soviet tank army towered over NATO's run-down forces. Western Europeans were deeply worried. They badly wanted help.

NATO's top Defence Planning Committee needed a maritime strategic framework on which to judge proposals for major new naval systems and equipment. They looked to Saclant, Admiral Harry Train, USN, who turned to his Deputy Chief of Staff, Operations, Rear Admiral Dan Mainguy. Thus it was a second-generation senior Canadian naval officer who wrote NATO's definitive "Concept of Maritime Operations." From 1980 it guided major NATO decisions and was largely adopted by the U.S. Navy. That same year a truculent Ronald Reagan was elected U.S. President and directed a massive build-up in American arms.

Changes in the world at large seemed to be registering on Canadians and their leaders. In 1983, even with galloping inflation and a huge deficit, the Liberal government moved. The new Aurora LRPAs were aloft and Air Command had its F-18 fighters and the army its Leopard tanks. It was high time for some ships. The Minister of Defence had said in 1977 that the first of six new patrol frigates would go to sea in 1985. But no funds were provided. Now, after years of delay and climbing cost, six were approved, with the possibility of a dozen to follow. This was scaled down sharply from the twenty-four urgently proposed for the navy in 1974. They would cost $3.9 billion and the first would go to sea in 1992.

In the 1984 election campaign, even the New Democratic Party's leader, Ed Broadbent, deplored the navy's near-demise. This was the first new construction approved in nineteen years, and the superlative navy ship design and system engineering expertise was long gone. Now Defence Headquarters had to put itself in the hands of industry, as the air force always had for planes. But along with navy expertise the Canadian industrial base had eroded. Various consortia set up their shops in Ottawa and competed for the frigate contract. They were fronted by Canadian companies but masterminded elsewhere. A surprising number of old navy hands were working for them in civilian clothes, but top management and policy were American.

It would be nearly ten years before new ships were at sea, and that forced a "Destroyer Life Extension Program" to keep sixteen old steamers going into the nineties at a cost of some $24 million each. Even that would take four years and it was little more than a charade. The ancient vessels got a lick and a promise, and updated detection, communications, and electronic warfare equipment. "Delex," as it was called, gave them a semblance of performance. They could fill surveillance slots and do fishery patrols, deploying one helicopter each. But with the weapons of the fifties they were incapable of defending themselves against air attack and were noisy sitting ducks for submarines. Even with their Delex they wouldn't have a prayer in a war like the one the Royal Navy fought over the Falkland Islands in 1982. Five ships were hit then, and three of them sunk, by French-made Exocet missiles.

Guided missiles had been around a long time. The first *Athabaskan* was hit by a guided bomb in 1943. *Athabaskan* the second went to the boneyard in 1966 with armament that could have done no better against Soviet missiles. One fired from an Egyptian gunboat had sunk an Israeli destroyer the year before. The third *Athabaskan* had Sea Sparrow missiles intended in the early sixties for the general purpose frigates. They could hit attacking aircraft but couldn't touch the wave-skimming Exocets that any Third World country in the eighties could buy straight off the shelf.

A "Tribal Update and Modernization Program" was also announced in 1983. The Tribals would become anti-air warfare ships, keeping a good ASW capability. The new Canadian patrol frigate would be the other way around – ASW primarily with one helicopter, and self-defence weapons against aircraft and missiles. As well, they would all have American Harpoons, proven guided missiles that could hit a surface target over the horizon. The "O" boats, the quiet, slow-paced hunter-killers from the early sixties, began cycling through an update, too.

In the early eighties the Arguses were replaced by eighteen new Auroras; at $1.03 billion it was the biggest peacetime defence contract in Canada's history. They were much better equipped than the Argus and easier to maintain and keep in the air, but for actual flying performance they were no giant leap ahead.

And there were fewer of them. Resources still had to be rationed among territorial surveillance (Arctic included once in three weeks), covering submarine activities in the Canadian ocean areas, training with Canadian ships and submarines, and periodic NATO exercises. None of these got enough.

The remaining Trackers clattered faithfully into the air carrying the bare equipment for inshore surveillance but they had no place in modern ASW. Sea King detachments rotated to the ships from two Air Command squadrons at Canadian Forces Base, Dartmouth. By the mid-eighties, after twenty years of extraordinary service at sea in wind and foul weather, the Sea Kings were in the same geriatric state as most of the ships from which they flew. In 1989 they were still flying off those little decks and had not had a single fatal accident in twenty-five years – remarkable airmanship and seamanship combined.

PACIFIC RIM

Vladivostok was the historic Russian naval base in the Pacific. Now the Soviets had a huge new base at Cam Ranh Bay in Vietnam. Their Pacific fleet by the mid-1980s had two ASW carriers, eighty-five major and 354 smaller warships, 134 submarines, and 500 naval aircraft. This vast fleet straddled the key routes of Pacific trade.

Vancouver was now the largest exporting port on the continent, handling more tonnage than Halifax, Montreal, Quebec, and Toronto combined. Arctic slope oil – one-fifth of the U.S. supply – moved in a vulnerable parade of supertankers from Valdez in Alaska to Puget Sound through the Maritime Commander Pacific's ocean area. He had no submarines and little more than half a basic training squadron to do his job.

THE NORTH

Huge mineral, gas, and oil deposits had been found in the Canadian Arctic in the sixties and *Manhattan*'s voyage proved they could be transported by sea. Lead/zinc mines at Nanisivik, north Baffin Island, started producing in 1977, then the Polaris mine at Little Cornwallis Island in 1982. In 1985 the first cargo of crude oil was tankered from Cameron Island. Economics would dictate when shipping would begin in a major way.

After 1960 American and then Soviet nuclear-powered submarines moved between the deep Arctic Basin and the Atlantic using the Parry Channel and the Ellesmere Island/Greenland route. They found their way, too, through the Canadian islands by way of Hell's Gate and Jones Sound. In September, 1985, the press reported that Canada was experimenting with a submarine listening system in Lancaster Sound. If not, it was long overdue. However, it wasn't the Soviet threat that tweaked the public's interest that year but a run through the Northwest Passage by the U.S. Coast Guard icebreaker *Polar Sea* without Canada's permission. Unlike submarines, which only another submarine could detect up there, *Polar Sea* was large as life. Citizens' groups and environmentalists flew north, dropped flags, and shook their fists. Arctic sovereignty was an issue. The Americans held this was an international waterway and Canada had no jurisdiction. By September, though, Canada had drawn straight baselines around the whole archipelago and extended Canadian law to the Arctic offshore.

The Polar 8 icebreaker the Liberals had talked about and shelved was dusted off and ordered for the Coast Guard. She was to be a huge vessel capable of year-round Arctic operation. She'd provide presence. She'd be invaluable when oil and mineral activity stirred. But real clout was up to the navy, and in the Arctic it had none.

Canada's claim to her Arctic waters is shaky on historic grounds. But, says Donat Pharand, leading Canadian expert in the law of the sea, "The Northwest Passage is a Canadian national waterway since its enclosure by straight baselines, without any right of innocent passage; however, if adequate control measures are not taken, it could become an international strait and the new right of transit passage would eventually apply in favour of all ships, including submarines." Adequate control measures? Submarines? Only a needling from south of the border ever turned Canada's attention seriously to her own North – at the turn of the century it was the whalers; in the fifties the potential for nuclear exchange; in 1969 it was *Manhattan*; in 1985, *Polar Sea*.

Yet at the northern gate lay a frozen arena roved by the submarines of the superpowers, where the fate of the world could be played out. To know what went on underneath the ice was the first step toward controlled reduction of forces in polar waters. If self-preservation, national sovereignty, and the lessons of history were heard, Canada must do something serious about Arctic naval defences or someone else most surely would. Historically, though, Canada has never been the keeper of her northern gate. Today she does not even have a turnstile to count the deadly players passing through.

SEVENTY-FIVE YEARS A NAVY

When the navy, past and present, gathered to celebrate its seventy-fifth anniversary in the summer of 1985, there was a Review of the Fleet in historic Bedford Basin. NATO's Standing Naval Force Atlantic was there in international strength, eight fine modern frigates. More came from France, Britain, Italy, Brazil, Sweden, and Finland. Thirty-four warships anchored in precise ranks in the Basin.

Added to this modern fleet was HMCS *Sackville*, the last of the brave little corvettes that had fought the great Battle of the Atlantic. She had been lovingly restored to 1944 fighting trim by old navy hands. There she swung at anchor in pale North Atlantic camouflage with the old green maple leaf and the Barber Pole stripes on her funnel and the White Ensign proudly flying aft.

As well as the most up-to-date ASW vessels, the visitors showed the latest in mine-hunting and anti-missile defences – two items of which Canada's navy had precisely none. Other than *Sackville*, in fact, only thirteen of those ships were Canadian. Two of the home team were support ships, three were Tribals. The rest were the ancients that made up most of Vice Admiral James Wood's Maritime Command. All told, on the east coast, he had twelve fighting ships, three submarines, and two operational support ships; out west were four destroyers and one support ship. Since 1963 his forces earmarked for Saclant had dropped from thirty ships and forty aircraft to fifteen and fourteen, respectively. As Admiral Wood said, four-fifths of the ships in his tiny navy would need protection from other navies to survive.

THE NEW SEA POWER

The awesome growth of the Soviet navy into the eighties wrought, next to the nuclear bomb, the biggest shift in world power alignment since World War Two. On the strategic side they added the mammoth Typhoon submarines, half again as big as *Bonaventure* and twice her speed, carrying twenty missiles with multiple nuclear warheads that would reach 4,500 miles. By 1985 close to 100 Soviet "boomers" prowled the depths of the polar sea, protected by geography, ice cover, and their massive fleet. The counterpoise lay in the American and British strategic submarines that roved the open sea.

There were 300 Soviet attack submarines, 100 of which were nuclear-powered. They included the huge Oscars, 15,000-ton deep diving battleships with submerged-launch missiles to strike at the American carrier battle groups. With 1,700 fighting ships the Soviet navy was the biggest in the world, just outbalanced by all the NATO navies put together.

While they had been so expanding there had been a tremendous increase in the Western world's dependence on seaborne trade, Canada's included. On any day over 3,600 ships plied the North Atlantic lanes alone – more than the U-boats sank in all of World War Two – and they were monsters compared to the ships of the 1940s. They carried the lifeblood, the economy, the standard of life, not just of Europe but of the Western world. Thus the Soviets, who did not have that dependence, had a great new strategic power. They could bring shipping, almost anywhere in the world, under siege. And if they won on the trade routes, not only Western Europe would be strangled. A noose would be drawn around North America's neck. If it should ever come, the West's war – on a worldwide scale now – could be lost at sea; the land-bound Warsaw Pact's could not. Admiral Gorshkov had called it right.

THE MERCHANTMEN

In 1987 the army, exercising for a time of rising tension, moved its Canadian Air-Sea Transportable (CAST) Brigade across to Norway in an exercise called

Brave Lion. Four thousand troops flew over, and their equipment, including 2,000 vehicles and heavy guns, ammunition, and combat stores for thirty days, got there in four chartered foreign-flag merchant ships.

The Norwegians had always agreed to provide the ships for this operation, but soon after Brave Lion Canada switched the CAST Brigade's destination to the Central European front. For sealift now Canada was on its own. No other nation would commit precious merchant ships for another's use in emergency, and there were simply no Canadian flag ships to do the job. In fact, there was virtually no ocean-going Canadian merchant marine.

The merchant fleet begun in the Great War almost disappeared in the twenties through lack of government policy. For the same reason the substantial "Park" fleet of World War Two faded away. While a respectable number of Canadian-owned ships sailed the oceans, lack of policy pushed them to foreign registry where they couldn't be controlled (or taxed) by Canadian law. European nations and the U.S. all subsidized their merchant fleets, preserving currency and a vital asset for emergency. On a small but embarrassing scale, in 1989 the Canadian government had to ship a cargo of PCBs to Wales for disposal – abortively, as it turned out – in a Soviet vessel. A country depending so greatly on the sea for its trade, its prosperity, its way of life, must depend on other nations for both the means and the security to use it.

CHALLENGE AND COMMITMENT

When the Progressive Conservative government, elected in 1984, announced the return to distinctive uniforms the navy took it as a symbol of recognition, a signal of a rebirth. But a main Tory election pledge had been to cut spending. The huge deficit, interest on debt, and the enormous weight of statutory payments left little room for fiscal footwork. Still, Prime Minister Brian Mulroney said firmly Canada would be a good ally to the U.S. and NATO, and that surely meant more navy.

When Erik Nielsen became Minister of Defence in 1985 and was briefed on the plans for new conventional submarines, he asked about a nuclear-powered alternative. Senior officers said they offered great operational advantages but with the high cost in relation to other needs they didn't believe the political will was there. To Nielsen, a tough politician and a strong man in cabinet, the matter of political will was his business and the admirals should get on with theirs. In fact, their recommendations had been influenced by American costs. A year of detailed study showed that a fleet of nuclear-powered, conventionally armed attack submarines of British or French design would be cost-effective for a three-ocean navy, would fuel major new industrial benefits, and was the only answer to naval control of the North.

By the time the study was completed Perrin Beatty was the Minister. His White Paper of June, 1987, opened with a statement by Prime Minister Brian

Mulroney that "No Government has a more important obligation than to protect the life and well-being of its people; to safeguard their values and interests. In Canada it is time to renew that commitment." Called *Challenge and Commitment*, Beatty's White Paper was Canada's first statement of defence policy since 1971 and the first ever to make a major point of how little Canada did about defence.

That was a political cut at the Liberals' long regime, of course, but the figures published every year by NATO, recording each ally's defence efforts, had changed very little since 1973. Canada stood eleventh in manpower (at 80,000), second last in Reserve strength (at 20,000), and fourteenth in expenditure of Gross Domestic Product (at 2.2 per cent). The United States spent three times that percentage, the U.K. over twice as much, and Netherlands 50 per cent more. Since 1960 Canadian GDP had risen steadily vis-à-vis Britain, Germany, France, and Italy. NATO still meant an attack on one was an attack on all. Canada enjoyed that benefit but, tops in living standard and with a network of social programs envied round the world, she was getting very close to a free ride. Other countries' taxpayers were carrying better-off Canadians on their backs.

The White Paper got to the nub of it with: "Social benefits, however, are the fruits of a secure and free society. This Government accepts the preservation of such a society as its fundamental responsibility and will, therefore, provide the resources necessary to make the Canadian Forces operationally effective and responsive to the challenges of the 1990's and beyond."

Defence priorities now were "maintaining strategic deterrence, credible conventional defence, protection of Canadian sovereignty, peaceful settlement of international disputes, and effective arms control." Deterrence included defence of North America and the ability to keep the sea lanes to Europe open. The Pacific had great new strategic significance, too. More naval forces were needed there, and the long-neglected Arctic must be seriously attended to as well. For the very first time in such a policy statement the fact came through that Canada, a maritime nation, must look to the sea – on all three coasts.

The old steamers would be scrapped as the new frigates commissioned. Proposed new forces started with a second batch of six patrol frigates. With the four revamped Tribals that was sixteen frigates in all. There would be several minesweepers. The old story was being retold in the Iran-Iraqi war with cheap, easy-to-sow mines stopping supertankers in the Persian Gulf. The small ships would be useful, too, for coastal and fisheries patrol, and would be manned mainly by the Naval Reserves.

To boost area surveillance on east and west coasts there'd be some towing vessels with underwater acoustic gear that would send the data to other ships and shore. A fixed sonar system would be deployed in the Arctic. There'd be six new Auroras, replacements for the Sea Kings, and some old Trackers would be re-engined and kept flying for their coastal role. But the big grabber in the whole paper was ten to twelve nuclear-powered attack submarines.

They were certainly the most cost-effective anti-submarine units available. Each was expected to be worth several conventional submarines and a good deal more than a frigate. In Arctic waters nothing else would do the job, and in no other way could Canada ever have prime alliance responsibility for her own northern ocean area. NATO, the USN included, had 107 nuclear attack submarines, so twelve new Canadian boats spelled significant naval muscle. With that came international influence, naval and political, with NATO, the U.S., and the world. The doors to the key inner councils of NATO opened to Canada once more.

But "nuclear" is a word that caught in most Canadians' throats and there was an erroneous public notion that nuclear weapons were involved. Canada had had nuclear-fuelled power stations for years and the record of thirty years of American and British nuclear propulsion at sea was clean. Still, spectres of runaway reactors like Chernobyl in the Soviet Union were readily invoked.

The price tag came a little later at $8 billion for ten to twelve boats. The choice was between the British Trafalgar (with power plant based on American technology, which needed U.S. permission) and the French Amethyste, with no strings. The whole naval program was to spin out over twenty years. It would be paid, Beatty said, out of "an annual real growth in the defence budget of 2 per cent per year after inflation." That was a lot less than the 3 per cent real growth averaged between 1975 and 1984. And when you got right down to it, nuclear submarines and all, the whole program was bare bones for a giant task. And it would be a very long time before the gap between commitment and capability was narrowed.

The nuclear-powered submarine issue drew far more public attention than the navy had had for many years. The second batch of six frigates was approved in late 1987 for delivery, perhaps, before the bottoms dropped right out of the old faithfuls. Again, even the New Democratic Party agreed with the strengthening of the navy, too small, ill-equipped, and overloaded as it was – but nothing nuclear, of course.

There was opposition in the States as well from the USN's powerful nuclear submarine navy-within-a-navy. They liked the free hand they'd always had in Canada's Arctic. They pooh-poohed the notion of Canadians playing with the big boys and ran a strong campaign in Congress to block British transfer of Trafalgar nuclear technology.

GUNS OR BUTTER

Beatty pressed for his program. When the first of the fine new frigates, HMCS *Halifax*, was christened in May, 1988, the polls – the overwhelming factor now in government decision-making – said two-thirds of Canadians felt the forces should have new equipment and 80 per cent said Canada should stay in NATO. But when it came right down to it, the bill would have to be paid in social benefits. Mulroney reversed course. He moved Beatty from Defence to Health and Welfare. By the November, 1988, election, cabinet had chosen to choose neither British nor French technology. Instead, just before dissolution, they proposed universal day care and edged away from the issue of defence.

In the campaign Liberal leader John Turner said he'd spend the submarines' $8 billion (offering no naval alternative) on day care and other social programs. Since President Reagan and Soviet Secretary Mikhail Gorbachev met in 1985, the winds had blown fair. Under the new leadership the Soviets had pulled out of Afghanistan, progressed mutual reductions in nuclear arms, and cut conventional forces in Europe. Why would Canada run against the tide?

The Tories won the election and their budget of April, 1989, announced major cuts in government spending to try and control the deficit. Thirty-eight per cent of those cuts came out of national defence, which accounted for less than 8 per cent of total government expenditure, and the next biggest chunk came from foreign aid. These two were the only areas where surgery would cause Canadians no social pain. The biggest item, the submarines, went overboard with no alternative naval program. Defence spending hit a dead low of 1.7 per cent of GDP. The only public outcry arose over closing some bases, notably Summerside, P.E.I., where the doddering old Trackers kept the local economy afloat.

It was another chapter in the same long story. Between 1947 and 1984, spending on the navy, compared with the total government expenditure, had dropped by 47 per cent; from 1969 to 1984, it had dropped by 63 per cent. Canada was in a period of remarkable economic growth. As it got richer, the less it spent on defence. And the navy, with its day-in day-out responsibilities at sea, had consistently trailed the army and air force for funds. The navy was, without a doubt, Canada's Cinderella service.

Ironically, there was too little actual spending scheduled in the first few years of the submarine program to make any serious impact on the deficit. In the two years since the White Paper there had been no fundamental change in Canada's economic strength so it was clear how shallow were her commitments, how pinched and self-focused was her vision of the world. The inner doors of NATO closed again. Prime Minister Mulroney had given up on defending his "fruits of a secure and free society." Canada's navy lolled in the backwater, becalmed.

THE NEW WINDS

While the superpowers worked cautiously on arms reductions, eastern Europe was astir. In Poland, a shipyard electrician, Lech Walesa, had been leading an heroic drive to break the economic chains of the Soviet-backed regime. Mikhail Gorbachev launched the Soviets themselves on a massive endeavour to restructure their inefficient, near-moribund economy, crushed for so long by an omniscient state and the burden of arms. He opened the government apparatus to participation and allowed freedom of action and expression quite unknown in their society. In 1989 Poland had free elections. Hungary followed. Huge popular demonstrations in East Germany forced the borders open and ejected the East German Politburo. Czechoslovakians ousted the Communist ruling party and scheduled free elections. The winds of freedom were blowing hard and the Soviet tanks stayed home. In November, in a height of euphoria, the Berlin wall was breached. Across Germany, families and friends who had not seen each other since 1961 were reunited. By year's end the iron-handed regime in Romania was overthrown.

In a few short incredible weeks the Iron Curtain had been drawn aside the only way it ever could – from the East. Since the end of World War Two the only possible endings to eternal East-West confrontation were mutual annihilation or the reassertion of basic human freedom inside the Soviet bloc. The task of NATO for forty years had been to hold the line until, in course of time, the human solution came to pass. And now the Cold War was over. NATO's warriors, two full generations of Canada's sailors among them, could be proud indeed of the part they played in the most crucial – and bloodless – victory in the history of the human race. Hindsight could say that Pierre Trudeau was right in 1968 to pull back and nurture Canadian society as Soviet strength grew greater. But politicians postured about NATO and defence and failed to develop any strategic vision. In the event, Canada at large could take small credit for the success that crowned those final twenty years.

BACK TO THE SEA?

Canadians, except in time of open war and the raw threat of the fifties, have turned their backs to their navy and the sea, just as they did with Nelson on his truncated column in Montreal. Laurier produced the vision but it failed in 1911, then in 1922, in 1946, in 1964, and again in 1989. Except for the brief, brave times, letting others do it has been the siren-song; Britain first, and then America and NATO.

But Canada's history was shaped by the sea. She grew, changed hands, was nurtured, protected, and finally thrived as an independent nation because of seapower. The seas brought people, nursed and nourished her. Her oldest industry, the fishery, time and again needed naval strength to be preserved, not infrequently from her neighbour. Shielded by others' navies she has stayed secure and grown strong on seaborne trade.

Great treasure lies beneath the sea around this longest coast of any country in the world. Territory, wealth, possessions, and seaborne trade must be defended against the hard reality of international life. The Cold War is over, but not the problems of the world. As NATO's armed might in likelihood recedes, with its job of forty years well done, Canada stands more on her own, less shielded in broad world affairs, and indeed more prone to domination by the United States. In fact, if all NATO nations cut their arms by 30 per cent and Canada stood pat, she would remain at the bottom of the heap.

But still, as a wealthy citizen of an ever-changing world, she must contribute to stability and lasting peace; and that includes the need for even-handed control of violence with armed strength. Our besieged fishery, global environmental problems, and the new membership in the Organization of American States will surely call for new commitments on the sea. Alliances with the like-minded are essential. But stripped of an effective navy through neglect, Canada has little to bring to the reality of a harsh and fast-changing world – a world in which the sea has the ever-profound influence that history clearly shows.

Except in wars too remote for most to remember, Canadians have given little time, small treasure, and less respect to their seamen-at-arms. But the remarkable fact remains: in war and peace the people in Canada's navy have served this country steadfastly and, quite astonishingly, very, very well. Their commitment has found no limits to the challenge of the sea. And simply, you will find no better sailors in the world than these.

The boundless ocean that makes our world a gleaming blue jewel from outer space holds the future of the nations. Indeed, the sea is at our gates. And the key is in the hands of those who heed its call.

Appendix A
Ministers and Service Heads, 1910-1989

MINISTERS RESPONSIBLE FOR THE NAVY

Ministers of Marine and Fisheries and the Naval Service

L.P. Brodeur	1910-1911
Rodolphe Lemieux	1911
J.D. Hazen	1911-1917
C.C. Ballantyne	1917-1921

Minister of Militia and Defence and the Naval Service

G.P. Graham	1921-1922

Ministers of National Defence

G.P. Graham	1922-1923
E.M. Macdonald	1923-1926
Hugh Guthrie	1926
Colonel J.L. Ralston, CMG, DSO, ED	1926-1930
Lieutenant-Colonel D.M. Sutherland, DSO, ED	1930-1934
Grote Stirling	1934-1935
I.A. Mackenzie	1935-1939
N. McL. Rogers	1939-1940
Colonel J.L. Ralston, CMG, DSO, ED	1940

Ministers of National Defence for Naval Services

A.L. Macdonald	1940-1945
D.C. Abbott	1945-1946

Ministers of National Defence

D.C. Abbott	1946
Brooke Claxton, DCM	1946-1954
R.O. Campney	1954-1957
Major-General G.R. Pearkes, VC, CB, DSO, MC	1957-1959
Lieutenant-Colonel D.S. Harkness, CM, ED	1960-1963
Lieutenant-Colonel G.M. Churchill, DSO, ED	1963
P.T. Hellyer	1963-1967
Leo Cadieux	1967-1970
Brigadier C.M. Drury, CBE, DSO, ED	1970 (acting)
D.S. Macdonald	1970-1972
E.J. Benson	1972
J.E. Dubé	1972 (acting)
Brigadier C.M. Drury, CBE, DSO, ED	1972 (acting)

J.A. Richardson	1972-1976
B.J. Danson	1976-1979
A.B. McKinnon, MC, CD	1979-1980
J.G. Lamontaigne	1980-1983
J.J. Blais	1983-1984
R.C. Coates	1984-1985
Erik Nielsen, DFC	1985-1986
Perrin Beatty	1986-1989
Bill McKnight	1989-

SERVICE HEADS

Directors of the Naval Service (Royal Canadian Navy)

Admiral Sir C.E. Kingsmill, RN (Retired)	1910-1920
Commodore Walter Hose, CBE	1921-1928

Chiefs of the Naval Staff (Royal Canadian Navy)

Rear Admiral Walter Hose, CBE	1928-1934
Vice Admiral P.W. Nelles, CB	1934-1944
Vice Admiral G.C. Jones, CB	1944-1946
Vice Admiral H.E. Reid, CB	1946-1947
Vice Admiral H.T.W. Grant, CBE, DSO, CD	1947-1951
Vice Admiral E.R. Mainguy, OBE, CD	1951-1956
Vice Admiral H.G. DeWolf, CBE, DSO, DSC, CD	1956-1960
Vice Admiral H.S. Rayner, DSC, CD	1960-1964

Commanders, Maritime Command of the Canadian Forces

(Integrated Forces, from July, 1964)

Rear Admiral W.M. Landymore, OBE, CD	1964-1966
Rear Admiral J.C. O'Brien, CD	1966-1968

(Unified Forces, from February, 1968)

Vice Admiral J.C. O'Brien, CD	1968-1970
Vice Admiral H.A. Porter, CD	1970-1971
Rear Admiral R.W. Timbrell, DSC, CD	1971-1973
Vice Admiral D.S. Boyle, CMM, CD	1973-1977
Vice Admiral A.L. Collier, CMM, DSC, CD	1977-1979
Vice Admiral J. Allan, CMM, CD	1979-1980
Vice Admiral J.A. Fulton, CMM, CD	1980-1983
Vice Admiral J.C. Wood, CMM, CD	1983-1987
Vice Admiral C.M. Thomas, CMM, CD	1987-1989
Vice Admiral R.E. George, CD	1989

Appendix B

RCN Ships Lost During World War Two

Date	Ship	Type of Ship	Commanding Officer	How Lost	Location	Remarks
25 June 1940	HMCS *Fraser**	destroyer	Cdr. W.B. Creery, RCN	collision with HMS *Calcutta*	Gironde River estuary	
9 Oct. 1940	HMCS *Bras d'Or**	auxiliary minesweeper	Lt. C.A. Hornsby, RCNR	unknown	Gulf of St. Lawrence	
22 Oct. 1940	HMCS *Margaree**	destroyer	Cdr. J.W.R. Roy, RCN	collision with freighter *Port Fairy*	North Atlantic	escorting convoy OL8
26 March 1941	HMCS *Otter**	armed yacht	Lt. D.S. Mossman, RCNR	accidental explosion and fire	off Halifax Lightship	
19 Sept. 1941	HMCS *Levis*	corvette	Lt. C.W. Gilding, RCNR	torpedoed by *U–74*	North Atlantic	escorting convoy SC 44
7 Dec. 1941	HMCS *Windflower**	corvette	Lt. J. Price, RCNR	collision with Dutch freighter *Zypenberg*	off Grand Banks	escorting convoy SC 58
10 Feb. 1942	HMCS *Spikenard*	corvette	Lt. Cdr. H.G. Shadforth, RCNR	torpedoed by *U–136*	North Atlantic	escorting convoy SC 67
7 Sept. 1942	HMCS *Raccoon*	armed yacht	Lt. Cdr. J.N. Smith, RCNR	torpedoed by *U–165*	St. Lawrence River	escorting convoy QS 33
11 Sept. 1942	HMCS *Charlottetown*	corvette	Lt. J.W. Bonner, RCNR	torpedoed by *U–517*	St. Lawrence River	
14 Sept. 1942	HMCS *Ottawa*	destroyer	A/Lt. Cdr. C.A. Rutherford, RCN	torpedoed by *U–91*	North Atlantic	escorting convoy ON 127
6 Feb. 1943	HMCS *Louisburg**	corvette	Lt. Cdr. W.F. Campbell, RCNVR	sunk by Italian aircraft	east of Oran	escorting convoy
22 Feb. 1943	HMCS *Weyburn**	corvette	Lt. Cdr. T.M.W. Golby, RCNR	mine	off Gibraltar	
20 Sept. 1943	HMCS *St. Croix*	destroyer	Lt. Cdr. A.H. Dobson, RCNR	torpedoed by *U–305*	North Atlantic	escorting convoy ON 202
21 Oct. 1943	HMCS *Chedabucto**	Bangor minesweeper	Lt. J.H.B. Davies, RCNR	collision with cable vessel *Lord Kelvin*	St. Lawrence River	serving with Gaspé Force
29 April 1944	HMCS *Athabaskan**	destroyer	Lt. Cdr. J.H. Stubbs, RCN	torpedoed by *T–24*	north of Île de Bas, France	serving with 10th Destroyer Flotilla
7 May 1944	HMCS *Valleyfield*	frigate	Lt. Cdr. D.T. English, RCNR	torpedoed by *U–548*	southeast of Cape Race	
8 Aug. 1944	HMCS *Regina*	corvette	Lt. J.W. Radford, RCNR	torpedoed by *U–667*	off Cornwall	escorting coastal convoy
21 Aug. 1944	HMCS *Alberni*	corvette	A/Lt. Cdr. I.H. Bell, RCNVR	torpedoed by *U–480*	English Channel	
25 Oct. 1944	HMCS *Skeena**	destroyer	Lt. Cdr. P.F.X. Russell, RCN	dragged anchor in a storm	Iceland	
25 Nov. 1944	HMCS *Shawinigan*	corvette	Lt. W.J. Jones, RCNR	torpedoed by *U–1228*	Cabot Strait	on independent A/S patrol
24 Dec. 1944	HMCS *Clayoquot*	Bangor minesweeper	A/Lt. Cdr. A.C. Campbell, RCNVR	torpedoed by *U–806*	near Halifax	escorting convoy XB 139
22 Feb. 1945	HMCS *Trentonian*	corvette	Lt. C.S. Glassco, RCNVR	torpedoed by *U–1004*	English Channel	escorting Channel convoy
17 March 1945	HMCS *Guysborough*	Bangor minesweeper	Lt. B.T.R. Russell, RCNR	torpedoed by *U–878*	English Channel	
16 April 1945	HMCS *Esquimalt*	Bangor minesweeper	Lt. R.C. Macmillan, RCNVR	torpedoed by *U–190*	near Halifax	on independent A/S patrol

*Ships lost by causes other than enemy U-boat action.

Sources: Director of History, Department of National Defence; K. Macpherson and J. Burgess, *The Ships of Canada's Naval Forces.*

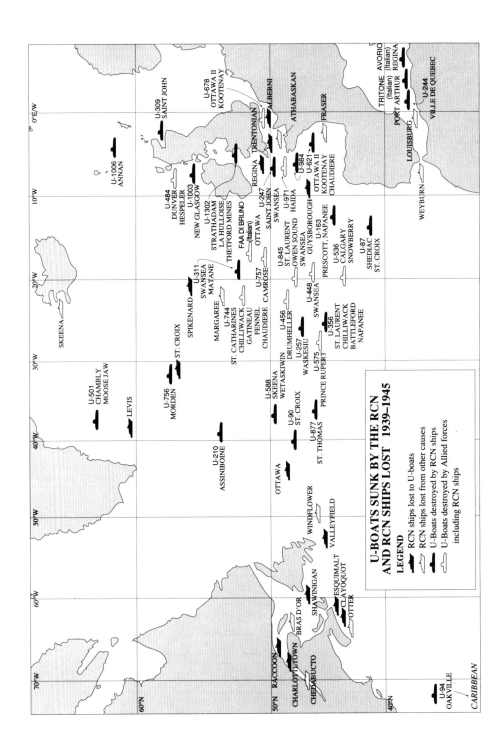

U-BOATS SUNK BY THE RCN
AND RCN SHIPS LOST 1939–1945

LEGEND

RCN ships lost to U-boats

RCN ships lost from other causes

U-Boats destroyed by RCN ships

U-Boats destroyed by Allied forces
    including RCN ships

Appendix C

U–Boats Sunk by RCN Ships in World War Two

Date	U-Boat	Ships	Commanding Officers
6 Nov. 1940	*Faa di Bruno* (Italian)	*Ottawa* HMS *Harvester*	Commander E.R. Mainguy, RCN
10 Sept. 1941	*U–501*	*Chambly* *Moose Jaw*	Commander J.D. Prentice, RCN Lieutenant F.E. Grubb, RCN
24 July 1942	*U–90*	*St. Croix*	Lieutenant Commander A.H. Dobson, RCNR
31 July 1942	*U–588*	*Wetaskiwin* *Skeena*	Lieutenant Commander G. Windyer, RCN A/Lieutenant Commander K.L. Dyer, RCN
6 Aug. 1942	*U–210*	*Assiniboine*	A/Lieutenant Commander J.H. Stubbs, RCN
28 Aug. 1942	*U–94*	*Oakville* U.S. Squadron 92	Lieutenant Commander C.A. King, RCNR
1 Sept. 1942	*U–756*	*Morden*	Lieutenant J.J. Hodgkinson, RCNR
27 Dec. 1942	*U–356*	*St. Laurent* *Chilliwack* *Battleford* *Napanee*	Lieutenant Commander G. Windyer, RCN A/Lieutenant Commander L.F. Foxall, RCNR Lieutenant F.A. Beck, RCNVR Lieutenant S. Henderson, RCNR
13 Jan. 1943	*U–224*	*Ville de Quebec*	Lieutenant Commander A.R.E. Coleman, RCNR
18 Jan. 1943	*Tritone* (Italian)	*Port Arthur*	Lieutenant Commander E.T. Simmons RCNVR
12 Feb. 1943	*Avorio* (Italian)	*Regina*	Lieutenant Commander H. Freeland, RCNR
4 March 1943	*U–87*	*St. Croix* *Shediac*	Lieutenant Commander A.H. Dobson, RCNR Lieutenant J.E. Clayton, RCNR
13 March 1943	*U–163*	*Prescott* *Napanee*	Lieutenant Commander W. McIsaac, RCNVR Lieutenant S. Henderson, RCNR
13 May 1943	*U–456*	*Drumheller* HMS *Lagan* RCAF Squadron 423	Lieutenant L.P. Denny, RCNR
20 Nov. 1943	*U–536*	*Snowberry* *Calgary* HMS *Nene*	A/Lieutenant Commander J.A. Dunn, RCNVR A/Lieutenant Commander H.K. Hill, RCNVR
8 Jan. 1944	*U–757*	*Camrose* HMS *Bayntun*	A/Lieutenant Commander L.R. Pavillard, RCNR
24 Feb. 1944	*U–257*	*Waskesiu*	Lieutenant Commander J.P. Fraser, RCNR
6 March 1944	*U–744*	Escort Group C4 *St. Catharines* *Chilliwack* *Gatineau* *Chaudière* *Fennel* HMS *Icarus* HMS *Kenilworth Castle*	Commander P. W. Burnett, RN Lieutenant Commander H.C. Davis, RCNR Lieutenant Commander C.R. Coughlin, RCNVR Lieutenant Commander H.V. Groos, RCN A/Lieutenant Commander C.P. Nixon, RCN A/Lieutenant Commander W.P. Moffat, RCNVR
11 March 1944	*U–845*	*Swansea* *St. Laurent* *Owen Sound*	A/Commander C.A. King, RCNR Lieutenant Commander G.H. Stephen, RCNR A/Lieutenant Commander J.M. Watson, RCNR
14 April 1944	*U–448*	*Swansea* HMS *Pelican*	A/Commander C.A. King, RCNR

Date	U-Boat	Ships	Commanding Officers
22 April 1944	*U–311*	*Swansea* *Matane*	A/Commander C.A. King, RCNR A/Commander A.F. Layard, RN
24 June 1944	*U–971*	*Haida* HMS *Eskimo* Czechoslovakia Squadron 311	Commander H.G. DeWolf, RCN
6 July 1944	*U–678*	*Ottawa II* *Kootenay* HMS *Statice*	Commander J.D. Prentice, RCN A/Lieutenant Commander W.H. Willson, RCN
18 Aug. 1944	*U–621*	*Ottawa II* *Kootenay* *Chaudière*	Commander J.D. Prentice, RCN A/Lieutenant Commander W.H. Willson, RCN A/Lieutenant Commander C.P. Nixon, RCN
20 Aug. 1944	*U–984*	*Ottawa II* *Kootenay* *Chaudière*	Commander J.D. Prentice, RCN A/Lieutenant W.H. Willson, RCN A/Lieutenant Commander C.P. Nixon, RCN
31 Aug. 1944	*U–247*	*Swansea* *Saint John*	Commander A.F. Layard, RN A/Lieutenant Commander W.R. Stacey, RCNR
11 Sept. 1944	*U–484*	*Hespeler* *Dunver*	Lieutenant Commander N.S. Dickinson, RCNVR A/Lieutenant Commander W. Davenport, RCNR
16 Oct.	*U–1006*	*Annan*	A/Lieutenant Commander C.P. Balfry, RCNR
27 Dec. 1944	*U–877*	*St. Thomas*	Lieutenant Commander L.P. Denny, RCNR
16 Feb. 1945	*U–309*	*Saint John*	A/Lieutenant Commander W.R. Stacey, RCNR
7 March 1945	*U–1302*	*La Hulloise* *Strathadam* *Thetford Mines*	Lieutenant Commander J.V. Brock, RCNVR Lieutenant Commander H.L. Quinn, RCNVR Lieutenant Commander J.A. Allan, RCNVR
13 March 1945	*U–575*	*Prince Rupert* USS *Haverfield* USS *Hobson* Aircraft: USS *Bogue* RAF Squadrons 172, 206	Lieutenant Commander R.W. Draney, RCNR
20 March	U–1003	*New Glasgow*	Lieutenant Commander R.M. Hanbury, RCNVR

Source: Directorate of History, Department of National Defence; K. Macpherson and J. Burgess, *The Ships of Canada's Naval Forces.*

BIBLIOGRAPHY

Albion, R.G., and Pope, J.B. *Sea Lanes in Wartime: The American Experience 1777-1945*. Hamden, Conn., 1968.

Appleton, T. E. *Usque ad Mare: A History of the Canadian Coast Guard and Marine Services*. Ottawa, 1968.

Audette, Louis C. Private Journal, Naval Recollections 1939-45.

___. "The Lower Deck and the Mainguy Report of 1939, " in Boutilier, *RCN in Retrospect*.

Beatty, Hon. Perrin. *Challenge and Commitment: A Defence Policy for Canada* (White Paper). Ottawa, June, 1987.

Bernier, Captain J.E. *Report on the Dominion of Canada Government Expedition to the Arctic Islands and Hudson's Strait*. Ottawa, 1910.

Berton, Pierre. *Flames Across the Border 1813-1814*. Toronto, 1981.

Botting, D. *The U-boats*. New York, 1979.

Boutilier, J.A., ed. *The RCN in Retrospect 1910-1968*. Vancouver, 1982.

___. *Matelot Memories: Recollections of the Lower Deck in Peace and War*. 75th Anniversary Conference, Halifax, 1985.

Bovey, Captain J. "The Destroyers' War in Korea, 1952-1953, " in Boutilier, *RCN in Retrospect*.

Brock, Rear Admiral J.V. *The Dark Broad Sea*. Toronto, 1981.

___. *The Thunder and the Sunshine*. Toronto, 1983.

___. Ad Hoc Committee Report on Naval Objectives, July, 1981, Directorate of History, Department of National Defence (hereafter DHist).

Brock, Rear Admiral P.W. "Commander E.A. Nixon and the Royal Naval College of Canada, " Boutilier, *RCN in Retrospect*.

Brodeur, Rear Admiral N.D. "L.P. Brodeur and the Origins of the RCN, " in Boutilier, *RCN in Retrospect*.

Bruce, J. *Back the Attack: Canadian Women During the Second World War – at Home and Abroad*. Toronto, 1985.

Burke, D.P. "The Unification of the Armed Forces, " *Revue Internationale d'Histoire Militaire*, 51 (1982).

Burrows, L., and Beaudoin, E. *Unlucky Lady*. Toronto, 1987.

Butcher, A.D. *I Remember Haida*. Hanstport, Nova Scotia, 1985.

Byers, R.B. "Canada and Maritime Defence: Past Problems, Future Challenges, " in Douglas, *RCN in Transition*.

Cameron, Captain A.K. "The Royal Canadian Navy and the Unification Crisis, " in Boutilier, *RCN in Retrospect*.

Cameron, J.M. *Murray, the Martyred Admiral.* Hantsport, Nova Scotia, 1981.

Corvus Publishing, *Canada's Navy Annual*, 1985/86/87/88/89.

Crickard, Rear Admiral F.W. "Three Oceans, Three Challenges," *Naval Forces*, 4, 5 (1985).

Critchley, H. "Canadian Naval Responsibilities in the Arctic," in Douglas, *RCN in Transition.*

Cuthbertson, G.A. *Freshwater: A History and a Narrative of the Great Lakes.* Toronto, 1931.

Davis, Rear Admiral S.M. "The St. Laurent Decision: Genesis of a Canadian Fleet," in Douglas, *RCN in Transition.*

___. "Technological Decision Making in the Canadian Navy, 1953-1965," Post-Doctorate Fellowship Studies, Queen's University.

Dobson, C., Miller, J., Payne, R. *The Falklands Conflict.* London, 1982.

Dönitz, Grosadmiral Karl. "Aufgaben und Stand der U-Bootswaffen," *Nauticus*, Berlin (1939). Translated as "The Submarine and its Tasks," *RCN Monthly Report*, No. 10 (1943).

___. *Memoirs: Ten Years and Twenty Days.* London, 1959.

Douglas, W.A.B., ed. *The RCN in Transition.* Vancouver, 1988.

___. "Alliance Warfare 1939-1945," *Revue Internationale d'Histoire Militaire*, 51 (1982).

___. "The Canadian-American Defence Relationship," DND Ottawa, 15th Dec. 1982.

___. "Canadian Naval Historiography," *Mariner's Mirror*, 70, 4 (Nov. 1984).

___. "Conflict and Innovation in the RCN 1939-1945," in Jordan, G., ed., *Naval Warfare in the Twentieth Century.* London, 1977.

___. *The Creation of a National Air Force.* Ottawa, 1986.

___. "Filling Gaps in the Military Past," *Journal of Canadian Studies* (Fall, 1984).

___ and Greenhous, B. *Out of the Shadows: Canada in the Second World War.* Toronto, 1977.

___ and Rowher, J. "The 'Most Thankless Task' Revisited: Convoy, Escorts and Radio Intelligence in the Western Atlantic, 1941-43," in Boutilier, *RCN in Retrospect.*

___ with Rowher, J. "Canada and the Wolf Packs, September 1943," in Douglas, *RCN in Transition.*

Easton, Alan. *50 North: Canada's Atlantic Battleground.* Toronto, 1963.

Eayrs, J. *In Defence of Canada*, Vols. 1-4. Toronto, 1974-1982.

Essex, J.W. *Victory in the St. Lawrence.* Erin, Ont., 1984.

Field, J.A. *History of United States Naval Operations: Korea.* Washington, 1962.

German, Commander A.B. "Fighting the Submarine: A Chronology," *Canadian Defence Quarterly* (Dec. 1985).

Glassco, J.G. (Chairman). *Report of the Royal Commission on Government Organization.* Ottawa, 1963.

Goodspeed, D.J. *The Armed Forces of Canada 1867-1967*. Ottawa, 1967.

Gough, B.M. "The Royal Navy's Legacy to the RCN in the Pacific, 1880-1914," in Boutilier, *RCN in Retrospect*.

___. "The End of Pax Britannica and the Origins of the RCN," in Douglas, *RCN in Transition*.

Graham, G.S. *The Empire of the North Atlantic: The Maritime Struggle for North America*, 2nd ed. Toronto, 1958.

___. *Sea Power and British North America 1783-1820*. Cambridge, Mass., 1941.

Granatstein, J.L. *Canada 1957-1967*. Toronto, 1986.

Grant, Vice Admiral H.T.W. "The Future Strategic Role of Naval Forces," lecture to National Defence College, 1948.

Greer, R. "Fiddy." *The Girls of the King's Navy*. Victoria, 1983.

Gretton, Vice Admiral P., RN. *Convoy Escort Commander*. London, 1964.

___. *Crisis Convoy*. London, 1974.

Hacking, N. *The Two Barneys (Captains B.L. and B.D.L. Johnson)*. Vancouver, 1984.

Hackmann, D. *Seek and Strike*. London, 1982.

Hadley, Michael L. *U-boats Against Canada: German Submarines in Canadian Waters*. Montreal, 1985.

___. "Inshore ASW in the Second World War: The U-boat Experience," in Douglas, *RCN in Transition*.

___. "The Impact of Public Policy on a Naval Reserve Division," in Boutilier, *RCN in Retrospect*.

Hellyer, Hon. Paul. *White Paper on Defence – 1964*. Ottawa, 1964.

Hill, Rear Admiral J.R., RN. *Anti-Submarine Warfare*. London, 1984.

Hughes, T., and Costello, J. *The Battle of the Atlantic*. New York, 1977.

Irvine, Lieutenant Commander T.A. *The Ice Was All Between*. Toronto, 1959.

Jane's Fighting Ships. London, annual.

Jones, Captain Basil, RN. *And So To Battle*.

Kealy, J.D.F., and Russell, E.C. *A History of Canadian Naval Aviation 1918-1962*. Ottawa, 1967.

Kellock, Justice R.L. Report on the Halifax Disorders, May 7th-8th, 1945. Ottawa, 1945.

Kert, F. "Privateering in Atlantic Canada During the War of 1812" (M.A. thesis, Carleton University, 1986).

Knox, J.H.W. "An Engineer's Outline of RCN History," in Boutilier, *RCN in Retrospect*.

Kronenberg, V.J. *All Together Now: The Organization of the Department of National Defence in Canada 1964-1972*. Toronto, 1973.

Lamb, J.B. *The Corvette Navy*. Toronto, 1977.

___. *The Triangle Run*. Toronto, 1986.

Law, Commander C.A. *White Plumes Astern*. Halifax, 1989.

Lawrence, Hal. *A Bloody War*. Toronto, 1979.

___. *Tales of the North Atlantic*. Toronto, 1985.

___. *Victory at Sea*. Toronto, 1989.

Lay, Rear Admiral H.N. *Memoirs of a Mariner*. Stittsville, Ont., 1982.

___. Report on Operation Crossroads. Ottawa, NSHQ, 1946 (H.T.W. Grant papers).

Leefe, J. "Atlantic Privateers," *Nova Scotia Historical Society*, 8, 1 and 2 (1978).

___. *The Atlantic Privateers, Their Story 1749-1815*. Halifax, 1978.

Leeming, Commander J.M. "HMCS *Labrador* and the Canadian Arctic," in Boutilier, *RCN in Retrospect*.

Leighton, R.M. *The Cuban Missile Crisis of 1962: A Case in National Security Crisis Management*. Washington, 1978.

Lund, W.G. "The RCN's Quest for Autonomy in the Northwest Atlantic," in Boutilier, *RCN in Retrospect*.

Lynch, Captain J.A.M., ed. *Salty Dips*, Vols. 1, 2, 3. Naval Officers Association of Canada, 1983/85/88.

Lynch, T.G. *Canada's Flowers: History of the Corvettes of Canada*. Halifax, 1980.

___. *The Flying 400*. Halifax, 1983.

Macdonald, Hon D.S. *Defence in the 70's: White Paper on Defence*. Ottawa, 1971.

Macintyre, Captain D., RN. *U-Boat Killer*. London, 1956.

___. *The Battle of the Atlantic*. Batsford, England, 1961.

MacKay, Captain G., ed. *Maritime Warfare Bulletin*, Halifax, 1985.

Mackenzie, K.S. *The Preparedness of Canada's Merchant Marine for Two World Wars, 1913-1947*. 75th Anniversary Conference, Halifax, October, 1985.

MacPherson, K., and Burgess, J. *The Ships of Canada's Naval Forces 1910-1981*. Toronto, 1981.

Mainguy, Rear Admiral D.N. *Concept of Maritime Operations*. Saclant. 1980.

Mainguy, Rear Admiral E.R., Audette, Rear Admiral L.C., Brockington, L.W. *Report on 'Incidents' on board HMC Ships Athabaskan, Crescent and Magnificent and Other Matters*. Ottawa, October, 1949.

McKee, F.M. *Volunteers for Sea Service: A Brief History of the RCNVR*. Toronto, 1973.

___. "Princes Three: Canada's Use of Armed Merchant Cruisers During World War II," in Douglas, *RCN in Retrospect*.

___. *The Armed Yachts of Canada*. Toronto, 1983.

Melville, T.R. "Canada and Seapower: Canadian Naval Thought and Policy 1860-1910" (Ph.D. dissertation, Duke University, 1981).

Metson, G. *An East Coast Port: Halifax at War 1939-1945*. Toronto, 1981.

Middlemiss, D.W. "Economic Considerations in the Development of the Canadian Navy Since 1945," in Boutilier, *RCN in Transition*.

Milner, Marc. *North Atlantic Run*. Toronto, 1985.

___. "Canada's Naval War," *Acadiensis*, 12, 2 (Spring, 1983).

___. "Convoy Escorts: Tactics, Technology and Innovation in the RCN 1939-43," *Military Affairs*, 48, 1 (Jan. 1984).

___. "Inshore ASW: The Canadian Experience in Home Waters," in Douglas, *RCN in Transition*.

___. "RCN Participation in the Battle of the Atlantic Crisis of 1943," in Boutilier, *RCN in Retrospect*.

Morison, S.E. *The History of U.S. Naval Operations in the Second World War*, Vols. 1 and 10. Boston, 1947 and 1962.

Morton, Desmond. *The Military History of Canada*. Edmonton, 1985.

___. "The Military Problems of an Unmilitary Power," *Revue Internationale d'Histoire Militaire*, 51 (1982).

Naval Historical Section. Notes on the Role of the RCN in the Great War. 16 July 1963.

Newman, Peter. *True North: Not Strong and Free*. Toronto, 1983.

Nixon, C.R. "Defence Budgets – A Review and Outlook," *Defence Associations National Network*, 5 Oct. 1989.

O'Brien, Vice Admiral J.C., and Rear Admirals R. Leir, J. Pickford, and R. Timbrell. "Have We Buried Our Navy?" *Canadian Shipping* (March, 1976).

Porter, Gerald. *In Retreat: The Canadian Forces in the Trudeau Years*. Ottawa, 1979.

Preston, R.A. *Canada and Imperial Defence*. Toronto, 1967.

___. "Marcom Education: Is It a Break with Tradition?" in Douglas, *RCN in Transition*.

Pugsley, W.H. *Saints, Devils and Ordinary Seamen*. Toronto, 1945.

Pullen, Rear Admiral H.F. *The Shannon and the Chesapeake*. Toronto, 1970.

___. "The RCN between the Wars, 1922-1939," in Boutilier, *RCN in Retrospect*.

Pullen, Captain T.C. "Parry Channel: The View From The Bridge, Then and Now," in P.D. Sutherland, ed., *The Franklin Era in Canadian Arctic History*. Ottawa, 1985.

___. *The Development of Arctic Ships*. London, 1981.

___. Reports of Summer Operations, HMCS Labrador 1956 and 1957, DHist.

___. *Northwest Passage 1906-1989, A record of ships, submarines and small craft known to have navigated the Passage to date*. Ottawa, 1989.

Raddall, T.H. *Halifax, Warden of the North*. Toronto, 1971.

Redmond, S.R. *Open Gangway: An Account of the Halifax Riots 1945*. Hantsport, Nova Scotia, 1981.

Roskill, Captain S.W., RN. *The War at Sea*, 3 vols. London, 1954-61.

Rotherham, Captain G.A., RN. *It's Really Quite Safe*. Belleville, Ont., 1985.

Russell, E.C. "History of HMCS *Labrador*," unpublished, DHist, 1960.

Sarty, R. "Hard Luck Flotilla: The RCN's Atlantic Coast Patrol, 1914-1918," in Boutilier, *RCN in Transition*.

___. "Silent Sentry" (Ph.D. dissertation, University of Toronto, 1982).

Schull, Joseph. *The Far Distant Ships*. Ottawa, 1950; reprinted, Toronto, 1987.

Sclater, W. *Haida*. Toronto, 1946.

Smith, M.G. *The King's Yard*. Halifax, 1985.

Snowie, Alan. *The "Bonnie."* Boston Mills, 1987.

Sokolsky, J.J. "Canada and the Cold War At Sea," in Douglas, *RCN in Transition*.

Soward, Lieutenant Commander (P) Stuart. "Canadian Naval Aviation 1915-1969," in Boutilier, *RCN in Retrospect*.

Stacey, C.P. *Arms, Men and Government: The War Policies of Canada 1939-1945*. Ottawa, 1971.

___. *Historical Documents of Canada*, Vol. 5.

Taylor, Andrew. *Geographical Discovery and Exploration in the Queen Elizabeth Islands*. Dept. of Mines and Technical Surveys, 1964.

Thorgrimsson, T., and Russell, E.C. *Canadian Naval Operations in Korean Waters 1950-1955*. Ottawa, 1965.

Thornton, Captain J.M. *The Big 'U': The History of HMCS Uganda/Quebec*. 1983.

Timbrell, Rear Admiral R.W. "Canadian Maritime Defence Requirements," *Maritime Affairs Bulletin* (Navy League of Canada), No. 2 (1977).

Tucker, G.N. *The Naval Service of Canada*. Vol I: *Origins and Early Years*; Vol. II: *Activities On Shore During The Second World War*. Ottawa, 1952.

Watt, Commander F.B. *In All Respects Ready*. Toronto, 1985.

Whitby, Michael. "Operations of the Tenth Destroyer Flotilla" (M.A. thesis, Carleton University, 1987).

Winks, R. *Canada and the United States: The Civil War Years*. Montreal, 1960.

Wise, S.F. *Canadian Airmen and the First World War*. Toronto, 1980.

Zimmerman, D. *The Great Naval Battle of Ottawa*. Toronto, 1989.

CHAPTER NOTES

CANADA'S NAVAL HISTORY HAS RECEIVED FAR LESS ATTENTION THAN THE very substantial amount paid to the military. Except for Admirals Brock and Lay, our senior naval officers have contributed no memoirs. Brock's is a self-revealing character study. Lay's, as he said, was written for his family rather than the record, but there are some gems among the tennis and cocktail parties. As noted in Douglas, "Filling Gaps in the Military Past," senior officers put thumbs down on historian Gilbert Tucker's draft of the official operational history of World War Two. At last, in the highly capable hands of Official Historian Dr. W.A.B. Douglas, it will be published in the nineties. Until very recently little was written about the RCN's considerable achievement in 1917-18 in assembling – on the flimsiest base – a ramshackle but sizable anti-submarine force. Tucker, official accounts, and general histories, which are mostly based thereon, largely ignore it and so lose its lessons on unpreparedness. After the Cuban crisis of 1962, no historical account was assembled. History – unpalatable or no – if left unpublished and hence unsung, leaves fatal gaps in a navy's and a nation's memory.

The following sources for large parts of this book I won't repeat under each chapter. Douglas's "Canadian Naval Historiography" gives a first-rate guide to the key naval issues and to the sources that illuminate them best. Gilbert Tucker's solid two-volume *Naval Service of Canada* is the major reference from the navy's beginnings to 1945 (except World War Two operations). Essential throughout is MacPherson and Burgess, *The Ships of Canada's Naval Forces 1910-1981*. Desmond Morton's *Military History of Canada*, though light on navy, provides a clear, succinct overall national context. Goodspeed's official *The Armed Forces of Canada 1867-1967* is a spare, factual account. Prime sources are the papers published in J. Boutilier's *The RCN in Retrospect*, from the 1980 conference on naval history, and in Douglas's *The RCN in Transition*, from the 1985 conference. They span the nineteenth century to the 1980s. Below, I will refer to specific articles in them by author's name as listed in the bibliography.

Chapter 1. The Tides of History

Graham's *Empire of the North Atlantic* gives a classic overview of the role of seapower in the evolution of Canada. McLennan's *Louisbourg from its Foundations to its Fall*, Raddall's *Halifax, Warden of the North*, John Leefe amplified by Fay Kert on Nova Scotia privateers, H.F. Pullen's *The Shannon and the Chesapeake* all illuminate the rousing early days. Cuthbertson's *Freshwater* gives a good perspective of the evolution, role, and exploits of the inland waters navies, French, English, and American. Their important part in the war of 1812 is given human highlights in Pierre Berton's *Flames Across the Border*.

Albion's *Sea Lanes in Wartime* shows the effect on trade and recalls seagoing activity and concerns of nineteenth-century Canadians. For alarums and excursions in the Civil War, see Winks's *Canada and the United States: The Civil War Years*. Melville's paper, "Canada and Seapower," is singularly revealing on Sir John A. Macdonald's naval thought and policy and the part played by Lieutenant Andrew Gordon. The Imperial forces at work on moving Canada toward a navy are clearly drawn in Gough's "The End of Pax Britannica."

Chapter 2. The Bare Beginnings
Rear Admiral N.D. Brodeur on his grandfather, "L.P. Brodeur and the Origins of the RCN," casts interesting light on Sir Wilfrid Laurier's time; P.W. Brock recounts a significant contribution to the early navy in "Commander E.A. Nixon and the Royal Naval College of Canada."

Chapter 3. The Great War
Sarty's "Hard Luck Flotilla," the Naval Historical Section's Notes, and the introduction to Hadley's *U-boats Against Canada* show the nature of the threat to Canadian waters and the poor level of preparedness for an important national role.

Chapter 4. Intermission
Rear Admiral H.F. Pullen writes from the perspective of the peacetime officer in "The RCN between the Wars." The view from the messdecks is reflected in Boutilier's *Matelot Memories* and by Hewitt and Manfield in Lynch's oral history, *Salty Dips*, Vol. 1. The navy is always a highly technical business and Captain Knox's "Engineer's Outline of RCN History" covers it very well from 1910 to the Tribals of the seventies. McKee's *Volunteers for Sea Service* recounts the shoestring struggles of the Volunteer Reserve. Canada's failure in maritime policy is covered in Mackenzie's *The Preparedness of Canada's Merchant Marine for Two World Wars*. C.P. Stacey's *Historical Documents of Canada*, Vol. 5, pins down Mackenzie King's (and Canada's) identification with appeasement, and the basis he shaped for unity in event of war: "no neutrality, fight alongside Britain, no conscription for overseas service."

Chapter 5 to 10. World War Two
The only official history to date covering RCN operations in World War Two is Schull's *The Far Distant Ships*, a highly readable, rousing story of exploits of ships and people, accurate chronologically but short on analysis with small heed to contentious issues.

Disinterment in the late seventies and eighties by historians including Alec Douglas, his West German colleague Jürgen Rowher, Lund, Milner, Hadley *et al.* has cast new, sometimes glaring, light. Zimmerman's *Great Naval Battle of Ottawa* examines the Headquarters failure to grasp matters technical and scientific that contributed so critically to Canadian ships' lag in battling the U-boats. Part 4 of Douglas's *Creation of a National Air Force* shows how far Canadian forces were from co-ordinated ASW and it contributes a lot thereby to the naval story.

Anti-submarine warfare, which has had such a major influence on Canada's navy, is a subject in itself though not treated separately in this book. The author's "Fighting the Submarine" is a chronology of the milestones, from tentative invention in the eighteenth century through the world wars to the eighties. The technical side of underwater detection from Great War beginnings through to the modern era can be found in D. Hackmann's *Seek and Strike* (including debunking of the myth that "asdic" was the acronym for Allied Submarine Detection Committee). RN Rear Admiral J.R. Hill's *Anti-Submarine Warfare* is excellent and concise into the modern era. Karl Dönitz's pre-war paper on U-boat operations, including wolf-pack tactics, and his memoirs written in prison post-war are both available in translation.

Hughes and Costello's *The Battle of the Atlantic* is a first-rate overview of a subject that has been expertly, assiduously, and comprehensively recorded from all but the Canadian point of view. Roskill and Morison wrote the official histories for the RN and USN and Roskill's work particularly is amplified generously by many books by key British participants, such as Macintyre, who disparaged the RCN's efforts, and Gretton, who admired them and understood their problems of equipment, training, and support. That the RCN's key part in the Battle of the Atlantic has been so little noted can be blamed less on lapses of British and American authors than on the failure of Canadians (including the navy itself) to write in depth about it themselves.

Lay tells first hand about 1940 in the Channel and the *Nabob* saga. For the burden of command, Alan Easton's *50 North* is a wonderfully written memoir, as alive as a novel. He commanded *Sackville* and *Saskatchewan* and his characters are real, though he changes the names. Perceptive journalist/photographer Bill Pugsley wrote *Saints, Devils and Ordinary Seamen* in 1945 fresh from experience living on the lower deck. Tony Law's memoir on his 29th MTB Flotilla was drafted (and drawn: he is an artist) in 1945, mellowed in the archives until 1989, and is nicely revealing. J. Essex recorded in 1984 his own story of that intriguing and little-known phase of the war in *Victory in the St. Lawrence*. Thirty to forty years after the events came Jim Lamb's *Corvette Navy* and *Triangle Run*, and Hal Lawrence's *Bloody War, Tales of the North Atlantic*, and *Victory at Sea*. They use their own and others' experiences most colourfully to evoke the spirit and feel of the times.

F.B. Watt's *In All Respects Ready* is the excellent, first-hand, and only published account of the innovative Naval Boarding Service in Halifax and contains a very moving picture of the merchant service at war. Wren "Fiddy" Greer's lively account of Canada's Wrens is supplemented by Jean Bruce's *Back the Attack*, on Canadian women at war. Burrows and Beaudoin's *Unlucky Lady* is the story of *Athabaskan*'s people – colourful, personal, not altogether accurate, but grippingly evocative. Basil Jones, the RN Captain (D) of the Fighting Tenth, writes very warmly of the Canadians, and of Harry DeWolf in particular, in *And So To Battle*. For *Haida*'s wartime story, see W. Sclater (1946) and A.D. Butcher (a new generation, writing in 1985, extending it through Korea). M. Whitby has studied the Channel operations from a more detached historian's viewpoint. For character and colour, the reminiscences (mostly officers') in the three volumes of Lynch's *Salty Dips* are a treasure trove, as is Boutilier's *Matelot Memories*.

Mr. Justice Kellock reported officially on the Halifax riots. Not until 1981 did J.M. Cameron write his sympathetic account of *Murray, the Martyred Admiral* on the Halifax riot; S.R. Redmond's *Open Gangway*, published the same year, took the other tack.

Chapter 11. The Sickly Season

Lay's report on Operation Crossroads gives a sanguine view of survival of fleets attacked by the atomic bomb. The need for a Canadian navy in the post-war, pre-NATO world (and the dearth of money to sustain it) was presented by the CNS, Vice Admiral Grant, in 1948 to the National Defence College in "The Future Strategic Role of Naval Forces." He also sounds a warning against visionaries without experience who propose unifying the forces as a cure-all. J. Sokolsky's "Canada and the Cold War At Sea" traces naval policy from this point on. Rear Admiral S. Mathwin Davis in *The St. Laurent Decision* shows how, in the pre-NATO doldrums, the distinctively Canadian post-war fleet was conceived. The navy's major social document, the Mainguy Report, is illuminated by the surviving commissioner, L.C. Audette, in "The Lower Deck and the Mainguy Report."

The Air Arm to 1962 is recorded in Kealy and Russell's official *History of Canadian Naval Aviation*. More controversial aspects – the early decisions, opposition by the RCAF, the senior officers' view of the air element – are recounted by Stuart Soward (who as a Lieutenant Commander (P) was technical adviser on the official history) in "Canadian Naval Aviation 1915-1969." The attitudes of the early days, the problems of RN aircraft, marginal training, and high accident rates I pieced together from talks with experienced naval aviators named in the Acknowledgements, including Bice, Burns, R. Creery, Edwards, Falls, Fotheringham, and Rikely, and reference to Rotherham's *It's Really Quite Safe*.

Chapter 12. Korea

The official account is Thorgrimsson and Russell's *Canadian Naval Operations in Korean Waters*. Field's *History of United States Naval Operations: Korea* provides the broad context from the American viewpoint. Volume 1 of Brock's memoirs gives the view from the bridge by the RCN senior officer in the early, most active period. Captain J. Bovey's "The Destroyers' War in Korea" recounts the train-busting time when he commanded *Crusader*.

Chapter 13. The New Navy

G. MacKay's *Maritime Warfare Bulletin* for 1985, published by the Canadian Forces Maritime Warfare School, includes: "The Canadian Development of Variable Depth Sonar" (D. Brassington), "The Marriage of the Small Ship and the Large Helicopter" (C. Dalley), and "Canadian Naval Contribution to Tactical Data Systems and Data Link Development" (D.N. MacGillivray and G. Switzer). Admiral Davis on "Technological Decision-making in the Canadian Navy" gives a remarkable picture of its shaping, including frigates and submarines and the considerations on nuclear power for ships and submarines. As Director General – Ships from 1960 to 1965, he was responsible for the design or construction of every warship active in the fleet today. With Knox's "Engineer's Outline" as a summary we have a clear picture of the quite remarkable technical achievements of this era.

On officer training, R.A. Preston surveys the whole span from earliest roots into the eighties in "Marcom Education: Is It a Break with Tradition?" A. Snowie's *The "Bonnie"* gives a spirited account of the beloved carrier's career, an excellent picture by a carrier pilot of day-to-day life on board with a real feel for the strengthening professionalism of naval aviation. Snowie's work illuminates as well Chapters 15 and 16 and on to the carrier's demise in Chapter 18. McKee continues to be a good resource on Reserves.

Chapter 14. The Northern Gate

"History of HMCS *Labrador*" written by departmental historian E.C. Russell is available to researchers at DHist but unfortunately is not published. *The Ice Was All Between* by *Labrador*'s navigator, Lieutenant Tom Irvine, comes with an expert's knowledge. So, of course, do Bernier's *Report* of 1910 and Captain T.C. Pullen's listed papers. A. Taylor documents discoveries in the Queen Elizabeth Islands. Captain Robertson's experiences came from personal interviews.

Chapter 15. The Brink of War

This most significant Canadian naval operation of the Cold War has been too well buried. Among a wealth of American material, Leighton's *The Cuban Missile Crisis of 1962* is a good reference. Typically, where Canada is mentioned it's only related to the failure of political decision-making. No copy of Admiral Dennison's "Historical Account of the Cuban Crisis," dated 29 April 1963, appears to have arrived in Canada until mine was downgraded and dug from Saclant's files in 1986. Sokolsky touches the incident briefly. The only comments of Admiral Rayner's to be found on the Cuban crisis are in evidence he gave to Parliament a year later regarding readiness, but not operations. Brock was Vice Chief of Naval Staff and his recollections in *The Thunder and the Sunshine* of personally directing readiness and operations are at odds with those of Rear Admiral Dyer and his staff. As Captain of *Mackenzie*, making ready for sea, I was quite close to developments. Sources are listed here, rather than in the bibliographic list:

Minutes, House of Commons Special Committee on Defence. Statement by Vice Admiral H.S. Rayner, Chief of Naval Staff, 15 Oct. 1963.

House of Commons, *Hansard*, 24, 25, 26 Oct. 1962.

Hon. Douglas Harkness papers, Memorandum: The Nuclear Arms Question and the Political Crisis Which Arose from It in January and February, 1963, National Archives of Canada (NAC).

HMCS *Bonaventure* (Captain F.C. Frewer) Ship's Logs and Reports of Proceedings, October-November, 1962, NAC.

Commander 5th Canadian Escort Squadron (Captain C.P. Nixon) Reports of Proceedings, October, November, December, 1962, NAC.

RCAF Station Greenwood (404 and 405 Squadrons), Historical Record, June-Nov., 1962, NAC.

RCAF Station Summerside (415 Squadron), Historical Record, Sept.-Nov., 1962, NAC.

Reports of Fallex 62 and Cubex. NSS 1630-2-13, 23 May 63, NAC, RG24.

Prediction of Operational Exposure Periods in ASW: ASW Operational Research Team Closed Circulation Report 34/62, NAC.

Cinclant Historical Account of Cuban Crisis, Admiral R.L. Dennison, USN, 29 April 1963, Directorate of History, DND.

Operations Cuba File 80/381, Message traffic. Statements File 73/1093, Directorate of History, DND.

Naval Board Minutes: Special Meetings 24 Oct. (2), 30 Oct. and 2 Nov. 1962, Directorate of History, DND.

W.A.B. Douglas, Director of History: The Canadian-American Defence Relationship, 15 Dec. 1982, Directorate of History, DND.

Personal interviews (ranks in October, 1962): Hon. D. Harkness, Rear Admiral K.L. Dyer, Commodore J. Pratt, Commodore J.C. O'Brien, Group Captain R. Gordon, Squadron Leader E. Voellmecke, Captain C.P. Nixon, Captain F.C. Frewer, Commodore R.P. Welland, Air Marshal L. Dunlap, Major General G. Walsh, Commander D.R. Saxon.

Chapter 16. Flying High
The "Brock Report" by the Ad Hoc Committee on Naval Objectives (1961) spells out strategic concepts and proposes plans for naval development through to the eighties.

Chapter 17. Integration and Unification
J.G. Glassco's Royal Commission Report is valuable background. V.J. Kronenberg documents Paul Hellyer's drive from White Paper through integration to unification. He assesses their effects (as of 1972) and notes other countries' reactions. Ten years later, Daniel Burke's "Unification of the Armed Forces" reinforces Kronenberg and details Rear Admiral Landymore's battle against unification. Rear Admiral Brock's highly personal account in *The Thunder and the Sunshine* contrasts with Landymore's views of the state of the fleet and arguments on unification in his briefs to the House Standing Committee on National Defence: 23 June 1966; 15, 16 February 1967, detailing his opposition to unification and his account of the altered testimony of 23 June 1966; 23 February 1967, on Hellyer's charges of disloyalty and the case against unification. Captain A.K. Cameron, who was secretary in the Atlantic Command to Admirals Dyer, Brock, and Landymore, concludes that the navy, since the war years, had failed to establish its relevance with Canadians, and hence there was no wave of real public support for its case. Morton underlines Hellyer's personal ambition and also concludes that Canadians didn't really care.

Chapter 18. Clipped Wings
Snowie's *"Bonnie"* recounts the last phase of the carrier's life very well. Soward argues that trade-offs between "air element" and "sea element" in the newly unified service and salt-horse thinking in Maritime Command conspired to ditch naval aviation in return for keeping a sizable small-ship, helicopter-equipped navy. Sokolsky recalls NATO's shift in the late sixties to graduated response and the clear call for stronger conventional – and especially maritime – forces. Saclant's 1969 Report: Relative Maritime Strategies and Capabilities of NATO and the Soviet Bloc, promoted strongly by NATO Secretary-General Brosio, put the case for much stronger naval forces as Trudeau launched his major cuts in defence.

Chapter 19. Change on Change
Lynch's *Flying 400* tells the story of the hydrofoil *Bras d'Or*. Gerald Porter's *In Retreat* comments on civilizing the Department, the continuing cuts, inflated rank structure, and language policy and practice. Bilingualism is covered officially by: Bilingualism Policy in the CAF, CDS Policy Directive P3/70, 27 February 1970; Program and Plan to Increase Bilingualism and

Biculturalism in the Canadian Armed Forces, 12 February 1971; and *Defence 72* (Ottawa: Queen's Printer, 1972). Preston is thorough on officer training in "Marcom Education." M. Hadley tells of adversity in the Reserve in "The Impact of Public Policy on a Naval Reserve Division."

Chapter 20. Troubled Times

Porter continues his indictment of defence policy and continuing neglect of the navy. Peter Newman pursues that theme more broadly in his *True North: Not Strong and Free*. Shrinking resources, aging ships, and increasing load were detailed in 1976 by retired Admirals O'Brien, Timbrell, Leir, and Pickford in "Have We Buried Our Navy?" Timbrell's assessment of the navy Canada should have in his "Canada's Maritime Defence Requirements" is very close to the report (never published) by a "Naval Board" of senior officers convened by Admiral Boyle to study the question. Porter recounts Boyle's travails, outspoken criticisms, and early retirement.

Chapter 21. The Eighties and Onward

Saclant's *Concept of Maritime Operations* written by Rear Admiral D.N. Mainguy lays the base for NATO nations' planning. Rear Admiral Crickard's "Three Oceans, Three Challenges" discusses response to Canada's trade and sovereignty issues. The Foreword to *Jane's Fighting Ships* (1988-89) by R. Sharpe gives a comprehensive position summary of the world's navies, including Canada's "giant stride" with proposed nuclear submarines. Harriet Critchley, in "Canadian Naval Responsibilities in the Arctic," discusses approaches to Canada's problem of sovereignty and defence in the Arctic, including an "Underwater Dew Line," nuclear submarines, bilateral sharing with the U.S., and multilateral arrangements within NATO. Rear Admiral Brodeur (retired) and others informed me on the development of the nuclear-powered submarine proposal. Defence Minister Beatty's White Paper of June, 1987, details years of underfunding and Canada's low standing in NATO. D. Middlemiss, in "Economic Considerations in the Development of the Canadian Navy Since 1945," documents expenditures on the navy over forty years as bottom of the service heap and steadily sliding in relation to GNP, total government expenditure, and share of the Defence budget. C.R. Nixon, recent past Deputy Minister of National Defence, in "Defence Budgets – A Review and Outlook," contrasts Canada's steadily increasing economic power in relation to friendly countries with her declining defence expenditure and the bleaker prospects following the federal budget of April, 1989.

ACKNOWLEDGEMENTS

DELVING INTO THE HISTORY OF CANADA'S NAVY BECAME A PLEASURE
with the help so generously extended by Dr. W.A.B. Douglas, the Official
Historian, Department of National Defence. His own publications – in keeping with his rare combination of scholarship of international repute and a
naval officer's solid sea experience – have filled many of the gaps in Canadian
naval historiography. His leadership has had a great influence over the last ten
years and more in developing studies in what was a sadly neglected field, and
he was unstintingly generous to me with his own time and talents.

On his staff, Mark Milner, Roger Sarty, Norman Hillmer, and Carl Chris-
tie were especially helpful while I worked on this book. So were Michael
Hadley, University of Victoria, with his special knowledge of the U-boat
men; Dean Allard, Naval Historical Center, Washington; Director Victor
Suthren, Hugh Halliday, and Fay Kert of the Canadian War Museum; Mari-
lyn Smith, curator of the Maritime Command Museum, Halifax; Colin
Shaw, Maritime Museum of British Columbia; F.D. Nelson, Base Historian,
CFB Esquimalt; M. Hamilton, curator of the Shearwater Aviation Museum;
Peter Seregei, National Defence Library; and staffs of the National Archives
of Canada, the Maritime Museum of the Atlantic, and the Imperial War
Museum.

Alec Douglas read my first seventeen draft chapters and his wise counsel
opened new channels and kept me clear of many shoals. For similar invaluable
help on subjects within their realms of unique knowledge I am most grateful
to Tom Pullen on the Arctic, Ken Dyer on the Cuban crisis, and Bill Landymore on integration and unification.

Leslie Smith and Andrea Schlecht were assiduous with their research.
Katharine Fletcher's execution of the maps was fine and precise. I must thank
Collins and Dial Press for permission to use graphic data on shipping and U-
boat losses from *The Battle of the Atlantic* by T. Hughes and J. Costello in the
maps on pages 81, 100, 114, 140, and 330; also, Dr. Douglas for the ship
dispositions on page 267. My editor, Richard Tallman, applied a surgeon's
skill to trimming a fat manuscript. Robert Paris helped me with translation.

My thanks to Mrs. H.T.W. Grant for allowing me access to Admiral
Grant's papers, and also to all hereunder – able seamen to admirals – who have
shared their personal experiences with me. I have used the first names by
which their shipmates knew them, no ranks, and for women their maiden

names. Among them are concealed a Privy Counsellor, some soldiers, air force types, and a master shipbuilder. The list includes:

Louis Audette, Camilla Balcombe, Al Bice, Dickie Bird, John Bovey, Douglas Boyle, Jeffry Brock, Nigel Brodeur, George Brown, Pat Budge, Helen Burns, Jim Burns, Barry Butler, Ruth Charlton, Joe Clark, Tom Clark, Gavin Clarke, John Coates, Ray Creery, Wallace Creery, Peggy Davis, Harry DeWolf, Larry Dunlap, Ken Dyer, Gordon Edwards, Ted Edwards, Bob Falls, Albert Fargo, Steve Foldesi, Pop Fotheringham, John Frank, Fred Frewer, George Fyfe, Ginger Geldard, Barry German, Don German, Andy Gillespie, Norman Goodale, Ralph Gordon, Douglas Harkness, Bill Hayes, Ralph Hennessy, Jimmy Hibbard, Bill Howe, Vern Howland, Norman Jolin, Bill Landymore, Tony Law, Hal Lawrence, Elsa Lessard, Sage Ley, John Lipton, Grace Lovatt, Mac Lynch, Allan MacConney, Dan Mainguy, Terrence Manuel, Bill Manfield, Jim McDougall, Andy McMillin, Jock McGregor, Paul Melanson, Stuart Meehan, Pat Milsom, Glen Moxham, Keith Nesbitt, Eleanor Nichols, Pat Nixon, J.C. Scruffy O'Brien, Bruce Oland, Donald Page, Scott Peddle, Jack Pickford, Debby Piers, Fred Polichuk, Jim Pratt, Bill Pugsley, Tom Pullen, John Ralph, Gus Rankin, Max Reid, Bill Rikely, Owen Robertson, Dick Ross, John Roue, Pat Ryan, Don Saxon, Bob Stephens, Iris Stinson, Alison Taylor, Bob Timbrell, Jean Verroneau, Ed Voellmecke, Geoffrey Walsh, Percy Warrilow, Jake Warren, Bob Welland, Vic Wilgress, Tug Wilson.

As well as doing the index and providing the perspective of a wartime Wren, my wife Sage gave me support beyond measure, the kind that comes with being a navy wife.

With all this invaluable help, what I have presented in this book is my responsibility alone.

Tony German
Kingsmere
Old Chelsea, Quebec
February, 1990

INDEX

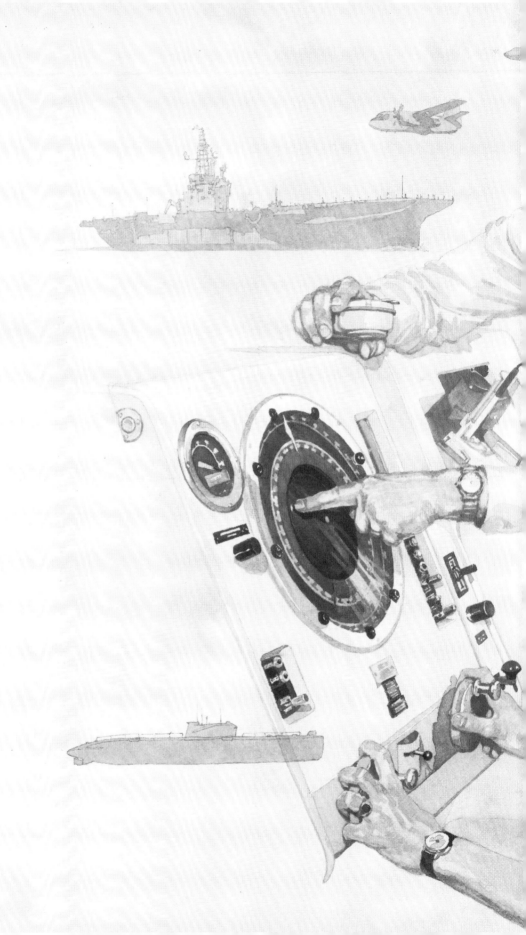